In order to communicate genuinely with most others and benefit from alternative ways of viewing the world, we need to learn languages. François Tochon describes the richness of language learning, how language is woven into culture, values and action. Even better, he provides a clear and systematic approach to deep language learning. Language learners and teachers will benefit greatly from this book.

—Stanton Wortham, Author of "Learning Identity: The Joint Emergence of Social Identification and Academic Learning", Associate Dean, University of Pennsylvania

François Victor Tochon has written an extremely important book. His Deep Approach to language learning / teaching provides the basis for developing a revolution in the teaching of second or foreign languages. His book sets forth the theoretical foundation for the deep learning approach, solid evidence that shows that the deep learning approach works, and most important practical and understandable guidelines on how to implement deep language learning. It is also consistent with Kurt Lewin's five-stage action-learning framework. The book is valuable for those in the language field but also for general readers who want to gain an introduction and overview of the field.

—Bertha Du-Babcock, Department of English for Business, City University of Hong Kong, China

Tochon makes a powerful case for dynamic language learning. His lively, visionary book explains how reproductive, boring approaches can be replaced by empowering processes for teachers and learners. Tochon's writing embodies the reflective, interactive learning that he advocates and charts so lucidly.

—Robert Phillipson, Author of "Linguistic Imperialism" and "English-Only Europe?", Copenhagen Business School, Denmark

As a language research, teacher, learner, and user, I realize the value of Professor Tochon's work and the improvement it will bring to language education. The Deep Approach will change the relationship between teachers and students as they become real partners, sharing in the fun while progressing through language learning. Let's start an adventure of language learning and get to know the world better!

—Ronghui Zhao, Chief editor of the book series "Foreign Language Strategy Studies", Director, Institute of Linguistic Studies, Shanghai International Studies University

In his latest book, *Help Them Learn a Language Deeply: The Deep Approach to World Languages and Cultures*, Professor Francois V. Tochon once again provides practicing language teachers, and, indeed, the profession-at-large, invaluable perspectives on the nature of the language learning process and beyond. In articulating the Deep Approach, it reflects the powerful dynamic potential that mastering language and cultivating cultural understanding represent to the world today, namely the hopeful prospect of "what a self-determined apprenticeship of languages could change in terms of the resources we provide to students, the way we consider evaluation, proficiency, and the role our discipline can play for internationalizing the mind and building peace" -- an aspiration truly to be pursued with energy, resourcefulness and commitment.

—*Gina Lewandowski, Middle School Teacher of French Spanish and ESL, Madison Metropolitan School District, Wisconsin, USA*

Acquisition of language skills occurs when students proactively learn the target language through appropriate and adequate facilitation by their teachers. The Deep Approach, as applied in this book, enables teachers and students to flexibly and meaningfully collaborate on language learning tasks, which will lead to the acquisition of language. This book shows clearly how language teachers can approach their instruction through the framework illustrated in this book. I would like to thank Professor Tochon for publishing this outstanding book, which is sure to revolutionize language instruction in the coming years.

—*Yuanshan Chuang, Director of Netpaw and APAMALL, Kun Shan University, Taiwan, ROC*

The Deep Approach is a new way to understand the World of languages; the learner is key as the engine to get motivated through the role played individually and with other peers as well as being an active part in the design of the Curriculum. The Deep Approach fosters a critical attitude in learners that has been consigned to oblivion for many years and that will provoke a change in the vision of key aspects such as culture, human rights or social justice. We lecturers do need to get immersed in this new and Deep Approach.

—*José Luis Ortega-Martin, Professor, Director of In-Service Training, Foreign Language Education, University of Granada, Spain*

WHAT OTHERS ARE SAYING...

François Tochon, a recognized leader in the renewal movement for "foreign" language education in the United States and beyond, provides a leap forward within the next mainstream of language education. His proposal of a self-determined apprenticeship of language learning recognizes the interface between government policies and classroom practices that has long been ignored in the field, to the detriment of the disenfranchised. Practitioners and scholars alike can benefit from the vision he brings, even as our field begins to benefit all of society in meaningful ways.

—*Terry A. Osborn, Author of "World Language Education for Social Justice", Dean, College of Education, University of South Florida Sarasota-Manatee*

I am often asked by Chinese students why their efforts and the time they have spent studying English have not given them the results they expected. As an English teacher, I have been frustrated by my lack of a satisfactory answer until I met Dr. Francois Tochon. Now I have the answer: Deep Approach. The conception of a self-determined apprenticeship in languages is a revolution against traditional language teaching methodology, which merely views a second language as a boring academic subject instead of a pleasant practical skill.

—*Gao Mingle, Director, English Education Center, Center for Linguistic Theory, and China Association of Language and Education, Beijing Language and Cultures University, China*

Tochon's conceptualization of the deep approach to the study of world languages, unlike most changes in foreign language education, is not simply a change in approach or methodology. It is far more fundamental than this – it is, indeed, a paradigm shift, that requires us to rethink virtually everything that we assume about the teaching and learning of languages. It is also one of the most exciting, creative and powerful ideas to emerge in our field in decades, and creates incredible opportunities for all of us.

—*Timothy Reagan, Author of "Language, Education, and Ideology" and "The Foreign Language Educator in Society" (with T. Osborn), Dean of the Graduate School of Education, Nazarbayev University, Kazaksthan*

The advocates for an effective U.S. policy for teaching and learning world languages could benefit from reading this critical contribution. Tochon's conceptualization of a "deep approach" is both timely and profoundly better for preparing learners for the globally interconnected realities they live now. Tochon provides viable options that show authentic language learning is profoundly connected to shaping thinking and social actions, as well as to further language and literacy learning. No longer can world language education be confined to merely a show of empty linguistic performances, rather needs to directed more towards building performances that truly put language to work on addressing sociocultural realities, forging ahead in the spirit of Dewey, Vygotsky, & Freire.

—Theresa Austin, Professor, Author of "Content-Based Second Language Teaching and Learning", School of Education, University of Massachusetts, Amherst

François Tochon's new book, *Help Them Learn a Language Deeply!*, is at once brilliant and humble. Tochon's humility enables him to transcend the arrogance that has traditionally permeated foreign language literature studies and relegated foreign language teaching to a sub-disciplinary status in the academy. Tochon's humility allows him to transcend the arrogance of disciplinary rigidity and status hierarchies while unabashedly embracing an interdisciplinary approach to language analysis and teaching that factor in cross-cultural variables. He convincingly argues for "methodologies associated with language arts and first language literacy [that] must now be integrated into the second/foreign language classroom for a deeper, integrated apprenticeship of languages and cultures. What makes *Help Them Learn a Language Deeply!* unique is the author's profound understanding of culture that goes beyond the elitist and often reductionist view of culture that, with rare exception, continues to dominate literary studies and to reproduce dominant values throughout the field of foreign language education.

—Donaldo Macedo, Author of "Literacies of power: What Americans are not allowed to know", Chair, Department of Applied Linguistics, University of Massachusetts, Boston

I find F. V. Tochon's book innovative and progressive, as well as original in the field of motivation and language learning. The proposed techniques and strategies enhance and stimulate effective learning; they are a great contribution to the complex field of motivation. I am sure that it will be welcome among educators and useful for language teachers and learners. Congratulations on the achievement!

—Daniel Madrid, Chief Editor of Porta Linguarum, Faculty of Education, University of Granada, Spain

As teachers and learners of languages we attend to language but we ignore what lies beyond—a complex of physical, spatial, interactional, institutional, political, and historical contexts that are present at every communicative moment. In deep learning, learners break free from such a narrow focus on language to develop skills that allow the creation of meanings in many different semiotic modalities that are embedded in context.

—Richard F. Young, Author of "Discursive Practice in Language Learning and Teaching", Professor, Department of English, University of Wisconsin-Madison, USA

Language learning in the contemporary era is complex, globally situated, and mediated by a wide array of fluid social practices, hybrid cultural environments, and emerging communicative modalities. Tochon's incisively argued volume acknowledges all of this and does a number of things very well: It highlights opportunities for the articulation of agency, is sophisticated in its treatment of culture and motivation, and relativizes historically constructed barriers between first and additional language learning. This book is innovative, insightful and an invaluable resource for students and teachers engaged in any aspect of language learning and teaching, applied linguistics, and world languages education.

—Steven L. Thorne, Department of World Languages and Literatures, Portland State University (USA), and Department of Applied Linguistics, University of Groningen (Netherlands)

Deep University Online !

For updates and more resources
Visit the Deep University Website:
www.deepuniversity.com
www.deepapproach.com

Certificate in Deep Education:
www.deepuniversity.com/graduatecourses.html

Copyright © 2014 by Poiesis Creations Ltd - *Deep University Press*
Member of Independent Book Publishers Association (IBPA)

All rights reserved. Permission is granted to copy or reprint portions up to 5% of the book (up to 22 pages) for noncommercial use under fair use agreement with the name of author, except they may not be posted online without written permission from the publisher.

For permissions, contact: publisher@deepuniversity.net

ISBN 978-1-939755-02-5 (Paperback)
Library of Congress Cataloging-in-Publication Data
1. Second Language Acquisition—Study and teaching. 2. Language and languages (Modern)—Study and teaching. Tochon, Francois Victor

Keywords: Foreign Languages Methods – Teacher Education – Language Learning – Foreign Language Teaching – World Language Education

Target audience: K-12 language teachers and Collegiate language instructors – language coordinators – curriculum designers – policy makers – graduate students - university researchers
Version 3
Translation of French versions of some parts of this text: Suzanne Mingo
Linguistic revision: Sunny Schomaker, Kristine Harrison, Jennifer Gray
Content revision: Gina Lewandowski, Mary Alice Sicard

Help Them Learn a Language Deeply

François Victor Tochon's Deep Approach to World Languages and Cultures

Deep University Press

Blue Mounds, Wisconsin

Also by François Victor Tochon

Educational Semiotics. Signs and Symbols in Education.
Deep University Press

Tropics of Teaching: Productivity, Warfare, and Priesthood.
University of Toronto Press

L'effet de l'enseignant sur l'apprentissage en groupe (Teacher's Impact on Group Learning). France University Press

La recherche-intervention éducative (Educational Intervention-Research). Quebec University Press

The Deep Approach: World Language Teaching for Community Building, with D. Hanson. Atwood Publishing

The Foreign Self: Truth Telling as Educational Inquiry.
Atwood Publishing

Video Study Groups for Education, Professional Development and Change. Atwood Publishing

Forthcoming

Tochon, F. V. (Ed.). *Language Education Policy, From Global Perspective to Local Practices.* Deep University Press.

Tochon, F. V., Ökten, C. E., Karaman, A. C., & Druc, I. C. *Teach a Language Deeply. The Deep Approach to Turkish.* Deep University Press.

Contents

Contents	9
Figures	14
Tables	16
Why the Deep Approach?	17

Preface
What Deep Language Learning Entails 21

Chapter 1
Deep Apprenticeship is Reflective, Adaptive,
and Self-Determined 29

Why Having Clear Goals Derived from Backward Planning is a Myth	30
Principles We Can Take from this Story	33
The Limits of Instructional Planning	38
Survey of the Book's Chapters	40

Chapter 2
Transcending Outcomes, Tasks, and Standards 45

A Brief Overview	46
What About Task Performances?	49
Playing with the Learners' Intentions	49
Product-Oriented Curricula	56
The Assets of Task-Based Planning	58
The Limits in the Definition of Tasks	59
Process-Oriented Curricula	61
Actual Planning as Teachers Live it	64
Limits of the Sequential Models of Planning	66
A Critical Analysis of the Zone of Proximal Development	69
Organizing Class Life Through Converging Activities: From Cartesian Analysis to Open Dynamics	71
Pragmatic Task Domains for Language Learning	73
From Four Skills to Task-Domains' Dynamics	75
In Short	79

Chapter 3
The Primacy of Text for Deep, Conceptualized Expression — 83

Project-Based Language Learning	87
The Good News with Whole Projects	89
The Bad News with Whole Projects	91
High-Caliber Outcomes in Light	92
The Shadow of Backward Planning	93
Hol-Act Organizers: Towards Compatibility	96
Tell Me About the Writing Workshop…	99
A Risky Definition	99
Content's Mastery, Procedural Transfer and Contextual Conditions of Expression	100
The Proactive Cloverleaf	105
The Workshop Dynamics	107
Dungeons and Spelling Dragons	110
First: Use your Head and Hol-Act!	111
Second: Negotiate the Hol-Act!	112
Third: Let the Kids Hol-Act!	119
In Short	121
The Writing Process as a Philosophy: Mike's Journal	123

Chapter 4
The Deep, Unified Taxonomy — 127

Deep Apprenticeship for Language Proficiency	129
The Whole is Greater than the Sum of its Parts: When a Person is of Many Parts	133
When the Affective is Objectified	135
No Learning Without Love	136
Gluing the Pieces Back Together	138
When Plans Dovetail: Validating Analysis Criteria	146
Definition of the Three Levels of the Unified Taxonomy	150
Reaching a Functional Coherence	152
Depth from Interdiscipline to Transdiscipline	153
In Short	157

Chapter 5
Forward Planning: Instructional Organizers for Deep Apprenticeship — 159

The Concept of Instructional Organizer	160
An Example from Research	166
Prior Knowledge, Students Lives and Motives as the Organizing Principles	166
Narrativors, Skillers, and Actualizers	168
Basic Principles of the Deep Approach to Language and Culture Learning	170
Illustration of the Forward Planning Model	174
An Actual Case: Vegetable Horoscopes	180
Discussion	187
In Short	191
Naturalizing as Curriculum Building	191
Adaptive Dynamics for the Language Class	193
Scientific Evidence on the Effectiveness of the Deep Approach to World Languages and Cultures	196

Chapter 6
Deep Pedagogy: Organizing Language Hol-Acts — 197

Deep Learning Requires Adaptive Teaching	199
How Projects Are Organized	201
Apprenticeship for Deep Learning: When Teachers Stop Working Against the Grain	202
Project-Based Language Pedagogy	203
Project Principles	205
Tasks in Deep Projects	206
Deep Pedagogy: Teachers as Coaches and Resource Persons with the "Me Project" as an Exemplar	209
A Conceptual Grammar to Create the 'Deep' Syllabus	214
A Syllabus with Empty Slots	216
How Is Evaluation Organized in the Syllabus?	221
In Guise of Conclusion	223

Chapter 7
The IAPI Model: Access and Voice for Identity-Building — 225

Interpret	226
The role of extensive reading	226
The role of reading aloud	232
The role of vocabulary	233
The role of films and visuals	233

Analyze	235
The role of grammar	235
Present	240
The role of writing	240
The role of oral expression	241
The role of audiovisual creation	243
Interact and Build your Identity	244
The role of educational technologies from iPBL to IDeep	244
The role of intercultural and transpersonal exchange	246
In Guise of Conclusion	249

Chapter 8
The Democratic Planner and Deep, Reflective Evaluation — 251

Self-Monitoring: A Difficult Project	253
Students' Input into Course Plans	256
Negotiation Without Noodles	260
Reflective Taxonomies Linked to Talk in Interaction	262
Evaluating Students' Deep Learning	265
The Reflexive Function of Level Evaluation	267
Limits of Instructional Design and Education Policy	269
Apprenticeship and Instructional Agreements	273
Avoid Dogmatisms	276
Autonomy: A Reflective and Complex Phenomenon	279
The Student Plans for the Protagonist	282
No Pain, No Gain: Many Difficulties to Overcome	286
In Short	288

Chapter 9
The Deep Turn Toward Wisdom and Autonomy — 291

The Deep Turn for Cross-cultural Understanding	293
Value Creation as One Characteristic of a Deep Approach	294
A Deep Approach to Linguistic Human Rights	297
Discussing Language Status in Teacher Education	299
Criticality in Content and Language Integrated Learning	301
The Deep Approach and Transformational Pedagogy	302
Avant-garde Methodologies for Social Change	306
Educating the Democratic Planner	307
Depth Is Not Stultifying	309
Self-Regulated Learning Strategies and Autonomy	310

Instrumentalized Autonomy	312
Pedagogy for Autonomy and Value Creation	312
Deep Creative Pedagogy Does Not Focus on Control and Order	315
The Theory/Practice Dilemma	317
Growth and Interiorization	320
In Conclusion	323

Conclusion 325

Learning How to Deal with Complexity	326
From Sequenciation to Complex Dynamics	327
Conceptualizing Social Action as Deeply Educative	329
Content-rich Experiential Learning	330
From Routine to Experience via Operative Images	331
Modeling Experiential Innovation	332
Crucial Changes Are Needed in the Teacher's Role	333
New Avenues for Deep Research	335
Final Warnings	337
To Sum Up: Why Do We Need a New Approach to Foreign/Second Language Teaching?	339

Decolonizing Foreign Language Education: An Afterword 343
Donaldo Macedo, University of Massachusetts Boston

Glossary 353

Appendix 379

1st Proaction: From Curriculum to Dynamic Activities	379
2nd Proaction: A Comedy Routine	380
3rd Proaction: Documenting a Profession	381
4th Proaction: An Informative Challenge	383
5th Proaction: On Your Own	384
6th Proaction: Commedia dell' Hol-Act	389

References 391

Index 434

Deep University Press Scientific Board Members 440

Author's Biosketch 442

Figures

Figure 2.1. The Outcome-Directed Teaching Model — 47
Figure 2.2. Character Under Active Surgery — 66
Figure 2.3. The Whole is More and Less Than the Sum of its Parts — 68
Figure 2.4. The IAPI Model and the Educative Project's Task Domains — 77
Figure 2.5. From the Beast to the Beauty: Transversal Connections — 79
Figure 3.1. The Big Picture — 89
Figure 3.2. Planning Mirrors — 102
Figure 3.3. Informal Learning through Spontaneous Expression — 108
Figure 3.4. Russian Dolls — 109
Figure 3.5. Tasks Distribution to Accomplish the "Dungeons and Spelling Dragons" Project — 114
Figure 3.6. In the Thick of Things. Narrative Diagram for "Dungeons and Spelling Dragons" — 115
Figure 3.7. All is Not Lost. Narrative Diagram for "Dungeons and Spelling Dragons" (sequence 2) — 116
Figure 3.8. Narrative Diagram for "Dungeons and Spelling Dragons" (sequence 3) — 117
Figure 3.9. A Well Deserved Rest. Narrative Diagram for "Dungeons and Spelling Dragons" (sequence 4) — 118
Figure 3.10. Spelling Dragons Organizers — 120
Figure 3.11. Text is the Primary Source of Deep Language Learning — 126
Figure 4.1. How Disciplines Interconnect within a transdisciplinary field — 131
Figure 4.2. A Thermometer of Learning: The Basic Categories of Bloom's Scale — 134
Figure 4.3. The Three Levels of the Unified Taxonomy — 150
Figure 4.4. To Make it Simple — 151
Figure 4.5. Embedment enacting the Unified Taxonomy In Educative Projects — 158
Figure 5.1. Model of the Authentic Teaching Situation — 163
Figure 5.2. The Student in the Authentic Learning Situation — 164
Figure 5.3. Instructional Embedment of a Theme into Operations to Develop an Action — 175
Figure 5.4. Thematic Pivot — 176
Figure 5.5. Instrumental Pivot — 177
Figure 5.6. Instructional Embedment with Dialogue

Recording as a Pivot	178
Figure 5.7. Class Council and Study Trip as Experiential Pivot	179
Figure 5.8. Moving Embedment in Which the Pivot Shifted from the Experiential Organizer (Actualizer) to the Proficiency Organizer (Skiller)	180
Figure 5.9. Moving Embedment in Which the Pivot Shifted from the Experiential Organizer (Actualizer) to the Thematic Organizer (Narrativor)	180
Figure 5.10. Instructional Framework on Characterization	183
Figure 5.11. My Vegetable, my Self	184
Figure 5.12. When Task Performance Is Not Enough	187
Figure 5.13. Deep Proactive Planning	194
Figure 6.1. Making Education Meaningful	201
Figure 6.2. Pragmatic Embedment of Narrativors, Skillers and Actualizers in the Realization of a Project	218
Figure 6.3. Organizers and Task Domains are Connected Together Through an Action Grammar	218
Figure 7.1. The IAPI Model Serves as Planning Template	226
Figure 8.1. A Question of Values: The imperfect match between school evaluation and life-anchored knowledge	271
Figure 8.2. Experiential Model Integrating Evaluation and Apprenticeship	272
Figure 8.3. Reflective Regulation Levels	280
Figure 8.4. The Action Plan: A Metaphor of the Physical World	281
Figure 8.5. The Many Faces of the Hero	282
Figure 8.6. Meta-Know Thyself: Self-Assessment as Reflective Experience at the Various Levels of Cognition	283
Figure 8.7. Writer's Cramp: Writing Self-Regulatory System	284
Figure 8.8. The Differential of Evaluative Formation: A Creative Carburator	285
Figure 9.1. Searching for the Included Middle or Third Space	318
Figure A.1. Choose the Pragmatic Embedment	389
Figure A.2. Organizers and IAPI Task Domains Help Decipher the Grammar of Projects	390

Tables

Table 2.1. Contrasting Industrial and Knowledgeable Views of Classroom Planning	55
Table 2.2. Birds of a Feather Flock Together	74
Table 4.1.a. Knowledge in Three Tenses	148
Table 4.1.b. Knowledge in Three Tenses	149
Table 5.1. Pastiche Planning – Preliminary project for "Mastering the writing techniques of character description"	181
Table 5.2. Creating a Pastiche: Actualized Instructional Strategy	185
Table 6.1a. Example of Schedule by Projects	212
Table 6.1b. Example of Schedule by Projects	213
Table 6.2. The Deep Syllabus - Deep Grammar of Project Planning	219
Table 8.1. Guidelines for self-exploration	258
Table 10.1. Dialectical Processes Inherent with Educative Projects	330
Table A.1. Project: Writing a Short Comedy Sketch	385
Table A.2. Pre-Professional Brainstorming: Profiling a Profession	386
Table A.3.a. Yours Truly - Project: Get an opinion letter published in the readers' page	387
Table A.3.b. Yours Truly - Project: Get an opinion letter published in the readers' page	388

Why the Deep Approach?

Immersing yourself in the Deep Approach to world languages and cultures will help you to:

- ➢ Understand how self-motivation could be the best incentive for deep language learning,

- ➢ Provide themes, motives, templates and incentives for self-directed learning and self-determination,

- ➢ Empower the student to be the curriculum builder by scaffolding possibilities and making the instruction flexible,

- ➢ Emphasize the learning process rather than pre-determined outcomes,

- ➢ Encourage individualized, peer-oriented, and project-based learning by focusing on cultural contents, value creation and social action,

- ➢ Consider grammar as story-telling about language, and

- ➢ Use formative, deep evaluation of integrated skills.

- ➢ Focus on value creation: highlight critical issues related to the respect of cultures, language status and discrimination, the colonial mindset and social justice, and linguistic human rights for peace building.

The Deep Approach establishes a link between language education policies and an open curriculum design focusing on values and creative proficiency in action rather than imposed outcomes. It places the learner as the curriculum builder.

The concepts I present in this book have been published in French, Spanish, Portuguese, and Vietnamese, but only some of them have been available in English. The reason why I could not transfer these concepts into English previously was the lack of a framework that could make the whole model intelligible to the Anglophone reader. I also wanted to test my hypotheses on American soil, which has now been accomplished through a large 4-year federal grant from the U.S. Department of Education. I am indebted to my outstanding colleagues and friends of the University of Wisconsin-Madison for their intellectual stimulation. Teaching and researching in an environment where close to 80 languages are being taught is quite an experience.

I am particularly indebted to graduate students, many of whom have been teachers and language instructors, who have read drafts of this book since 2009, have implemented the Deep Approach in their practice and have given me invaluable feedback. A forum was created on the Deep Approach website for K-12 teachers and collegiate language instructors who wanted to share their experiences with the new approach.

I am also thankful to many colleagues for having invited me to present keynote lectures and give workshops on the approach at the following places: the Conference of the National Council for Less-Commonly Taught Languages (NCOLCTL); at the European Conference on Education Research (ECER) in Berlin; Startalk language teacher education at PENN; Boston University; the Language Institute of the University of Columbia; CelCAR and the Turkish Flagship Program at Indiana University-Bloomington; the World Conference on Teaching Turkish in Bishkek (Kyrgyzstan); the Language Center of the University of Chicago; and many universities abroad, such as Granada (Spain); Porto (Portugal); Lyon, Marseille and Reims (France); Akershus-Oslo (Norway); Queensland and Griffith in Brisbane (Australia) Shanghai International Studies University and Shanghai Normal; Zhejiang and Zhejiang Normal; Beijing Languages and Cultures; and Beijing Foreign Studies University; Nanjing (China); NCKU and MUST (Taiwan).

Since January of 2000, I have been working at the University of Wisconsin-Madison as professor in a department of Curriculum & Instruction that has been consistently ranked first in the nation since 2001 according to the U.S. News and World Report; I also give one course a year in the Department of French & Italian, most usually to train teacher assistants to new approaches in the field. I headed the World Language Education program from September of 2001 to June of 2007, and then Graduate Studies in World Language Education.

Researchers in my department usually do not do mainstream research, but prepare what will be tomorrow's mainstream. I trust that this book presents the mainstream of tomorrow. This will be the type of apprenticeship that we will be facilitating in the coming decade due to the nature of economic and technological change, of population changes, of increasing internet resources, and the backlash against the view imposed by narrow-minded economists and politicians alike who support short-term interests in terms of standardized performances, gains, profitability, international mimicry, and shallow education.

The Deep Approach is being tested in many American colleges and in Turkey at Yildiz Technical; Bosphorus and Istanbul Şehir in Istanbul; Çanakkale; METU in Ankara; and Suleyman Demirel in Isparta, as well as in many countries such as China.

Deep University supports a deep approach to learning with online Summer courses and a Graduate Certificate in Deep Education. See:

- http://www.deepuniversity.com/graduatecourses.html

- The Deep Approach website is here:
  http://www.deepapproach.com

- As an example, the resources we created for the Turkish language are here:
  http://deepapproach.wceruw.org/

The Deep Approach team publishes a newsletter and Book Series for authors who investigate the approach. We are on Twitter, and we have a Facebook group.

❖ Our Facebook group is here:
http://www.facebook.com/groups/deep.approach/

❖ Twitter: http://twitter.com/Deep_Approach

Preface
What Deep Language Learning Entails

I started my career teaching German to sixth graders in a French-speaking middle school. I had been teaching for about a month when one day, the assistant principal made a surprise visit to my class, unannounced. We had pushed all the chairs, desks, and tables into the corners of the classroom, and I was sitting on the floor in a circle, with the 16 kids in the class. I was holding a pen, presenting it to my child next to me, telling him in German: "This is a pen." "Ah, this is a nice pen," he was to respond. "Yes, this is a beautiful pen, I like it"—and he had to give the pen to the next student using the same sentences. We would continue with a variety of objects, then mix the objects and go in both directions at the same time, which caused some ruckus and laughter because the children were hearing competing messages.

After class, the assistant principal asked me why I was not using the textbook he had given me for the class, titled **Wir Sprechen Deutsch**. *I told him I was not aware the textbook was a requirement. He also said that sitting on the floor might generate bad habits and the parents might complain. German was not an optional discipline in Switzerland and if my students did not succeed with State exams, it would be difficult for them to move on to high school. I then skimmed the textbook. Many chapters looked boring and made learning look like a mere repetitive practice. Nonetheless, there was something good about them: the chapters were organized by themes. In the next class, I listed the themes on the chalkboard, and asked the students to choose the theme they preferred. We formed groups that would specialize in one thematic chapter, would learn it, find other German resources on that topic (there was no internet at the time), create tasks for an educative project, and teach the chapter to their peers.*

The Deep Approach was born. It took me years to conceptualize the new process and convey what a self-determined apprenticeship of languages could change in terms of the resources we provide to students, the way we consider evaluation, proficiency, and the role our discipline can play for internationalizing the mind and building peace. This book is an introduction to this action-based, deep learning approach to other languages and cultures, which can increase sensitivity toward human history, our environment and the role of Education for a better society. As action is used here for value creation, and language apprenticeship, this approach can be considered trans-actional: it implies reflecting on the way of acting, with tasks being subordinated to transdisciplinary projects. This in turn will facilitate a new approach to the earth and history through education starting with the vehicle of language.

Experienced language teachers as well as specialists in Second Language Acquisition (SLA) and foreign language education (FLE) might be surprised and even amazed when reading this book with its number of iconoclastic ways of handling the field, which I need to justify here. Our understanding of what a language is has taken on a new *complexity* that I wish to address. The frontier between first and second languages becomes blurred in a multilingual society. I will rarely allude to "second/foreign languages"; if I do, it will be in terms of world languages—any language of the world—which includes English[1].

In this book, speaking of language learning at large will be to emphasize that nowadays language classes are often a mix of native speakers, heritage language and bilingual students, some of whom

---

[1] English as a foreign language (EFL) or Teaching of English to Speakers of Other Languages (TESOL) should be considered a different field from English as a Second Language for English Language Learners (ESL/ELL). EFL, in general, is proposed for secondary schools in countries that speak other languages than English. ESL addresses issues related to immigrant children in English-speaking countries, which generally relates to early childhood education and elementary education, more rarely to secondary school and post-secondary settings. Moreover, EFL is evolving towards English as Lingua Franca (ELF), with a focus on multilingual, non-native speaker communication practices. This new orientation can help reconceptualize world language education at large, as the purpose of a lingua franca (such as Turkish for Turkic countries) implies a focus on meaning rather than on form (Willis & Willis, 2007).

already speak two languages at home. Teachers must adapt to a large variety of contexts. Knowing who the students are is of utmost importance to find a good fit between who they are, what their interests and learning needs are, and how they will learn. Additionally, methodologies associated with language arts and first language literacy must now be integrated into the second/foreign language classroom for a deeper, integrated apprenticeship of languages and cultures. This goes along with the *Modern Language Association*'s emphasis on the need to better integrate literature with language learning. As well it is a reaction against the marginalization of foreign language education (Reagan, 2002): the family of language education needs to unite forces.

Apprenticeship will be the term I shall use: learning languages in action, by doing, which will imply cross-cultural pragmatics and a critical reflection on values and linguistic capital. In the forthcoming chapters, the reader may recognize the influence of the works of Pierre Bourdieu, John Dewey, Henry Jacottot, Charles S. Peirce, Ivan Illich, Jean Lave, Henri Lefebvre, Jean-Louis LeMoigne, Edgar Morin, Basarab Nicolescu, Jacques Rancière, Donald Schön, and; closer to the Second Language Acquisition and world languages reader, Dick Allwright, Michael Byram, Rod Ellis, Ofelia García, Claire Kramsch, Ryuko Kubota, B. Kumaravadivelu, Donaldo Macedo, Terry Osborn, Robert Phillipson, Tim Reagan, Elana Shohamy, Tove Skutnabb-Kangas, Dave and Jane Willis, and Anna Wierzbicka. I am in agreement with late Leo van Lier and Richard Young on the need to reframe applied linguistics within the broader scope of applied semiotics—the science of meaning making—, a thesis I have been defending since I was editor of the *International Journal of Applied Semiotics* and president of the special interest group in educational semiotics of the American Education Research Association.

I am indebted to all of these researchers, yet what I am presenting here is unique and different. I also express my gratitude towards numerous experienced teachers and teaching assistants whose feedback, experiences and conversations were illuminating. Particular thanks go to language teachers such as Suzanne Mingo, Mary-Alice Sicard and Gina Lewandowski who have provided feedback on early versions of this manuscript to increase its readability towards the K-12 teacher community, and to the doctoral students whose comments stimulated me to improve this text during the last four years.

The attempt here was to define what could be the next main stream. I have tried to meet the challenge of gathering modern and postmodern trends within an integrative framework that describes their included middle. Rather than keeping with a dualistic view of paradigmatic wars, Lupasco's principle of the included middle, or third space, integrates apparently opposed elements at a higher (still relative) level. As well, the flexible and adaptive model I propose is in a sense a consequence of numerous contacts with language policy research, as it is an expression of what could be done to deepen language curriculum and instruction in ways that are respectful to language and culture differences. The bibliography at the end of the book demonstrates that the argument is well informed and up-to-date. Yet, I apologize for the number of researchers in language policies and world languages that I could not review for lack of space. They will be the focus of other works.

In this book, I reconceptualize language learning in two ways: first, as an expression of dynamic planning prototypes that can be activated through self-directed projects. Second, the proposal is an attempt at integrating structure and agency to meet deeper, humane aims. The dynamism of human exchange is meaning-producing through multiple connected intentions among language task domains. Here, language-learning tasks have a cross-cultural purpose which then become meaningful within broader projects that meet higher values and aims such as deep ecology, deep culture, deep politics and deep humane economics. Applied semiotics will be a tool beyond the linguistic in favor of value-loaded projects that are chosen in order to revolutionize the current state of affairs, in increasing our sense of responsibility for our actions as humans vis-à-vis our fellow humans and our home planet. In this respect, this book presents a grammar for deep instructional planning that is also, a grammar for action. Understanding adaptive and complex cross-cultural situations will be the prime focus of such a hermeneutic inquiry.

I suggest that students use thematic organizers to guide their projects. A thematic organizer is a specific subject-matter focus that matches students' self project and interest and will serve as a pivot to build self-determined, educative actions. The study of how experienced teacher organize their curriculum revealed that they not only use thematic organizers but also instrumental organizers or *skillers* and experiential organizers that I called *actualizers*. These aspects are developed in this book. Organizers have no meaning without the complex, associated dynamics of the situation. Handling connections across language tasks, I suggest, will be a matter of the teacher's experience in the field, i.e. in the classroom. The concept of curriculum organizers comes from field pragmatics: their understanding emerged from more than three hundred visits and classroom observations I have made, as well as interviews with teachers on their instructional planning during the last twenty-five years in different countries such as Argentina, Belgium, Canada, China, Ecuador, France, Japan, Peru, Spain, Switzerland, Turkey, the United States, and Vietnam.

I feel the time is now ripe for clarifying the stakes of language *complexity*—that language is plural rather than one—and self-directed learning in the world language arena. Therefore it is timely as well as new. What is new here is the emphasis on the deep transformational dynamics of learning—in which learners become social activists for other languages through the interactive practices of wisdom pertaining to various cultures. Thematic organizers transcend their structural definition and soon become flexible, pragmatic ways of guiding students' choices without reifying the concepts enacted in the projects, which are like personalized standards. Thus pragmatic organizers come from the field and transform the field into wor(l)d maps.

Here is what makes this approach distinct:

❖ The students are placed in charge of building their own curriculum and projects to achieve their own desired expertise, using accountability measures through instructional agreements.

❖ The basis of the students' curriculum building is the teacher's provision of literary and multimedia resources organized adaptively. The teacher becomes expert in scaffolding and facilitating feedback.

- ❖ Knowledge is not a 'thing' that can be taught as an object: it is understood as deep, subjective and intersubjective, inseparable from the identity process. Depth is defined in opposition to the commodification and commoditization of knowledge. Educative projects are open and become ways of preventing knowledge crystallization and sedimentation. Rather, it is about situated knowledge in action.

- ❖ The focus is on deep processing, not standardized outcomes similar for all. There is room for diversity and flexibility, non-native speaker comfort, code-switching, and unique perspectives.

- ❖ It targets transdisciplinary values for a more sensible and wiser world—this way language learning becomes the means toward conflict resolution, ending war and poverty, re-greening the planet, and turning to politics for the human. Yet, rather than a dualistic view, the principle of the included middle (or third space) is applied, through which two apparently opposed elements can be integrated at a higher (still relative) level.

The Deep Approach is a convergence of what worked best in earlier approaches. Its holistic scope allows for more student autonomy and works for the planet and society while working on the language.

The instructional principles I believe in for teachers are to:

- ➢ Go by the results of motivation research, and provide incentives for self-directed learning and self-determination.

- ➢ Help students build their curriculum through their own literacy-based thematic units, indexing all language modalities to each other. As an instructor, merely scaffold possibilities; make your landscape as flexible as possible for the student to choose, select, and frame on his or her own. Use online modules rather than a textbook or supplement with a large variety of multimedia resources for blended learning.

- ➢ Emphasize process rather than outcomes; refer to instructional organizers in forward planning rather than goals or outcomes in a backward planning.

- Encourage individualized, peer-oriented, and small group project-based learning, focusing on cultural content and social action;
- Give primacy to text. Consider grammar as storytelling about language; target extensive reading/viewing and intensive writing/recording.
- Use deep formative feedback and empowerment evaluation. Integrate self-evaluations and peer-evaluations.
- Focus on value creation: highlight critical issues related to the respect of other languages and cultures, language status and invisible or open discrimination, the colonial mindset versus principles of social justice, and linguistic human rights for peace building.

In summary, understanding the Deep Approach is seeing Education and schooling in an "avant-garde" way!

Chapter 1
Deep Apprenticeship is Reflective, Adaptive, and Self-Determined

> *Because of exam-oriented education, students have become rootless.* (Liu, 2010)

This chapter scaffolds understanding about a series of premises that are crucial for a good grasp of the breadth and scope of the Deep Approach project.

When I started teaching, the reference model for teacher planning was to use well-defined objectives. Nowadays with outcomes-based standards, the situation has not changed much: the teacher is in a position to direct and control learning through a prespecified curriculum and a textbook. Curricula are usually imposed by the foreign language department, the program coordinator, or the head teaching assistant.

In the early 1970s, I read Robert Mager's book on "Preparing Instructional Objectives" and was baffled that he could claim that, once outcomes are clear and the sequence of instructional goals is on paper, not much is left to do as a teacher. This present book can be considered a response to Mager. It shows how much is left to do if you target responsive practice. Planning travel on the basis of a roadmap and moving forward adaptively may be as important as knowing the goal. I illustrated this point in a short story that I presented in China at a workshop on the Deep Approach at the beginning of the Year of the Rabbit[1].

---

[1] The Chinese version, 什么是深度反思性学习？is here: http://www.deepapproach.com/chinesestory.html

Why Having Clear Goals Derived from Backward Planning is a Myth

Once upon a time, there was a rabbit, who, after saving eight gold coins, was preparing to seek his fortune in the world. Before leaving, he sought the advice of a wise, old rabbit, who told him this: "Don't listen to advice; think for yourself, and think deeply."

Our rabbit, baffled by the old rabbit's advice, leapt from field to field, deep in thought. He stopped for the night at the top of a hillock where he could admire his surroundings. In the morning, as soon as he opened his eyes, he saw he was not alone. A weasel was staring at him.

"Good morning, rabbit! Where are you off to?"

"I'm thinking of how I can go and seek my fortune."

"You are a lucky rabbit. I will guide you on your journey. You need a clear starting point, a goal, and a method."

The weasel instructed him to make a backward map that began at his destination. The lesson lasted several days. When she felt he was ready, the weasel cried, "Perfect! You owe me three gold coins."

The rabbit found himself alone, disheartened at being poorer, but now he knew how to set a goal based on a starting point composed of clear outcomes, which made him very proud of himself. He started on his first goal: that by the end of the day, he should be able to reach the hill about five miles off in the distance without spending another coin.

Poor rabbit! A group of children from the village pestered him so much that he had to avoid the village, which took him in the opposite direction of the hill! During his escape, he lost one gold coin. After a pensive journey where he thought deeply about the unexpected, he finally approached the hill, but he was stopped by a river that would most certainly keep him from his destination on the far-off hill. He sighed sadly, heartbroken, and camped for the night. As he opened his eyes in the morning, he saw he was not alone. A beaver was staring at him.

"Hello, rabbit! Where are you off to?"

"I'm thinking of how to seek my fortune."

"You are a lucky rabbit because I'm going to teach you how to walk. You can't get anywhere if you don't know how to walk. You can move to the left, you can move to the right, you can navigate by sight or by sound. But you must first breakdown your journey into pieces and handle them one at a time."

The rabbit pondered on this for a while and recognized in the words of the beaver the advice of the weasel, but the beaver's advice seemed more brilliant. He groaned hesitantly, "But how much will this cost, my friend?"

The beaver was so persuasive that the rabbit devoured his lessons. He learned how to divide the journey into individual steps in order to get a feel for it. His schooling lasted several days. When he felt the rabbit was ready, the beaver announced, "You have finished your lessons. You owe me three gold coins."

The rabbit found himself alone, disheartened at being poorer by three gold coins, but he now knew how to breakdown an outcome into parts and find the solution to each individual problem. The beaver had given him charts, rubrics, testing forms and every instrument imaginable. The rabbit decided to cross the meadow, towards a ribbon of smoke that rose in the distance. He started off, applying what he had learned, taking extra care not to spend another coin.

Poor rabbit! He knew everything about backward planning, but he stopped after each leap, not knowing how to proceed with the next step or tool to use, or how to compare the earlier leaps with the later ones. Nothing was as he expected. Each blade of grass, each stream terrified him. Another gold coin disappeared when he lost his footing, the rabbit being too absorbed in his charts. And he lost hours milling over each step of the way, weeping the whole time. Nothing of his journey was predictable, so he found himself reduced to improvisation.

Suddenly, he remembered the wise old rabbit. He realized the weasel and beaver were wrong. No longer bound by one theory or another, he felt free! He frolicked as he pleased, deciding spontaneously what followed each leap. He reacted in the moment. He understood that a weasel or a beaver couldn't teach a rabbit how to move as a rabbit, and he was angry to have paid dearly for his lessons. His past came back to him. In comparing the attitude of the wise old rabbits he knew, he saw the common link. Flexible, old rabbits laid the pathway by adapting to the circumstances, without useless instruments.

As night fell without a hitch, he approached a large fire. A man sitting there stared at the rabbit hungrily.

"Hello, rabbit! Where are you off to?"

"I'm reacting to my surroundings, so I can seek my fortune."

"You are a lucky rabbit. I'll let you in on a secret: you've reached the end of your voyage. If you break the spell, you will be master of time and space. Jump into the fire, it's the only way to seek your fortune."

The rabbit, wiser than before, sat to reflect deeply on this for himself, also thinking of the old rabbits, who were terrified of men. "All advice is an illusion, only take what is useful."

From his experiences and deep thoughts, our friend the rabbit had developed his own strategies. He understood that there was no knowledge for everyone. He declined the invitation and went on his way, certain to find his fortune.

The moral of this story: If one doesn't think profoundly, having goals doesn't help. Backward planning before experience itself is delusive.

In the story, the wise old rabbit represents the Deep Approach—a way for students to self-guide their learning. The beaver is an earlier model of structured planning—it costs a lot but... The weasel presents the backward planning of more recent pedagogy...similarly costly and time-consuming and ...The man in the story who tells the rabbit to jump in the fire could be interpreted as the extreme version of teaching for the test that many teachers face today. The way that best fits the young rabbit's path is forward planning on the go, focusing on content input and output as a process, not a pre-specified, restrictive goal.

Note that, in this book, I use the words 'input' and 'output' in a way that matches the definitions provided by Curriculum Theory because of its focus on organizing open apprenticeship activities. From a Curriculum perspective, instructional units can be planned as conceptual entries through forward planning (input focus in planning) or as measurable outcomes through backward planning (focusing on outputs in planning). In contrast to this definition, SLA researchers differentiate the 'structured input activities' of processing instruction (Cardieno, 1995; VanPatten, 2004) considered since Krashen (1985), Gass (1997) and Carroll (2001) as being superior to instruction that was traditionally based on language production (or output) through drilling practices. However, there are other ways of making good use of output than drills. For example, open expression may reinforce self-evaluation and increase proficiency.

Swain (1985) proposed the output hypothesis suggesting that L2 production could affect acquisition, which was supported by Skehan (1998), Ellis (2003) and Toth (2006), among others. The idea was that production "pushed" learners from the "semantic processing" that comprehending input entails to the "syntactic processing" required to encode meanings (Swain, ibid, p. 249). The idea that production (output) helps acquisition is now well accepted (Swain, 2000): it (1) pushes learners to note the gap between what they want and can say; (2) provides opportunities to express oneself, test and encode meanings and get feedback; (3) routinizes encoding procedures; (4) allows learners to develop their own voice; and (5) generates reflective meta talk with increased awareness about the language. This book proposes an approach in which scaffolded production in open projects chosen by the learners becomes the key to language acquisition. Within this perspective, learning by doing in the production mode redefines acquisition in terms of apprenticeship.

Principles We Can Take from this Story

THERE ARE NO WORTHY OUTCOMES WITHOUT DEEP THOUGHT. Learners often feel that they are taught by theories that ignore contextual difficulties. For example, standardized models are often created off-practice, and can lead to neglecting adaptive qualities, necessary for working with others in co-created contexts. Such a theoretical ideal is partly unsustainable in the reality of the classroom. At the very least, it deserves to be complemented.

PEDAGOGY IS A LANGUAGE OF PRACTICE. In order to understand language learning in practice, a body of research should study the thoughts of students when they plan their learning, and as they work to realize their projects. Self-directed, project-based learning is under-researched. The results of this research paradigm would lead to a vision of a new way of teaching for proficiency, directly inspired by the reflections and practices of students' spontaneous actions and genuine projects.

REFLEXIVE LEARNING ADAPTS ITSELF TO STUDENT PROJECTS. Reflexive apprenticeship represents a dynamic process: students reflect in the moment and make decisions for projects that play a mediating role in the apprenticeship of the language. Deep pedagogy places reflection in the foreground.

DEEP TEACHING REQUIRES FLEXIBLE PLANNING. Learning is much more complicated than assimilating easily digestible content, taxonomically organized according to a Cartesian ideal that breaks difficulties into smaller chunks. Students can conceive plans for their own that are flexible. Learning is a negotiated process that gives a sense to the resources in organizing them in educational projects relatable for the students, allowing for the instructional material's integration.

DEEP LEARNING IS REFLECTIVE AND DOES NOT REQUIRE A NORMATIVE FRAMEWORK. Contrary to models, which impose normative frameworks, complete with fixed outcomes, reflective pedagogy does not respond to a focus on prescriptive rigor. It includes the capacity for the student to adapt the academic goals in reference to a moving context applied to projects, drawing on a repertoire of knowledge, which allows the anticipation of problems and assuring a personal progression. Deep, reflective teaching is an open form of scaffolding and feedback centered on the process of learning. The goal is autonomous, creative reflection and action while developing proficiency.

As an example illustrating this last principle, here are the reflections of Jingjing, a World Language teacher who received a copy of the aforementioned rabbit story, which had been translated into Chinese for the "Rabbit Year":

> After his experiences with the weasel and the beaver, the little rabbit finally understands that "all advice is an illusion, only take what is useful" and finds his fortune. This story reminded me of similar ideas in Chinese philosophy. Chinese philosophy presents several education principles. The first principle is "inexpressible". One teacher was once asked: "What is the first principle?" He answered: "If I were to tell you, it would become the second principle." That means if a principle can be told in the process of teaching, it cannot be the useful knowledge to learn. In the fable, the old rabbit told the little rabbit not to listen to advice and think for himself, this act can be interpreted as an understanding of inexpressible education.
>
> Then, the method of cultivation is also non-cultivation. In some aspects of Chinese philosophy, to do things without deliberate effort seems to be the best way to achieve goals, and the adequate confidence in oneself is equally important. So actually, learning does not impose a normative purpose, and sometimes, the teachers should wait for the students to learn reflexively, like the old rabbit did. The old rabbit did not tell the little rabbit any details about the journey and didn't tell him what should be done step by step as the weasel and the beaver did. But the little rabbit carried the first advice with him on his journey. The old rabbit teacher used the non-cultivation to some extent and successfully let the little rabbit find the most suitable way for himself.

This example illustrates the importance of and the unforseeable turns in the Deep Approach process and its inexpressibility. Chinese philosophical thought supports the non-normalizing aspect of the Deep Approach, as would do recent philosophical explorations, such as Jacques Rancières' (1991) study of the need for students to find their own learning path.

Obviously, the attempt at describing the indescribable is a complex endeavor. In Eastern philosophy, one way of approaching such depth is inspired from what depth is not. Here is a little survey to grasp the Deep Approach by what it is NOT. Note which points strike you as important.

1. Directive teaching and controlled learning do NOT lead to language proficiency.
2. Backward planning is NOT the easy way to language fluency.
3. The emphasis on oral communication has been at the cost of depth in language learning.
4. The place of grammar is neither clear nor balanced in current language teaching methods.
5. Language tasks rarely target sociocultural situations in their context.
6. Language courses rarely provide exposure to the regional and social varieties of the target language.
7. Deep culture and cross-cultural pragmatics are minor topics in language classrooms.
8. The way we teach cultures in a language classroom context is commonly not respectful of their varieties and complexity.
9. New technologies are rarely used in the language classroom to make students self-sufficient in their learning.
10. The teacher rarely works as a facilitator and the students almost never build their curriculum and their progression themselves.
11. Language programs do not adapt to students' determination.
12. Situations in which students freely build up on their projects represent a very minor part of what most foreign language departments propose.
13. Most languages courses are based upon extrinsically motivated activities.
14. Depth is more important than coverage in most languages courses.
15. Evaluation is rarely helpful and empowering in language classrooms.
16. Literature is not well integrated in language courses.

What, how and why should students learn? Is it better for them to learn rules by rote or to express their creativity? Is the post hoc focus on form(s) the final say on what should be enacted in a classroom context? Should they be storing information in their memory or be encouraged to find answers for themselves? The current context of education does not allow much freedom for reflective activity that respects the natural flow of learning. These approaches may be complementary, and it becomes a matter of affirming their respective merits. This directly concerns the management of instructional content. Planning is, in large measure, responsible for the way in which our students' lives are organized. A highly structured plan risks developing automatism, whereas a project with more complexity may trigger something like an awakening. All these questions require a closer study and serious reflection. What are the underlying values that are being targeted?

While in the United States it is legitimate to believe that the emphasis on the 5 Cs standards (Communication, Comparisons, Connections, Cultures, and Community) within their presentational, interpretive and interpersonal aspects constitutes an advancement over previous methods in the promotion of foreign language learning—an emphasis that is now shared across K-12 grade levels as well as college instruction—, the European Reference Framework for Foreign Languages has developed in the community of language instructors a sense that the communicative functions of the language are not sufficient and must be put into situated action. Indeed, it indicates that linguistic communication competences must be re-thought within broader competences whose contexts and conditions may vary to mobilize strategies adapted to the tasks that need to be accomplished (CECR, 2001, p. 15). Richer (2009) posits that this new, post-communicative framework based upon action theory must be understood more as a rupture from the past, rather than a simple, soft and cosmetic move away from the usual communicative jargon. It offers a perspective that is eclectic and post-methodological because its focus is the take-over by the learners of their teaching, whatever means can concur to develop the needed, situated proficiency in its context. More than an "actional" turn, this framework represents a turn towards self-direction and the acknowledgement that the language instructor cannot do much if the learner is not actively part of the decision-making process.

Thus from the somewhat simplistic perspective of communicational competences emerges a new panorama of what needs to be done for the complex action/project competence, a process which presents the major challenge and paradox of having to be explored and perfected in large part *without the teacher*. The whole turn challenges one basic premise that was taken for granted by generations of language instructors: that language classes should be planned by the teacher (and by extension with the close guidance, supervision, curriculum and agreement of the foreign language department). To understand how revolutionary the move is and why it deserves the denomination of post-method, let us consider a minute what instructional planning is. Indeed the linking of research on language learning in action and field practice, especially for teachers in training, is vital.

The Limits of Instructional Planning

Instructional planning has so far been at the core of the life of language teachers. It is highly influenced by textbooks, and therefore, represents market forces over individual empowerment. Textbooks, as well as teacher planning, present anticipation of instructional events, an organization of content that precedes interaction. In this sense, planning is an evolutionary fiction that projects itself beforehand onto unpredictable future interactions of instructional life. Thus, planning is a conceptual simplification of reality. Its models marry diverse theories to produce a concrete, practical action.

At the moment of instructional action, planning has, to a great extent, a transformational face because it must respond to immediate situations whose referents are past experience and prior knowledge. To be sure, this knowledge may appear hybrid and any work on planning courts the danger of applying different epistemological frames onto an action that a learner will explain using terms from a cross section of theories. Curriculum planning, then, has its own way of knowing, is an epistemology of synthesis with the risk of artifice. Its legitimacy resides in convergence and the pragmatic fusion of ideas. It would be a mistake to fault planning for slighting the roses when it blends them with the marigolds and dahlias; the florist creates art out of the harmony of confrontation. Accessed by metaphor, pedagogical relations transcend the realm of behaviors; they can be guided only by an approximate estimation, a project. Planning lies on this side of the meaning constructed from experience; it is a way to make sense of things. It conscientiously fuses these many theories, which apprentices (students) amalgamate at will to understand and to deepen their understanding. The quintessence of planning resides in the common denominator; and some risks are associated with reductive meanings. Concepts, with use, become divorced from their pragmatic contexts and become trite. Abstractions become objects of discourse. This *thing*ification makes them meaningless.

Research on language learning in action should hereafter be linked to field practices. The investigations into the categories and constructs used by language students to organize learning experience ran counter to the predominant normative trend. Nonetheless, the number of studies in this area of research has increased steadily. Enthusiasm for the description of actual practices is explained in part by the recurring problems encountered by master program designers and innovators who attempt to prescribe changes without coming to grips with the importance of teachers' and students' knowledge, beliefs, values and interests in the instructional process. Innumerable practical problems arise from the deliberate ignorance of working mental models, and of the rationales of situated practice (Lave & Wenger, 1990). Other practical problems are related to teachers' training: experienced teachers advise education students to leave theory aside when they are in the field, i.e. the classroom; and in higher education, teacher training is practically nonexistent. The approach that I propose may remedy this situation, which can be attributed to partial irrelevance of training models and their frequent lack of connection with practice, unless intensive practicums are organized in close connection with methods courses.

Another issue is the novice teacher's inherited mindset. Teachers are meant to teach. A teacher must be interrupted in some way to leave room for student self-determination and decision-making. Teachers make huge efforts to adapt their syllabus in a way that will fit the comfort level of their class. However, such attempts are limited as long as the student is not part of the planning process. In the classroom, the written program is transformed into an active one and the interpretation of the curriculum is crucial in choosing what to teach. This interpretation is a part of the genesis of a learning plan. But how can a teacher interpret content from the perspective of twenty or so students? It must be close to the students' mental models for them to be able to grasp it. Any training that does not take into account the practical problems related to the adaptive transfer, by each learner, of abstract contents into action is doomed for failing to use the full resources of the learner. Therefore we first need to address how to stimulate engagement and language development in the classroom through strategies we learned from motivation research and SLA research that point to the inadequacy of the present approach.

In principle, education is an applied science. Problems are generated the moment theory loses touch with the learners. For this reason, instructional models should draw closer to field practice. Mixed studies, conjugating ethnomethodological analyses, experiential approaches, teacher professional stories, action research, case studies and experimentations should pave the way for the conception of methodologies that reflect more closely the wisdom of practice. This work pursues this intent inasmuch as it is the product of video study groups (Tochon, 1999), participatory action research (Tochon & Ökten, 2010) and ethnomethodological research on the experience of seasoned teachers. Its models were verified by exploratory practice (Allwright, 2003), by virtue of the connection between theory and its field integration. They correspond to the latest developments in world language education and Second Language Acquisition, but more importantly, they work in practice.

Survey of the Book's Chapters

In this book, a rather rigorous description is undertaken—this being characteristic of any attempt at verisimilitude and trustworthiness, if not generalization—of what is happening in expert language instruction (Tsui, 2003). Instructional planning in practice equates to describing the unverbalized, implicit dimension of teaching.

Chapter 1 was an introduction to the nuances required for transdisciplinary action and value creation in instructional design. That said, planning has its limits, as shown in the second chapter.

Chapter 2 : « A compelling chapter » expressed a teacher. « Absolutely vital to forming an understanding of the theoretical bases of the Deep Approach. » A number of curriculum researchers and theorists proposed to define instructional outcomes in a way that would make assessments comparable. However models born from Cartesian logic are often inadequate relative to language-situated competence, they do not account for all its complexity. The deep learning process, defined as apprenticeship, gives rise to a variety of outcomes that cannot be anticipated. Therefore, evaluation is open and focuses on creative work.

Chapter 3 addresses the critical roles of text to language learning and its correlate, project-based learning, clearly key features of the Deep Approach. Because they directly challenge deeply embedded orally-based conversational learning practice, they are introduced directly and without equivocation. I indicate how and why text and the writing process should be the primary focus of deep language learning. Writing is used as a form of expression that leaves a trace where analysis and reflection are used as tools to encourage further improvement. Writing precedes oral exchange. Oral exchange must be considered the by-product of reading and writing in the language, as reading and writing are the seats of knowing.

Chapter 4: As Kurt Lewin emphasized, there is nothing more practical than a good theory. A number of researchers have designed educational classifications integrating the cognitive, the socio-affective, and the psychomotor aspects of learning. Their levels have some important points in common: the first level is usually related to the mastery of disciplinary content and is confined to the short term; the second level concerns thinking strategies and instrumental skills that can be transferred from one subject area to another; and the third level pertains to the long term, representing transdisciplinary competences in concrete situations. The articulation of the discipline/interdiscipline/transdiscipline levels supports transversal approaches, i.e. a better relation between the subject areas and a social application of contents.

Chapter 5: An inquiry conducted with some thirty teachers suggests that, contrary to the principles established by most planning models, seasoned practitioners do not sequence their lessons linearly but by integrating task domains. This integration allows the simultaneous attainment of a variety of outcomes, not just one. The characteristics of the Deep Approach and its core principles are highlighted.

Chapter 6: "An important chapter for the teacher so that she can develop the global perspective needed for facilitating and guiding the student on the various levels." In the Deep Approach, the learners are in charge of their own learning; they are, in large part, in charge of the curriculum decisions, such as planning educative projects, choosing themes, films, and texts, as well as grammar complements they need for their projects. The teacher becomes an advisor or counselor and facilitator and provides extensive feedback. Thus, what articulates teaching and learning is intensive viewing and its conversational feedback, extensive reading, and extensive writing workshops for individual and group projects. A series of examples are proposed.

Chapter 7: Self-determination and the awareness of one's own way of knowing and learning is the cornerstone for the possibility of deep apprenticeship. When students are allowed to plan their own productions, they organize their knowledge autonomously and develop their reflectiveness. In an educative production, the students are brought to evaluate themselves. The path to self-evaluation is acquired gradually, by experience. Studying the directives develops a working methodology as well as reflexive aptitudes. In the final learning phase, evaluative metacognition becomes a fundamental competence.

Chapter 8: The deep process can't be reified. In the internationalization of the mind, value creation is of utmost importance. This positioning first suggests that it is no longer possible nowadays to think disciplinary without re-connecting content to the issues that we live as a world, a society, not only as inhabitants but as members and partners of planet Earth. Language is the conduit for connecting humanity across states, and peace building across cultures. Therefore language study should not be constructed for the exclusive purpose of proficiency: it can foster the wisdom, courage and compassion of cosmopolitanism for peace. This "Deep Turn" in language education goes with Ikeda's (2010a) suggestion of changing the standards model toward 6Cs standards with the overarching C of Cosmopolitanism.

Make no mistake: the age of methods has passed, but of course, the teachers remain (Reagan & Osborn, 2002). The rigor of the arguments posed in this work should not overshadow the fact that a methodology blends with the teacher's knowledge. Any application is an individual, unique, non-reproducible experience. Thus, a planning synthesis is an arduous, controversial task that too often skirts the context and the student-teacher relationship. The aim of this work is not to oversimplify the realities of learning but to lead the reader to reflect upon them in a way that helps reconceptualize one's practice.

Many language instructors are used to teaching in a way that involves decontextualized exercises, which have proven ineffective for Second Language Acquisition. Empty slot exercises, vocabulary and morphologic manipulation, and an overemphasis on formal aspects of the language are most often developed at the cost of meaning, communication, and depth. They make learners passive, as the teacher makes the curriculum decisions. Therefore, the first step to a deeper approach is for teachers NOT to teach. Teaching as usual must be interrupted. Then what are the teachers doing? This book is a response to this question.

Chapter 2
Transcending Outcomes, Tasks, and Standards

> *Welfare bureaucracies claim a professional, political, and financial monopoly over the social imagination, setting standards of what is valuable and what is feasible. This monopoly is at the root of the modernization of poverty.*
> Ivan Illich (1970, p. 3)

This second chapter examines the status of instructional planning in a survey of common theories: what has happened in research on outcome-based teacher planning?

Concerns that education should prepare learners for 21st Century skills have prompted policy makers to focus on ways of designing classroom instruction with special attention given to measures of effectiveness. Outcome-based education reflects a belief that the best way for students to get educated is first to determine where they are and where they want to go—then design instruction backwards, starting from the goal. The terms outcomes, standards and goals often are used interchangeably, and there is disagreement about their meanings, whether they determine contents, student or school performance. Most often it creates a schooling system in which instructional decisions are centralized and imposed top-down.

Thus instructional design has enjoyed such tremendous success in the past decades, that it has come to a general, "backward design." Most teachers are trained to that model. A thorough analysis however reveals how the outcome-based organization of instructional sequences does not answer to a proven functional principle or to an epistemology proper to the content involved.

Models born from Cartesian logic are often inadequate relative to language-situated competence; they do not account for all its complexity. The deep learning process, defined as apprenticeship, may give rise to a variety of outcomes that cannot be anticipated. Therefore, evaluation is most useful when it is open and focuses on creative work.

This chapter proposes an approach, which was reverse-engineered from the spontaneous practices of expert language teachers. The concepts proposed bring a response to the limitations of outcome-based curricula, task-based learning, and educational standards. This chapter also offers a new perspective on ways of organizing classroom practice, which are genuine to seasoned teachers of world languages.

A Brief Overview

Let's try to take a leap backwards to when behavioral thinking first became dominant in the social sciences. The outcome-based teaching model appeared at the turn of the century with Bobbit (1918), and was later influenced, first by Skinnerian behavioral trends of research, then later by the development of cybernetics. Its premises evolved over a century, in tandem with developments in scientific thinking. The consensus at the time was that input-based instruction was not sufficient to allow for learning assessment in a way that would enable school districts and states to compare the results of education across schools or nationwide. Traditionally, children were required to read and write extensively, and when learners were ripe for assessment, they could be required to write a long text. Evaluation criteria were often fuzzy; in contrast with the earlier input-based learning traditions, behaviorists emphasized output.

A number of curriculum researchers and theorists, such as Benjamin Bloom (1956), Robert Gagne (1974), and Robert Mager (1975), proposed to define instructional outcomes in a way that would make assessments comparable. Instruction had to be criterion-referenced; for example, outcomes were derived from a performance, which reflected the competences developed by learners. This systematic model was based on a clear definition of tasks that would permit analytic control. For this reason, at times, it has been judged inflexible. To increase flexibility, one development has been to integrate more supple regulations in the planning of behavioral outcomes. From a school administration perspective, the outcome-based model offers considerable advantages. It is meant to increase efficiency by enabling the teacher to analyze comparisons between actual results and planned intentions (Figure 2.1). This teaching model is learner-centered because it proposes verification of the student's acquisitions by observing measurable behavior, i.e., performance of tasks with criteria for their acquisition.

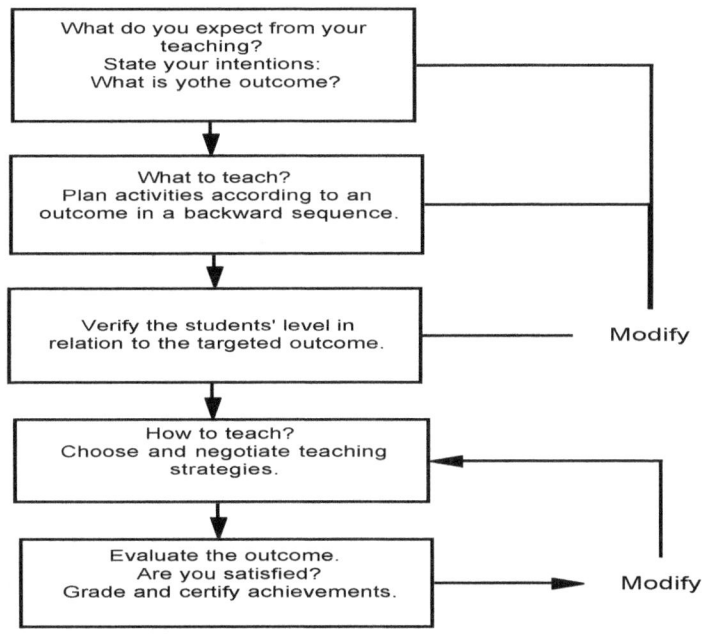

Figure 2.1
The Outcome-Directed Teaching Model

Despite reductionist tendencies, an outcome-based analytical model does not exclude aspirations of self-fulfillment. Its possibilities for integrating self-direction appear minimal however because of the anticipation-of-results process. The technology is claimed to have a neutral purpose, which should make the concept of outcomes' analysis adaptable to many contents and activities. As a result, divergent schools of thought in education have appropriated the outcome-based model. It can be applied to a framework that is pedocentric (child-centered), sociocentric (group-centered), or traditional (knowledge-based). At one extreme lies programmed instruction that presupposes complete understanding of the learning processes.

Here, the freedom of choice for students and teachers is highly limited. Conversely, an unrestrained socio-pedagogical approach may reflect a libertarian conception of the learner as an autonomous decision-maker. Between these poles lies a third possibility: defining flexible, feasible educative projects that would reconcile the curriculum outcomes with the subjective needs and intentions of the student. Another serious issue is that these ways of reflecting on instruction are usually subservient to schooling as a system, which has its own rationale of efficiency and continues to function, regardless of environment and global needs. Teachers are forced to function within principles of what is supposed to be effective within the normalized and standardized view conveyed by national exams, not by priorities regarding good life on earth. Can teachers and educators continue to do business as usual when the planet is in danger?

Outcomes—and standards—have been introduced in school programs as a classical way to organize and administer content. The present standard-based instructional design, for example, addresses the issue of control in learning by ordering thinking processes into performance-based planning, often proposed based on tasks (Ellis, 2003). Still, researchers and practitioners are not convinced. Can the incompatibility that sets the task-performance at odds with global proficiency be reconciled? Can learning remain a global process in the face of outcome-based instruction? How do affective, sociocultural and ecological factors fit in? For example, in language instruction, how can the problems associated with its segmentation into sectors of activities (four skills and 5Cs) be addressed? A planning model that is more reflective of learners' interactive thinking and of the realities of practice must be worked out.

This chapter outlines a response to these questions. It shows how to organize instructional intentions within a global framework that develops proficiency. Educative projects are meant to unfold within the context of real communication. This implies certain risks because not everything can be planned. The innovation presented in the chapter is to explicitly state intentions that remain subordinate to the projects of transformation and change. This chapter shows how language acquisition units can be constructed and negotiated within the context of proficiency-based, whole acts. It indicates how to connect two levels of planning: organizing tasks and the general dynamics of action within meaningful projects.

Two definition points should be emphasized. (1) The word "intention" will be often used instead of "goal" and "outcome"; this is to reveal learning as an intentional process, when intentions are from within. The teacher's role will be to model learners' genuine intentions through tasks, domains, and levels of achievement. Speaking about intentions rather than outcomes sheds light on the paradox of handling intentions of others in school programs. (2) In this book, "thematic units" are described, rather than instructional sequences. This is to illuminate the non-linear function of learning negotiations.

What About Task Performances?

A bureaucratic mindset marked the beginning of outcomes-based education. The idea was to rationalize instruction. Descartes' principle of dividing difficulties in smaller segments was applied. Students would study only the skills not yet mastered. The level required was defined by the criteria clarified in the expression of the outcomes. Feedback was provided. Repeated practice was organized in sequences with feedback loops. Progress was controlled by the development of competences. Well-defined outcomes allowed the school administrations to prove that a minimal common level had been reached. Its way of looking at curricula was based on the premise that the clarity of the outcomes would increase the focus on what was important in the curriculum.

Playing with the Learners' Intentions

For nearly a century, many corners of the world have contributed literature expanding the theory of outcome-based instruction, giving rise to standards. This abundance of information can be attributed to a number of factors: the simplicity of the theory; the precise nature of its predictive, evaluative approach; its coherent objectives coordinating the means to an end (classifications of goals are discussed chapter 4); its system logic and its learner centered operational reliability. An outcome does the following: it describes an educative intention in the form of an anticipated set of results on the part of the student, which allows for accountability, and it defines the achieved intention in terms of task and performance (i.e. expected product). Whether in curriculum planning, in the development of content programs, or in lesson preparation, outcomes have been used for over a century. They have been used to clarify and specify educative aims and standards.

In spite of its apparent widespread use in curricula and in school administrations, the standard-based planning model remains, for a number of reasons, a controversial issue. Its origins are rooted in psychology, wherein intelligence is reduced to observable performance. Observable performances have a widespread use in examinations and state-level tests. Socially and politically, the implementation of this model poses problems, specifically within the framework of compulsory education. Operational criteria are an area of contention. A well-defined learning outcome should include a precise description of the desired tasks as well as the conditions and criteria for evaluating said performance. There have been some efforts recently to better define what is a task. For example, Ellis (2007) tries to clear misunderstandings in specifying that tasks are goal directed, that their main focus is on meaning with a clearly defined outcome, and that it is the role of students to choose the resources to complete their task. However, experience in the content areas of humanities has shown that the fragmentation of teaching into tasks that specify minimal performances entails a blurring of important high-level goals. A teacher may stall at an intermediate-level task (say, transcribing and punctuating oral recordings) without apparent success, having forgotten the value of a broader activity that could better motivate the student, and assist the student's assimilation of details. Splitting program contents into operational intentions often favors the cognitive aspect of learning at the expense of more complex, reflective, and socio-affective goals. We can point out the danger of mechanizing education, speaking against fragmentation incurred by the overspecification of outcomes. One way out might be to use a taxonomy of socio-affective goals and engagement, which in itself is also a domain of contention (Zembylas, 2005, 2006a).

Paradoxically, the plethora of literature dealing with educative outcomes has broadened the scope of reflective thought on the subject, but has not overcome the difficulties related to their implementation. In any case, certain subject areas, such as humanities or social studies, are more sensitive to difficulties caused by the use of the outcome-based model than others that lend themselves more readily to segmentation. Yet even in fields, such as mathematics, it is now well understood that the fragmentation of the discipline into abstract universals is at the root of numerous instructional problems. The teacher who attempts to apply standard outcomes to the course of instruction soon encounters the discrepancies between theory and practice. It becomes evident that any theory omits a quantity of factors that arise in the field. If the teacher applies operational rules rigorously, learning steps begin to multiply, as any diagnosed unlearned aspect should be carefully reviewed before going ahead in the program. Then, the implementation of evaluative strategies, as well as evaluation itself, becomes for practical and logistic reasons, nearly impossible. The outcome focus was refined and made somewhat more flexible in terms of standards. It did not help much.

Teaching does not operate *in abstracto*. I have witnessed classes of elementary students terrified by nationally-imposed diagnostic tests and students weeping because every day, during the first two weeks of the academic year, they would be tested on what they did not know. Every night, parents would try, with a high level of anxiety, to prepare their children for the diagnostic test of the following day. Teachers could not begin by teaching classroom routines, which are so important at the beginning of the year, because of the time taken by these tests. Happily enough, foreign languages are out of this loop.

Educators had been warned about the perverse effects of outcome-based education. After two decades of teacher training, focusing on well-defined instructional goals, a research review of what teachers thought about these instructional models, published by Shavelson and Stern (1981), indicated that tens of thousands of teachers had been trained to use the outcome-based model. However, a large majority of teachers reported that this was not really the way they think and act the way they conceive of learning. Outcome-based planning (often named backward planning because of its backward process from the end task) is foreign to school practitioners. Genuine classroom planning is in large part social and interactional (Rogoff, Baker-Sennett & Matusov, 1994). Even after years of in-service training and efforts to accomplish the logical sequence of goals, most teachers admit that they rarely succeed in applying the outcome-based model in practice. I have met hundred of teachers who, informally, have observed the exact same phenomenon. At the same time, they felt guilty for not being able to apply the model that was given to them. The logic of science does not match the complexities of classroom practice. Since then, studies on these matters have involved thousands of teachers in many states. Similar responses were noted. The teachers did not oppose the principle of goal-based planning; on the contrary, they tried hard to make it succeed. Nonetheless, each trial was met with an inability to keep within the goal-directed anticipations of classroom events.

In response to the contradictions of outcome-based systems of thought, evaluation should focus on the customized learning process, rather than generalized task performances. Other criteria, based on ability, values, commitment, etc., would be valid in the medium-to-long range. The articulation of intentions, in terms of "can-do" verbs, is highly debatable, as these are prone to individual interpretation, thus jeopardizing the reflective relation between a task indicator and its intention. A better way to articulate intentions might be in terms of content aims and emphasizing process, rather than product. It seems more important for both teachers and learners to plan holistic forms of action than standard-based outcomes. This was confirmed long ago by most research on teacher planning (Clark & Peterson, 1986).

Currently, divergent schools of thought dominate conceptions of language classroom planning, represented in broad terms by partisans of standard-based performance, task-based-teaching and learning, and those of "socially situated competence": "it is the actors themselves, their expectations, who determine and shape the content of the competences required to perform successfully in individual professional contexts" (Alvarez, Guasch & Espasa, 2009, p.322). The classification and sequencing of educative outcomes adds a further complication. As we will see in Chapter 4, in the education sciences, taxonomy is characterized by a hierarchical, systematic, and logical classification of instructional goals.

The classification is rooted in the principle of selecting products targeted by the teaching process. As can be expected, no single taxonomy of intentions has earned unanimous endorsement. Classifying educational outcomes addresses namely the issue of ensuring an exact derivation of public education law within masters programs and within operational intentions in study guides and classroom teaching. Classifications of outcomes should enable, for example, values of autonomy to be expressed and become operational within school programs. Research on this question is partly misleading. Though curriculum literature has explored this subject to a high degree over the past sixty years, educative classifications are simplified reifications of what happens in schools; they have yet to become contextualized, adaptable instruments. This is still true regarding attempts to classify the basics of pedagogical-content knowledge (Shulman, 1987), or to classify types of cognitive knowledge (Marzano, 2001). The vocabulary of education is not defined to such an extent that it can be rigorously classified. Education is still an emerging, applied science.

Underlying educational standards are reifications of competences, as if one could 'learn' a competence. What we now understand, almost one century after Bobbit (1918), when well-defined outcomes have been extended and solidified into standards, is that a managerial view of education tends to reduce the scope of what is being taught and learned in our schools. The tendency has been increasingly to teach to test, and teach only core knowledge. Children became more and more limited in their development by the pre-specified goals that were assigned to them (Tochon, 2011d). In contrast, the focus of past curricula on input and acquisition processes opened the world of the child to the infinite possibilities for exploration of contents in personal and unique ways. Such a rhizomatic approach—like a root multiplying creatively—would seem a better fit with the Internet age. Indeed, for slightly more than one decade, communication technologies enable teachers and students from all parts of the world to contact people of other cultures in real time (Du-Babcock, 2003), which provides a fluid perspective on the curriculum. In contrast, standards have established norms that everyone must follow. Today, standard outcomes—a complex derivative of instructional outcomes—often provide a trite and shallow picture of what deep schooling should really be. 'Power point learning' only surveys core knowledge in each discipline. Under the pretext of equal chances for all, now children seem programmed to mimic the same outcomes. The potential for creativity has been partly lost. All children should be provided equal chances to learn, in their own way and at their own pace, what they are intrinsically motivated to learn, with reflective guidance and feedback, and with a mindful and social view of accomplishment.

In other fields of knowledge, such as engineering, technical standards provide agreed-upon criteria on the format of products: car bumpers must have a standard height across car types and makes to be effective, for example. Standards have been created in different professions to make sure degrees gained at one institution equate the degrees of other institutions; thus, allowing mobility under the realm of globalization. This is the language heard today in almost any government administration around the globe. Standards have been proposed and refined for each discipline. Since they are more flexible than instructional goals, the evaluation criteria function as thresholds. The burden of proof that each standard outcome was reached is transferred onto the learner. It opens the door to alternative forms of assessment, such as portfolios.

Nonetheless, the types of knowledge proposed are pre-formatted, which is a strong constraint that keeps the prevalent top-down, managerial view over more bottom-up and adaptive approaches. Innovation and creativity are limited. Learning cannot be personalized or individualized, except within the narrow limits of the standard definitions. The format is pre-cast and the ways of learning imposed. There is no way students could become curriculum builders.

The current administrative straitjacket in schools and universities alike brings a paradoxical constraint: its focus on accountability and assessment has drastically reduced opportunities to seriously improve the depth of learning. In 1999, Reigeluth proposed what would become "the bible for the development of many instructional designers in the years that followed"(p.1). His elaboration theory contrasted the industrial age understanding of curriculum planning and the information age access to complexity. In agreement with the dichotomy analyzed in Table

2.1, this chapter proposes an approach that fits with the 21st Century mindset.

Few studies have undertaken a comparative description of the problems associated with standards in practical contexts (van Roekel, 2008; Tochon, 2010a). One might think that standard-based instruction has rarely been fully realized in actual classrooms. Reforms are usually not followed with 'after-sale service', meaning sufficient in-service training, feedback, and reform improvements. Budgets do not allow real bottom-up feedback. Curriculum standards do exist, but we still do not really know how to use them. We cannot even hope to define, for the student, all criteria of success. It is an impractical approach and it carries many unresolved scientific problems.

Table 2.1.
Contrasting Industrial and Knowledgeable Views of Classroom Planning

INDUSTRIAL SOCIETY	KNOWLEDGE SOCIETY
Standardization	Customization
Centralized control	Autonomy with accountability
Adversarial relationships	Cooperative relationships
Autocratic decision making	Shared decision making
Compliance	Initiative
Conformity	Diversity
One-way communications	Networking
Compartmentalization	Holism
Parts-oriented	Process-oriented
Teacher as "King"	Learner (customer) as "King"

From C. M. Reigeluth (1999)

We must go beyond the idea of fragmentation and recognize the social context within which the attainment of a standard is determined and conditioned. This context is a factor largely misrepresented by tests. Meanwhile, the classroom teacher must make decisions and act accordingly. The teacher's planning must take psychosocial factors into account and must, above all, be rooted in the daily activities of the classroom.

Product-Oriented Curricula

Let's examine further the history behind outcomes-based education. Before the behaviorist wave reshaped curricula with well-defined goals, most school curricula were based on notions, themes, and concepts that had to be explored and learned. Curriculum content would be taught as deeply as time would allow, and teachers would give lots of feedback with formative evaluations. It is only afterwards that the teacher would consider summative assessment, which would be pondered by the experience every child had in relation to the content they explored.

The major difference between the earlier trend and the new trend may have escaped the scrutiny of most educators: it was not so much the focus (process versus product) that was radically different, it was this unique characteristic that students, who were taught notions and thematic contents, could go at their pace in their own direction, while outcomes and standards would homogenize the types of contents and the levels of achievement for all. Under the cover of a democratic argumentation, which at first seemed sound and appropriate, difference suddenly became outcast in the system. The attempt at making things even for everyone prevented the wide variety of learning paths that students had been allowed to follow in the past. The types of content, and the levels of learning were leveraged while we thought they were more open to higher cognitive functions. In reality, the reduction of complexity increased rote learning and restricted the opportunities for children to learn whatever they liked to learn. Now, learning was normed. Curricula became more and more normative. Content diversity largely disappeared. Individual trajectories were not permitted anymore in a timetable overloaded with tests on the basics.

We currently need a third way for education, instead of a return to tradition, and a major conceptual reframing of what second language acquisition really is. Our ways of understanding learning have become obsolete. Learning a language is much more complex, open and nuanced than most current theories propose. It is rhizomatically organized, like those rhizomes or roots that multiply in all directions from the branches of certain bushes and trees. Learning is in large part self-determined and follows a natural evolution. How do we account for such spontaneous development moves?

Research on school evaluation has increased coherence in the ways practitioners assess learning. However, coherence has been obtained at some cost. The fuzzy evaluation of the 'pre-Bobbit' teachers was adaptive to a variety of situations, in which students could express different content and types of learning. For example, writing a composition or a long essay would evaluate any sound application of the developed disciplinary content. Not everybody was expected to perform the same tasks or express the same arguments on the same content. Students could learn their own way and choose the path they liked. There were individualized pathways. Evaluation was more humane in the sense that the whole person could be considered. Before B. F. Skinner brought the idea of operant conditioning and verification of learning through observable behavior, most curricula were built as lists of notions to be developed, and there were "notional master plans" for each discipline, unfolding concepts that would simply be proposed as teaching and learning topics. Evaluation was on the depth of understanding. Now children are assessed for their skill to mimic expected behavior.

Many children feel threatened by high-stakes testing and cannot perform their best in those situations. Common standards for all in product-oriented curricula may resemble an industry-framed, assembly line production. Everybody is taught to act in a herd-style manner. This limits the freedom to think otherwise. The idea that each child is unique and deserves his or her own learning path has been lost. Standards are pre-set. Children are fabricated within the same mold. Teachers also often feel that outcomes-based schooling has restricted their actions to mimicked shallow performance standards. With the types of lesson plans that many school administrations require, and with the overloaded curricula, they must fill slots and be accountable for their productivity, with much less ability to genuinely co-construct content that fit the children's needs.

What can be done in this context of restricted time and overloaded curricula? What lessons can we learn from the past? As we have seen, by the time the idea of an outcome-based rationale had gained acceptance in teacher education institutions, several studies amply showed that, of the thousand of teachers trained on this model, very few actually used it in practice. Goal-directed instructional design did not fully take into account teachers' nor learners' practices. Moreover, it ignored the necessary adaptation to student contact and the interactive context of the classroom. It presented a theoretical ideal that was disproved every day by field experience (Clark & Yinger, 1987).

The standards movement is currently repeating the same errors. In 2008, Dennis van Roekel, the president of the National Education Association noted: "We can think of standards in two ways—as goals that guide instruction or requirements that must be met. In either case, the education standards currently being used in this country are neither worthy goals to follow nor sufficient requirements to provide a quality education for all students." The logic of economical sciences is not a good fit for education.

Let us now briefly examine one specific type of outcome-based teaching, which has become mainstream in World Language Education: task-based teaching and learning.

The Assets of Task-Based Planning

Task-based teaching and learning (TBTL) closely followed the developments of research in the field of Second Language Acquisition. Tasks stimulate interactions and natural acquisition processes (Prabhu, 1987). They usually reflect real-life language use, and, in this sense, their open and authentic versions are compatible with a Deep Approach to language learning. They are often organized with a pre-task phase that introduces the topic and the task to clarify the meaning of guidelines; a task cycle that involves action, planning and report; and then a language focus on the nature of the text or recording that searches for comparisons and possible additional connections (J. Willis, 1996). Tasks are compatible with goals that define their purpose; tasks are considered work plans for learner activity (Ellis, 2003). Such plans shape meaningful instructional materials. They define a leap that requires some forms of action or problem solving to bridge a gap that requires language use and *focus on meaning*.

Willis & Willis (2007, p.5) add that tasks can focus on isolated forms to study vocabulary or grammar, or imply a *focus on language* "in which learners pause in the course of a meaning-focused activity to think for themselves how best to express what they want to say". In a Deep Approach to proficiency, students should become curriculum builders. Then the focus would most often be on language as a self-sufficient analysis with the necessary tools at hand, and on meanings in action. *Focus on form* is rarer and may help when the teacher feels the need to intervene to scaffold the realization of projects and facilitate the educative process. Meaning-focused projects involve language use before form is analyzed. Self-study and focus on language come next, and peer review has as much importance as the teacher's in-depth feedback on process as well as language to promote accuracy. This means that tasks could be used with a deeper aim. Deep understanding of the process through which one can reach accuracy is more important than the formal details: the focus is on the generation of correct communication and constant improvement of production, not on formal exercises.

TBTL researchers are currently trying to broaden their model is adding complexity to the tasks, as projects do when adding the four different task domains. Exploratory research on the impact of task complexity suggests that participants demonstrate greater accuracy and lexical diversity when task complexity is increased. More complex tasks proved to be more effective in inducing developmentally advanced constructions and promoting interaction-driven language learning (Révész, 2012).

The Limits in the Definition of Tasks

A few researchers tend to favor closed tasks as a way to improve Second Language Acquisition, for example Long (1991) and Ellis (2003). However, most tasks are broadly defined: narratives of experience and digital storytelling are examples of open tasks that require negotiations of meaning, interaction, and possible turn-taking. Open tasks have potential for deep learning. More could be done to support self-directed learning. Even though research acknowledges the existence of two-way tasks, which are the products of negotiation amongst learners for their production, and despite neoconstructivist claims of mainstream current research, TBT researchers do not allude to the potential importance of tasks *defined* by the learners.

Deep understanding characterizes deep learning (Akbar Hessami & Sillitoe, 1990). The focus is on what is signified, and the arguments proposed, with a linking process to prior information and to everyday experience (Morgan, 1993). For example there are deeper ways of reading texts, and there are deep differences in the way learners approach texts (Marton and Säljö, 1976; Biggs, 1993; Entwistle, 2000). Ramsden (1992) contrasted the deep and surface approaches to learning. Surface learning focuses on forms and signs, while deep learning focuses on meaning. Surface learning associates facts and concepts without reflection while deep learning relates theoretical concepts to daily experience. The emphasis is external and fragmented for the surface learners as it relates to the demands of assessment, while it is internal and holistic for the deep learner. Therefore the approach proposed in this book targets deep education (Tochon, 2010b).

Another issue is the inability of the task models to anticipate open learning. Actual tasks may not match the workplans and therefore "may not result in communicative behaviour" (Ellis, 2003, p. 9). Tasks may lack a cultural component or any social component. Tasks can be disciplinary or interdisciplinary, but they are rarely transdisciplinary (see chapter 3 for a definition). Some programs use speech acts or language functions as tasks with a list of content free actions that can be applied to a variety of situations. Each function or speech act is systematically related to grammar patterns. These tasks have a predetermined, linguistic focus that Ellis named 'focused tasks' (Ellis, 2003). D. Willis (1996) noted the dangers of this particular approach: explicit grammar teaching implies simulations, rather than actual tasks; then control over form supersedes focus on meaning. Furthermore, when tasks are closed and precisely fabricated, the learner enters the logic of replication, rather than creation (J. Willis, 2004).

The definition of what a task is is becoming so vague that anything, such as a topic or a theme, can be formed into a task, to the extreme that any language utterance is connected to life. Within the prevalent mindset of totally controlled environments for learning, many tasks may come to be considered as a form of direct instruction, fabricated for the classroom and artificially imposed on the student. However, in a project-based approach, the inclusion of open tasks would reenergize their meaning and stimulate intrinsic motivation in the direction of authentic proficiency.

The last three sections have examined the assets and limitations of outcomes-based education and the potential of an open task-based model if it targets creative and holistic action. Holistic language units imply whole discourse functions, including the pragmatic intent and social roles (Fetzer, 2007). Second language researchers try to understand how the exchanges that learners generate in communication lead to further acquisition. For example, Doughty and Long (2003) advocate task-based language teaching design principles for distance learning; yet, since most task-based research is interactionist, it does not focus on the holistic language units generated by learners. Learners tend to use language holistically. This book addresses this concern. The next sections propose ways for teachers to customize learning, providing autonomy with accountability and shared decision making, cooperative and diverse initiatives, networking and whole acts focusing on the learning process.

Process-Oriented Curricula

There are new attempts at understanding what Yinger, in 1987, had named the "language of practice". A body of ethnomethodological research studied the genuine logic of teachers in their lesson-planning and during classroom interactions (Calderhead, 1987 and 1996; Tochon, 1989a, 1990a, and 2001). The results of the paradigm of teacher thinking in the 1980s and 1990s were so convincing that classroom practice was reconceptualized in terms of reflective activity. This understanding has developed since the late 1990s in World Language Education (Richards & Lockhart, 1996; Meijer, Verloop & Beijaard, 1999), and lately, it has been transferred to the field of Second Language Acquisition (SLA), with broad reviews on teacher knowledge, such as Tsui (2003) or Borg (2003), published in *Language Teaching no 36*. The backlash to accountability standards and outcomes-based education at the end of the nineties skewed the whole discussion on teaching and learning in the direction of assessment.

The focus on process is radically different from the emphasis on outcomes, yet it can be complementary. We are not dealing with a straightforward opposition but a difference in perspective. Indeed, processes lead to production. The leap is that there can be a broad variety of products from one single process. Teaching by the process does not pre-determine products. Learning about process is to art and craftsmanship what learning production is to industry. The former strives for passionate knowledge in a highly skilled and unique apprenticeship, while the latter is an attempt to normalize learning products, a form of repetitive obedience organized in the quest for uniformity. Paying attention to the process is a sure way to marvel in learning whatever the topic, while focusing on products may engender boredom in the learning system. A large number of students tend to think that learning the indicators of performance will suffice—why make the effort to discover other content? With rigid goals, and the impossibility of discovering one's own purpose, motivation often dies. The learner should be given a right to the process as much as on its products. Otherwise, motivation, being mostly extrinsic, will push students to superficial learning. None of it will last for long.

Education is more subtle than simply transmitting contents, in an order from simple to complex. Lesson plans are the result of dynamic interaction, and are constantly being adjusted to include instruction variables, such as modes and paces of learning, evaluation, and contextual factors. It is a deep process negotiated with the students as an ever-evolving project and mediated by the teacher, who gives meaning to the content by fitting them into an integrative learning environment conducive to transfer. Seasoned teachers tend to construct educational activities holistically, based on the learner's previous knowledge, motivation, and level of interest. Teaching-in-practice develops a twofold agenda that includes content management and face-to-face negotiation. The teacher continuously alters classroom plans according to constant feedback, balancing the conflicting needs of guidance and independent learning (Tochon & Munby, 1993).

Thus, a better understanding of classroom life has emerged from research on teacher thinking, which was mainly qualitative in nature. Teaching acquires depth when the learner plays a significant role in curriculum building. Deep teaching does not primarily respond to a concern for prescriptive rigor. In a broad sense, it includes the teacher's ability to personalize instructional processes in reference to a changing context. It borrows from a repertoire of organizational patterns that allow the teacher to both anticipate problems and ensure progress, while quickly responding to the context of interactions. The use of standardized assessment is rather irrelevant in deep pedagogy, as it often grounds learning on extrinsic motivation and short-term retention, which is soon forgotten and is not meaningful. Deep language pedagogy emphasizes the relevance and meaningfulness of the content and tasks chosen and developed by the students. Project-based units are viewed flexibly on the principle of non-linear spirals that respond to students' own impulses to learn (McManus, 2000).

Process philosophy would inspire the teacher to link new knowledge to prior experiences within an understanding of the value of societal and environmental improvement, thereby positing sociocultural themes that are respectful of the identities of the students involved in the creative process of learning. In the Deep Approach, students contribute considerable input, and are the curriculum builders. It may be difficult at first for some instructors to interrupt their repertoire of grammar presentations and exercises, and realize that their students need to build their own projects (Damron, 2009). The teacher needs to change roles with the students, framing instruction to increase coherence in projects, scaffolding understanding and facilitating the apprenticeship process. The task criteria are chosen by the student, not the teacher. An educative contract is negotiated. The focus is on the process, rather than the outcome, which is a moving target. It evolves along the way, as the students gain a better understanding of what corresponds to achievable and desirable aims of their holistic endeavor. Students can express their preferred way of learning. They learn from themselves and about themselves in order to build their curriculum with the help of the teacher. This is in contrast to sequential learning, which is sliced into small pieces based on extrinsic motivators; here, the work flows and the fewer interruptions, the better. A wide variety of resources and feedback are available for an optimal process (Csíkszentmihályi, 1990). Learning becomes a form of engagement.

This section has emphasized the value of a focus on the learning process rather than the outcomes. The next will examine the difficult position of the teacher, pulled on both sides.

Actual Planning as Teachers Live it

The education sciences use the term "planning" rather liberally in different contexts. "Planning" may mean formulating educative goals in school programs. It may also mean the use of anticipatory mental models, which may relate the pre-active to post-active teaching continuum. The latter concept—inspired from Jackson (1968) in one of the first ethnographic studies on teacher thinking— will be retained for the purposes of this book. Preaction is understood here as being closely related to interaction and not a very formal preparation. It is proactive in the sense that it is full of virtual multiplicities of action.

Authors who worked on instructional design believed that defining intentions constitutes a complete planning model for the teacher, and even a good application program for learning. ("Once you have distributed a copy of your goals to your students, not much else remains to be done" expressed Mager in 1962). These theorists did not take into account the complexity of the pedagogical field. In world languages, for example, a terminal intention may become the focus of a diversified approach, according to sender/receiver, oral/written domains of tasks. Therefore, the ordering of intentions within a teaching plan may indeed differ from their realization.

It is an astonishing fact that many theorists who have worked arduously at determining rigorous operating principles for standardized instruction have neglected the contradictions inherent within the preactive construction of instructional interactive contexts. For example, a teacher must ask what must the student have the ability to do in order to successfully achieve the desired outcome? No two individuals will analyze an outcome using identical elements. There is a tendency to identify more intermediate goals than are required to achieve an outcome. At this crucial phase of planning, the teacher is adrift, advised to simply carry out the appropriate exercises. The most guidance the teacher is likely to receive would be a recommendation to order intentions from simple to complex, referring to Gagne's (1985) levels of learning, for example. Robert Gagne posited principles of organization based on simple logic. The characteristics of the teaching plan will vary according to the product targeted by the teacher. He did not specify how or in what they might vary. Most researchers and curriculum designers adopted a deductive approach to planning: they have elaborated *a priori* planning models, and they were supposed to work top-down. In the face of these theorists' inability to consider the realities of teaching in the field, as well as the inadequacies of prescriptive models, a body of descriptive research has evolved to examine interaction in the classroom and to create planning models that complement teachers' thinking. These models needed to integrate some bottom-up flexibility.

More recent models of planning following the 5Cs foreign language standards imply an embedding of comparative and communicative tasks, interdisciplinary connections and community experiences within cultural goals, but no details are provided on the specifics of how to enact these standards (Sandrock, 2002). Nonetheless, research into the inductive analysis of teachers' planning has been energetic. Which models are used spontaneously by practitioners? Millions of teachers received professional training based on the communicative approach or standard-based learning, but very few actually employ it consistently. Practitioners are generally in favor of these models, but confine their utility to novices only. Eclecticism prevails. The modes for describing what is being done and is to be done vary greatly. A single teacher could use many descriptions concurrently, according to varying temporal sequences or categories: daily items, weekly themes, short notes, diagrams, concept maps, and so on.

No satisfactory planning model has been proposed so far, despite outstanding efforts—in this discipline—by the American Council for the Teaching of Foreign Languages (ACTFL) and state departments of public instruction to innovate in this domain. Researchers currently agree that the standard-based model does not much reflect the practice of experienced teachers, but no better solution seems to have been worked out (proposals are analyzed in this chapter and in Chapter 5). Researchers should probably go beyond description and build a framework that is valid in the medium and long terms. This book engages in the search for such a framework.

A teacher's planning must steer a course between the extremes of an exhaustive dissection of outcomes, and a loose task-based, holistic project. A pragmatic question thus arises: Is there a middle ground? Is there compatibility?

Limits of the Sequential Models of Planning

To respond to this major question, analyzing a concrete instructional situation may shed some light on the matter. Using a physical and psychological sketch of a fictional character in a world language class, I will apply an outcome-based analysis. The teacher, whose students might be thirteen to fourteen years old, selects a few pertinent, intermediate tasks: searching for new vocabulary, writing the profile of a peer, characterizing and assimilating related vocabulary, developing a character within a story. Should the teacher adopt an instrumentalist logic, they may associate the phases of planning to programmed, formative evaluations in an effort to adhere to the principles of mastery learning. Thus, the teacher might add a few remedial loops to the instructional plan. These loops might be interactive, where the teacher intervenes and corrects the student's work-in-progress. Some might be retroactive, where non-achieved intentions are taken up again. This type of instructional sequence may well resemble the one depicted in Figure 2.2.

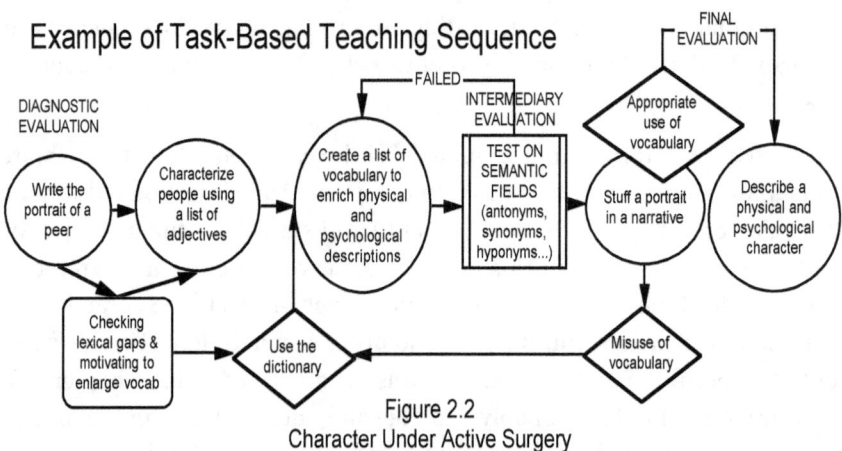

Figure 2.2
Character Under Active Surgery

The teacher would feel satisfied with their effort at conceptualizing the sequence, which may seem promising at this point in task organization. However, many problems would arise in actual practice. World language instruction differentiates several domains of tasks (often referred to as the four skills). Must the four skills be dealt with independently of personal expression activities? Do we favor a communicative approach over the sentential, structural approach? Should writing be separate from the teaching of reading? Teaching terms such as "conjugation" (or "verbs and tenses"), "vocabulary", "spelling", "grammar" are being brought into question in light of discourse approaches and pragmatic linguistics, which may not recognize these divisions.

These distinctions constitute many aspects of language functioning that threaten to obstruct the achievement of the targeted outcome. Must they be integrated? Many teachers separate the study of language-as-a-tool (focus on forms) from that of language-as-communication (focus on meaning; see Willis & Willis, 2007). How can this be dealt with within a coherent plan? Must several task levels be distinguished? The sequence shown in Figure 2.2 is derived from an instrumentalist point of view, i.e. the application of a highly structured, evaluative theory disconnected from context. This sort of caricature of mastery learning would likely run into many difficulties because it almost ignores communicative interaction and the teaching realities in the field. The priority, which should be learning, may be unduly replaced by evaluation.

The itinerary required to develop a task such as "Writing a Character Sketch" may be more complicated than it seems at first. This end outcome may be divided into a multitude of subgoals related to strategies included in various teaching task domains (See Figure 2.3). So what of instructional progression? How to choose? How to prioritize?

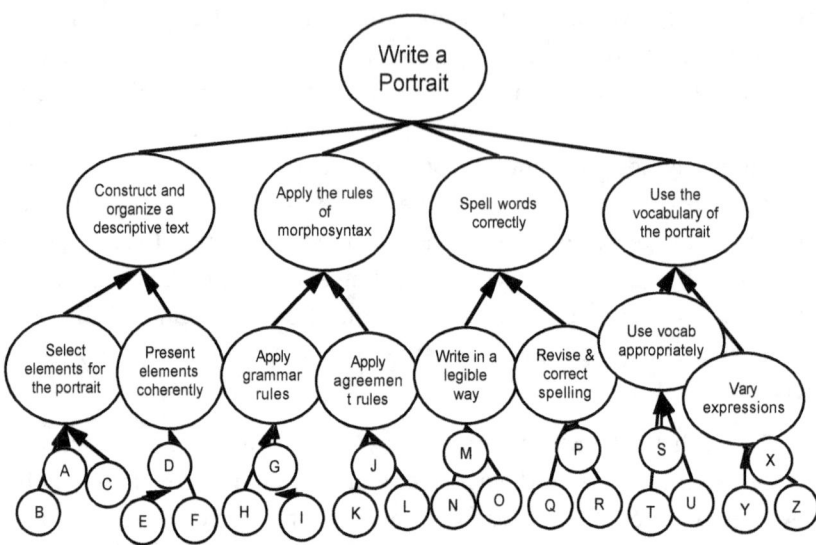

Figure 2.3
The Whole is More and Less Than the Sum of its Parts

Figure 2.3 presents the hierarchy of sub-tasks required to reach an outcome successfully, such as writing a portrait. The choice of elements suggested in Figure 2.3 may initially be criticized as arbitrary. No motivating socio-affective goals are included. The transformational vision is absent. In short, it is incomplete. The sum of all lower level learning does not equal the achievement of the end task. The intermediate levels contribute to the final success, but do not guarantee success. The whole surpasses the sum of its parts! This schema also lacks any interactive, organizational guideline that would transform its structure into a complex dynamic learning system or project. In this absence, the whole is equally less than the sum of its parts, as shown by the paradoxical system equation S # S or S < > S. Finally, the nature of the message and of its receiver influences the content of the written production and its complexity at all levels. That is, the communicative situation is absent.

One might be misled into thinking that the determination of the student's learning needs, in view of developing a specific approach, would be relatively easy. This is not the case. Understanding the task and identifying the student's level are not sufficient to deduct a teaching strategy. In the first place, evaluation of a student's real competences is difficult to verify. Secondly, educative intentions are interconnected, and needs cannot be treated separately. Furthermore, the students and their needs change constantly, as does the gap between the student activity and the pursued outcomes. Therefore, we cannot use disconnected interventions as a means of determining a student's needs. Teaching as practice must constantly refer to the overarching, transformational goal of education. This alone will permit a valid evaluation of the student's needs in the area of knowledge related to a specific, intermediate-level outcome being integrated. In this way, discourse-level language learning requires that no single language component be studied outside the context of a precise communicative need. This need indicates how and to what degree a language characteristic must become a focus of learning.

A Critical Analysis of the Zone of Proximal Development

In the field of Second Language Acquisition, it was inferred from Krashen & Terrell (1983) and their emphasis on formal instruction of the 'natural order' of acquisition, from Krashen's (1985) notion of comprehensible input that implies 'i+1' progress, and other authors using Vygotsky's work, that instructors must select textual materials to read and analyze that are situated within the Zone of Proximal Development (ZPD) of their students. Research results suggest that students learn within a range of possibilities of learning that are close to their current level; they need to be challenged but not too much. However this comfort zone can be extended with extensive practice. Our experiences within a Deep Approach indicate that extensive and complex reading alone can unlock higher levels of understanding and lead to progress of up to one or two OPI thresholds in two semesters depending on the students (Tochon, Ökten, Karaman & Druc, 2012).

Instructional designers have inferred from the 'i+1' ZPD principle that *instructors* can and must choose for their students the appropriate level of reading. What instructor could be able to do so? Each student has his or her own level and variety of vocabulary, various seats of excellence and weakness, different backgrounds with a heterogeneous range of prior learning experiences, which make it almost impossible to really specify the ZPD of each of them or the 'i+1' forthcoming steps of achievement. This is a myth among instructional designers, which perpetuated a whole industry of textbooks that are based on the assumption that someone can choose the right level and the right steps for students.

The same profitable error of interpretation had been prevalent after Jean Piaget's studies on researched steps in psychological development (Piaget, 1960). I shall not enter into the controversy of generalized epistemic profiles and their arguable classical order here. Suffice it to say that pedagogists justified their work and brought this interpretation to the forefront by applying the steps best matching the students' possible profiles. Our entire educational system is based on many such errors of judgment.

Duly informed by decades of research, we have learned that, indeed, students grow incrementally for a number of reasons (neurological and cognitive, psychological, attitudinal, etc.). This leads them to choose—from whatever experience—those aspects that are within their next level of interest, possibility and challenge. They do not learn beyond their ZPD, and their instructor, in most cases, can't find where the ZPD for another person is. It is from within the ZPD that one can choose. This choice depends upon a number of factors, such as past experiences and prior knowledge, inclinations and dispositions to learn from certain types of texts, epistemic modalities or ways of knowing, styles and topic preferences, mastery over a certain vocabulary or structure, etc. Students who have the freedom to choose their own readings learn *more* from them and develop new strategies with increased motivation (Madrid, 2002). This was a fundamental principle in Piaget's active learning (1974); it characterizes flow learning (Csíkszentmihályi & Selega-Csíkszentmihályi, 1990).

This example leads us to conclude that the common, outcome-directed analytical model of progression disregards the complexity of the learning situation. It is too precise; it limits creativity by predetermining cognitive progress. Yet its principles of progression are too vague. It seems too linear to offer problem-solving situations that encourage the development of higher-level cognitive and socio-affective strategies. An identical criticism might be addressed towards any sequencing based on the abstraction of conceptual knowledge.

Having read the preceding points, one may come away with the impression that a teacher cannot adopt a pre-established sequential activity. Rather, the teacher must simultaneously act on different levels. It has become a matter of habit to start from the simple end of the spectrum at the risk of becoming simplistic and boring the students. *Why not begin from the more complex, and link the complex and the simple in a constant indexation of relevant connections with students' tasks? That proaction transcends planning. Proactive planning is just a framework for adaptive classroom dynamics.*

The following part of this chapter supports this proposition: *in order for educative planning to be viable and useful, the tasks' organization must be partly driven by interactions. Priorities should evolve in a responsive way.*

Organizing Class Life Through Converging Activities

From Cartesian Analysis to Open Dynamics

Most teachers were taught to plan their lessons rationally. For example, Figures 2.2 and 2.3 are guided by Cartesian logic. Rene Descartes' Discourse on the Method (1637) held up these four precepts as dogma: 1) the verification of veracity; 2) the division of problems into segments; 3) the gradation of simple to complex; 4) exhaustiveness. The course of teaching proposed in Figures 2.2 and 2.3 demonstrate hierarchical thinking. In the instructional design way of thinking:

1. The choices made by the "model-teacher" (or the computer application) are based on a more or less universal agreement regarding the objectivity of the strategy and direction.
2. The teacher (or the applied linguist designing learning activities) splits up teaching into smaller, less difficult units.
3. The teacher (or the designer) establishes a simple-to-complex gradation.
4. The teacher (or the designer) believes to have exhaustively described the instructional intentions.

These four Cartesian precepts are breached in various scientific fields by open systems science. This research trend describes complex realities and advocates a qualitative analysis of the field, taking into account the singularity of potential events. It describes the dynamics of living systems. These dynamics involve interactive processes, which act simultaneously on many levels and whose functioning proceeds from an intentional, relevant choice of action. Four characteristics of this dynamic and open perspective, inspired by Jean-Louis Le Moigne (1984), may apply to new ways of conceiving learning activities:

1. **Relevance**: One true path that objectively attests the one best way (or the best and only way) does not exist. The teacher must be less concerned with evidence of certainties than with the relevance of a path of activity that will adapt to real circumstances in relation to the described intentions.

2. **Holism**: The segmentation of steps and outcomes leads to reductionism and may be an obstacle to accurate perceptions of learning as a whole. The analysis of structures and the dissection of components blur their functional aspect. Understanding the parts does not necessarily entail the functioning of the whole. The object of learning interacts dynamically with a context, a situation, a speech community. An appreciation of this environment may be the condition required to understand functionally the object in its dynamics.

3. **Direction**: The gradation of simple to complex is often justified by a causality principle (stimulus-response; cause-effect; condition-action). Yet every student is unique and different. How can one prejudge learning activities by a single logic, a single gradation? Rather than making decisions based on knowledge of causes, the teacher is asked to make decisions on the knowledge of consequences. Since the same causes will not necessarily provoke the same effects, this simple-to-complex Cartesian precept may be replaced with an adaptive precept: interpreting the object through its movements, without seeking to anticipate its behavior by some law that is part of some future structure. The learner should attempt to understand the activity and the resources it mobilizes in relation to the end project, which is freely attributed to the object through situated interactions.

4. **Connectedness**: Figures 2.2 and 2.3 are indications that exhaustiveness is an illusion. Is anticipatory exhaustiveness at the planning stage of a project useful or desirable? The exhaustiveness principle favors the addition of elements rather than a path of functional, dynamic and connected units. The definition and selection of topics and connected units that are relevant in relation to a learning project are sufficient. This is the principle of connectedness: acknowledging that all representation is one option in reality, not by omission, but deliberately. In consequence, it appears legitimate to look for some clues that may guide the selection of presumably relevant connected units and to exclude the thorough inventorying of elements to be considered. For example, the election of instructional task domains in world languages is partly arbitrary. It consists in selecting units of knowledge, which we suppose will be relevant in language instruction: reading, writing, etc.

Nunn (2006, p.71) emphasized that "To achieve 'competence', language learners need more than just atomistic linguistic knowledge, however essential this may be. They also need to practise putting together the parts." The four open systems precepts (relevance, holism, direction, connectedness) will promote a radical change should they be integrated into instructional planning. This is no less a change than the passage from the Cartesian paradigm to a paradigm of open dynamics; in other words, a move towards a more situated logic. Applying these principles makes it possible to go beyond a Cartesian organization of performance to the complex dynamics of situations, considering context and pragmatic interactions. Instructional planning can pass from the static design of outcomes to a dynamic framework based on pragmatic organizers.

Pragmatic Task Domains for Language Learning

It was suggested that the organization of language performance be driven by a connectedness and a convergence of tasks within global projects. The contents then become energized along an axis defining a relevant, preferred plan of action. In practice, instructional domains of tasks are determined (Table 2.2). The domains defined in this book are the result of empirical investigations I made among language teaching practitioners. Experienced teachers tend to include speaking/listening activities in a large interpersonal, oral exchange domain of tasks. They connect oral activities with reading, writing, and basic activities. The basic language focus activities combine traditional categories, such as vocabulary, spelling, grammar and verbs. Focus on form usually comes after the task has begun. It is a post hoc activity. This book emphasizes the importance of creating the conditions for an independent focus on language, by the learners, based on a wealth of resources. Differentiating basic aspects of language comes from a post- or metacommunicative analysis of language. That is, these operations should directly follow or be integrated into the act of communicating. Reaching this communicative convergence, which characterizes proficiency, constitutes the axis of language activities dynamics.

Table 2.2. Birds of a Feather Flock Together

Global Interactive Dynamics			
Oral Exchange	Reading	Writing	Focus on Language
End Task	End Task	End Task	End Task
Aspect A	Aspect B	Aspect C	Aspect D
Intention A1	Intention B1	Intention C1	Intention D1
Intention A2	Intention B2	Intention C2	Intention D2
Intention A3	Intention B3	Intention C3	Intention D3
Etc.	Etc.	Etc.	Etc.

The tasks domains enumerated in Table 2.2 constitute pragmatic categories. By pragmatic, I mean both intentional and practical. They relate to bottom-up professional language, not a theoretical, top-down one. The "four skills" had been proposed by cognitive psychologists based on theoretical distinctions. The four task domains in Table 2.2 are the result of ethnographic research on the genuine practices of experienced language teachers. It is their language of practice. The language curriculum often refers to the four basic skills: listening, speaking / writing, reading and the 5C standards or, in Europe, the Common European Framework of Reference for Language Learning. However, the key role of interpersonal exchange and the basics of language instruction justify, in the eyes of language teachers, the division shown above. The reason why the proposals in this book will work in the classroom is that they come from the observation of experienced teachers. The four pragmatic domains of tasks (oral exchange, reading, writing, and language focus) are fundamental in teaching other disciplines than world languages as well, for example, social studies. They represent process domains for teacher education. This opens the door to content-based learning. World language education should be a crucial part of world education: an education to the world, including earth, and a healthy society.

To sum up, the four skills categories that had been proposed by cognitive theory—oral reception (listening), oral production (speaking), written reception (reading), written production (writing)—are theoretically coherent; however, they don't really work in practice, except for testing. To plan activities for the classroom, most language teachers prefer a pragmatic categorization of their actions. Oral Exchange, Reading, Writing, and Focus on Language can be considered interconnected task domains. They don't work in isolation.

From Four Skills to Task-Domains' Dynamics

Educators who emphasize identity growth provide a deeper dynamic for personal and group projects. When students plan their own educative projects, they do it as a whole. They proceed from a broad theme and describe an action. The language instructor can help them describe the tasks needed for the realization of their project. For that purpose, the instructor defines the tasks that pertain to the different language modalities. There are various ways to do this. My studies with expert teachers indicated that they liked linking practical tasks in domains such as reading, language techniques, writing, and oral exchange.

Bringing the language techniques back into the picture can legitimately focus on spelling, word formation, verb morphology, tenses and aspects, sentence and discourse construction, with certain conditions; the analytical focus is placed, either as a pre-activity (vocab prep before reading for example) or preferably, as a post-activity to support the learner's reflection and raising of metalinguistic awareness. Task-based planning AND language techniques must be topically connected to educative projects involving oral, reading, viewing, and writing activities. Integrating listening and speaking in a broader oral exchange category allows for interpersonal dynamics, which the four skills (speaking, listening, etc.) actually neglect.

Acknowledging the change in the way of planning language instruction is a first revolution in the field. It relieves many teachers from the intense guilt that was generated for not being able to follow the communicative approach *à la lettre*. Teachers were still doing grammar (with guilt); indeed, there was some evidence that it made a difference, depending how it is integrated. For example, prior mastery over grammar is the best predictor of the ability to bridge one oral proficiency threshold during intensive Summer immersion abroad (Davidson, 2010a). However, *focus on forms* represented, for many, a backlash to grammar-translation.

Immersion programs take various forms, such as "one-way," "two-way," and indigenous immersion, partial/total, early/late, and 50:50/90:10 (Fortune & Tedick, 2008). Immersion teachers tend to focus on subject matter content at the expense of language teaching, which is the reason why teacher training focuses on integrating some language focus with the new contents. Cammarata & Tedick (2012) explored teachers' lived experience and report what multifaceted struggle teachers live, involving identity, stakeholder expectations, and better understandings of how their work can relate both aspects simultaneously. The Deep Approach brings a response in that respect because it rebalances the task-domains of instruction in ways in which they complement each other within students' content-based projects.

The way task domains have been conceived in this deep, project-based approach has evolved with time. I first noticed that teachers had their own way of doing this that did not fully integrate the four skills. Seasoned teachers supported listening and speaking skills within a broader interpersonal task domain related to oral exchange. They would not develop task domains independently, but in relation to each other: extensive reading with writing tasks and some integrated focus on language techniques, as appropriate to the types of texts and discourse genres used or developed, with oral exchange conducive to projects that express content knowledge grounded in the reading and writing tasks. Thus, the initial model for building projects within this Deep Approach was based on the following task domains: oral exchange, reading, writing, and language techniques. It actually corresponds to ways of organizing language tasks that can match the Common European Framework of Reference for Language Learning, Teaching, and Assessment (Council of Europe, 2001). Nowadays, the situation is somewhat complicated by technology as multimedia use enmeshes language modalities. The current language of practice in American World Language classes identifies curriculum acts that are interpersonal, interpretive (reading and viewing), and presentational (writing, recording and creating), with an autonomous language focus or a guided focus on form. This led to revising the initial model for project planning, to match current practices. This planning model integrates ACCESS and VOICE as two major components of any identity-building, developmental project.

The model's name, IAPI, comes from the acronym of its tasks domains: I for Interpret, A for Analyze, P for Present, I for Interact (see Figure 2.4). It is not a remake, but an enhancement of the ACTFL model, which takes into account years of research on seasoned language teachers' practices. This model, based on classroom observations and interviews of teachers on their classroom planning not only makes more sense, it works in practice.

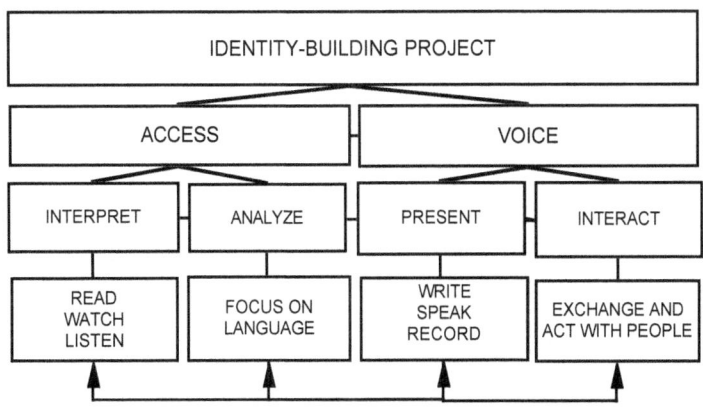

Figure 2.4
The IAPI Model and the Educative Projects' Task Domains

Moreover, it is a good fit with the 5Cs standards: oral interpersonal exchange opens a window for community building, intercultural work, comparisons and communication, within a model that constantly connects categories together. This, in addition to the 5Cs standards, leads to consider sociocultural and political as much as linguistic factors.

This book provides examples of a dynamic planning based on pragmatic instructional organizers. These organizers are process-oriented to contrast with outcomes, which are product-oriented. Outcomes are a particular type of organizer related to tasks evaluations. With organizers, verification of a task's accomplishment operates within the whole dynamics of the project negotiated with the students. Projects are always negotiated. They also are compatible with educational standards (Mitchell, Foulger, Wetzel & Rathkey, 2009).

The instructional flexibility of experienced teachers is based upon ways of connecting and alternating tasks domains (Tochon & Dionne, 1994). Connecting parallel activities in the various domains may enhance knowledge indexation and learning transfer among students. The alternation and embedding of task domains is a basic adaptive strategy of experienced teachers (Tochon, 1993). The use of integrated concepts in the different instructional domains compels the learner to use comparative strategies and to transfer knowledge from one tasks domain to another. Such thematic connections across task domains can be thresholds towards larger projects (Figure 2.5).

Learning can be targeted from different perspectives, according to the variety of domains in use. For example, the learner would find it advantageous to work on character descriptions, not only in writing, but in reading and oral exchange as well and give it a transdisciplinary extension within the project of learning about various partners' characters. The instruction gains a degree of coherence, and critical thinking is developed through the dynamics of transferring the content of one domain to another. This can be done as a preparation to a broader thematic project chosen by the learners individually, in pairs or in small groups.

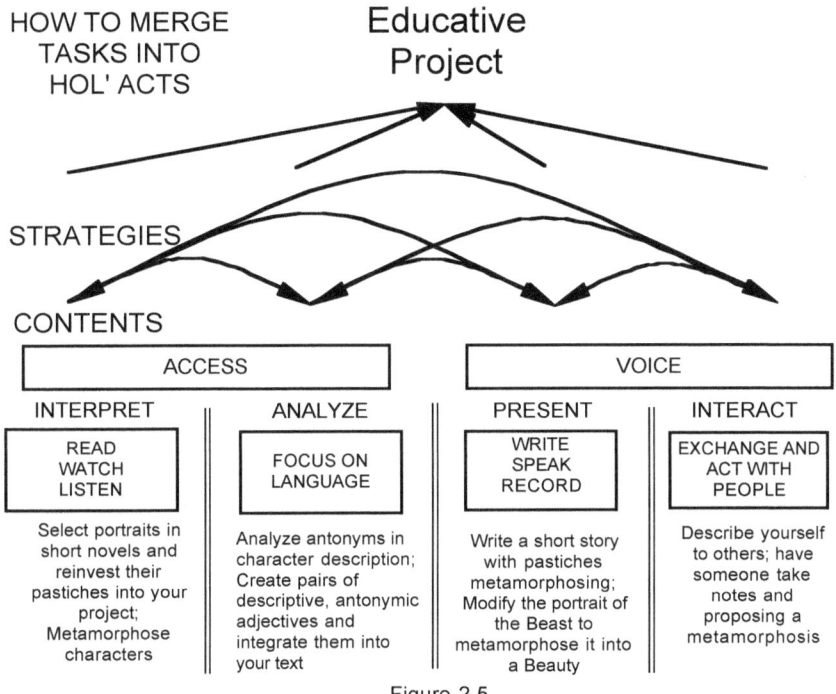

Figure 2.5
From the Beast to the Beauty
Transversal Connections

Bringing these strategies together into a personalized project provides the learner with an additional source of motivation. The strategies converge into a framework that may develop, for example, a characterization competence. The difference between Table 2.2, Figure 2.5, and the linear plan in Figure 2.2 lies in the thematic convergence of task domains within a unifying, dynamic project. The project assigns dynamism to its task domains by bringing them together in joined strategies.

In Short

This chapter has demonstrated that most perspectives focusing on outcomes are static and propose closed systems of planning. Even with feedback loops such as in figure 2.1, curricula and learning goals imply systems that are viewed in a quite simplistic way, with formalisms that reduce the complexity of interactions in daily life. However we could envision templates for resourceful interactions that generate complex learning, such as in real life. For that purpose a new dynamic must be created in the classroom. Instruction must be open to emerging events organized spontaneously by the students. Curricula should not be entirely pre-formatted. Students should be free to choose their own processes. Processes should be emphasized over products.

While researchers in literacy and early childhood education, language arts, applied semiotics and L1-L2 cross-sections may have studied learning in school settings and teacher cognitive planning from the perspective of complex and open systems since the 1980s (for example Tochon, 1989a) the integration of Dynamic Systems Theory (DST) as a framework for Second Language Acquisition is recent. For example, Scott, Liskin-Gasparro & Lacorte (2009) consider that language teaching should not be a closed environment. While language teachers focus on what goes on in the classroom as a sheltered space in which they have some control, they avoid thinking about outer spaces and account for the larger and more complex environment in which languages are situated. A broader and more flexible way of handling resources could open the classroom system to the subtleties and ramifications of how language, identity, and power are construed and enter a form of transdisciplinary re-framing, as attested in stories emerging from narrative inquiry. The narrative descriptions imply a conceptual framework that is non-dualist, eclectic, and that accommodates the complexity of real life situations. One compelling argument Virginia Scott makes (ibid) is that the native language should be welcome in the second language classroom, as code-switching builds up thresholds towards real proficiency. Dynamic systems theory legitimates genuine conversational environments that allow for scaffolding and improvements rather than the strict L2 enforcement usual in the communicative approach, which for years prevented students from sound practice in classroom situations. Double talk is indeed important in ordinary circumstances that require gesture, semiotics, and trials in first and second language modes. This contributes to a more relaxed learning climate with an emphasis on what is really important, which is a deep and spontaneous acquisition of interpretive, presentational and interpersonal competences.

Diane Larsen-Freeman gave a plenary address at the American Association for Applied Linguistics in 2010 (published 2012) on the need to introduce twelve key principles of Complexity Theory in our understanding of educational linguistics. Further she emphasizes the importance to avoid the disciplinary fragmentation of knowledge and transcend the narrow and normative focus on the disciplinary. Systemic complexity emerges from interaction and takes multiples routes to manifest, in a non-linear way. Among the key authors she refers to is Edgar Morin, whose abundant work is well-known in Francophonie and Hispanic countries but has not been translated in English, to the exception of Morin (2008), a few interviews and articles, his *Seven complex lessons in Education for the future* also present on YouTube, and two early book of sociology. Morin's major work on Complexity as Method is not accessible in English. The American reader tends to confuse DST with early cybernetic system theory, while there is as much difference between the closed algorithms of early cybernetics and the complex heuristics of today. Complexity is a transdisciplinary theme that migrated from physics and physical sciences to social sciences, as illustrated by the study of Crozier & Friedberg (1977), an early work on DST that is exemplary of the subtle power of any agents on complex social systems. Thus DST in social sciences refers to open and complex human systems in interaction. The type of understanding such knowledge builds that can inform policy makers, curriculum makers, educators, teachers and learners and any social agent.

De Bot, Lowie, Thorne and Verspoor (2013) propose Dynamic Systems Theory as a comprehensive theory of second language development. They express that, from a DST point a view, second language *acquisition* is an obsolete concept, because of the bidirectionality of change and the need to envision language as process rather than product. They posit that Second Language Development (SLD) would be a better denomination for the field, as complex subsystems change continuously at various levels of granularity, and the dynamics of language development occurs within the brain-body-world continuum rather than in isolated cognition. They emphasize the unpredicatibility of acquisition processes and the need to consider language growth as a multifaceted process stimulated by resourceful environments, which is a stand we adopted in 2008 when we started creating resources for a Deep Approach to Turkish (Tochon, Karaman, Ökten & Druc, 2008 and 2012). The templates proposed in the Deep Approach to languages and cultures (in Chapter 5 for example) derive from DST understandings and principles. Further the Deep Approach opens SLD to principles of quantum theory illustrated by Nicolescu's inclusion principle, which will be developed in Chapter 8. The proposed dialectic would be to incorporate the Deep Approach into school pedagogy by gradual degrees, either through targeted adaptation by pre-service programs or controlled integration into standard classroom use, or some combination of the two.

To summarize, instructional planning is a crude approach to learning, because it is so static. Instructional flexibility is the basis of interactive learning. To be proactive, planning must be open to dynamic changes and new connections. In the field, there is no best way; learning becomes a personal matter. Proactive planning gives just a sketch of possible connections between concepts and tasks domains. It supports spontaneous instructional variability. Teachers cannot afford the time needed to articulate all their operational outcomes, nor to apply instrumentation to every action. On the other hand, they can imagine a close connection between the components of language and language modalities that would favor comprehension and strategic apprenticeship. To dynamize a planning structure, one must organize its transcendence and ensure that a global functioning involves the convergence of task domains.

To anticipate the next chapter, let me add that the deep planning model embraces interdisciplinary transfer and transdisciplinary expression in order to transcend the limitations of prior instructional models. Instructional organizers are flexible ways of planning action. The intentional organization of knowledge then follows open processes rather than being restricted to specific products. Pursuing the same lines of reflection, the third chapter focuses on the fusion of both methodological trends, that of outcome-based instruction and of action-based instruction, trying to find an included middle at a higher level.

Chapter 3

The Primacy of Text for Deep, Conceptualized Expression

Two philosophers were arguing about a flag. One said: "The flag is moving." The other said: "The wind is moving." Another philosopher happened to be passing by. He told them: "Not the wind, not the flag: the mind is moving."

The Communicative Approach has instilled among teachers a common sense perception that language learning is all about oral communication. In contrast, I will posit in this chapter that text has precedence over oral utterance. No deep language learning can occur without intensive writing and extensive reading. Among various forms of self-determined projects that may deeply enhance linguistic, cultural and strategic competence, the writing workshop and the reading club play a key role, right from the beginning of language studies.

One major claim at the basis of a Deep Approach to languages and cultures is that texts are the basis and primary source of deep language development. The concept of 'text' is used in this book in the linguistic meaning of any form of inscribed or recorded utterance. Deep communication requires having access to authentic and complex documents and a grasp of personal and social texts through a deep level interpretation of their pragmatic features that may vary across situations, contexts and time periods. Thus the Communicative Approach as usually practiced is a threshold towards deeper layers of understanding that text can provide. This does not deny the usefulness of the communicative threshold but expresses the deep need to transcend it fast if linguistic and cultural depth are to be reached.

This statement is valid for both first and second language learning. When 33% of graduating high school seniors do not meet college-readiness benchmarks in English and 48% in Reading (ACT, 2012), and 60% adults barely reach the Advanced Low level in language proficiency, such language and culture competence levels suggest that the next generations might have problems at conceptualizing even simple issues in their own lives, since verbal IQ is correlated to vocabulary size. This is precisely the problem created by narrow reforms that reduce the content bodies to the bone. Unless we change the trend, we are globalizing power point thinking.

Texts, in the form of writings or recordings, are the foundation of analytic work that expands the potential for conceptualized expression of the language learner. Oral communication gains depth through its entextualizing (writing or recording), which scaffolds language expression in a way that is crucial for language apprenticeship. Thus this chapter is all about reversing other delusive trends that had prevailed for decades, countering Saussure's (1916/1977) exclusion of writing and the prohibition of the mother tongue in the second language class, often compared to a situation in which we deliberately ignore the L1 elephant in the L2 classroom.

In this respect, Levine (2011) notes with humor: "The 'cultural turn' in language education of recent years has helped move language teaching and curriculum design away from many of the rigid dogmas of earlier generations, but the issue of the roles of the learners' first language in classroom interaction is far from settled. Some follow a strict 'exclusive target language' pedagogy, while others 'resort to' the use of the first language for a variety of purposes. But underlying both these competing views is the perspective of the first language as an impediment to second-language learning" (p.1).

Two principles of the Deep Approach are that (1) you learn the second language in relation with your first language, to the support of which Levine (2009) and Kramsch (2009) have brought convincing arguments recently; and (2) deep language learning implies a thorough approach of texts, personal texts, shared texts and texts of others, matching Derrida's (1974) grammatological understanding of the primacy of texts over oral utterances.

This chapter explains how and why the writing process should be the primary focus of deep language learning. Writing is used as a form of output that leaves a trace where analysis and reflection are used as tools to encourage further improvement. Writing precedes oral exchange. Oral exchange must be considered the by-product of reading and writing in the language, as reading and writing are the seats of knowing. This principled way of linking knowing and languaging has received recent support in work on a sociocultural literacy approach (Kern, 2000; Byrnes, 2005; Allen, 2009). If advanced language learning and deep proficiency are to be targeted, writing must have primacy. Writing stabilizes discourse and practice and develops agency. Writing is to be understood here in a broad sense. It relates to the inscription, "entextualizing" (Young, 2001) or textualization of knowledge. Recording is another form of inscription, of inscribing knowledge within a record for further reflection, reference and use. Videography may also be considered a form of text or inscription on tape, DVD or hard disk in whatever file format.

The previous chapter demonstrated a crucial point: the four skill categories that represent the fundamentals for the Common European Framework and serve as the basis for proficiency tests in many countries are theoretically coherent, but they don't really represent actual learning practice, only testing. When most language teachers plan instructional tasks, they prefer a more pragmatic categorization of learning activities. They do not refer much to oral reception (listening), oral production (speaking), written reception (reading), written production (writing) as distinct skills. The categories they use in practice are oral exchange (merging listening and speaking into instructional tasks), reading and watching, writing and recording, and basics (or rather, language techniques: vocabulary, verbs, grammar, and spelling). In America, due to the way standards have been organized, teachers refer to Interpretive, Presentational and Interpersonal dimensions, as these dimensions are how, in part, accountability measures are enforced. Yet, in practice, teachers add at least one dimension that is not present in the framework proposed by the American Council for the Teaching of Foreign Languages: reflective analysis, which focuses on language meaning and sometimes on form. The analytical dimension, proper to the integration of language techniques, is key to the development of writing (Manchón, 2009).

The strongest predictor of proficiency growth before study abroad is the mastery of grammatical structures (Davidson, 2010b); however, grammar represents for many a backlash of traditional approaches, focusing on *forms* rather than stimulating metacognition and metalinguistic awareness. As I mentioned at the end of the first chapter, bringing the Analysis category into the picture legitimizes the focus on words, verbs, tenses, grammar, and spelling *on certain conditions*: language focus is placed either as an individual or group pre-activity (for example, vocab prep before reading) or preferably, as a post-activity to support learner's reflection and metalinguistic awareness raising (Willis & Willis, 2007). Language analysis must be topically connected to the oral, reading and writing tasks in their interpretive, presentational and interpersonal expressions (Hirvela, 2004; Weissberg, 2006). Integrating Listening and Speaking within the broad Oral Exchange category allows for the interpersonal, the transdisciplinary and the transpersonal. Oral interpersonal exchange opens a window for community building, intercultural work, comparisons and communication (Tochon & Hanson, 2003) within this project-based approach that constantly connects task domains together, and contributes to sociocultural and political, as well as linguistic factors (Matsuda, Ortmeier-Hooper & You, 2006; Holliday, 2008).

The present chapter is an attempt to define the writing workshop in proactive terms and to describe the pragmatic, instructional organizers that can help create a learning environment favorable to conceptualizing in the target language. Teaching by whole projects and the task-based planning model were previously considered differing ways of organizing learning, however complementary they might be. The writing workshop – and, more broadly, any expression workshop – may be situated at their junction. In the following section, a brief overview of these two trends (tasks and projects) is presented, in which their respective merits and flaws are examined. Three levels of interaction that lie at the heart of the expression project are defined, in order to objectify learning conditions that elaborate biographic (story-based), situated knowledge and experience (Tochon 2011). These three levels of learning have been the targets of cognitive psychology research into reading, writing and problem-solving. Tochon (2003b) analyzed the dimensions of experiential knowledge: (1) biographic and diachronic, and (2) situated and synchronic; they enter into dialogue through the apprenticeship of narrative. Both dimensions imply declarative and procedural knowledge of implicit and explicit natures. Within educative projects, such as writing workshops, a dynamic relation between learning and collaborative planning is proposed, showing that planning must fulfill certain conditions for a balanced learning activity (Boss & Krauss, 2007).

In the latter part of this chapter, an analysis of the content organization in a writing workshop will help determine: a) the conditions surrounding language learning, and b) the learning conditions underlying the empiric, personal and holistic knowledge that characterizes expression in relatively autonomous situations. An example of the integration of this framework is provided: a junior-high level writing workshop titled "Dungeons and Spelling Dragons". Process mapping is proposed in a series of tasks chosen and carried out by a group of secondary school students who created "Dungeons and Spelling Dragons", an organizational chart of learner-centered guidelines for a project of creative writing. This example defines the three levels of interaction that lie at the heart of holistic learning: the mastery of declarative knowledge, the transfer of procedural strategies, and the expression of situated understanding. These levels allow the fusion of the aforementioned trends within a holistic action, encompassing three levels of an educative production - the discipline, the interdiscipline, and the transdiscipline. This educative project integrates numerous tasks at various levels within a unifying experience. It develops thematic contents, strategic operations, and experience in action.

Project-Based Language Learning

Historically, the Dalton Plan (1911), as well as the Winnetka method, operated the fusion between the school master plan and the students' needs by specifying formative contracts within self-regulated projects. Within a thematic activity, students organized their own work programs and were committed to acquiring concepts within a set time. Many researchers credit John Dewey for the basic principles of Project-based Learning (PjBL), expressed in his 1916 book "Democracy and Education: an introduction to the philosophy of education". Indeed Dewey supported the pragmatic claim that education must create situations of apprenticeship in which students learn by doing. Problem-based learning (PBL) as well derives from Dewey's pedagogy organized through projects (Roschelle, 1999). Project methodology itself was initiated by David Snedden in science education and then developed and disseminated by a student of Dewey named William Heard Kilpatrick, in a 1918 pamphlet to which Alberty (1927) referred.

Meanwhile, John Dewey fought against the segmentation of content, as well as the fragmentation of subject matter, by focusing on action-centered learning within interdisciplinary themes. His project methodology had many repercussions in the United States and Canada. In Eastern Europe and Russia from 1923 to 1930, the so-called "complex method" also functioned on the basis of a productive action. The students learned to manage their personal framework and received responses tailored to their needs. Celestin Freinet (1960) drew inspiration from these methods. In this line, the French Ministry of National Education defined, from 1973 to 1987, many types of holistic actions called educative projects. They were differentiated according to the action's initiator (teachers, students, groups, businesses, local political representatives) and their field of application.

The introduction of PjBL into world language education and Second Language Acquisition can be traced back in the 1990s. It has been reviewed by Beckett (2006). It was applied successfully in EFL and ESL (Alan & Stoller, 2005; Hosie, 1999; Lee, 2002), in English for specific purposes (Fried-Booth, 2002) for adult learners in particular (Mathews-Aydinli, 2007), and was considered the most appropriate approach to content-based second language teaching (Bunch, Abram, Lotan & Valdes, 2001; Hall Haley & Austin, 2004; Stoller, 2002). Indeed higher order thinking and critical thinking are enhanced when language socialization is organized in a community setting or a communication network (Tochon & Hanson, 2003; Beckett & Miller, 2006).

We live a period in the history of Education at which enhanced control is required at all levels to match quality standards. This managerial view of curriculum planning entails a paradox: more we try to control our students' learning, shallower and narrower it becomes. On the contrary, when we provide more freedom of choice to our students, they strive creating their own projects close to their life interests, with much intrinsic motivation. The writing workshop is a way of planning shared projects that make students socially active, allow for multi-literacies, and personal as well as interpersonal expression, while perfecting the formal apprenticeship of writing proficiency in the language within a project-based learning framework.

Writing workshops stem from the idea that writing can be shared in groups of individually active authors, in a long term process that requires students to come back to their writing ideas and their form again and again to perfect them, consult each other and, why not, publish the results in whatever format they may choose: blog, webpage, exhibit, PDF, eBook, or paperback. Even beginners can start in this direction.

The Good News with Whole Projects

Holistic actions lie within the gratification of learners' subjective aims (self-plan) and educative aims (curriculum-plan) in an attempt to reconcile these two plans emerging—one from the school project and the second, from the project of the self (Bru & Not, 1987; see Figure 3.1).

Self-plan   Curriculum-plan

Educative project

Figure 3.1
The Big Picture

Whole projects are products of negotiations. They aim at producing a group activity that will satisfy individual aspirations and meet social needs. They present the advantage of integrating learning in a meaningful way, rather than fragmenting it, of linking knowledge to a problem or situation to be resolved. In this way, world languages can be developed within a broader framework that implies social justice, for example (Osborn, 2007). This is the good news. Learners do not develop content for their own sake but immediately recognize their practical value in the context of an action.

At the procedural level, a whole project has the advantage of linking the content of various subject areas (for example, task domains pertaining to various language modalities) within a common framework that promotes transfer (Larmer, Ross & Mergendoller, 2009). It may also develop instrumental maneuvers, i.e. high-level strategies.

Three psychological and motivational theories have explanatory power in legitimating such project-based approaches. All three illuminate why this approach is so powerful to motivate students. These theories are self-efficacy theory (Bandura, 1986), attribution theory (Weiner, 1986), and self-determination theory (Deci, Vallerand, Pelletier & Ryan, 1991). According to all three motivation theories, educative projects offer ways to increase learning dynamics because they benefit from students' intrinsic motivational impulses. Self-efficacy requires that learners set their own course of action, develop cognitive and metacognitive strategies in practice with successful peers who model actions and convince them that they really can do it to achieve their goals. Students need to know that they are in control of the determining factors of their success. Attribution theory indicates the crucial role of the teacher in emphasizing that the learning process is a source of pleasure and accomplishment, not only the goal, yet the outcome and the rationale for choosing the outcome have to be clear. Prolonged effort is the key reason for the success of expert professionals, according to numerous studies on professional achievement, rather than help or chance. The source of achievement is inside, not outside. This is learned through ownership over personal and team projects. Self-determination theory emphasizes students' needs for team relationships, autonomy, and self-directed competence.

The application of situated knowledge and its autonomous creative management in holistic actions contribute to learners' empiric, personal and overall development. Writers' workshops ease effort and stimulate intrinsic motivation and autonomous choice within a noncompetitive working environment that develops responsibility (Harris, Graham & Mason, 2006). In this respect, whole projects supply the basis for a pedagogy of identity-building and self-actualization. This advocates for the emancipation from education's reproductive role, the learners' creative autonomy, discovery in a context of freedom, and an integrated, animating pedagogy. This is the good news.

The Bad News with Whole Projects

There is nothing intrinsically bad in educative projects. The purpose of this section is not to break the trend. On the contrary, as we have seen, it has numerous merits. Nonetheless a non-dogmatic view of pedagogy entails that educators should be aware of the pros and cons of the models they use and promote. No model is perfect. Some concepts come at the right time and provide worthwhile motives for change in an interesting direction, but ten years later may have become buzzwords that people do not try anymore to understand deeply. They become trite and vanish, until a new reading is proposed and a new cycle of adjustment appears necessary.

The whole project trend does reflect a pedagogy that advocates for a production-oriented activity. Task-centered production has an educative role at the cognitive level, as well as the socio-affective, and possibly, kinesthetic levels. One flaw is inherent to the approach itself: directional globalization tends to overlook systematic mastery of individual concepts. Criticism of this type of teaching is directed at (a) the disregard for content, (b) the slow pace of learning by discovery, and (c) the action's potential for ideological deviation. This model has been criticized for its vagueness and lack of rigor. Very fashionable for a time, it fell partly into disrepute in Eastern Europe and the United States because of its lack of methodology and competitiveness considered necessary in the training of scientists, technicians or skilled laborers.

Looking at the level of procedures, the whole project's inductive maneuvers may lock learners into a tentative stage where they may waste undue time. They need to move rapidly from field experience to a reflective phase and a mental conceptualizing of experience. The whole project proceeds from a pragmatist psychology that might promote a false representation of cognitive development. In a global action, the temporal succession of experiences does not fully correspond to a rationale psychogenesis, which may require alternating inductive and deductive phases.

In the final analysis, the conditions of a learner's educative project are often determined by the teacher's inclinations. Concrete action inscribed onto the ideology of actualization can founder in dogmatic control, manipulation and indoctrination. A subtle link between the idea of autonomy and action aimed at developing autonomy in others exists; advocating freedom excludes its imposition. Holistic activity-centered pedagogy rests on a fundamentally contradictory basis since the best holistic action remains, which arises spontaneously, freely, from the learners. But how does one teach within such a vague frame? The dangers of this approach come from the systematization of affective goals, where it may be difficult to systematize individual growth and self-actualization in mass education (Jung, 1973; Maslow, 1998).

The preceding points have outlined the advantages and the flaws of project-based teaching on the levels of contents, procedures and contextualization. These positive and negative aspects are inherent to the psychosocial model of an approach, which promotes autonomous expression. In the proceeding points, the problems related to the specification of educative intentions within holistic actions are examined. The goal of this analysis is to find complementary aspects in both trends. Deep pedagogy, as proposed in Chapters 5 and 6, is an attempt to respond to these valuable criticisms. There should be ways to specify project processes and the tasks attached to each language domain. We should provide better scaffolding and more precision and rigor in the self-determination of a course of action.

High-Caliber Outcomes in Light

Instructional tasks, outcomes, and standards were examined in the second chapter. To summarize, intentions may become operational through tasks or standard outcomes. They allow a clear communication of a teacher's expectations. In this approach, knowledge is organized in a rational progression of simple to complex, in correspondence to hierarchies of classified goals. Its review led to questioning such linear approach.

From a procedural standpoint, planning successive learning sequences required to reach a terminal task or outcome would allow a progressive assimilation of knowledge. However, its contextualization in a multimodal practice is needed (Young, 2010). Transfer-related intentions can be made explicit in order to develop a work method, for which evaluation may be instrumental. The implicit factors that lead to a specific outcome can be clarified in individualized work contracts, and subsequently, can fit the learning to the needs of the learner.

Regarding contextual knowledge, efforts targeting the specification of intentions may contribute to the whole project and encourage an experimental attitude in education. The improved evaluation of materials, academic results, and subsequently the output would increase the efficiency of the learning process. This subordinates the means to the end. Thus, the system presumably improves itself through feedback (Hyland & Hyland, 2006), and both the teacher and the learner are self-taught.

Generally speaking, the evolution of outcome-based thinking proves that this analytical model does not dismiss outright all humanist aims. For example, learners' operant conditioning has been reshaped by the Rogerian tendency to focus on the "clients" and their informal development (Rogers, 1986). Also, stimulus-response has been remodeled as an integrated component of cognitive development through conditions of action and their triggering factors.

The Shadow of Backward Planning

In Chapter 2, we have seen that the rational sequencing of outcomes is a myth. Regarding content, backward planning and analysis, either modeled on tasks or standards lies on the theoretic principles of an evaluation that targets educative intentions, all epistemological considerations aside. In other words, this is an evaluation that may be blind to the actual learning process and the nature of the content.

Content evaluation is overlooked by the outcome-based approach. Evaluation must be integrated into the specific orientation of the subject matter; it must be framed within a specific way of knowing. Determining the linear logic of an ideal course of study is not enough. An orientation for the pedagogical process is required as well; in addition, the verification of achieved intentions requires an instrumentation that the teacher cannot hope to create. Lastly, backward planning favors behavioral and cognitive intentions, to the detriment of socio-affective and socio-cultural intentions because priorities are skewed. Memorized knowledge is preferred over synthesis or expressive competences. It is obviously easier to evaluate numbers or vocabulary than it is to evaluate a summarizing competence or creativity.

As far as procedural operations are concerned, the linear simple to complex progression has not been proved to be the ideal planning concept. Some complex tasks are more helpful to develop proficiency: "(1) increasing task complexity, with respect to the planning time continuum, produces significantly greater fluency... and lexical complexity; (2) increasing task complexity, through the provision of ideas and macro-structure, produces significantly greater lexical complexity but no effect on fluency" (Ong & Zhang, 2010, p. 218). Establishing linearity is equivalent to imposing assimilation by operant conditioning and a taxonomic shift[1] that results in reflex action rather than purposeful learning. Learners no longer control their method of learning, nor their own syntheses -everything has already been decided, at least theoretically. The crucial choice of content and strategies are each teacher's own make. The one guideline provided for organizing instructional sequences is that of requisites: what must the student be able to do in order to achieve the desired behavior? The application of the theoretical model is even more arduous in the teaching of languages and human sciences than it is for scientific subject matter, which lends itself

---

[1] The push-down principle or principle of reduction: according to the law of least effort, cognitive responses tend to "slide" toward the lower end of the taxonomic scale. What was initially a complex problem-solving situation becomes, by force of habit, a simple regurgitation of stocked responses.

more readily to segmentation. When minimal tasks are defined, general intentions become blurred. More often than not, rigorous instruction on the basis of well-designed outcomes is simply neither viable nor possible without constant adaptations.

Where context is concerned, an extensive fragmentation of outcomes proves to be inapplicable in the classroom. Paradoxically, such over-specification that can be seen in many state master plans is called "operational" but is inoperative. The aims of technocratic efficiency and the attempts at quasi-scientific objectivity contrast with the lack of attention to the relation between teacher and learner and of the sometimes turbulent context of heterogeneous classes: although teachers are most often well intentioned, they rarely feel confident to address issues related to the diversity they have in their classes (Ortega-Martin, 2004). The chasm between theory and practice swallows up those teachers who attempt to apply the model and discover this insurmountable contradiction: by ordering intentions into a hierarchy, they lose sight of the true priorities. Their extensive reflection on theory centers only on the transfer of knowledge in a string of successive outcomes, and does not take into consideration the factors probed by social psychology and empiric observation: the conditions and contextual realities of communication, and the interactive, socio-affective aspects of learning. Research on teacher planning indicates that teachers are seldom preoccupied with outcomes, unless standardized assessments force them to teach to test (Sacks, 2000). This is perhaps due to a lack of time, perhaps because the required effort is deemed too great for minimal results, perhaps even because of perceived risks: the risk of a technical approach that robs learners' motivation, the risk of students cramming for tests when the goal and its behavioral indicator are confused (mistaking performance for competence), and the risk of inflexibility. With such a constrained approach, students are exposed to sets of predetermined instructions, when they should be creating, deciding and constructing for themselves. This also suggests new directions for research on writing (Ransdell & Barbier, 2002), as developed in the second part of this chapter.

To sum up, a brief review of teaching through whole projects and of the outcome-based backward planning model stresses the advantages, as well as the flaws, inherent to these two ways of organizing classroom activities. These two approaches do not ordinarily converge; however, analysis indicates that specifying the organization of intentions may improve projects, and that, conversely, the subordination of intentions to an integrative action forestalls the fragmentation of learning. Therefore, it is advisable to retain the advantages offered by both approaches. The synthesis of these two trends could be conceived as an interrelation between levels of learning; content is then activated by strategies that ensure, within a specific context, the conditions of expression.

In a classroom setting, the holistic writing activity affects the junction where the learner's subjective needs and the objective needs of the curriculum intersect. The learner can then move from language to symbolic competence (Kramsch, 2006). The compatibility of subjective and objective requirements can be achieved by embedding the organization of intentional acts, tasks or outcomes into a whole project arising from the students' wishes as individuals, in small groups or as a class.

There are pros and cons in both educative models. Why not take the best from each? The advantageous characteristics of these approaches may merge in a well-defined proactive concept. Let us consider the detail of that analysis.

Hol-Act Organizers: Towards Compatibility

Teaching based on whole project draws upon the flexible and adaptive practice of "reflecting-in-action" (Schön, 1987). Students' interests are integrated into the curriculum. It effects the fusion of the self-plan and the school plan, resulting in higher classroom dynamics. The thematic management of content situates knowledge, and a concrete experience ensures its assimilation around specific genres (Hyland, 2004; Byrnes & Sprang, 2004). The weakness of this holistic approach lies in the oversight of mastery, making it rather uncompetitive in a technical or scientific field. There might be fewer problems in world languages and Language Arts, yet structural knowledge makes a difference. Outcome-based designs, on the other hand, keep track of knowledge so systematically that it risks boring the learner with repetitive activities, if outcomes of a higher level are not targeted: those outcomes that would, in fact, be developed through holistic action, which includes specified organizers that would operate at various levels. That is the *Hol-Act* process.

Learning by discovering, in the context of a whole project, stimulates motivation. However, from the standpoint of procedure, a deductive phase should follow this inductive phase, in order to avoid prolonged experimental fumbling. The specification of transfer organizers would promote the development of the instrumental competences required for a successful action. In an outcome-directed analysis, the organization of strategies corresponds to a linear principle, from simple to complex. This excessive rationality in backward planning, subordinate to an ideal of exhaustive foresight, seems inadequate in the classroom and leaves the learner no room for finding her/his own path of learning.

Depending on contextual conditions, the extremes of both trends verge on ideological manipulation. In principle, the initiators of a whole project, as well as the tenets of outcome-based instructional design declare an aspiration of "neutrality in teaching". The first group claims to allow learners autonomy in their choices and creation of their own ideals (the whole project being an ideal to realize); the second group claims neutrality by virtue of rigor and a scientific method. At this point, a fundamental debate must be reviewed, if only briefly. An instructional option is never neutral. Any educational system is the external manifestation of a culturally-biased thought model (Kuhn, 1962; Woolgar, 2002; McLaren, 1992). On one side of the debate, certain instructional specialists accuse the whole project trend of being a demagogic option of creativity, fulfilling a need for satisfaction among students, rather than emphasizing efforts towards excellence. A methodology which is loosely structured, therefore, is of little educative value. On the other side, some whole language specialists condemn a technical rationale in the outcome-directed standard-based design, which subjects learners to an industrialized society's goals (Edelsky, 1990). To state the problem more clearly, the criticisms are linked implicitly or explicitly to oppositions that are:

-political: mistakenly, since one could point to a leftist "exploitation" of the outcome-based model of analysis as well as "right-wing" administrative definitions of whole projects;

-philosophical, as in the autonomy assigned to learners and the recognized role of consciousness in the learning process;

a considerable effort should be made to reveal the pragmatic complementarity of both approaches. It is high time for compatible views on the teaching-learning process (Lemke, 1994). Knowing that a model cannot be neutral, one may prevent structuralist reductionism by enlarging the intentional acts to constructive values voiced by and negotiated with the students.

Any method can be perverted or abused, but an explicit clarification of intentions may present fewer dangers than the unstated and implicit. In addition, efforts towards outcome-based analysis should be context-adaptive. Moreover, they should hinge on the clarification of higher-level aims, to which outcomes are subordinated. This priority should remain at the forefront. In the context of a holistic action, negotiation should deal clearly with a clarification of intentions, as well as with ways of realizing the end project. One trend's strength could mitigate the weaknesses of its complementary approach. That being said, no one has yet found the ideal method. The ideal is not in methods; it is certainly in the way learners live and mutually care when things are co-organized, so that time is used with a generous attitude and a goal to share achievements. Defining pragmatic organizers may just help this community of learning to happen.

In sum, the issues of the whole project and educational outcomes have, in this chapter, been surveyed in a manner that suggests the dialectic complementarity of each approach's inherent strengths and weaknesses. This analysis has implicated three levels of relevance: content, procedural operations, and contextual conditions of actualization. It did not acknowledge a fundamental element common to both approaches: both are directional, i.e. oriented toward a final achievement, which is historically explainable by the pragmatic roots of both trends. It is important that the ultimate achievements are stated and that the outcomes are clearly subordinate to these high-level achievements. The specification of thematic resources to meet content needs, procedural operations and contextual conditions would improve both approaches of learning and bring them together. This is what I propose hereafter in terms of well-balanced holistic actions. The hol-act process is emphasized in the rest of the chapter. Now, let us see how it applies to the world language writing workshop.

Tell Me About the Writing Workshop...

A Risky Definition

The unexpected, the spontaneous creative urge, the involuntary sensory surges, and other unplanned factors determine, in large part, the success of a writing activity. A pragmatic definition of the writing workshop will challenge those researchers who attempt it. They must abandon the preconceived schema of the linear organization of learning and confront a complex, dynamic model (Kroll, 2003). While remaining within the restrictions of an analysis of learning conditions alone, they must plan creativity, allowing for the possibility of creative events that transcend planning. Subjective experience must be objectified to some degree in order to define the conditions of organization.

Exclusive of planning, every expressive situation is unique. In practice, the management of the workshop environment (socio-affective, relational) depends upon the topic, context, biographies, the teacher, learner and peer relationships, implying human flux and change and spontaneity in writing. The planner is not concerned with idiosyncratic environments but rather with their underlying common denominator. Which pragmatic organizers are most likely to generate an expression workshop? By defining the common parameters of a learning situation, the planner effects a desired breach in the instructional process itself in order to make this situation typical, and then reproducible. This is a questionable design because situations are never really typical. As soon one designs learning activities in typical terms, one loses sight of contextual and biographic features. So as to be transferred in a new context or classroom situation, plans have first to be typically decontextualized. Thus, for a practitioner, a measure of practice has to be injected into any planning model.

The best that can be done is to propose to students different avenues of organizing interactive elements, preserving their mobility in a flexible model. This might help in maintaining lively learning dynamics. The option presented here is to help students define their own writing projects as multiple forms of an identity search. They need to define the elements that they intend to focus on and creative writing situations. This will allow a flexibility of experience. Attempting to circumscribe a precise set of intentions can never be easy or entirely satisfactory. However, it remains the condition necessary for writing workshop scenarios, aside from the consideration of specific content knowledge (textual, morphosyntactic, semantic, pragmatic, psycholinguistic, etc.), as well as contextual and biographic singularities.

Content's Mastery, Procedural Transfer and Contextual Conditions of Expression

One of the important advantages inherent to the project-based, holistic action model of teaching is its allowance for subjective expression. That is its "good news" side. Its corresponding weakness is related to the non-objectification of content. In complete contrast, the outcome-driven instructional design systematically plans knowledge but generally neglects the learner's freedom of choice and expression. This book targets a compatibilist area in the middle, a return to the cognitive, socio-affective and situational dimensions of pedagogy in a pragmatic model of well-specified intentions.

Many researchers have directed their efforts toward expanding the outcome-driven planning model. Among them, Eisner (1969) proposed breaking the domination of mastery objectives by specifying higher goals like transfer and expression. Intentions related to transfer would include interdisciplinary, instrumental procedures, such as "self-documenting", "researching", "conceiving a work plan", "applying directions", and so on. Intentions related to expression describe the conditions of expression in transdisciplinary, creative contexts, for example, "writing your biography", "working in a group setting on creating language passports", "art painting and debating your representation of a novel", "organizing a eco-exhibition", "sharing and evaluating critically a presentation", to name a few. An explicit description of these three levels: content to be mastered, procedures to be transferred, and contextual conditions of personal expression would expand the goal-directed planning model and would also encompass all aspects of a holistic project.

Many researchers in the field of cognitive psychology as applied to curriculum agree on the description of three levels of knowledge that are generally activated by a reading or writing activity: a) **declarative knowledge** that is content-specific and related to concepts and facts, as well as knowledge of the organizational models (what to learn); b) **procedural knowledge** that is related to processing declarative knowledge, such as in planning (how to apply); c) **contextual knowledge** that pertains to appreciation of variability and decision-making in a given situation (learning context: why and when to learn or apply learning and how to evaluate - Winograd & Hare, 1988; Resnick, 1991). These levels coincide with the levels described by this instructional model. Mastery of content is linked to declarative knowledge, transfer operations and strategies correspond to the elaboration of procedural knowledge, and creative expression determines the situations likely to activate contextual knowledge.

A planning model prescribes certain types of actions to achieve a desired result. This tri-level prescriptive model (mastery of content, transfer procedures, situated expression) seems to correspond to knowledge strategies that can stimulate deep learning (Oxford, 1994). It appears to be supported by a considerable body of descriptive research (Jones, 1990; Paige, Cohen & Shively, 2002). The study of the inductive processes activated by writing, reading or problem-solving show that learners link new information to prior knowledge through flexible mental models (Holland, Holyoak, Nisbett & Thagard, 1994). This applies to new, flexible views of planning as well. Mental models have active properties, and allow planning in action. Learner-centered curriculum frameworks recognize the diversity of the students, who seek a wide array of goals, such that it seems more appropriate to create personal learning environments than imposing the same outcomes for all (Dolence, 2004). In this way, this book proposes a planning model that allows instructional flexibility (Tochon & Dionne, 1994). Many processes involved in a reading activity apply equally to writing. Before undertaking a writing activity, the writer will access prior knowledge of structures, such as types of text, genres, writing plans, settings, cultural norms, and knowledge of future audiences. Many levels of meaning are considered: the organization of the text, the style, the level of language, etc. The construction of these elements guides learners in their writing; they are constantly comparing them to prior experience and knowledge, to their goals and to their eventual audience. Much as in a reading activity, prior knowledge evolves as the learner reads, where the meaning of the text is constructed (Scardamalia & Bereiter, 1986).

The writing workshop requires three phases of planning: (1) the internal planning on the part of the workshop's monitors (students can monitor a project), (2) the instructional (external) planning of directions and its negotiation, and (3) the internal planning on the part of the learners involved in the expressive activity (Figure 3.2).

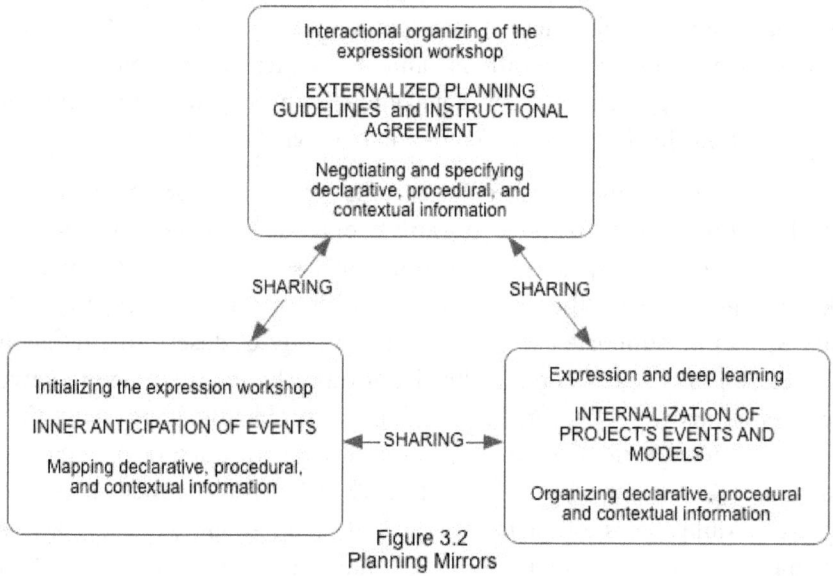

Figure 3.2
Planning Mirrors

Internal planning transpires spontaneously and can be aided by *pragmatic organizers*, which are procedures that link declarative knowledge to contextual conditions. In a writing activity, defining the required declarative knowledge, the procedures to activate and the contextual conditions are an example of a body of activity organizers. They can be elaborated as intentions of mastery, transfer and expression.

The writing workshop is furthermore an identity project (Moje & Luke, 2009), which must be anchored into the personal aspirations and motives of the apprentices of expression, or it won't reach its motivational peak. Self-determination stimulates engagement (van Lier, 1996) and is even a requirement for its successful follow-up (Ware, 2003). These aspects will be emphasized in Chapters 5 and 6. It matches a dynamic in which writing is not only sense-making, but also 'self-making and world making' (Bruner, 2001, p. 25).

Writing projects are more and more organized online in the form of blogs, portfolios and e-journals. While it is not my intention here to develop issues related to language learning with technologies and computer mediated communication because this domain is wide enough that an entire book on this very issue would be required, notwithstanding I can briefly allude to the potential of narrative associated to new technologies, with caveats that I have expressed in Tochon (2010c and 2011b). The 2007 MLA report calls for language studies to "provide substantive training in language teaching and in the use of new technologies in addition to cultivating extensive disciplinary knowledge and strong analytic and writing skills" (p. 7). A technology is not a standalone practice: it cannot exist without a way of understanding the technology and its purpose, i.e. an epistemology. One area that seems promising despite the limitations of current technologies and the ways they affect human health, are the uses of narrative within virtual worlds. Bruner (1986 and 1990) among others has developed interesting characteristics of narratives that suggest their deeply rooted connection with our situated and experiential way of learning about reality, as highlighted by Neville (2010).

A. Specific mental states, instances and events connected through time form the basis of a *story*. They can be expressed in words, images and films, abstract animations, and theater to form the "basic story stuff, the events to be related in the narrative" (Bruner, 1986, p.19) in a way which appears medium-independent. Narrative is the "form of not only representing but of constituting reality" (Bruner, 1991, p. 5).

B. The organization of events within a narrative in order to form a story defines its *plot*. It is a conceptual scheme "by which a contextual meaning of individual events can be displayed" (Polkinghorne, 1995, p. 7). The plot, in Bruner's words, is "the story as told by linking the events together" and "how and in what order the reader becomes aware of what happened" (1986, p. 19). It is an interpretation of how the narrative fiction enfolds.

C. *Narrative sequences* are medium specific story constructs that build up the narrative landscape. The story builds up a landscape of action according to the predicates and arguments of a story grammar, and a landscape of consciousness in which those in the action "know, think, or feel, or do not know, think, or feel" (Bruner, 1986, p. 14).

A number of educational technology researchers are using narrative with a plot and a storyline to develop three-dimensional digital game-based learning environments for second language acquisition (Neville, 2012). They express the need to develop for world languages experiential contexts that Blake (2008, p.135) identified as a form of "critical and rhetorical literacy," allowing learners to exploit what Gee (2007) named an "internal design grammar" (p. 28), along an articulate "intentionality of instruction" (Zheng et al. 2009, p. 505). It is not excluded that such attempts might contribute one day to the development of narrative-based environment for deep language learning.

The Communication standard that has been overemphasized because it was relatively easy to evaluate its interpretive, presentational and interpersonal modes, needs to embrace interdisciplinary transfer and transdisciplinary expression in order to transcend their limitations. The interdisciplinary level relative to transfer defines instrumental procedures that are useful in many branches of learning and fulfill the Connection C of the 5 Cs standards. The transdisciplinary level relative to personal expression defines the contextual conditions of a creation and may involve the Culture and Communities Cs of the 5 Cs standards. The three levels of intention pertaining to the planning model coincide with the three levels described by research into the processes linked to the arts of reading, writing, and problem-solving. This concurrence allows the definition of field and pragmatic organizers for expression workshops within an expanded vision of a variety of possible outcomes, making it compatible with the actualization of competence through performance, and thus, achieving proficiency. From a curriculum design standpoint, pragmatic organizers are flexible and can be composed of directional modules in an intentional, functional organization of knowledge.

The Proactive Cloverleaf

The expression workshop fits the definition of a specific educative project. Writing is one aspect of self-expression. The writing workshop is a framing activity, i.e. a span of work directed toward a common production. In the course of this action, immediate needs are met and this workspace becomes, in tandem with exchanges and discoveries, a period of reflection on language. Unlike instructional lessons, workshops are communicative and expansive; their content is spread over many interlinking sessions. Workshops include diversified strategies, and individual and group research is a dominant element. The writing workshop involves characteristics of a holistic action directed at a language production. It entails a quality approach to Second Language Acquisition, as it integrates characteristics that Kramuch (2009) emphasized: it contrasts with the usual brisk pacing of language courses and provides the necessary maturation of an enactment that is not rushed but goes along with the bodily need to "re-member, re-thread, re-cognize" (p. 202). Time is different in the expression workshop, which provides "opportunities to disrupt or subvert expectations" (p. 203).

Creativity requires the manipulation of meaningful materials, so it is a meaning-making competence. In the writing workshop, this material is a text with a purpose and an audience, implying a strategic development of formal content in a situation of active communication. A writing activity involves processes of regulation related to content mastery, procedure transfer, and contextualized expression. In addition, the definition of the writing workshop described in this chapter is compatible with writing-process models. It is also perceived as a strategy of activation and development of biographic, situated, and experiential knowledge, focused on a production that stimulates identity-building processes. Its planning framework is built on flexible and non-linear processes, allowing sub-processes to cycle back on each other while achieving the more global project of communicating the intended message to a potential audience.

As described, the writing workshop incorporates three main levels of knowledge and contributes to the development of all three within one holistic action. It functions by subordinating well-articulated transfer and content organizers to that of expression, which is the primary organizer. An example of this incorporation is given later in this chapter. This descriptive analysis can lead to a model of a writing workshop, i.e. a set of operating instructions, with, of course, all the reservations stated earlier. The monitoring conceptualizers of the writing workshop negotiate and specify the Hol-Act's three levels with the other participants, thereby increasing the probability of success. However, the socio-affective factor cannot be planned; this aspect is related to interpersonal dynamics and remains unpredictable. In this model, the writing workshop's conditions are defined through the organization of the three levels of activity. The instructional management of the model can either stress content mastery, operation transfer, or contextual conditions of expression. A particular management may proceed from content to context, or inversely, from context to content, or act globally on all three levels.

Curriculum designers had long insisted upon content; then, performance was emphasized. Another curriculum trend postulated that content should not be developed outside a context of meaningful communication. This more inductive movement in the acquisition of language was supported by Chomskyan innatist views and whole language approaches (Hudson Kam & Newport, 2009; McKenna, Robinson & Miller, 1990; Edelsky, 1990). The pendulum's swing has returned to standard outcomes and task performance, but current research is focusing on situated, subjective strategies and multilingual knowledge in complex settings, such as curriculum-based ecosystems (Barab & Roth, 2006) and personal affordances in cross-cultural encounters (Kramsch, 2009; Tochon & Ökten, 2010). The model suggested here advocates a balanced expression of these levels: content knowledge/strategic transfer/situated personal expression. The nature of the relation between levels is subject to variability.

Within a holistic action, there is a tendency to overestimate the value of the final product, to the detriment of the creative process itself. Over the course of decades, research has concentrated on finished products, rather than on the expressive process of composing with its subjective insights ...identity and social transformations... itself (Halverson, 2010). When the process is not precisely scaffolded and guided, there appears a danger of limiting the holistic action to momentary spurts of creativity in the absence of an instructional agreement on the details of action. In planning an expression workshop, the use of pragmatic organizers that pertain to all three levels of activity should ensure a degree of interaction between the various levels of knowledge processing. This constitutes the Hol-Act in projects.

The expression workshop is an interactive project centered on meaningful language production, which supports cross-cultural identity building and new visions of the social and multilingual self. It has been defined as the integration of three levels of pragmatic organizers that target the activation of declarative, procedural and contextual expressive processes. The writing workshop is a particular case of an expression workshop. It becomes operational by the subordination of transfer and mastery activities to a global activity of situated expression. These levels of organizers are developed interdependently; no single level is preferred over another in this non-linear planning model.

The Workshop Dynamics

A workshop functions on the basis of its dynamics; this aspect draws on its planning in a way that may transcend its initial intentions. The interface between planning and learning is communication. A workshop will function optimally on the basis of guidelines corresponding to the content being mastered, the procedures being transferred, and the conditions pertaining to its context of expression. In most planning models, the guidelines must be followed in sequence. In contrast, the writing workshop, like any holistic action centered on expression, unfolds dynamically by meaningfully interacting among levels of knowledge. Declarative knowledge gets contextualized through transfer procedures. In addition, a context will sometimes stimulate the emergence of prior knowledge, which then becomes the object of a transfer procedure.

Writing is a dynamic, spontaneous act whose process can vary from moment to moment, from one context to another (Figure 3.3).

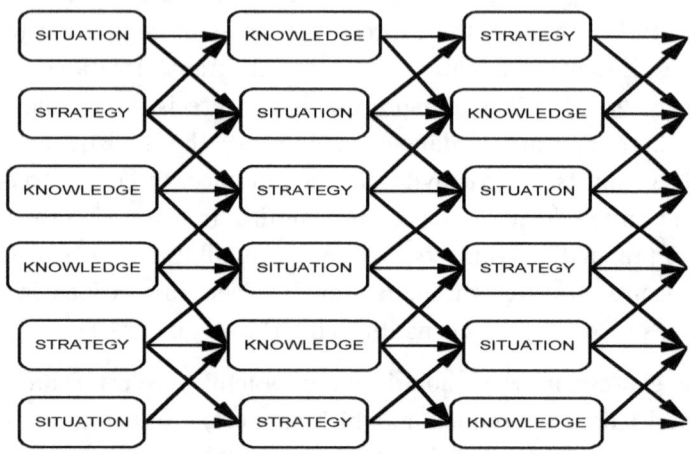

FIGURE 3.3
Informal Learning through Spontaneous Expression

This is why an attempt to objectify expressive intentions within these levels as organizers of mastery, transfer, and expression cannot possibly result in a linear methodology. Apprenticeship develops in non-linear phases. The least awkward and most convenient representation of expressive Hol-Acts might be the interlocking of a tri-level taxonomy of tasks. Its pragmatic organizers function in a cyclical, recurring interrelation, and it is neither really useful nor realistic to plan them in sequence. Feedback is often provided in writing by the teacher (Goldstein, 2005), and it increases accuracy (Bitchener & Knoch, 2010). It is, at any rate, difficult to foresee which level is being developed at a given moment. It is enough to specify intentions dealing with each level of a task. The subordination of the three levels to any holistic action is the genesis of the Hol-Act model (Fig. 3.4).

This planning model defines the levels of activity in one creative project. Each level formulates its negotiated guidelines in as many pragmatic organizers as needed for consensual action. These organizers are pragmatic because they organize shared intentions through guidelines. A guideline is a clearly-stated direction; participants in the creative action may, at any time, refer to the guidelines to verify their progress and direction. The guidelines arrange the three levels of knowledge into a dynamic interrelation, which corresponds to the contextualized activation of the model, i.e. to an expression Hol-Act. They constitute a negotiated instructional agreement, which can be expressed in a rubric.

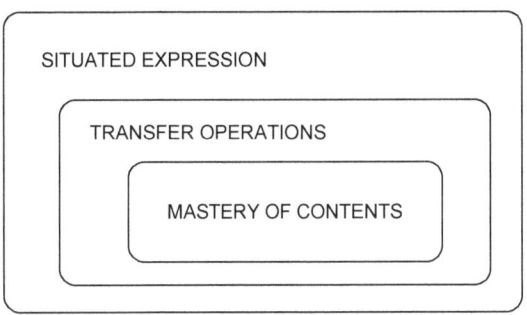

Figure 3.4
Russian Dolls

In short, workshop instruction activates the levels defined by the deep planning model. The interlocking levels determine a non-sequential arrangement of tasks within a whole project. This non-linearity preserves a freedom of individual endeavor. In fact, over-specifying the temporal sequence of the mastery, transfer, and expression organizers may block spontaneous operations, differentiated strategies, and individual approaches. While it is true that rhythm, rehearsal, and regular, ritualized concerted actions can support such collaborative endeavors; an educative model aiming at creative learning should avoid automatism.

Language learners are sometimes considered a monolithic group whose learning ability is dictated by the number of years studying the target language. Little attention is given to historical factors that enter into this process. As the number of heritage learners grows, there is a need to adapt the language curriculum and face issues related to the language background, cultural ways of knowing and learning, and interests. Achievement depends upon the ways the curriculum addresses these issues or not. Koike and Palmiere (2011) found that learners behave differently in oral versus written contexts and differ in pragmatic production from each other in both contexts: "It is often assumed that oral production can easily be reproduced in the written modality." Their study "indicates that pragmatic language use is difficult for these learners to express in the written modality, and that difference should be recognized in class activities and assignments" (p.101). Learners cannot simply rely on a transfer of their L1 writing skills to L2 writing. The writing transfer is quite complex in its use and implies epistemological as well as pragmatic changes.

This result questions whether methods that encourage systematic sentence transfer and contrastive comparative approaches can really promote learning and proficiency in writing. On the contrary, practices such as journaling or personal storytelling, which may be shared through e-mails or a blog, are effective ways for the teacher to follow and support the learner's progress evidenced by the evolution of mastery over form as well as insights into self-directed writing (Stewart, 2010).

Dungeons and Spelling Dragons

What is the writing workshop, how does it work and why is it better for students? An anecdote may illustrate it. Here is an example, which was planned in concert with the students on the basis of their interest in the forms of adventures present in videogames.

These students were in trouble regarding French spelling and wanted a way of reviewing the rules of writing correctly in the French language. The teacher was aware that their request was about introducing a low impact learning method since learning spelling rules may only improve spelling when related to intensive writing practice with regular feedback loops. But the students asked for it, and the issue from the teacher's viewpoint was to find a way to integrate such sequence of rule revision within a unit that would support extensive reading and intensive writing, two fundamental aspects of the Deep Approach.

Intensive practice was the key. Thus the review of French spelling rules, the teacher suggested, could be organized as a quest within a complex writing workshop that would stimulate a dynamic of exchanges among the students. The result was much better for the students than simply receiving a list of spelling rules with exercises: it was for the students to create original rule-based exercises in an intensive writing practice which would scaffold challenging tests for peer students along a concerted storyline. The workshop was to embed the rule explanations in a narrative followed by series of challenges brought in sequences by three characters that would impose to the hero reader adapted challenges associate with practices and corrective feedbacks. The game, much more complex than simply answering empty-slot exercises, was to create such practices and integrate them smoothly into a plot with characters that would legitimate taking this or that path within a narrative written by the students in cooperative groups, each having specific rules and roles.

The workshop planning phases that were shown in Figure 3.2 are illustrated below in the form of a writing workshop entitled "Dungeons and Spelling Dragons". This workshop involved a group of fifteen low-achievers, in a 4th year (senior) French class.

First: Use your Head and Hol-Act!

These students were fond of the "Choose Your Own Adventure" genre of books and videogames. They also needed to work on spelling skills and accurate syntax. At the beginning of the school year, half the students were unable to write more than ten lines, regardless of the subject. These initial conditions were a determining factor; they resulted from objective needs of the language program (in regard to textual writing) and from subjective needs related to students' motivations. A basic situation was thus defined, leading to the emergence of a needs-unifying concept. The Hol-Act was an integration of the School-Plan and the Self-Plan of these students. The idea of a holistic action arose after a "decomplexification" phase, which consisted of a series of non-graded tests. These showed that the students were able to write coherently and at some length if the subject interested them sufficiently, and if they did not feel as though they were being judged or evaluated. At the same time, the students were asked to closely observe character descriptions and settings in texts they were reading, thus enabling the assimilation of descriptive elements. The holistic project is therefore conditioned by four deterministic elements: subjective needs, objective needs, the achievement possibilities of the students, and their prior knowledge.

The phase of internal planning consisted in arranging these work conditions into a production-based project. The following organizing elements had to be determined and specified: (a) the content (declarative knowledge); (b) their processing under a common framework, in order to develop procedural writing knowledge); (c) the situated experience, i.e. the contextual conditions for the management of the content and writing procedures. These activity organizers developed after a survey of needs and interests in an internal planning process, crystallized spontaneously in the teacher's thinking during the course of one weekend. They emerged as a kind of mental tally of the obvious problems and their possible solutions.

Second: Negotiate the Hol-Act!

Within this precise context, it was not possible to have the students take full responsibility of the curriculum, but their ideas were integrated in the plan, and there were consultations at every step. There was flexibility in the system's dynamics. The idea of Hol-Act was discussed with the students to determine whether they were sufficiently motivated to accomplish a class writing activity. Their reception to the idea was favorable, so in response to their suggestions, this writing production activity was proposed the following week: write a "Dungeons and Spelling Dragons" book for students of their age who might be experiencing similar difficulties with the target language. Accordingly, this book would constitute the general organizer of expression in which all the activities' organizers would be embedded.

The action's external planning consisted of negotiating and writing down guidelines. These would develop the action by specifying content, its processing and contextualization modes. This holistic action developed in terms of targeted activities that were later verbalized into written practical organizers. The experienced teacher does not seem to require a detailed specification of performance outcomes. As far as the external planning is concerned, the most important factor is the clarity of the guidelines and their correspondence to the organizational levels: the content to be mastered, the operations to apply to content and the global context of action. More often than not, planning will correspond spontaneously to these three levels of consideration, as this taxonomy corresponds to seasoned practice (see Chapter 4).

In the case of "Dungeons and Spelling Dragons", the declarative and procedural tasks were to organize a number of adventures in a succession of "spelling battles" (presenting rules, exercises and games, copying texts and finding errors) that led to "remedial battles" or to various rewards (a visit to an island paradise, for example), according to the determined program. Following some discussion with the students, they planned, with the teacher, the episodes of the story in the form of a large concept map. Some 45 rules were chosen as a work reference, and each student was responsible for three rules related to three rounds of exercises and remedial work. Some recap exercises had been planned as well (CLOZE exercises to pinpoint spelling difficulties, using short newspaper articles). This chapter does not claim to analyze the relations between morphosyntax and semantics, or to deduce particular consequences of arbitrary dichotomies between form and function; therefore, these terms are used in accordance with their definition in a context of language teaching. It should be stressed, however, that a project-based model integrates language basics into a context of real communication, which seems more productive than the traditional dissection of contents.

From a descriptive standpoint, the students developed contrasting settings and characters on the basis of earlier practice locating these elements in texts. The story episodes had been discussed and agreed upon in class. Choices were open; the teenagers—seven girls and eight boys—opted for a male hero. The hero's adventure would last five days, during which he would quest for the five volumes that make up "Dungeons and Spelling Dragons" in French: "Livre d'Or Tograf."

Each student was responsible for one third of the hero's day: from 7 a.m. to noon, at which time the hero lunched; from noon to 5 p.m.; or from 5 p.m. to 10 p.m., at which time the hero retired for the evening, tired but happy for having found a new volume. The students decided that the hero would have a magic calculator that could transport him into the past, the future, or into outer space.

This guideline granted every student a large measure of creative freedom. Every student followed three organization charts composed of ten episodes. Together, the thirty episodes defined the course of one third of a day. Therefore, the structure of each third of a day was similar (definitions, types of questions, remedial cycles, corrective steps, successful or unsuccessful responses, etc.), but this structure was completed by the students according to their imagination and the rules they were mandated to teach (Figure 3.5).

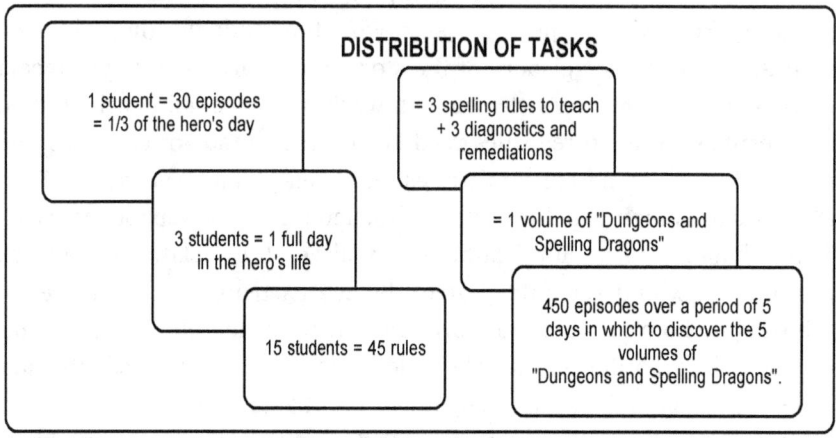

Figure 3.5
Tasks Distribution
to Accomplish the "Dungeons and Spelling Dragons" Project

For space reasons, the 30 steps are presented hereafter in four figures. Figures 3.6, 3.7, 3.8 and 3.9 show the writing guidelines (narrative diagram including steps 1 to 30, applicable to every student) that were given in the course of the expression workshop.

Part of the reasoning behind the "Dungeons and Spelling Dragons" process was that students who wished to teach spelling to other students would become more aware of the realities of teaching it. A second argument supporting this project pertained to the benefits produced by copious amounts of monitored writing: improved spelling as part of successful communication, and the development of higher-level competences. The motivation prompted by this holistic action was strong enough to enable every student to write twenty pages of text, which actually corresponds to sixty pages when the two re-writing phases are taken into account.

Step 1
Frame the protagonist according to preceeding sequence (asking information from the classmate who wrote it); state what has happened, what remains to be done, identify the positive and negative elements, the protagonist's (=you) situation, secondary characters, i.e., who, what, where, when, and why. The protagonist has a magic calculator that she/he may use throughout her/his quest.
An event is produced. Describe it. This is the beginning of a new adventure. The event brings about an encounter (with positive results? negative?) and the protagonist receives (how?) a message: a short text (to be written, maximum of 8 lines) that must be copied without error. The message refers to a future event. Once the message is copied, the protagonist finds a vehicle (which?) and proceeds to step 2

Step 2
The protagonist has arrived and finds a surprise. What? Why? The adventure is under way: How? By what means? Someone presents the protagonist a challenge (=1st rule to learn). The protagonist must repeat it mentally three times and must try to write it down from memory. An event is produced: (A spell? Time travel?) Where is the protagonist? Where is she/he going? Who is met along the way? Someone asks the protagonist a question relating to rule no. 1: she/he must choose between two responses (two paths? two directions? two messengers?) Choice = step 3 or step 4.

Step 6
The protagonist loses the battle; describe the dire consequences. What will she/he do? Where will she/he go? Describe in nightmarish detail. Some being (animal? space alien?) brings back rule no. 1 (from where? why?) and summarizes it, including the exceptions. The protagonist can now get back on track. Someone (who?) asks she/he ten new closure questions related to rule no. 1. Answers are found in Step 8. 8-10 correct answers = Step 7; less than 8 = Step 3.

Step 8
Correction key for closure exercise in Step 6.

Step 3
The protagonist's reply is erroneous: (either the wrong road was chosen or wrong direction taken). The protagonist is transported to a frightening place and meets a terrifying creature -or some other strange events unfold (Which? How? Describe them).
Finally, the protagonist receives help (from whom? how?) and is given rule no. 1 again (by what means?); this helpful character shows the protagonist the correct solution and explains the mistake.
But a test is coming. Someone (who?) warns the protagonist of a confrontation. Describe the confrontation. To win, the protagonist must answer ten questions (a closure exercise relating to rule no. 1). When finished the test, the protagonist checks her/his answers with the help of step 5: 8-10 correct responses = go to step 7; less than 8 correct = go to step 6.

Step 4
The protagonist's reply is correct, or, the appropriate path or direction was chosen. She or he is transported to a heavenly place (or meets some celestial being; perhaps some wonderful events arise). Describe in detail.
The protagonist receives a special present (from whom?) to tackle a new challenge. Describe the challenge (same one as in Step 3, same questions). Depending upon the outcome (see answers in Step 5) go to Step 7 (8-10 correct answers) or Step 6 (less than 8 correct answers).

Step 5
Correction key for the challenge (in Steps 3 and 4). After verifying your answers, calculate the score and go back to point of origin...

Step 7
In the Thick of Things
Figure 3.6 Narrative Diagram for "Dungeons and Spelling Dragons"

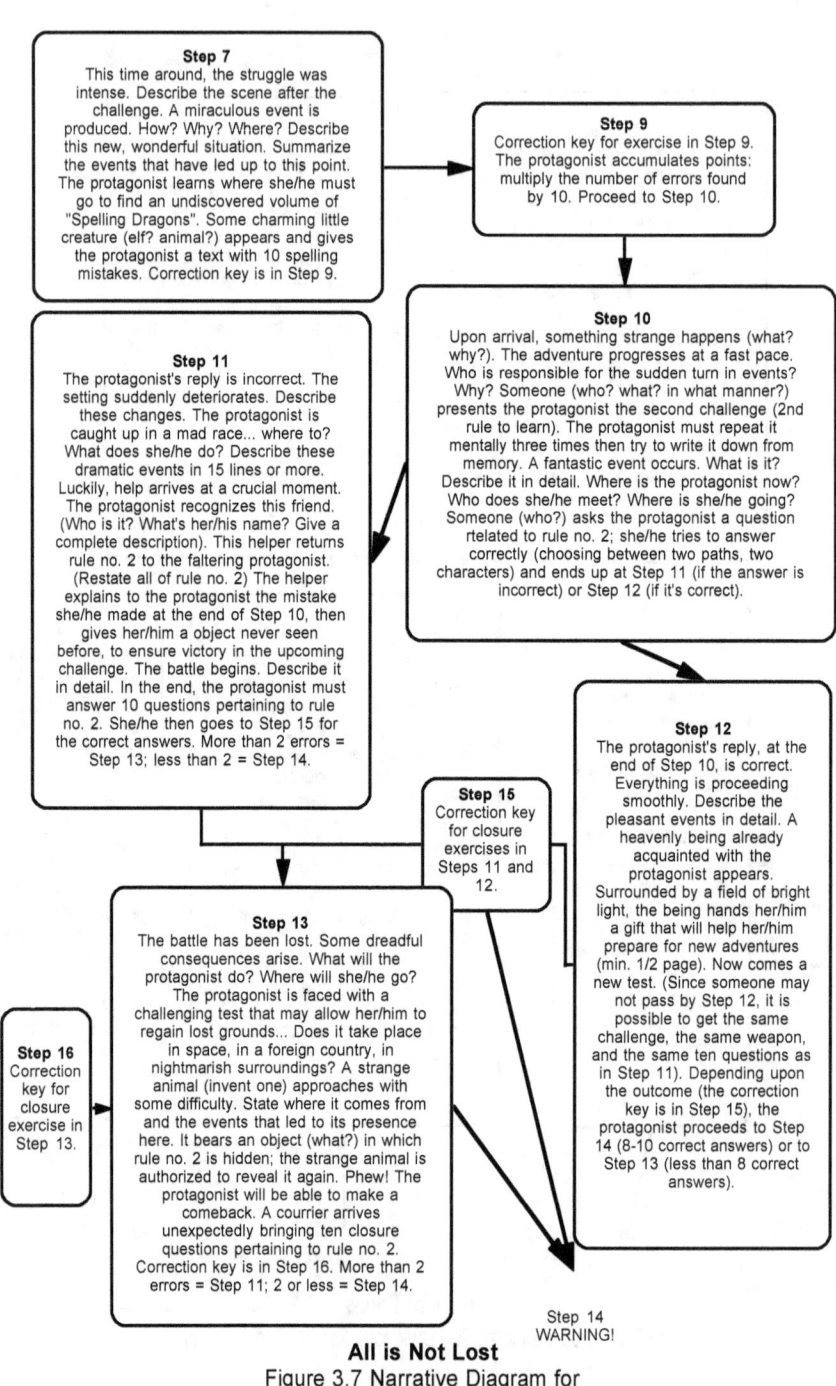

All is Not Lost
Figure 3.7 Narrative Diagram for
"Dungeons and Spelling Dragons" (sequence 2)

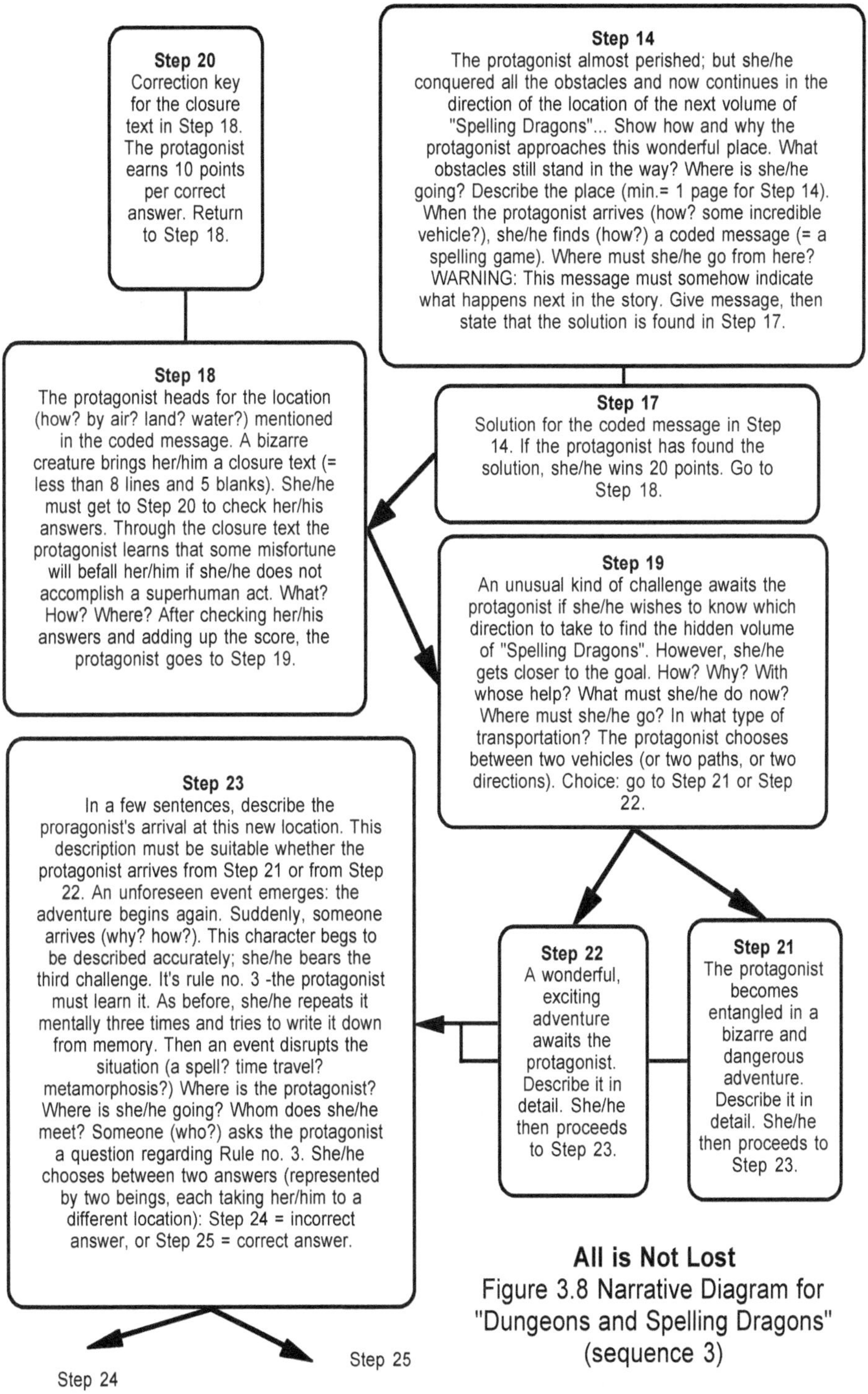

Step 20
Correction key for the closure text in Step 18. The protagonist earns 10 points per correct answer. Return to Step 18.

Step 14
The protagonist almost perished; but she/he conquered all the obstacles and now continues in the direction of the location of the next volume of "Spelling Dragons"... Show how and why the protagonist approaches this wonderful place. What obstacles still stand in the way? Where is she/he going? Describe the place (min.= 1 page for Step 14). When the protagonist arrives (how? some incredible vehicle?), she/he finds (how?) a coded message (= a spelling game). Where must she/he go from here? WARNING: This message must somehow indicate what happens next in the story. Give message, then state that the solution is found in Step 17.

Step 18
The protagonist heads for the location (how? by air? land? water?) mentioned in the coded message. A bizarre creature brings her/him a closure text (= less than 8 lines and 5 blanks). She/he must get to Step 20 to check her/his answers. Through the closure text the protagonist learns that some misfortune will befall her/him if she/he does not accomplish a superhuman act. What? How? Where? After checking her/his answers and adding up the score, the protagonist goes to Step 19.

Step 17
Solution for the coded message in Step 14. If the protagonist has found the solution, she/he wins 20 points. Go to Step 18.

Step 19
An unusual kind of challenge awaits the protagonist if she/he wishes to know which direction to take to find the hidden volume of "Spelling Dragons". However, she/he gets closer to the goal. How? Why? With whose help? What must she/he do now? Where must she/he go? In what type of transportation? The protagonist chooses between two vehicles (or two paths, or two directions). Choice: go to Step 21 or Step 22.

Step 23
In a few sentences, describe the proragonist's arrival at this new location. This description must be suitable whether the protagonist arrives from Step 21 or from Step 22. An unforeseen event emerges: the adventure begins again. Suddenly, someone arrives (why? how?). This character begs to be described accurately; she/he bears the third challenge. It's rule no. 3 -the protagonist must learn it. As before, she/he repeats it mentally three times and tries to write it down from memory. Then an event disrupts the situation (a spell? time travel? metamorphosis?) Where is the protagonist? Where is she/he going? Whom does she/he meet? Someone (who?) asks the protagonist a question regarding Rule no. 3. She/he chooses between two answers (represented by two beings, each taking her/him to a different location): Step 24 = incorrect answer, or Step 25 = correct answer.

Step 22
A wonderful, exciting adventure awaits the protagonist. Describe it in detail. She/he then proceeds to Step 23.

Step 21
The protagonist becomes entangled in a bizarre and dangerous adventure. Describe it in detail. She/he then proceeds to Step 23.

Step 24

Step 25

All is Not Lost
Figure 3.8 Narrative Diagram for "Dungeons and Spelling Dragons" (sequence 3)

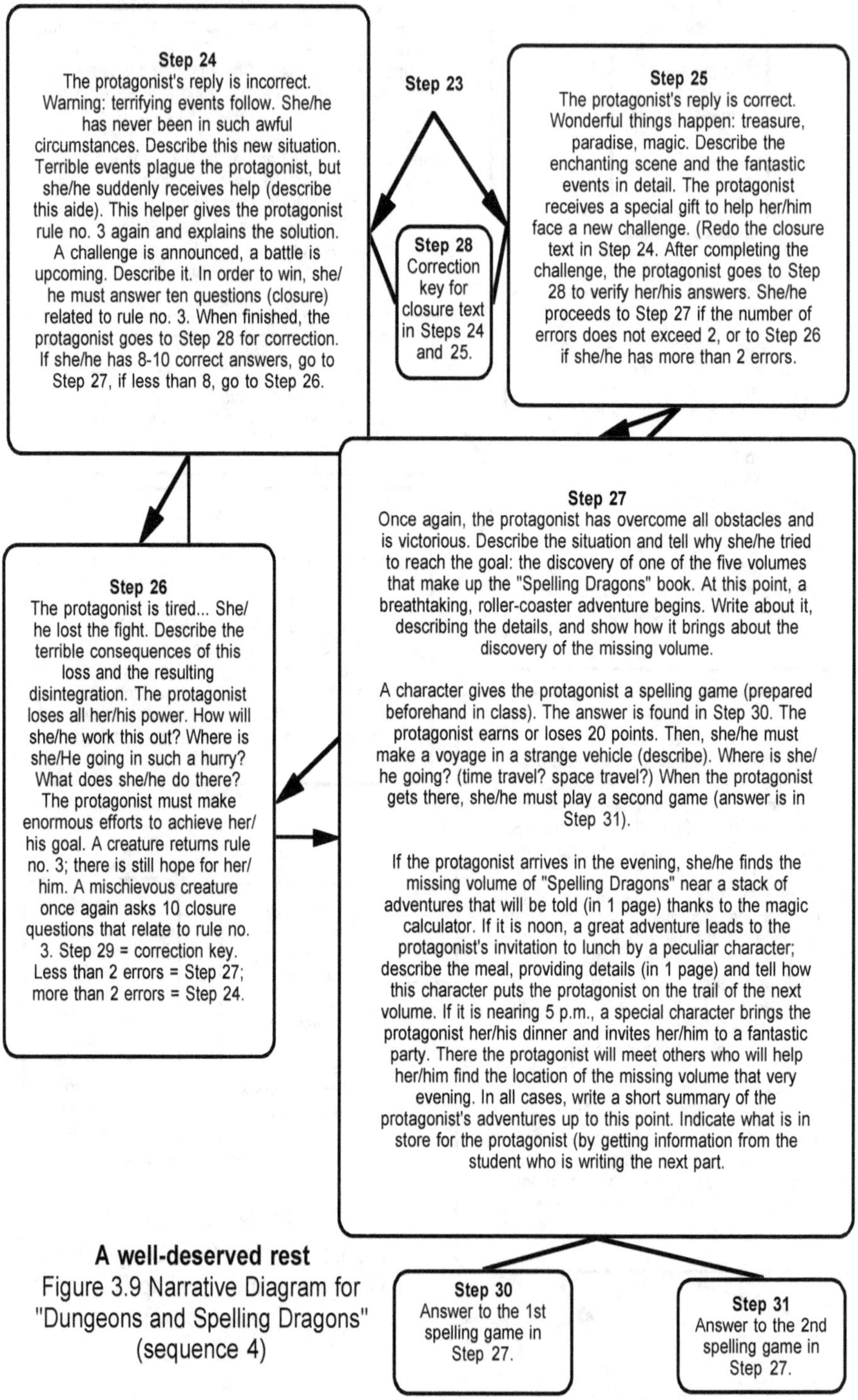

Step 24
The protagonist's reply is incorrect. Warning: terrifying events follow. She/he has never been in such awful circumstances. Describe this new situation. Terrible events plague the protagonist, but she/he suddenly receives help (describe this aide). This helper gives the protagonist rule no. 3 again and explains the solution. A challenge is announced, a battle is upcoming. Describe it. In order to win, she/he must answer ten questions (closure) related to rule no. 3. When finished, the protagonist goes to Step 28 for correction. If she/he has 8-10 correct answers, go to Step 27, if less than 8, go to Step 26.

Step 23

Step 28
Correction key for closure text in Steps 24 and 25.

Step 25
The protagonist's reply is correct. Wonderful things happen: treasure, paradise, magic. Describe the enchanting scene and the fantastic events in detail. The protagonist receives a special gift to help her/him face a new challenge. (Redo the closure text in Step 24. After completing the challenge, the protagonist goes to Step 28 to verify her/his answers. She/he proceeds to Step 27 if the number of errors does not exceed 2, or to Step 26 if she/he has more than 2 errors.

Step 26
The protagonist is tired... She/he lost the fight. Describe the terrible consequences of this loss and the resulting disintegration. The protagonist loses all her/his power. How will she/He work this out? Where is she/he going in such a hurry? What does she/he do there? The protagonist must make enormous efforts to achieve her/his goal. A creature returns rule no. 3; there is still hope for her/him. A mischievous creature once again asks 10 closure questions that relate to rule no. 3. Step 29 = correction key. Less than 2 errors = Step 27; more than 2 errors = Step 24.

Step 27
Once again, the protagonist has overcome all obstacles and is victorious. Describe the situation and tell why she/he tried to reach the goal: the discovery of one of the five volumes that make up the "Spelling Dragons" book. At this point, a breathtaking, roller-coaster adventure begins. Write about it, describing the details, and show how it brings about the discovery of the missing volume.

A character gives the protagonist a spelling game (prepared beforehand in class). The answer is found in Step 30. The protagonist earns or loses 20 points. Then, she/he must make a voyage in a strange vehicle (describe). Where is she/he going? (time travel? space travel?) When the protagonist gets there, she/he must play a second game (answer is in Step 31).

If the protagonist arrives in the evening, she/he finds the missing volume of "Spelling Dragons" near a stack of adventures that will be told (in 1 page) thanks to the magic calculator. If it is noon, a great adventure leads to the protagonist's invitation to lunch by a peculiar character; describe the meal, providing details (in 1 page) and tell how this character puts the protagonist on the trail of the next volume. If it is nearing 5 p.m., a special character brings the protagonist her/his dinner and invites her/him to a fantastic party. There the protagonist will meet others who will help her/him find the location of the missing volume that very evening. In all cases, write a short summary of the protagonist's adventures up to this point. Indicate what is in store for the protagonist (by getting information from the student who is writing the next part.

A well-deserved rest
Figure 3.9 Narrative Diagram for "Dungeons and Spelling Dragons" (sequence 4)

Step 30
Answer to the 1st spelling game in Step 27.

Step 31
Answer to the 2nd spelling game in Step 27.

Third: Let the Kids Hol-Act!

The students were given a guided freedom of expression. They were compelled to respond to many levels of demands built into their project. The development and organization of content and the group effort required by the writing activity led students to gain a better knowledge of each of these levels. For example, the use of the magic calculator brought the students to agree on a cooperative mode of action (applying contextual knowledge), to unify their individual themes and to agree on the verb tense to be used (proceduralizing declarative knowledge). Also, the person addressed would necessarily be the 2nd person singular "you". The fact that the dog-lion-robot of a student followed the hero in one morning episode meant that the next student would need to deal with this character. As all students wrote their parts in parallel, writing could not be sequential: they had to continuously read others' work and complete their own part to make the whole coherent. Each student, together with the writer of the previous chapter or the next one, would need to decide whether to take up this or that character in the afternoon episode or justify his disappearance (applying contextual knowledge). The student then had to transpose these elements into the new unit (transferring items by means of procedural knowledge). For example, the characteristics of the dog-lion-robot, as it appeared in the previous unit, had to be considered as well (declarative knowledge and making the following episodes coherent with it).

During writing, the students needed to refer to declarative content, procedural activation of this content, and verification of their contextual relevance. The strategically organized guidelines allowed each student to develop three levels of knowledge in an active situation. The project's accomplishment attests to these three actualization modes (Figure 3.10). Hol-Acts mean situated learning (Lave & Wenger, 1990).

In brief, the writing workshop titled "Dungeons and Spelling Dragons" was planned on three levels, actualizing three types of knowledge. It demonstrates the functionality of the planning model presented. The Hol-Act model is operational. It makes it compatible to developing basics along creative productions, enhancing cognitive strategies along the way. Language focus activities pertained to mastery organizers, the descriptive and narrative procedures constituted transfer organizers, and the expression organizers contextualized the conditions of communication both in writing and among the students, and created a homogeneous, whole action. Many guidelines corresponded to each planning level. Of course, this model would have to be adapted to each classroom situation. Hol-Acts belong to field dynamics and are never totally reproducible.

EXPRESSION ORGANIZERS
-producing a story;
-inventing a programmed mini-course and integrating it into the story;
-inventing spelling games based on models and integrating them into the story;
-interacting with peers in order to ensure the correspondance of all the parts to a global production;
-developing collaborative strategies that will promote the making of a coherent whole;
-taking on the role of reader-hero for peers and helping them in the writing and composing of the story;
-regulating the different levels of communication;
-self-evaluating one's work according to the various levels of guidelines;
-evaluating the work of peers;
-adapting one's own writing to peers' and teacher's judgement.

TRANSFER ORGANIZERS
-applying the descriptive, narrative, communicative and instructional guidelines coherently;
-writing detailed descriptions of characters and settings;
-keeping track of all the characters involved in the narrative;
-organizing a coherent course of action for the hero through concept maps;
-including and justifying "spelling battles and tests" at the end of an episode;
-structuring exercises based on the guidelines;
-establishing clear guidelines for the reader-hero at the beginning of exercises and with subsequent corrections;
-constructing formative evaluation and corrective sequences;
-describing the rewards and punishments to the reader-hero in accordance with the story episodes and the outcome of exercises;
-ensuring an internal correspondance within the episodes and sequences, and other parts of the story.

MASTERY ORGANIZERS
-self-correcting the spelling in one's texts;
-respecting the syntax of simple and complex sentences;
-using the narrative present tense and 2nd person singular;
-punctuating one's texts correctly;
-using text organizers and markers rationally;
-applying the spelling rules studied in the making of integrated exercises.

Figure 3.10
Spelling Dragons Organizers

In Short

This chapter has provided a pragmatic definition of the expression workshop, albeit a limited definition, due to the degree of generality that is required. The holistic project-based model and the outcome-directed planning model were examined, underlining their respective strengths and weaknesses. It was then shown that the writing workshop is situated at the convergence of these two trends, and that it may be described as a holistic action actualizing three levels of knowledge in interaction. Three types of pragmatic organizers will allow the balanced conception of a language expression workshop. These organizers prepare the classroom dynamics of the writing activities: mastery of content, transfer strategies, and situated expression. These three types of organizers represent efforts to map out the mental models actualized by expressive activities in the composition process of a project. In fact, mastery organizers targeted mostly memory applications and declarative knowledge; transfer organizers developed specific procedural knowledge; and expression organizers developed situated knowledge. The external planning negotiation can therefore closely match the internal planning in order to favor deep learning.

This instructional workshop model becomes operational when the mastery and transfer levels are subordinated to a holistic act of expression. An example of this dynamic relationship between group planning and deep learning was given in the workshop "Dungeons and Spelling Dragons" (modeled after the "Choose Your Own Adventure" books and videogames). Although there is already good evidence about the benefits of expression workshops and integrated language, future research may clarify the impact of Hol-Acts experiences on apprenticeship processes and the quality of the expression.

The Deep Approach is about scaffolding opportunities for students to express themselves and, through this process, to discover who they are while increasing proficiency. Deep expression is the motivation engine. The discovery of the intrinsic impulse to create helps learners specify who they are and who they want to be. It is part of a branding process in which fragments of identity are gathered in a focused endeavor. This process is at first fuzzy, subtle and complex, and requires a lot of flexibility on the part of the teacher, and flexibility in the curriculum itself. As has been demonstrated in Chapter 2, everything cannot be specified in advance.

Now let us briefly examine the limits of this model. Clarifying the processes involved in a deep approach to learning into an instructional model may generalize a way of thinking that might at a certain point become dogmatic. Generalizing the approach may imply a risk of curriculum fixation. The transposition of cognitive apprenticeship research into systematic instruction might appear an attempt to "robotize" human intelligence. Indeed, instructional planning emerges from the passage from descriptive to prescriptive approaches of learning. And it is difficult to predict the impact of systematizing higher-level learning into generalized instructions. This is why it is proposed:

- to negotiate the task organizers in order to take subjective needs into account; students should be able to choose their topics and contents;
- not to impose sequential learning, but to provide the opportunity of learning through various interactive procedures and in differing orders.

Systematic proposals for instruction are shaped by teacher's knowledge and students' actions, making it a lively dynamic. Learners should be trained to progressively become curriculum designers, as educative conceptualizing is creative act. It is what happened here when the students started conceptualizing their writing guidelines in a map.

The Deep Approach to language and culture learning inherits key aspects of project-based learning and proposes an original format and theory. It is different from mainstream project-based learning, in that

(1) the projects and their focus are initiated by the students, not the teacher;

(2) the task domains that scaffold the instructional process are precisely defined in the phase of initial planning along with the criteria of accomplishment.

Language is always more than language, as semioticians like to express. The Deep Approach is framed within applied semiotics, rather than applied linguistics *stricto sensu*, which is part of semiotics. Semiotics is about any meaningful sign; indeed, meaning can be conveyed through multiple channels, not only through voice. Dewey's pedagogy is process-oriented; it focuses on meaningful life projects and is a nice fit with applied semiotics. It was influenced by the semiotics of Charles S. Peirce, the founder of pragmatism, with whom John Dewey had courses at Johns Hopkins University. In contrast to language instruction that imposes fast pacing for swift and controlled surface learning that is assessed in the short run—with the risk that results might not last—Dewey proposed student-centered, empirical projects focusing on long-term, life achievement within interdisciplinary perspectives.

Practical problem-solving is a process open to constant revision, feedback and verification. Its empiricism is the ground for a reflective attitude of inquiry that is fundamental for moral, transdisciplinary growth. In language and culture studies, project-based apprenticeship creates new ways of conceptualizing how courses should be organized for proficiency, that is, real-life linguistic and intercultural competence. This approach "challenges mechanistic models of curriculum and pedagogy predicated on linear thinking, control and predictability." Projects indeed imply "understandings of futures in and for education that are open, recursive, organic and emergent" (Bussey, Inayatullah & Milojević, 2008). One difference between Dewey's pedagogy of experience and the Deep Approach is that here we deal with complexity in a way that allows project apprentices to read situations, select relevant insights and affordances, and choose their focus of engagement (Pennycook, 2001).

The Writing Process as a Philosophy: Mike's Journal

The Deep Approach entails a focus on process. Process philosophy is a key to the Deep Approach. The emphasis is on the free flow of the shared creative process that takes a textual dimension with feedback loops that help improve it. Self-regulation is crucial otherwise the learners will always depend upon a teacher. Autonomous, smart learners may create autonomous, smart citizens: the types of citizens that provide leverage, restore democracy and are not easily deceived. A deep understanding of cultural texts is the threshold.

After a phase of scaffolded and shared planning with templates that help frame projects, the entire learning process starts with students autonomously negotiating their roles in the whole endeavor to help, in their own way, reaching the targeted achievement levels that they specified themselves. This training leads to the possibility of life-long autonomous learning. Students are taught a way of constructing their identity. They are trained into an approach they may later use when dealing with life situations.

Building a Roof

Think of the writing workshop or any other classroom plan as a process rather than a concept. Think of it as a house with many rooms but no roof. The participants all have equal shares in this house and propose to build a roof. This is now their goal. Everyone participates in this common purpose to the best of their ability. Inside the house, the participants can move about freely, going from one room to another without restriction. Miraculously, all the rooms connect by means of communicating doors that swing both ways. In each room, the participants will find things they need to achieve their goal: nails, hammers, saws, wood, precision instruments of measure, and the like. Directions are posted here and there so that no one gets lost; or if they do (it is quite a maze!), they are soon back on track. Everyone cooperates in every step of the roof-building. Some need to learn how to drive a nail with a hammer, others must overcome the difficulties of a woobly saw, and some who already know how to measure and fit pieces together will gladly help others to know as well. The participants are seldom discouraged and all are anxious to see the finished work. When at last the roof is in place, the participants are proud of what they have accomplished. They now stand outside their house and proclaim: "We did that!".

If writing were conceived as a product, then static aspects of writing would be broken down for analysis with the risk of loosing sight of the whole. Writing as a process entails recursive feedback loops in which self-determined stages of achievement are perfected. Obviously there always is an underlying social framework behind any personal choices, which means that autonomy and choice are relative terms. Like in the example of roof building above, at a point in time the students makes an agreement to collaborate and work in a certain direction. But even though choices are not unlimited there are still alternatives, and our schools need to provide such alternatives.

The writing workshop offers choices to students. Whole and then local revisions guide the writers while they look forward to new accomplishments within the social context of their team, brainstorming the unfolding of a story together. The story, the curriculum, are not imposed to them. They can develop the way they want in a negotiated direction. They set up their own criteria of achievement and are bound to achieve them by a humane instructional agreement. The path is more important than the goal because they develop a method that could keep them motivated in whatever they do. Deeply, the approach is identity-based. It is not totally sequential as students negotiate every stage (planning, prewriting, drafting, revising) with each other, and the stages are re-visited repeatedly as creative situations enfold them in the narrative imaginary (Figure 3.11). Creation leads to Reading-Writing connections in the expression of whole aspects of identity that are incrementally more coherent as revisions increase focus and textual cohesion. Textual cohesion in the act of creative writing thus becomes a factor of identity coherence.

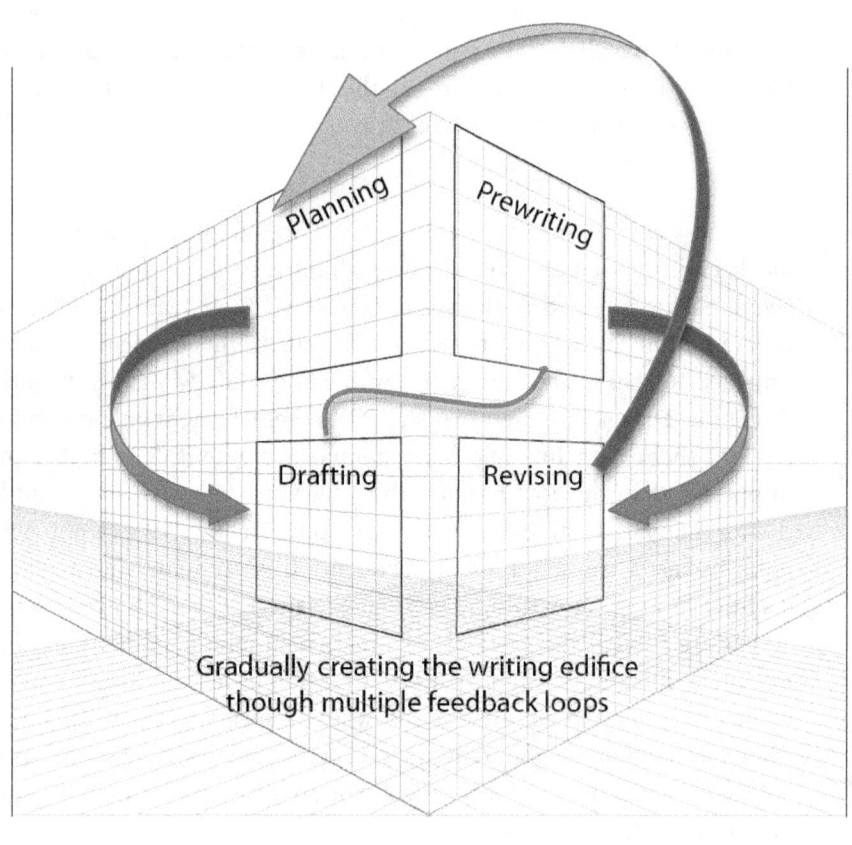

Figure 3.11

Text is the Primary Source of Deep Language Learning

Chapter 4
The Deep Taxonomy

Transdisciplinarity might be thought of as a challenge to space-binding and time-binding learning.
Knowledge Organization (1995, 22-2, p. 82)

This chapter explores the hidden structures of the curriculum from the perspective of practical categories enacted in the process of learning and teaching. It highlights a new way of considering education, which integrates three levels of achievement: the disciplinary, the interdisciplinary, and the transdisciplinary. The embedding of these three levels offers the opportunity to unify the classifications of educational processes (or taxonomies) and provide a deeper, more humane view of what should and could be done in education, integrating the cognitive, the sociaffective, and the kinesthetic. This semiotic approach unifies the mind, the heart and the body and transcends traditional approaches to learning and teaching. Transdisciplinary action allows for social and self-actualizing goals in the world language class.

The previous chapters of this book showed how to organize instructional tasks within a global project that develops proficiency as well as deep knowledge of the target culture. The innovative idea presented was to negotiate flexible, educative agreements that remain subordinate to the goals of transformation and change. Language units can be inscribed within the context of whole acts. The second chapter analyzed how and why writing and recording should be the primary focus of language learning and teaching. Such inscriptions leave a trace where reflection is used to stimulate further improvement. Teaching by whole projects and the task-based planning model were previously considered competing ways of organizing learning; the expression workshop may be situated at their junction point. An overview of these two trends indicated the key role of three levels of interaction. This taxonomy lies at the heart of the expression project and characterizes learning conditions that underlie an integrated apprenticeship. It provided empirical clues for the analyses proposed in this chapter.

Bourdieu (1969) defined 'intellectual fields" as dynamics created by agents (e.g., teachers, scholars, researchers, etc.) responsible for disciplinary formation that compete in co-defining what counts as "intellectually established and culturally legitimate" (Ringer, 1990, p. 270). From this perspective, concepts, notions and knowledge are inscribed in fields from which they cannot be decontextualized; as such conceptual networks are enmeshed in practices and practice-related ideas. This understanding should stimulate critical thinking and deeper learning in students as they grasp genre-based systems of thought. A school genre is a discursive pattern that has been institutionalized by commonly shared discourses on practice, as they characterize the forms of expression proper to an intellectual field (Schneuwly & Dolz, 1997 ; Tochon, 2000b).

In this chapter as well as Chapters 5 and 6, I will emphasize the importance of a non-linear planning model that touches on three operational levels. I argue that three levels of operation define teachers' and learners' field of action, which in turn articulates curriculum & instruction as a field of knowledge sharing and school genres' attunement. Educational classifications highlight the problem of the level of operation targeted by an instructional outcome. Simple abilities, such as knowledge of specific facts, are subordinate to more complex competences, such as analysis, synthesis, or evaluation. The wide scope in which intentions are expressed in school programs can be illuminated. Some outcomes simply target content. Others target thinking operations, and others still are related to complex actions.

Research into integrated classifications of instructional goal stresses its relevance to the tri-level planning model that defines curriculum-in-action. The first classifications of the cognitive, affective, and psychomotor areas that were published imposed fragmentation of the human being. Since then, many researchers have developed unified systems. Interestingly enough, most unified taxonomies of educational goals are spread over three specification levels which, though defined by various authors, share some important characteristics: 1) the first level is related to subject-matter content and has short-term aims; 2) the second level is related to thinking strategies that can be transferred from one domain to another; 3) the third level is related to long-term goals because it targets learners' creativity and experience actualized in a context of active communication. The embedding of three levels of knowledge shall herein be supported by a general theory of the educative action, this being directly linked to the classroom realities of teaching.

Deep Apprenticeship for Language Proficiency

While cognitive apprenticeship uses situated modeling, scaffolding, collaboration and coaching to develop proficiency within the boundaries of a particular discipline (Collins, Duguid & Brown, 1989), social apprenticeship stimulates various forms of interaction and socialization through cooperative projects to enhance knowledge, skills and experiences within contexts genuinely and informally created by the learners through peer negotiations and collaborations (Ding, 2008). Deep apprenticeship encompasses both cognitive and social aspects within a content-based, transdisciplinary perspective. The model of deep apprenticeship that I propose here fulfills disciplinary, interdisciplinary, and transdisciplinary goals. These levels define a unified taxonomy of learning processes. Such an apprenticeship model fits well in language studies if proficiency is the target (Tochon, 2013 and 2014). The following sections develop the conceptual basis for this model.

Back to the time when educational researchers were trying to homogenize curricula through classifications of instructional objectives, it had appeared important to divide the totality of learning into its cognitive (Bloom et al. 1956; Anderson & Krathwohl, 2001; Noble, 2004), socioaffective (Krathwohl, Bloom & Masia, 1964), and kinesthetic parts (Harrow, 1972), which provided pacing for such broad group work. This enterprise allowed curriculum designers to attune their criteria and ensure that the work proposed from state to state would target similar complexity levels. However, this division encouraged the development of the cognitive to the detriment of the other aspects of human learning. Nowadays, we are witnessing a comeback to socio-affective goals and emotional learning, which itself contains its own challenges (Zembylas, 2006b). Developing the affective domain is necessary for the transdisciplinary development of feelings, values, ethics, and aesthetics (Turk, 2002). Affective learning implies changes in emotions, attitudes, and values that characterize thinking and behavior, with the "internalization of transdisciplinary values including service, social justice, the dignity and worth of the person, the importance of human relationships, integrity and competence" (Neuman Allen & Friedman, 2010).

The initial idea of unified taxonomy came from Tochon's (1988) research on experienced teachers; then, research on taxonomies supported this discovery. There had been work on the classification of educational goals that unified all three aspects of human learning, and possibly more. The concept was developed in Tochon (1989e and 1990b) with a comparison of 12 unified classifications of educational goals integrating the cognitive, the socioaffective, and the kinesthetic. Most of these classifications were three-layer taxonomies. This review ended with a proposal for an integrated taxonomy that could take into account the characteristics of all the unified taxonomies reviewed. The unified taxonomy was defined as the embedding of three levels of intentions implicitly present in most curricula:

Discipline – The subject-matter of instruction or branch of instruction or learning, defined by the Merriam-Webster Dictionary as: (1) "the treatment suited to a disciple or learner; education; development of the faculties by instruction and exercise; training, whether physical mental or moral." This first definition matches the etymology of the word discipline, which emerged in the early 13th Century from French origin "descepline" from the Latin "disciplina", meaning "instruction given to a disciple" (discipulus). Its sense of "treatment that corrects or punishes" came in the 14th Century from the notion of "order necessary for instruction."

Interdiscipline – Instructional matters that involve two or more academic, scientific, or artistic disciplines: the interdisciplinary viewpoint analyzes, synthesizes and harmonizes links between disciplines into a coordinated, synthetic and coherent whole, establishing a new level of integration of knowledge (Choi & Pak, 2006).

Transdiscipline – The prefix trans- means beyond, over, across, to or on the farther side of[1]. To go beyond and over disciplinary frontiers, disciplines need to be recombined within a new focus. It is not mere juxtaposition: it moves holistically towards integration through world- or life-related themes or topics. The process transforms existing compositions, breaks them down and recombines them to form new ways of understanding. On occasions, this process leads to Ah-ha experiences when new knowledge emerges (Kerne, 2005). Transdisciplinarity integrates the natural, social and health sciences in a humanities context, and transcends their traditional boundaries. It is holistic, in that it encompasses the disciplines and transcends disciplinary viewpoints.

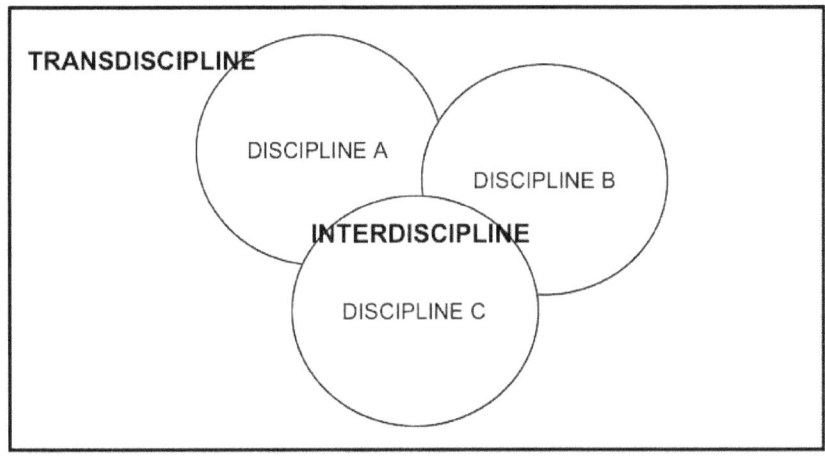

Figure 4.1
How disciplines interconnect within a transciplinary field

Any curriculum would implicitly include these levels of content and could be organized in a way to encourage disciplinary, interdisciplinary

---

[1] *Multidisciplinarity* has a different definition, as instruction draws on knowledge from different disciplines but stays within their boundaries; then the process is additive, not integrative (Klein, 1996).

and transdisciplinary apprenticeship. The most complete review so far on taxonomies, including unified taxonomies, has been published by Tristán & Molgado (2006). The analysis of how curricula classify instructional contents in several subject-matters has reinforced the idea that most current curricula tend to merge cognitive, socioaffective and kinesthetic goals and differentiate three layers of competence, which could be visualized in Figure 4.1.

Figure 4.1 is a simplified representation of the logical articulation between the disciplinary, the interdisciplinary, and the transdisciplinary. Interdisciplinary work emerges from co-disciplinary collaborations, connections and comparisons; it is situated within the realm of the disciplines as a cross-section of two or more disciplines. The concept is more complex than it might appear, as the cross-sections between music and mathematics or physical education and foreign language need, in many cases, to be created through collaborations across fields; moreover, the nature of what is interdisciplinary may be very different, depending the disciplines involved (Lenoir, 2006).

Transdisciplinarity relates to what permeates all disciplines (the sap within all disciplinary trees) and transcends the field of the disciplines, as it targets self-actualization and social action and transformation. Any discipline is—within its own realm—potentially developing an interdiscipline and a transdiscipline; however, the emphasis on each level can be shallow or profound. A deep approach to education would offer a balanced emphasis on all three levels. These three levels of intentions can be understood as pragmatic organizers or organizing intentions that shape teaching practice and the apprenticeship—within any discipline— of deep identity-building projects. The unified taxonomy can be considered as a frame for curriculum organizing or a way to grasp subject-matter complexity and move knowledge from access to voice into action. These matters are crucial if we are to change our school programs for a better world: a world that has learned to communicate across disciplinary boundaries and ways of knowing, with self-actualized individuals who are able to step aside from their own culture and consider action for social justice, ecology, and a civilized world. The alternation of reflection and exploration is key in an apprenticeship model that utilizes proficiency growth as a pretext for the development of wisdom in action.

An analysis of the relationships between integrated classifications forms the basis of a deep, general classification useful for the practitioner. This taxonomy distinguishes between disciplinary, interdisciplinary, and transdisciplinary levels of learning; these, in turn, correspond to three levels of educational activity. The specification of these three levels in curricula would help enhance learners' acquisition of instrumental strategies, interdisciplinary group work among teachers, and the genesis of holistic actions for deep, situated learning.

The Whole is Greater than the Sum of its Parts When a Person is of Many Parts

In Education, taxonomy is defined as a logical, systematic and hierarchical classification of educative intentions. This classification rests on explicit principles of selection. Many classifications have been designed, but few are functional. The most widely known taxonomy was developed by Benjamin Bloom and his colleagues. It is also the one most widely referred to in education, in spite of its imperfections. Bloom's (1956) classification can still be a useful tool for teachers. Referring to this type of classification can help them avoid restricting their teaching to a single level of educative activity. The levels of the educational classification are ordered from simple to complex (Figure 4.2).

In order to forestall the risk of fragmenting educative goals, such a classification adheres to a high level of generality. It distinguishes between cognitive, affective and psychomotor areas. This arbitrary distinction, useful as it may have been for educative purposes, manifests a preference for some cultural priorities in education. This distinction provoked a shift of priorities, in favor of the best-balanced scale of goals: the cognitive scale. One manifestation of this is probably the growth of cognitive research on learning. Because this aspect of human knowledge is the easiest to classify, research on educational classifications favored the cognitive aspect of education.

Bloom's cognitive classification is composed of six categories that proceed from simple to complex: knowledge acquisition, comprehension, application, analysis, synthesis, evaluation.

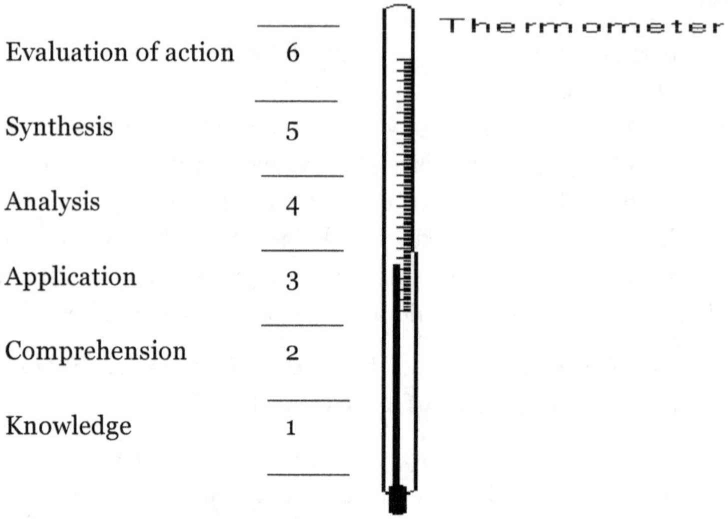

Evaluation of action	6
Synthesis	5
Analysis	4
Application	3
Comprehension	2
Knowledge	1

Figure 4.2
A thermometer of learning
The basic categories of Bloom's scale

The authors of this first classification were primarily concerned with its utility in the teaching field. To make their choice of categories, Bloom and his collaborators used test questions and exercises as a starting point. These categories were not mutually exclusive and disagreements arose between authors on the classification of identical problems. For example, some test items could be classified in two categories. Bloom's taxonomy may be imbalanced due to the predominance of the inferior levels, but no better domain-based classification has yet been devised, despite slight improvements in later models. Guilford's model is more complex, has a more solid theoretic base, and is founded upon factorial analysis, yet it is nonoperational. Marzano's (2007) model shares some of Guilford's characteristics. Nevertheless, taxonomies had a so great influence that it surpasses the trend for educative goals specification. It made the educational community aware of the high ranking of memorized knowledge in school settings, and of the lack of stimulation given to the higher-level cognitive processes.

To summarize, the classification of cognitive aims demonstrates the taxonomic concept's usefulness and potential. However, its classification criteria barely respect the principles of coherence (instructional, psychological, logical, and objective) the authors had selected. From this standpoint, the classification of affective aims corresponds more closely to the description of the coherent continuum of interiorization.

When the Affective if Objectified

Krathwohl, Bloom and Masia (1964) introduced their classification of the affective domain with strong reservations. The principal difficulties they encountered were in determining an increasingly complex order, and objectifying an area that eluded explication. Affective aims are ordered in such a way that each category of affective behavior presupposes the realization of the preceding behaviors along an **interiorization** continuum. Interiorization is at the basis of deep learning and its understanding is of utmost importance to teachers.

Interiorization combines long-established concepts. It is defined as the process of acquiring values and attitudes, leading to the gradual adoption of the desired action. Interiorization allows the establishment of a relationship between the different affective actions and their organization in a sequence. At the first level of the continuum, the individual is **conscious** of a phenomenon because it is **perceived**. At the next level, the individual is ready to **receive** the phenomenon. The individual then **responds** to the phenomenon with a **positive feeling**. This feeling can become strong enough to lead the individual to **seek** occasions that will elicit a response. At some point in the process, the individual **conceptualizes** his or her action and feelings and **organizes** them in a system. This system becomes increasingly complex, as it becomes the individual's **conception of life**.

The gradual process of the interiorization of affective aims does correspond to the stages of character development. Maslow's (1959) principle of self-actualization, or the rational-altruistic type defined by Peck and Havighurst (1960), corresponds to the ultimate stage of human maturity. But this raises an ethical problem. The moment they become educative goals, the ideals of self-actualization may well be related to manipulation and indoctrination, imposing idealistic views and practices on pupils, and that, paradoxically, on the prejudice against free will and autonomy. It is paradoxical because self-sufficient thinking and autonomy is one component of self-actualization. Krathwohl and his collaborators grant equal importance to the development of conformity and to that of nonconformity. Their multidimensional concept of interiorization evokes the passage from simple to complex, from concrete to abstract, as well as from external to internal control. Thus, Krathwohl's internalization of affective goals parallels the Vygotskian psychopedagogical school's process of "mentalization", proper to the theory of activity. It suggests that behavioral hierarchies of a goal may be compatible with defining education in terms of activities.

Briefly, Krathwohl, Bloom and Masia's classification present education's implicit aims within the process of a progressive interiorization of values. This interiorization ultimately results in the individual's social commitment. From a theoretic standpoint, the interiorization continuum ensures the coherence of this classification; from a practical standpoint, the specification, out of context, of higher-level affective aims may transform the educative field into an area of systematic indoctrination, unless the learner is given complete autonomy in choosing commitments.

Cognitive and affective classifications correspond to different principles of coherence. It is nevertheless important to relativize their differences by focusing on the similar structure of these two scales.

No Learning Without Love

The distinction between cognitive and affective domains is an arbitrary one; affective aims have a cognitive component and vice versa. Krathwohl and colleagues (1964, p.61) state: "Some of the most interesting relationships between cognitive and affective domains (as well as some of the most convincing proofs of their interrelationship) are those where the achievement of a goal within one domain is considered a means of achieving a goal in the other domain". It is highly probable that every emotion has its cognitive counterpart and that cognitive aims often serve to attain affective goals.

The classification's authors note that a large measure of what is called good teaching rests in the teacher's aptitude to reach affective goals by challenging students' beliefs through discussion and debate. This idea is rooted in Piaget's theses about the necessity of cognitive conflict for the development of knowledge. Inversely, affective aims can be used as tools of motivation prior to the attainment of cognitive aims. The joint pursuit of affective and cognitive goals can result in curricula that alternately use one domain to develop the other. Krathwohl and his collaborators compare this strategy to that of a person scaling a wall by means of two ladders placed side by side, the rungs of each ladder being too far apart to allow this person to reach them easily with a single step, an analogy close to some of Foucault's comparisons in his 1970-71 course on the willingness to learn (published in 2011). The two scales of cognitive and affective aims intermix, every cognitive aim having an affective counterpart and vice versa. There exists a correspondence between every level of the two classifications. This is not at all unexpected since an individual is a whole, integral entity, and the cognitive – affective - psychomotor trichotomy can only be justified by analytical and operational uses. For example, a person who is receptive to poetry (or geology or mathematics) will manifest a positive response to that subject-matter, which may increase his or her ability to develop higher cognitive learning in that field of knowledge.

The differentiation into three systems of categories may be explained by various reasons. First, it frames cognition as an independent domain. Second, school programs function principally on the cognitive domain. Third, the cognitive domain seems easier to research and categorize. Fourth, purely cognitive aims may only give rise to fragmentary perspectives on learning. Bloom and his colleagues gave room to the forgotten domains (affective and psychomotor) that are related to important aspects of personal actualization. But this concern actually worked against the primary intention. The distinction of three domains that were originally fused favored the cognitive aspect to the detriment of the affective and psychomotor domains. The last fifty years have seen a tendency to forget the latter two domains to the advantage of the cognitive domain only. In regards to the third domain, the psychomotor classification seems largely ignored and has not spawned the research or response necessary to assess its value.

In practice, the teacher would be at some loss if attempting to manage each domain separately from the others. Classifications provide a language based on definitions that allow comparison and communication. However, the complexity inherent to the three existing scales each comprising five or six highly detailed levels excludes all but analytical and theoretical uses. A classification by domains revealed to be too complex to yield applications really useful to the practitioner in the field. Turning now to classifications that preserve the integrity of the learner, these most often determine three levels of learning whose specifications proceed by different strategies but are remarkably similar.

Gluing the Pieces Back Together

The separation into three domains is arbitrary and artificial. It denies the situated nature of cognition and the integrated wholeness of the human person. In Tochon (1989e), I expressed the need for a unique, polyvalent taxonomy that would fuse the traditional domains and would constantly remind educators, curriculum authors, and test makers of the necessity to consider the whole individual. Oddly enough, traces of research into classification by integrated categories can be found in the work of many authors who developed the outcome-directed planning model. Most of these integrated taxonomies are composed of three hierarchical levels of educational goals (see Table 4.1). They are integrated in the sense that they blend the cognitive, affective and psychomotor domains into one unified approach of learning.

Only the common denominator that binds the various unified taxonomies, i.e. the one that recurs from one system to another, shall be retained for the purposes of this chapter. The differences that do exist cannot, for reasons of space, be analyzed here. Any attempt at generalization has its disadvantages; it runs the risk of using its sources metaphorically since it is impossible to thoroughly explore each author's thinking. An analysis based on characteristics, such as those depicted in Table 4.1 necessarily omits a complex host of variables. However, this limitation does not preclude an essential fact: these systems share a surprising number of common factors, enough to support the thesis stated above.

Miller (1962) proposed three integrated levels that are dovetailed: tasks, operations, functions. These levels of analysis relate to a task description; they do not represent a system of domain classification. However, they do correspond to a rough sketch of a functional, unified hierarchization. For Miller, a specialist in task analysis, a function can be divided into operations that can themselves be split into tasks. The first level implies the specificity of the achievement of a short-term task. The second level indicates a superior operational sphere, a general aptitude that is transferable to various situations. The third level concerns individual functional competences in a situation that has been created by the long-term development of aptitudes pertaining to the first two levels. To give an example, the targeted function of radar operator includes learning many operations, such as calculating wind speed, which will, in turn, include simpler tasks, such as measuring the tangent of an angle. The tasks/operations/functions triad can be considered as a simplified classification that integrates Bloomian domains. In Miller's work, a human being is considered as a functioning totality. A function (operation, tasks) integrates the cognitive, affective and psychomotor domains.

Bloom and his colleagues have solidly demonstrated the need to distinguish between inferior and superior levels of educational processes. Eisner's (1969) trichotomy pursues in a slightly different vein: he indicates that higher-level goals may not be easily evaluated. **Mastery** intentions pertain to the circumscribed universe of the accessibly knowable and the operatively definable. These goals can be completely foreseen and pertain to the lower levels of Bloom and his colleagues' classification. **Transfer** intentions are related to those activities learned in one domain that can be applied to another. These intentions pertain to knowledge processing, for example, to analysis and synthesis. No one can foresee all potential situations for the application of transfer intentions; thus, they cannot be fully specified. Intentions of **expression** describe problematic educative situations that imply creative thinking and activities. This type of intention is more evocative than prescriptive, also more complex and difficult to operationalize. It implies the mastery of particular content and the use of acquired transfer strategies. Furthermore, the learner transcends the two first levels of intentions through a creative effort and subsequent personal actualization. Thus, the three levels form a continuum directed to the development of individual initiative. Eisner's trichotomy (mastery, transfer, expression aims) has been quite successful and has been adopted by teachers of creative writing and language arts.

Hoetker (1970) identifies three levels of performance that are a function of transfer strategies:

1) **Can do**: what the student is capable of doing, relative to an operational goal. This level pertains to specific situations and implies non-transferable, domain-specific knowledge.

2) **May do**: what the student may achieve using transfer in new, unfamiliar situations. This level of transfer strategies, applicable to many types of performances, transcends the bounds of specific contents.

3) **Will do**: what the student will be capable of achieving in adulthood, relating to action within a complex situation. This long-term predictive level includes the first two levels in the adult individual's life situations. As in Eisner's classification, Hoetker's classification of educational intentions distinguishes between the short, intermediate and long terms in the learning process.

Tuckman's (1972) integrated classification discerns **objects** to which are applied **processes** relative to **domains**. **Objects** pertain to facts or data specific to objects, ideas, or people. **Processes** are related to interdisciplinary operations effected on objects, and activating memory, application, evaluation and communication strategies. **Domains** refer to the functional components of an individual and include perceptive, cognitive, affective, and psychomotor aspects.

Rowntree (1974) developed three types of goals in relation to their degree of permanence and to the level of content specificity:

1) **Content goals** related to instructional sequences defined by short-term performance in a specific subject-matter. These goals are determined by the concepts, principles or applications that are specific to a content element being memorized or understood.

2) **Methodological goals** pertain to the instrumental procedures required for the research, organization and interpretation of

information. These goals target strategies related to transfer and are developed over the intermediate term. These strategies apply to specific contents but are not limited to any single subject-matter. They are applicable to various learning situations but will often require periodic reinforcement to maintain their operationality. They deal with the "how-to-do" of learning **life-skill goals**.

3) Long-term, **life-skill goals** pertain to long-lasting competences needed for social action and involving value integration. These goals are trans-educative in the sense that they target adaptability to diverse social contexts beyond the school years. Unlike the goals of the first two levels, life skills are not related to content or to cognitive strategies alone; they result from the development of a integral individual. Life skills embed content and methods and transcend them.

De Block's (1972-1973) tridimensional model separates content from method (or learning strategies) and the student's subjective culture. These three levels of learning may vary in the way they are related to transfer, according to student's self-sufficiency.

-**Content-related goals** have a high degree of specificity within a subject-matter and operate on a differentiated scale, based on instruction limited to simple facts.

-**Method-related goals** pertain to transfer strategies that lie at the heart of the learning process itself; these go beyond accumulation of subject-matter knowledge and integrate the different subjects. They are basic to integrative education.

-**Student-generated goals** emerge from a global transfer through the generalization of individual values to all domains of action as a whole. These goals start from specialized functions and end up as the harmonious, general education; this is expressed in a subjective, individualized cultural growth raising self-actualization. Student-generated goals integrate method-related goals pertaining to the learning strategies, as well as content-related goals.

De Landsheere and De Landsheere (1976) have reworked the classifications of Tyler, Gagne, Eisner and McClelland, elaborating and sorting out as a mainframe the mastery, transfer and expression intentions.

In second-language instruction, Rolinger et al. (1976) clearly differentiate the learning of **basic content** (phonetics, structures, vocabulary) from that of **communicative strategies** and **situations**, in which proficiency is demonstrated—a frame implying whole language in use. The first level is specific to the teaching of a particular subject-matter (second language); the second pertains to the use of strategies, such as "selecting information" that imply the transfer of contents learned in a given situation. The third level includes actions from the two first levels and defines the general frame of contextual functioning in communicative situations, such as the introduction of friends and family in a second language. This last level aims at developing proficient and situated actualization modes in a foreign language.

D'Hainault (1977) makes a distinction between three types of approaches to learning: intradisciplinary, interdisciplinary, and transdisciplinary. The **intradisciplinary** approach is the most common one; it follows the logic of a subject-matter. According to D'Hainault, this approach would be justified by the convenience of organizing teaching in simple to complex sequences in a single matter. There would also be parallels between the structuring of knowledge in a learning situation and the structure of the subject-matter being taught. The structural **interdisciplinary** approach organizes learning by means of general concepts or strategies that are applicable in many domains. This approach to learning tackles content, according to an organizing principle shared by many subject-matters; it focuses on the mental instruments (concepts, strategies, structures). The **transdisciplinary** approach determines a learning situation based on contextualization strategies that arise from intellectual and socio-affective experience in life-situations. This approach is directed towards situations that the student may run into outside school; it proceeds from very general social, affective and intellectual actions and provides an image of the fulfilled human being (Netten & Germain, 2002a). This perspective is centered on the student's self-realization as an individual; it conforms to educations' integrated goals and is adjusted to the roles and functions the student will have throughout life.

The Lyon school of educational thought in France expresses three levels of learning goals based on multiple experiments in action-research: the **contents**, the **abilities**, the **competences**. (See Meirieu, 1984; Gillet, 1986; CEPEC, 1987). These authors note that by focusing on learning, in the sense of accumulating knowledge, the goal-directed planning model has drawn the teacher's attention to content-related objectives. But content is only one aspect; it is ultimately as important to lead the student to develop strategic abilities and situated competences. They propose an advanced and flexible goal-directed planning model. Their tri-level scale makes meaning with content in directing the act of learning towards the mastery of complex actions relevant in a host of professional or scholastic situations. Learning progressions are organized by integrated modules within global teaching situations that include content objectives, strategic abilities, and situated competences as indicators of a successfully executed task (Gillet, 1991). An **ability** signals the learner's development in the procedural transfer and management of content. It represents a work hypothesis for the planning teacher; it is an open possibility for progress. A **competence** is a complex, interiorized system of learning that represents an ultimate realization embedding many tasks. A competence is the point where contents and abilities synchronize in an integrated actualization. The achievement of a competence is the non-linear situated result of multiple content and learning strategies.

Cardinet (1989) examines the common teaching options that underlie a group of existing curricula and notes that educative aims can be formulated in many ways according to how the contents taught within a subject-matter (logical organization) are linked to general cognitive strategies (psychological organization) or to the contextualized application of knowledge in a given situation (functional organization). His analysis of curricula underlines three types of complementary teaching intentions:

1) **content** intentions pertaining to the concepts and lexicon of a subject-matter, as well as to the lists of elements related to the focus of study, including rules and relations established within a content area;

2) **strategy** intentions referring to transformative aims within the student, in the form of interdisciplinary abilities, expressing psychological, transferable aptitudes.

3) **function** intentions target the autonomous mastery of the life-frame, a social role or a problematic situation; these intentions activate disciplinary knowledge and interdisciplinary thinking strategies within a real-life context that implies actualized values, production, communication or creativity.

Allal's (1986) classification may be mentioned as well. It includes four levels of intentions: 1) mastery of content and basic knowledge; 2) elaboration of strategies; 3) self-monitoring; 4) social interaction. The third and fourth levels are integrated in situated actions. This typology, even though less balanced, takes up the essential points presented in the preceding unified taxonomies.

In an ethnographic study of thirty seasoned language teachers defined as experts by their administrators and teacher educators, Tochon (1993b) found that such expert teachers have three ways of transforming curriculum knowledge for the purpose of language instruction: they reshape curriculum knowledge through thematic stories, operational skills, or experiences that help students actualize knowledge in a social action. On the basis of these research results, Tochon distinguished three types of instructional organizers: disciplinary storytelling organizers (or *narrativors*) which transform the master plan or curriculum into stories that can be shared and gather instructional contents ; interdisciplinary skill builders (or *skillers*), which are intended to develop transferable skills in the learners ; and transdisciplinary actualizers of experiences enacting aspects of the curriculum. Narrativors transform the curriculum into stories of experience, skillers transform the curriculum into task operations, actualizers transform the curriculum into interpersonal and transpersonal projects and experiences and actualize social, affective, cultural and ecological goals. Thus, it was discovered empirically that the entire curriculum is remolded with the help of key organizers to which all other tasks are subordinated. Narrativors, skillers, and actualizers consist in layered forms of instructional intervention embedding the cognitive, the socio-affective and the psychomotor, and thus match the definition of an integrated taxonomy.

Tristán & Molgado (2006), in their thorough review of the concept of integrated taxonomy proposed by Tochon, added to the aforementioned classifications those of Romiszowski (1981), LOGSE (1990), Hauenstein (1998), and Paquette (2002).

The general law organizing the educational system in Spain has been elaborated in a way that integrates three levels of content: conceptual, procedural, and attitudinal (LOGSE, 1990). It targets competences that are cognitive and intellectual, emotional and related with personal balance, as well as interpersonal and social. (1) The conceptual level includes facts, concepts, principles and theories. (2) The procedural level consists of algorithmic and heuristic strategies that are of interdisciplinary nature—but may be applied within a discipline as well. (3) The attitudinal level includes (3a) general values for action, such as competences useful for psychological, moral and civic development (trust, autonomy, conviviality, life goals...) and (3b) attitudes vis-à-vis the content's subject-matter , either scientific, practical, or artistic, such as they may lead to actions defined by the socioaffective taxonomy of Krathwohl et al. (1964).

Hauenstein (1998) proposed a taxonomy that integrates the cognitive, the affective, and the psychomotor into unified, composite behavioral learning processes and actions. Instructional objectives are understood as processes targeting human development within a holistic approach. The composite behavioral domain facilitates the integration of objectives within the development of the whole individual. The integrative levels can be understood as (1) acquisition and assimilation; (2) adaptation; and (3) clarification (**desempañar** in Spanish) and aspiration. They aim to teaching the whole individual. "We do not develop in a balance of emotions, knowledge, and physical skills. Some of us will attain high levels of physical skills but low levels of emotional development. Similarly, others will develop high levels of knowledge and emotional sensitivity but will attain a low level of physical dexterity. The challenge for teachers is to attend to whole development and help students attain a balance of cognitive, emotional, and psychomotor development" (Petrina, 2007, p.23).

Paquette (2002) defined three levels of educative action in distance learning: specialized abilities, specific processes, and general metaprocesses. The taxonomy slightly differs from the previous ones but still aims to integrate three levels of educative action. Along these lines of thought, Paquette, Rosca, Mihaila and Masmoudi (2006) propose a service-oriented framework with three sorts of operations to support learning and knowledge management, based on

1. Basic operations on a resource;

2. Resource life cycle operations where a resource is composed, prepared for use, used in action, and analyzed, providing feedback to start new resources life cycles.

3. Global system generation operations extending system with new resources to produce learning experiences and management.

To summarize, many authors affirm the need to integrate the cognitive, socio-affective and psychomotor domains within educative aims. Almost all establish three integrated levels of planning, as shown in Table 4.1 (a & b). In that table, the horizontal axis corresponds to the authors and the vertical axis to the shared characteristics of their classifications. A (V) marks the presence of a shared characteristic that pertains to the author's definition of a particular level. The characteristics that constitute the vertical axis are retained from definitions given by the authors of the most important and well-known trichotomies.

This table shows three levels of action in a synthetic formula. The first level pertains to short-term intradisciplinary organizers related to the contents to be mastered. The second level addresses interdisciplinary procedures of an instrumental nature and thinking strategies that invoke transfer. The third level is related to transdisciplinary action in the complex creative expression of competences, implicating self-actualization and contextualized interaction.

When Plans Dovetail
Validating Analysis Criteria

The first part of this chapter indicated that the classifications of educative intentions constitute a useful analytical tool that can help teachers organize their action. But the division of cognitive, affective and psychomotor domains, as well as the scales' complexity, has hindered the application of taxonomy in the practice of teaching. Nevertheless, this unresolved matter remains important because of the necessity to progress beyond the cognitive domain and attain the higher-levels of achievement and self-actualization.

Simplified classifications that integrate the cognitive, affective and psychomotor domains will most often adopt a tri-level scale. The correspondence that exists between these three levels among numerous authors is established in Table 4.1 (a & b) by the inclusion of common criteria of definition under different terminology.

On the next two pages, the criteria of analysis in Table 4.1 (vertical axis) are derived from definitions found in the most widely known trichotomies. This correspondence is all the more striking in that the various authors arrived at their definitions via very different approaches.

1. Eisner, De Landsheere & De Landsheere, and D'Hainaut proceeded by **deduction**, by first identifying the aims that are relative to the mastery in a subject-matter, the aims that are transferable from one subject-matter to another, and those that lead to open activities of creative production.

2. Cardinet discovers three general categories by **induction**, analyzing existing curricula.

3. Lyon's school of teacher researchers started from a **pragmatic** strategy that was focused on practices in the field of teaching; their definitions resulted from action-research in teaching. Tochon's unified taxonomy was also derived from the empirical study of the curriculum categories used by seasoned teachers.

4. Tochon deciphered pragmatic organizers in the teachers' verbal protocols through an **empirical investigation**.

Table 4.1.a Knowledge in three tenses

Integrated Taxonomies	LEVEL 1					LEVEL 2					
	Intra-disciplinarity	Mastery domain	Short term course	Content-related	NAME	Inter-disciplinarity	Transfer operations	Middle term course	General	Cognitive or	NAME
Miller	V	V	V	V	Tasks	V	V	V	V	V	Operations
Eisner	V	V	V	V	Mastery	V	V	V	V	V	Transfer
Hoetker	V	V	V	V	Can do	V	V	V	V	V	May do
Tuckman		V		V	Object	V	V	V	V	V	Process
Rowntree	V	V	V	V	Content object	V	V	V	V	V	Method goal
De Block				V	Cultural Content	V		V		V	Learn method
Landsheere	V	V	V	V	Mastery	V	V	V	V	V	Transfer
Rolinger	V	V	V	V	Basics		V	V		V	Communic capacity
D'Hainaut	V	V		V	Intradiscipline	V	V		V	V	Interdisc capacity
Romiszowski	V	V	V		Stimulat Percept.	V	V	V		V	Memory operation
Cardinet	V	V	V	V	Content	V	V	V	V	V	Think strategy
Allal	V	V	V	V	Mastery	V	V	V		V	Strategies
CEPEC	V	V	V	V	Objective	V	V		V	V	Capacity
Tochon	V	V	V	V	Discipline	V	V	V	V	V	Interdiscipline
LOGSE	V	V	V	V	Discipline	V		V	V	V	Interdiscipline
Tochon	V	V	V	V	Narrativors	V	V	V	V		Skillers
Hauenstein	V		V	V	Acquis&assimil	V		V		V	Adaptation
Paquette 1	V	V	V	V	Special ability	V	V		V		Specific process
Paquette 2		V	V	V	Basics	V	V	V	V	V	Operations

Table 4.1.b Knowledge in three tenses

Integrated Taxonomies	Trans-disciplinarity	Integrates socio-	Implies situated	Long term course of	Implies production	Implies self-	Implies social	Integrates levels 1 &	NAME
Miller	V	V	V		V	V	V	V	Functions
Eisner	V	V	V	V	V	V	V	V	Expression
Hoetker	V	V	V	V	V	V	V	V	Will do
Tuckman	V		V					V	Domains
Rowntree	V	V	V	V	V	V	V	V	Long-term life-skill
De Block	V	V	V	V		V	V	V	Subject culture
Landsheere	V	V	V	V	V	V	V	V	Expression
Rolinger	V	V	V	V	V	V	V	V	Proficiency
D'Hainaut	V	V	V	V		V	V	V	Transdisciplinary Competence
Romiszowski	V	V	V	V	V	V	V	V	Improvisational planning
Cardinet	V	V	V	V	V	V	V	V	Situated functioning
Allal	V	V	V		V	V	V	V	Self-regulation & social interaction
CEPEC	V	V	V	V	V	V	V	V	Competence
Tochon	V	V	V	V	V	V	V	V	Transdiscipline
LOGSE	V	V	V	V	V	V	V	V	Personal & social balance
Tochon	V	V	V	V	V	V	V	V	Actualizers
Hauenstein	V	V	V	V	V		V	V	Improvisation & aspiration
Paquette 1	V	V	V	V	V	V	V	V	General Process
Paquette 2	V	V	V	V					Global generation

LEVEL 3

Since these researchers arrived at converging theorizations, their definitions correspond to common criteria. This convergence reinforces the validity of the model shown in Figure 4.3 because the criteria of definition for the three levels have been successively validated by vastly different approaches—deduction, induction, and pragmatic action-research. These levels of classification deal with educational intentions in the field of curriculum and instruction. These curricular goals fit with the three levels emphasized by authors working on strategic teaching and learning. They also involve affective and social expressions of self-actualization.

Definition of the Three Levels of the Unified Taxonomy

The trichotomic construct born from this analysis corresponds to the three levels of the educative action. The logical relationship between these levels is illustrated in Figure 4.3.

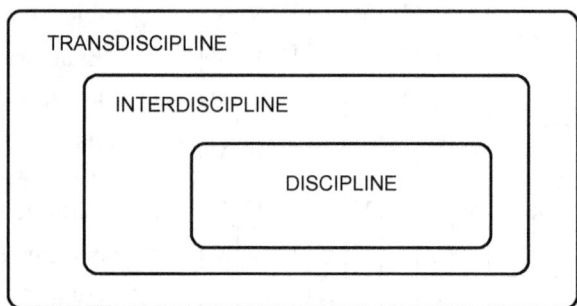

Figure 4.3
The Three Levels of the Unified Taxonomy

These three levels can be identified by the following definitions:

Discipline corresponds to the content of a specific, separate field of knowledge, as represented by a subject-matter (for example: mathematics, art, Spanish, biology).

Interdiscipline corresponds to a structural intersection between many types of subject-matter, in the form of instrumental, transferable strategies (for example: taking notes, organizing an argument, researching information, planning, comparing data, deducing or inducing conclusions, applying guidelines, transposing data onto a graph).

Transdiscipline encompasses disciplinary contents and organizing principle of interdisciplinary strategies. It integrates and transcends these two levels in that it relates to the whole learner in a contextualized actualization that is at once cognitive, socio-affective and psychomotor (for example: adapting oneself in a collaborative situation, enacting values for social justice, solving ill-defined problems in a real-life situation, taking responsibility for one's actions in a professional context, affirming oneself and voicing values, working within a group to achieve ecological goals). This last dimension confers its depth to the unified taxonomy.

Figure 4.4 present the curricular embedment of the three layers of instructional action.

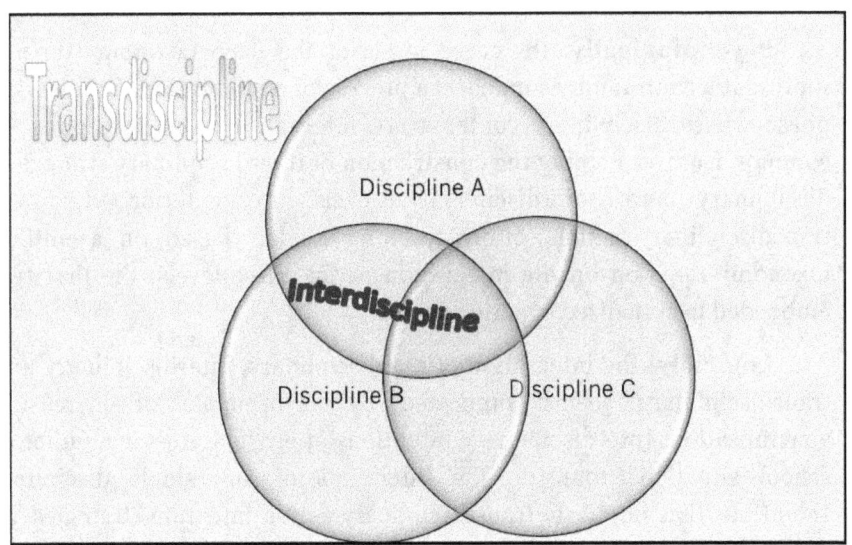

Figure 4.4
To make it simple

Reaching a Functional Coherence

In the first part of this chapter, the principles underlying the classification of cognitive and affective intentions were studied, stressing the difficulty of attaining adherence to a body of coherent, functional principles. For purposes of reflection, and as an introduction to "revisited" thinking on this matter, the following points illustrate some of the possibilities of a general, unified classification.

Instructionally: the educational institution clearly targets three levels of tasks; these levels have firm grounds in the teaching practice and in learning processes. They correspond to distinct school genres. All three levels are expressed in curricula, although the use of these categories may not always be emphasized as it is here. In a study with thirty seasoned teachers planning simulations alternated concurrent and short-term retrospective verbalizations, Tochon (1993) discovered that these levels were frame organizers of spontaneous teacher planning.

Psychologically: the three levels of the deep taxonomy do not represent a continuum as much as a process of equilibration. Following a phase where disciplinary contents are internalized, the perception of common features helping the construction of interdisciplinary strategies, disciplinary and interdisciplinary levels are exteriorized in a transdisciplinary action. Many teaching models based on a unified taxonomy function on the integration of the three levels, the first two embedded in actualized experiences.

Logically: the integration of the disciplinary, interdisciplinary and transdisciplinary seems supported by a principle of increasing generalization. Interdisciplinary intentions apply to a greater number of school situations than do the intentions of any single discipline. Intentions that implicate transdisciplinary action integrate strategies, as well as the mastery of specific content. A temporal logic underlies this ordering because the long term encompasses the intermediate and short term.

Objectively: this hierarchy favors situated action and personal expression over transfer, and transfer over straightforward mastery of contents. This balance among basic, strategic and experiential goals would seem a desirable educative situation.

The criteria that define the integrated classification are validated by inductive, deductive and pragmatic research approaches. This general classification has shown a functional validity, as it is already used empirically in curricula, as well as in certain formative methodologies arising from action-research. Practical applications of the unified taxonomy are presented in the next chapter. Various researchers in World Language Education have found useful applications of this work, for example, Germain and Netten (2005). The classification is supported by principles of instructional, psychological, logical and objective coherence, principles that should bear confirmation by further research.

Depth from Interdiscipline to Transdiscipline

I have now presented the unified taxonomy. I qualify this taxonomy as 'deep' for two reasons. First, it addresses the deep epistemic flows of knowledge that give sense to academic life: it is all about ways of knowing, as disciplinary conceptions are of epistemological nature. Second, it reaches a deeper dimension at which knowledge acquires a creative purpose and a dynamism. This level was named 'transdisciplinary.'

This section explores the transdisciplinary dimension further. It is the third space of the educative act. The concept of third space has been developed by Henry Lefebvre (1991) to designate a space which goes beyond polarities: "subjectivity and objectivity, the abstract and the concrete, the real and the imagined, the knowable and the unimaginable, the repetitive and the differential, structure and agency, mind and body, consciousness and the unconscious, the disciplined and the transdisciplinary" (Soja, 1996, pp. 56-57). Kramsch's (1994) conception of third space in second language education inherits from Lefebvre understanding. Bhabha's (1994) third space is similarly a space of hybridity where both self and Other meet, creating a dynamic subspace (Ikas & Wagner, 2008). For Bhabha, who refers to Jameson's (1991) 'quantum leap' in the representation of the future beyond despotic times and spaces, it is a space of enunciation and interpretation, and the seat of expression.

Where dominance resides, there are negotiations and an effort to legitimize difference and identity. Social identification and academic learning can deeply depend on each other: students' identities and roles emerge during the year in the classroom through subtle adjustments around curriculum issues (Wortham, 2006). Expression creates a space to reach an alternative form of discourse where identity can be projected (Castells, 2004); such identity projection allows social actors to redefine their position in the third space, within an 'imagined space' (Taylor, 1999), where the 'imagined' identity takes shape in the interplay of language and power through voice (Park, 2008). Thus, the transdisciplinary explores identity in hybrid projects that involve self, Other, and knowledge in action through specific forms of engagement.

The transformation of curricula toward interdisciplinarity acknowledges "the limits of understanding in the sciences and of the human condition when one employs just one—however sophisticated and well-developed—set of practices, traditions, and ideologies that goes by the name of an established academic discipline" (Cook-Sather & Shore, 2007, p.1). One discipline can inform the way another discipline writes its own subject-matter. Cross-sections across disciplines highlight the role of knowledge formatting and ways of knowing (or epistemology) in the definition of any discipline. From this perspective, "If a faculty is a way of doing things well because of innate or learned capacities, if a discipline is a delimited body of knowledge, an object of study, or a methodology and discipline is teaching, instruction, or tutoring, and inter means between, among, amid, in between, and in the midst, then we propose that interdisciplinarity practiced by a faculty should mean teaching, learning, and doing research among and between and in the midst of those of innate or learned capacities" (ibid), which would emphasize the 'skilling' dimension and connectivity of such reflective intersection.

When handled properly, interdisciplinary connections are considered high-leverage teaching practices, as they promote higher-level learning. Interdisciplinarity is thus being promoted as a way to enhance classroom learning as well as teacher education (Cummings Hlas & Hlas, 2012). Practice-based curricula in teacher education focus on actual practices and guide student teachers in comparing their own practices, for example after school supervision visits in portfolio discussion and video study groups (Tochon & Black, 2006, 2007). This focus implies that experiences will be deciphered and deconstructed before and after practice to support teacher learning (Lampert, 2010). This approach has strong partisans in the world language education community (Glisan, 2010). It is highly compatible with Deep Education, as it situates student teachers as researchers on open and creative projects and implies "sustained inquiry about the clinical aspects of practice and how best to develop skilled practice" (Grossman & McDonald, 2008, p.189). Preparing cosmopolitan learners within the new paradigm described in the National Standards implies that the teachers must be much more than individuals who orchestrate mechanical language practices. As the facilitators providing resources for learning, they help students design their interactions with communities beyond the classroom, and provide feedback and assistance so students can monitor their progress (Shrum & Glisan, 2010). Making systematic connections across task domains (writing, literature and readings in general, grammar analysis and interpersonal activities) is not a new idea as such but it has never been applied systematically as the template to balance tasks within self-determined educative projects. Following the MLA Task Force report of 2007, there are efforts to create better integrated curricula that are interweaving literary and rhetorical analyses, stylistics, and culture and maximize the use of language literature (Barrette, Paesani & Vinall, 2010), "however, notes Huhn (2012), the call for change in the 2007 MLA report has not manifested itself in the literature of our profession." Teachers are still waiting for a model that helps them making the quantum leap. The present work is an effort in this direction.

The Trandisciplinary Charter attempted to address the constant growth of knowledge, which makes a global view of the human being impossible (de Freitas, Morin & Nicolescu, 1994). Gibbons (1998, p. 8) points out the main properties of the transdiscipline:

- Its evolving framework guides problem solving and it is generated and pursued in the context of its application, rather than being developed first and then applied by practitioners in a top-down fashion. The project's conceptualizing cannot be reduced to disciplinary sections and may be difficult to map within restricted

disciplinary views.
- Knowledge production is accomplished in the process of its creation.
- Transdisciplinarity has its own dynamics. It is a form of integrated research and problem solving on the move.

Transdisciplinary practice is a prior condition for the conceptualization and invention of new institutional forms (Genosko, 2003). The transdisciplinary project challenges "the spiritual and material self-destruction of the human species" (Charter, online). It considers that "life on earth is seriously threatened by the triumph of a techno-science that obeys only the terrible logic of productivity for productivity's sake". Consequently, increasing quantitative knowledge, with an increasingly impoverished inner identity, lead to the rise of obscurantism with huge personal and social consequences. Specifically, the exponential growth of knowledge and access to it increases inequalities between the haves and have nots. "Transdisciplinarity concerns that which is at once between the disciplines, across the different disciplines, and beyond all disciplines. Its goal is the understanding of the present world, of which one of the imperatives is the unity of knowledge" (Nicolescu, 2005, p. 2)

Transdisciplinarity integrates its immanent critique within its creative process. Immanent critique is a method of post-negativity. It retains Adorno's (2008) insistence that contradictions and tensions operate as a constituent force within any idiom of expression and it recognizes that sociality within network cultures and creative economies is configured, not according to dualisms, but rather to patterns of distribution, rhythms of tension, transversal social relations, modulations of affect and transdisciplinary institutional practices. In this sense, immanent critique understands the antagonism of the binary constituents of discourse as a processual force of affirmation distinct from the "negation of negation." (Rossiter, 2006, p. 5).

This final section allowed us to explore the genesis of the concept of transdisciplinarity, and its connection to a creative space that merges oppositions and dualisms into a deeper layer of understanding. Transdisciplinarity operates at the junction of what is perceived as reality (ontology) and the way of knowing it (epistemology). It situates the flow of knowledge in transformative action. This is the last of the demonstration in this chapter: the deep approach to education requires the transdisciplinary, which confers to the model wisdom in action as a key component of education.

In Short

A large part of research in education uses taxonomies. Indeed, we can't do research without using ordered categories of understanding. They provide a grammar of educational practice. Research on the classification of educational intentions is thus useful; it is necessary for analyzing educative processes. The relevance of this issue had been somewhat diminished by the difficulty in applying complex, diversified scales. The taxonomy of education, as "revisited" in this chapter, may help practitioners to ask the right questions about their teaching intentions. It may help language teachers balancing disciplinary basics with interdisciplinary strategies and situated experience within a deep learning model. Furthermore, it invites teachers and educators to question their action in terms of deep concerns, such as wisdom, impacts of schooling on the world as we live it, students' autonomy, and social action.

The analysis of educational classification proves that many authors of integrated classifications establish three relevant levels for instructional actions, whatever their research orientation is. These authors provide definitions for the three-scaled levels of learning and teaching; these definitions concur most frequently when the authors' own criteria are applied to the body of hierarchies. The thesis proposed here, that an implicit taxonomy underscores curricula and the schooling orientations, is corroborated by the predominance of specific constants appearing in a number of authors. The overlap that occurs between deductive, inductive, and pragmatic research supports this book's hypothesis that there exists a hierarchized classification underpinning curricula and the functioning of educational institutions.

This chapter merely displays the functional levels in the educative system. Also, it is grounded in empirical data. Consequently, the classification should be manageable and useful for the teacher-practitioner. The unified taxonomy may make teaching closer to deep learning processes, as evidenced by research on critical thinking. The three levels of learning correspond to specific teaching intentions. For example, as will be seen in the next chapter, students' projects can be built on various forms of embedment of themes, operations, and experiences gathering all three levels of the unified taxonomy (figure 4.5).

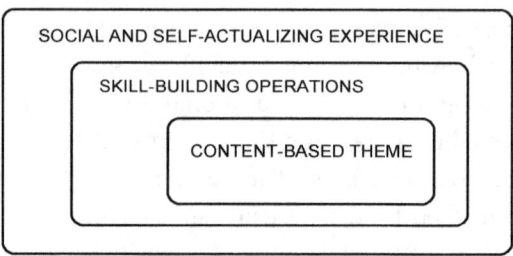

Figure 4.5
Embedment enacting the unified taxonomy
in educative projects

The specification of these scaled intentions, in school curricula may well stimulate the initiative of interdisciplinary teams, the integrative approach among subject-matters, the facilitation of transfer, and the use of methods that open onto transdisciplinary, transformative action. The latter effect would allow the learner the opportunity to integrate knowledge, contextualize deep learning and apply it to actual, meaningful situations in society. As we will see in the next chapter, projects fit disciplinary content together through interdisciplinary strategies, connected in a transdisciplinary action. Such connections ensure learning dynamics of a new genre, able to revolutionize the way we think about schools.

It is a call for an education that develops in learners a wisdom linked to reflective practice, as well as proactive instruments to solve the problems humanity will face during the coming generations due to the uncivilized and undemocratic behavior of a minority of psychopaths within the governing bodies of the present and past generations, as demonstrated by the scientific study of political and financial ponerology (Lobaczewski, 2007).

Chapter 5

Forward Planning: Instructional Organizers for Deep Apprenticeship

Successful organizing is based on the recognition that people get organized because they, too, have a vision. Paul Wellstone

When applied to outcome-based analysis, the precepts of the Discourse on the Method *create contradictory results. The organization of instructional units must itself evolve into an adaptable,* forward model. *In overemphasizing outcomes, curriculum designers and teachers forgot the value of curriculum input. Broadly, they forgot the construction of values.*

This chapter contains proposals for radical changes in the modes of planning instructional units, into which the complexities of the value-laden communicative contexts are factored. This change involves, by virtue of its interactional nature, an adaptive movement forward, directed toward world-related, life-related projects. The chapter outlines a flexible, action-based approach to planning deep, value-loaded experiences. Responding to the limitations of outcome-based curricula, the Deep Approach gives rise to a variety of outcomes that are mapped proactively, as the process unfolds. Evaluation is open and focuses on creative work. Pre-cast assessment would restrict learning to shallow and formal learning. On the contrary, thematic apprenticeship places the emphasis on the quality and depth of the acquisition process within the accomplishment of projects. This new perspective on ways of organizing learning will bring fresh air in world languages education. Research behind the Deep Approach to languages and cultures model is detailed with guidelines and examples from classroom practices.

In order for instructional planning to be viable and useful, the tasks' organization must be partly driven by interactions. Priorities should evolve in a responsive way. Therefore, the proposal is to focus on processes, rather than outcomes. There will be outcomes, but the focus is on the process to stimulate a deep approach to learning. In contrast with instructional goals that define learning outcomes, instructional organizers define apprenticeship processes, which may offer varied outcomes and adapt to self-directed orientations.

The Concept of Instructional Organizer

Instructional organizers are process-focused intentions; they are ways of connecting curriculum items to build learning projects: through thematic stories, strategic skills, or interpersonal experiences. Here is a brief history of the concept.

First let us distinguish it from advanced organizers, famous in the field of literacy. 'Advance organizers' were used by Ausubel to describe any structural information that could be presented in advance to the learner to ease the learning process (Ausubel & Robinson, 1969). Advance organizers anticipate action a bit like movies anticipate events through advanced clues and indicators that take their full meaning as events develop. Advanced organizers are beneficial to low-achievers and students who have limited knowledge of the domain (Mayer, 1979). Ausubel (1978) had discovered organizers that anticipate information and pre-structure knowledge for the reader or the listener. Mainstream research and applications have focused on their role in pre-reading activities, as graphic organizers and concept maps. The concept proposed here has some similarities because it relates to the dynamics of text superstructures, in which instructional planning is considered as a text genre.

Psycholinguists highlight the role of semantic organizers: abstract textual superstructures scaffold reading (Frederiksen & Breuleux, 1989; Reigeluth, 1999). Since 1984, I had been interviewing teachers on their classroom planning, comparing the prior lessons plans, the observations of planned lessons, and what had happened during the lesson. This research, pursued in different countries, gave rise to publications in various languages. I proposed the concept of the 'instructional organizer' in Tochon (1988).

The study of the teachers' mental models highlighted how language teaching enfolds around key instructional organizers, according to a conceptual grammar that was based on the curriculum items used as ontology (Tochon, 1991a; Tochon & Dionne, 1994). This led to applications such as INCA (Interactive Classroom Analysis, Tochon & Brandon, 1996). Carl Frederiksen, who had created the first cognitive grammar of learning in the field of reading at McGill University, noted in a personal communication that this semiocognitive grammar of language teaching was a world first.

Other researchers in Second Language Acquisition followed a different track and analyzed the organizational patterns of instruction in a different way. For example, Ellis & Friend (1991) referred to instructional organizers as "teaching routines used to help students understand what is being learned and to integrate new information with that which is previously learned"(p. 96). This definition is close to Ausubel's concept in the sense that the purpose is to help students discriminate important from unimportant information, relate new information to prior knowledge, and store the new information in an organized way. On the basis of empirical studies, Ellis (1991) established three ways to enhance the organizational patterns of instruction and assist students in the phases of acquisition, organization, and retrieval: advance organizers, lesson organizers, and post organizers. The lesson organizers present the structure of the lesson. For example, the teacher may use numbers to indicate the presence of steps, provide structural information on what is being presented to highlight its importance, draw associations and integrate prior information, or clarify instructional expectations. The post organizers provide a neat closure to the learning session, such as wrapping up contents, evaluating acquisition, presenting homework, and forecasting forthcoming acquisitions (Ellis & Friend, 1991). These elements focus on well-defined products related to pre-defined contents. They do not offer much maneuvering margin to the learner in terms of personal or group projects: the instructor's curriculum dictates the learner's curriculum. This is very different from the concept that is being advanced in this chapter.

Early in my career, I was a teacher researcher in a junior high school, and as an instructional consultant, was in charge of the language reforms at these grade levels for eight years. I was intrigued by the way the genuine practices of seasoned language teachers self-organized in an adaptive way to integrate students' insights meaningfully. The adaptive nature of educative projects caused me to reflect in terms of processes, rather than goals. This led me to analyze, in a study, the function of time in teaching (Tochon & Munby, 1993). Time plays a crucial function in teacher planning. The teacher in action is interweaving prior knowledge with present interactions at many levels. For example the teacher planned to discuss a text but is interrupted by students who ask about the context in which it was written. Then the plan needs to be adapted. Teacher planning is constantly evolving to better match the students' needs. Instructional time is curricular and diachronic when the teacher retrieves prior knowledge: the focus is past knowledge within the teacher. Teaching time is relational and synchronic when the focus is the ongoing interpersonal exchanges stimulated by knowledge (figure 5.1).

The model rests upon the two axes of instructional planning and interactive pedagogy. Where the axes of Figure 5.1 meet, the structural limits of binarism are transcended. The axes are complementary yet they enable the conceptualization of fundamentally different mental spaces. The discipline's inner cultural space "enminds" action (if I may coin a term modelled on "embodies"). This content-specific enminding of teaching action operates along the timeline preceding and following the action. Action is but an expression of this inner "mind" of the disciplinary understanding of upcoming situations and events in a classroom.

On this dimension, the disciplinary mind is diachronic: it is historic and follows the inner narrative of the events experienced through different classroom situations. It is on this axis that experience is semanticised, that is, enminded in the particular vocabulary and genres of a particular subject matter. This first axis, one of disciplinary goal-setting, intersects with the second axis, that of the present tense of pedagogy, in which, for instance, inner intentions may be transformed in specific outer actions. This is the axis of pragmatisation, that is, the actualisation of meaningmaking experiences. Synchronic (present-tense) interactions move the inner world of the disciplinary culture forward and make it evolve. Thus there is an interconnection between the here and now of pedagogy and the historic mind of a discipline. The disciplinary culture evolves in learners' minds, teachers' minds, schools' inner cultures, and the inner world of research and scientific knowledge.

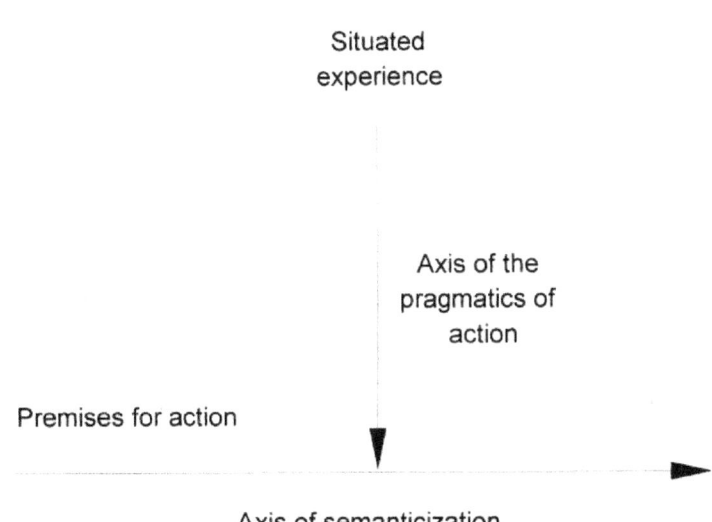

Figure 5.1

Model of the authentic teaching situation

An enhanced, non-binary version of this reflection on time in teaching is presented in Figure 5.2. The latter figure explains why the plans of the former are constantly being readapted, which indicates why the standards model (NSFLEP, 1999) must be reconciled with the realities of the field.

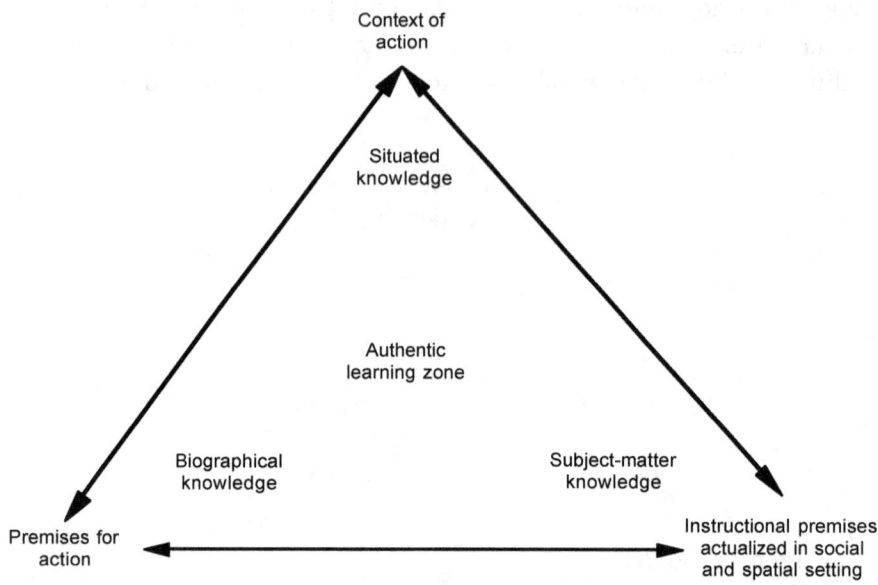

Figure 5.2
The Student in the Authentic Learning Situation
(Tochon, 2000b)

Educative projects and writing workshops are sustained by processes that I name instructional organizers. Objectifying these subtle instructional processes that constantly adapt to learning and thematic resources made me aware of objectification: naming perceived realities tends to sanitize them from their context and transforms abstract and diaphanous nuances into reified objects people will take for granted. The analysis might be 'true' in a certain context but may in part become a 'lie' when it is simplified for teacher training. I analyzed how metacognition had been reified in curricula and was treated as if it were an object (ibid, 2002). By instructional organizers, I did not mean structural units that would convey classroom concepts and genres in a unilateral way, but rather, faint and abstract processes of conceptualizing that shape classroom interactions in a way conducive to learning (Tochon & Ökten, 2010).

My study of instructional organizers and the transformations of knowledge in curriculum planning was supported by federal grants in

Canada for 10 years. I moved to the University of Wisconsin-Madison in January of 2000, and very soon, the responsibility of the World Language Teacher Education program allowed me to grasp, within different linguistic environments, how standards were shaping practices and were reshaped by these practices. Throughout these years, this study shed light on the genuine instructional propositions of seasoned language teachers in various settings (French L1, French in bilingual settings, French as a Second Language, Basic French, English as a Second Language in Francophone settings, French immersion, and later, Chinese, German, Italian, Japanese, Portuguese, Spanish, Russian, and Turkish). My understanding of the nature of instructional organizers evolved over time. First conceived as the moving superstructures of teachers' instructional planning (Tochon & Dionne, 1994), they were later understood as context-bound pragmatic organizers, expressing learning intentions and generating interactional transformations of subject-matter knowledge.

My earlier studies focused on locating the instructional organizers used by experienced teachers to form a sense of commitment among learners gathered around educative projects. Examples are provided in the subsequent sections of this chapter. Instructional organizers are a crucial expression of genuine forward planning, which is what teachers spontaneously do when they think about forthcoming learning situations. They anticipate instructional action and form plans based on commitments. Experienced teachers often allow their students freedom to choose their form of engagement. They can opt for specific commitments and negotiate instructional agreements that have a strong motivational component that leads to some form of identity investment. They may correspond to personal urges that merge into a sense of the social contract. Commitments are indications of levels of engagement. Their impulse cannot be restricted to the cognitive level. They are also philosophical, and, as such, involve the heart, as well as the mind and the body into a sense of oneness in action. Commitments correspond to a Chinese concept: /xin/, heart-mind-emotion (Zhao, 2009). Commitments are organized. Simply said, their organization in a classroom context responds to student-based curriculum decisions and is the result of engagement in particular areas of knowledge transferred into action.

In this section, I have proposed to expand prior work on instructional organizers, lesson organizers, and organizers of practice into a concept engaging the heart-mind-emotion into action. Situating students as curriculum builders, such organizers would articulate commitments to fulfill particular aspects of the social contract. In a sense, instructional organizers are commitment operators, as they help learners negotiate and articulate their educative projects.

An Example from Research

Prior Knowledge, Students Lives and Motives as the Organizing Principles

One of my initial studies was based on a simulation with 25 experienced French teachers. The goal was to explore this unfolding interpretive process. The simulation consisted of making a lesson plan orally according to four goals that were chosen to correspond to different levels of difficulty, to see how teachers would spontaneously organize such mini-curriculum: (1) Placing commas correctly in punctuating a text; (2) developing an interview guide to create a dossier on a given topic; (3) forming and exploring a lexical field (for example, love, loving, lovely, lovable...), and then, a semantic field (for example love, care, dedication, attraction...); (4) analyzing the structure and acting forces of a narrative. The teachers explained how the class would be organized around such mini-curriculum, describing the contextual constraints and their manner of teaching with concrete references to actual experiences. They also explained how they shaped learning tasks through wider meaningful projects, and the types of dynamics they would promote. They provided lived examples from their own experiences in classroom situations. The goal was to see how language teachers' thinking would genuinely unfold into an organizing process.

My interviews and classroom observations with hundreds of novice and seasoned teachers in different languages and language areas focused on the strategies of the language teachers. These teachers were selected using criteria justified by research literature on 'expert' teachers (Tochon,

1991c; Tsui, 2003). 'Resource' persons were chosen to act as institutional experts (districts specialists, teacher educators, leaders in the language areas). They were chosen for their qualifications in the subject area, their responsibility as master teachers supervising student teachers, and their acquaintanceship with numerous colleagues. They were asked to recommend 5 to 10 particularly outstanding teachers of whom they knew. The full list of those recommended was then cross-checked with the following criteria: holding a specific degree, as well as certification in the language discipline researched, and at least seven years of experience in the language discipline. A random sample was then taken from the list, which had been shortened according to the aforementioned criteria.

These teachers were considered a sample of the most highly qualified teachers in the institutions studied. The selected teachers were contacted for semi-structured interviews. When classroom observations were organized, a 'preactive' interview was organized before class, then I would observe the class interactions, and a 'postactive' interview would follow. Interviews were recorded and transcribed for thematic analysis, content analysis, or grounded theory mapping. The length of each interview was between 100 and 180 minutes; they were deep interviews, aiming to decipher the meaning of teacher planning and its actualizing.

Inevitably, there were idiosyncratic elements in classroom planning, as it is so closely related to teacher and learners' identities, the context, and history, which shape the interpretive metaphors that guide teaching. However, there were constants as well. For example, the quasi-totality of the expert teachers interviewed expressed the ability to intelligently improvise their courses. They had such a repertoire of strategies and resources that they could adapt from moment to moment within the interaction, and switch to particular points independently from their planning. Classroom planning was at heart, a response to students' suggestions, rather than formally on paper. This was true even when the institution required a prior written plan or proposed a rigid curriculum grid with a schedule. It seemed normal to seasoned teachers to constantly adapt the contents to interactions and suggestions from students.

Actually, students were, in large part, their own curriculum builders. Such connectivity was organized in a way that would reshape the curriculum to students' best aspirations. These teachers were highly knowledgeable in the discipline taught, cared deeply for their students, and were exemplary overall. Their improvisation was not the type you might find among some novice teachers who simply do not know what comes next because they do not remember their plans or part of the information necessary to convey proper content. The seasoned teachers practiced a well-rounded, well-organized improvisation. These expert teachers had more materials than needed in their bag to adapt at will when the need would appear.

Narrativors, Skillers, and Actualizers

Focusing for many years on finding the key organizing frames of such careful improvisation, I discovered a few ways these smart teachers transformed the curriculum into a spontaneous, smooth and flowing learning experience, which allowed for students' self-determination through individual and group projects. Principles derived from research on teacher expertise that characterize the Deep Approach to languages and cultures. Seasoned teachers transform the curriculum into thematic stories, operational skills, or actualizing experiences. Hereafter, they will be defined in terms of theme, operation, and action. Their functioning is special and legitimates the use of three neologisms. Instructional organizers exist for the three levels of the unified taxonomy: disciplinary, thematic *narrativors*; interdisciplinary, strategic *skillers*; and transdisciplinary, experiential *actualizers*. Narrativors transform the language curriculum into stories of experience, skillers transform the curriculum into task operations, actualizers transform the curriculum into interpersonal and transpersonal experiences. The entire curriculum is remolded with the help of key organizers to which all other language tasks are subordinated.

What is a narrativor? A narrativor is a narrative organizer that provides expression to a story-making intention. Thus, the narrativor is an instructional, story-making organizer; it is intended to develop declarative knowledge (therefore, content) in the form of themes, images, anecdotes, or stories. This narrative way of transforming curriculum knowledge has been empirically verified (Tochon, 1993b). *Examples*: "She understood this point of grammar when she developed it in the story she had gone through this morning". "I emphasized a theme which related the book to daily life". "Imagine a terrifying and sinister haunted house and start describing its props". *Question*: Is any storytelling a narrativor? No. Storytelling must be guided by curriculum connections and lead to such discernment that it clarifies the processes and goals of strategic strategic tasks and action. Practical wisdom derived from narrativors provides a better retention of the key tasks and action. There are conditions for stories to stimulate curriculum (disciplinary) transformations; namely narrativors must be integrated with skillers and actualizers and provide the needed conceptual "glue" that will stick contents to real life situations. As curriculum metaphors, narrativors smoothly grip the road of life yet don't stifle creative storytelling.

What is a skiller? A skiller is a procedural organizer that provides expression to a skill-making intention. Thus, the skiller is an instrumental organizer; it is intended to develop procedural and strategic (interdisciplinary) knowledge that focuses on a skill, an operation or a procedure forming a component of a task or an action. *Examples*: "How to organize a loose-leaf binder; a table of contents is completed every time they receive a new paper". "Practice these directions regularly to improve your summaries". *Question*: Is any exercise a skiller? No. Only praxis will allow learners to develop skills. Praxis is a form of reflective practice, with an awareness of the learning process that implies metalearning (learning about learning). There are conditions for assignments and tasks to aid students in building skills. Namely, they must be embedded with actualizers and narrativors and connect various task domains.

What is an actualizer? An actualizer is a situated, contextualizing organizer that provides expression to an experience-making intention. Thus, the actualizer is an instructional, experiential organizer; it is intended to develop situated knowledge by focusing teaching on actions, on the relationship with life and the world through concrete experiences. *Examples*: "We shot a film together". "We were in situations close to their everyday life." "Go in the streets and question the people". *Question*: Is any experience an actualizer? No. Experience must be guided by wisdom and theoretical understanding. Wisdom is a form of self-reflection and reflective learning associated with an ethical rule of conduct. There are conditions for experiential projects to actualize higher levels of engagement and awareness within learners. Namely, actualizers must be integrated with skillers and narrativors and provide transdisciplinary intelligence.

To sum up, narrativors, skillers and actualizers express the three levels of the deep taxonomy analyzed in Chapter 4. In a sense, they represent the deep taxonomy in action.

Basic Principles of the Deep Approach to Language and Culture Learning

Thus several patterns and stable processes appeared in the study, which constitute basic principles of the Deep Approach to language and culture learning:

1. *Curriculum transformation.* These expert teachers helped students transform the curriculum into thematic stories, operational skills, or whole acts, which led to self-actualizing and social experiences. Thus, instructional organizers existed at three levels: disciplinary, thematic *narrativors*, interdisciplinary operations as *skillers*, and transdisciplinary action as *actualizers*. Narrativors transformed the language curriculum into stories of experience, skillers transformed the curriculum into task operations, and actualizers transformed the curriculum into interpersonal and transpersonal experiences. The entire curriculum was remolded with the help of key organizers to which all other language tasks were subordinated.

2. *Embedding and multitasking principle.* When faced with a curriculum, these teachers tried to organize links between the various goals to mold them into a whole that would give them a meaning. This embedding allowed the learners to save time by dealing with several tasks simultaneously, and to allow full impact for a few priority tasks. Multitasking was organized through tasks' embedding. Embedding was directed by a task taxonomy that intertwined disciplinary, interdisciplinary, and transdisciplinary

processes, unifying cognitive, socioaffective, and behavioral goals. Examples of such embedments are provided in Figures 5.2 and 5.5.

3. *Student-initiated curriculum.* The teachers reported that they knew the students and their interests. They used their input to select those elements that were able to satisfy both students' interests and needs in the curriculum. In many cases, they negotiated the curriculum with the students or they gave to the students' teams the liberty to choose their projects and the way to proceed.

4. *Connection principle.* Language modalities that defined task domains were interconnected wherever possible. This was accomplished by the development of themes inherent to the discipline and interdisciplinary instrumental skills within transdisciplinary projects, which targeted autonomous apprenticeship. Very concretely, some teachers would take a marker and would highlight or circle curriculum elements that could be bridged through integrative tasks. Thus, the teachers selected curricular elements that were apt to be linked together, integrating tasks that both they and their students enjoyed.

5. *Task-domains organizing principle.* Language modalities were used as task domains. The meaning of content was constructed as it related to its expression in different instructional modalities that defined domains of tasks through access and voice. These domains of practice differed from the 4 skills of cognitive psychology.

6. *Transdisciplinary principle.* The teachers targeted a higher order of achievement, self-actualization, and social action. Classroom actions had a moral and transformative purpose and were not limited to the disciplinary contents. They were used for a higher, more profound purpose, which is a critical component of a Deep Approach that distinguishes it from other approaches or methodologies.

7. *Operation principle.* Teachers made content operational in a general action. Actions were specified by projects. Projects

involved strategic operations that pertained to various task domains.

8. *Engagement and identity principle.* This principle derives from the transdisciplinary and connection principles. Tasks and action do not make much sense unless they are moved and energized by personal engagement and a strong attraction to what is being done. Action thrives in passion for knowledge with a sense of self-determined service that contributes to identity building. Therefore, the steps towards further progress in personal and social projects are dictated by a zone of proximal identity development (ZPID—Tochon & Lee, 2010), which blossoms through committed relationships.

9. *Pivot principle.* The learning units were built from instructional organizers that operated strategically at the time the plans were actualized. They acted as pivots to unite the different task domains and language modalities. The pivot could be a theme, an instrumental skill necessary for task operation, or a general action. Learning units may shift imperceptibly from one pivot to another to give a sense of cohesion, continuity, and progression. A variety of instructional organizers could coexist. The organizer, acting as pivot, could change quickly, depending on the interest and motivation of the students. Examples are provided in Figure 5.8.

These principles delineate the major discoveries related to the grammar of action of expert language teachers. They were subsequently confirmed in 2009-2012 Title VI Research awarded by the U.S. Department of Education (Tochon, Ökten, Karaman & Druc, 2012). I synthesized its research results in an instructional model that defines the Deep Approach to language and culture learning. It clarifies several steps that teachers can use to help their students build their own language projects.

A. Know your students; ask about their interests and their lives. Create a personal connection with students. Ask for their input and situate them as curriculum builders. Work on team building and their sense of ownership of the curriculum. Indicate what the broad lines of what is possible and appropriate for their level in terms of curriculum development are. Help them specify agreements with the self that support successful learning and language proficiency. Release their anxieties related to language learning. Do not be judgmental.

B.   With the active participation of the students, explore themes that meet both academic goals and students' personal aims. Help them transpose the study plan into task domains by pre-setting certain bridges across domains. They should choose themes, operations and actions that match their interests and motivations, and circle the academic topics that could be linked into whole projects. Help them map and build individual projects, small group projects, or whole class projects. See the examples and templates presented in Figures 5.3, 5.4, 56, 5.9, 5.10, and in the Appendix at the end of this book.

C.   Establish together core projects with Access and Voice joining the IAPI task domains (see Figure 2.4 at end of Chapter 2, and Figure 5.12 hereafter) according to a common guideline (thematic, instrumental, or experiential). IAPI is the acronym of Interpret, Analyze, Present, and Interact. Projects are broad activities that embed a variety of tasks within the modalities proper to Access (Interpret and Analyze) and Voice (Present and Interact).

D.   Negotiate a group plan or individual plans, and create instructional contracts. For a project to be successful, it must integrate the project of the Self with the students. If the projects of the Self of the students differ, then they should be gathered in subgroups that form their own projects. Thus, the role of the teacher shifts towards facilitating students' project achievement that leads to proficiency and deep language and culture understand.

E.   In a collaborative effort, establish detailed instructions for the plan or plans chosen. Model them according to the eight aforementioned principles of the Deep Approach. As a guide, detail what will be done in the four task models and propose a map of embedding instructional organizers with a thematic, strategic, or experiential pivot.

To sum up, clear principles guide the curriculum transformations in the passage to practice operated by seasoned language teachers. Their grammar of action has been deciphered and provides some clues for a revolutionary approach to language and culture learning.

Illustration of the Forward Planning Model

This section provides examples of forward planning with conceptual organizers that allow instructional flexibility at all three levels of the deep taxonomy: themes molded through narrativors, operation articulated into skillers, and whole actions (Hol-Acts) guided by actualizers. Here is an illustration of the model. It indicates how instructional organizers may work at three levels that match the deep taxonomy. First the instructor should tell the students how to use the IAPI template to create their projects.

1. During the first phase of transposing the curriculum into priority instructional organizers, the learners gather resources and order the elements of the curriculum matching the standards by considering how the different instructional modalities within specific task domains may correspond to each other. For example, character description in the writing/recording domain could be linked to oral sketches on labeling and stereotyping, working on adjectival suffixes. Having described what would be done in terms of oral exchange, reading/viewing, writing and language techniques, they look for thematic, instrumental or experiential links. With a pencil, they can circle curriculum elements in each task domain that could be linked to other elements in other task domains into a coherent thematic project.

2. The learners prioritize a few instructional organizers that will become strategic for their projects. They gather a number of thematically related tasks, spread out over a learning period, around which subordinate actions will be grouped, which may, in turn, become pivots later on. For example, they may cluster a series of characters into a brief drama that they will play to describe a stereotypical situation and its resolution.

3. The teacher may suggest several types of instructional organizers to the students (themes, operations, or actions) and have them choose a group action or individual actions. It is what we did in the Turkish language modules[1]: students could adapt the proposed templates. The guideline is to 'operationalize' one level that receives particular emphasis, whether thematic, instrumental, or experiential. These three levels overlap and are almost always present, but one of them acts as priority pivot or strategic organizers (Figure 5.3).

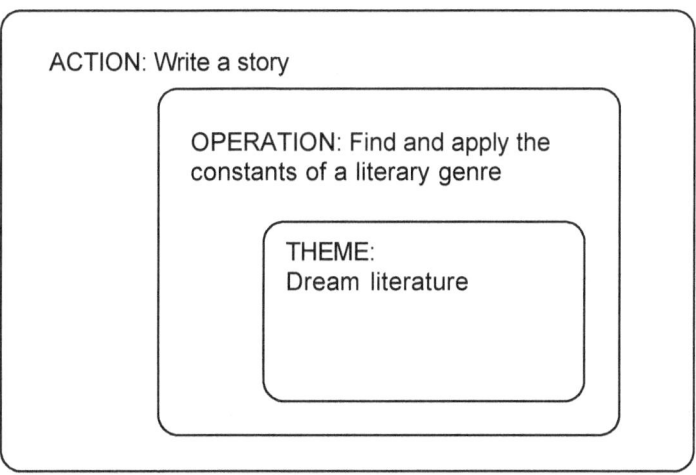

Figure 5.3
Instructional Embedment of a Theme
Into Operations to Develop an Action

4. To give priority to the level of contents of the discipline, the learners should choose a thematic organizer, integrating the IAPI task domains. For example, in Figure 5.4, a project is proposed with "Dreams" as the thematic organizer. In each IAPI task domain, a series of tasks are proposed, which are described in each column. Project tasks embed the broad theme within an action, which will require a series of operations on specific contents.

---

[1] Presented here: http://deepapproach.wceruw.org/modules.html

THEMATIC ORGANIZER

Dreams

DREAM-RELATED PROJECTS				
ACCESS		VOICE	
INTERPRET	ANALYZE	PRESENT	INTERACT
READ WATCH LISTEN	FOCUS ON LANGUAGE	WRITE SPEAK RECORD	EXCHANGE AND ACT WITH PEOPLE
- Read about the history of surrealism - Read short surrealist texts - Watch one surrealist film	- Find dream writing techniques - Find the techniques particular to immanent dream literature (fantastic) and transcendent dream literature (the world of wonder) - To analyze texts and productions, apply the typology of dream literature: narrator's position, setting atmosphere, narrative grammar - Use illocutionary linguistic means to create appearance, doubt or hesitancy	- Create and present a powerpoint on the role of dreams in surrealism - Write about a dream - Transform a realistic short story - Write a dream short story, either entering another world (the world of wonder) or transforming reality (fantasy or fantastic)	- Exchange through Powerpoint presentation and select the best slides to make one outstanding powerpoint; discuss its structure and contents - Relate a dream and discuss its life connections with your peers - Oniric Story-telling: Improvise dream-like changes in real-life stories

Figure 5.4
Thematic Pivot

When they prioritize the interdisciplinary operations level, the learners can select some tasks from each IAPI domain that converge toward the practices and development of a single instrumental organizer. For example, dialogue is instrumental in the project presented in Figure 5.5.

INSTRUMENTAL ORGANIZER
Dialogue

DIALOGUE-RELATED PROJECTS			
ACCESS		VOICE	
INTERPRET	ANALYZE	PRESENT	INTERACT
READ WATCH LISTEN	FOCUS ON LANGUAGE	WRITE SPEAK RECORD	EXCHANGE AND ACT WITH PEOPLE
- Read dialogues by humorists - Watch videos presenting comic dialogues - Listen to your peers reading and playing comic dialogues	- Analyze the strategies of theatrical emphasis and the comic style - Punctuate a dialogue - Respect oral punctuation - Change language register (low, standard, elaborate) - Transpose a comic dialogue into indirect speech and vice versa	- Audio record a reading of a comic dialogue - Write the dialogue between glass, toothbrush and toothpaste about the impact of fluoride on the brain - Write the dialogue of the shirt, pants, and tissue about the owner's identity	- Improvise a dialogue between characters on a TV program (with the sound turned off) - Play the dialogues you wrote - Improvise sketches involving contradictory characters - Act out a comic sketch

Figure 5.5
Instrumental Pivot

Forward Planning and Instructional Organizers

Here too, the three levels overlap, but one has priority and acts as a pivot or strategic organizer (Figure 5.6).

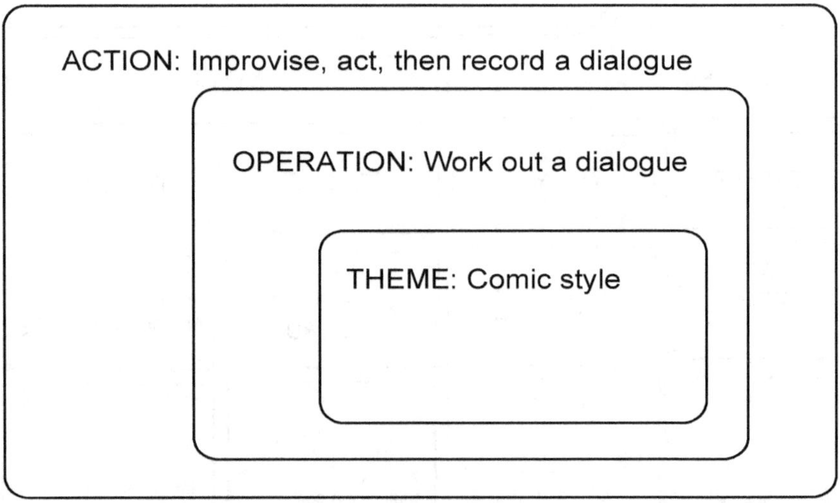

ACTION: Improvise, act, then record a dialogue

OPERATION: Work out a dialogue

THEME: Comic style

Figure 5.6
Instructional embedment with
dialogue recording as a pivot

5. To prioritize action, the students can negotiate a project that integrates their subjective needs and the needs of the world language curriculum; an experiential pivot is chosen (figure 5.7).

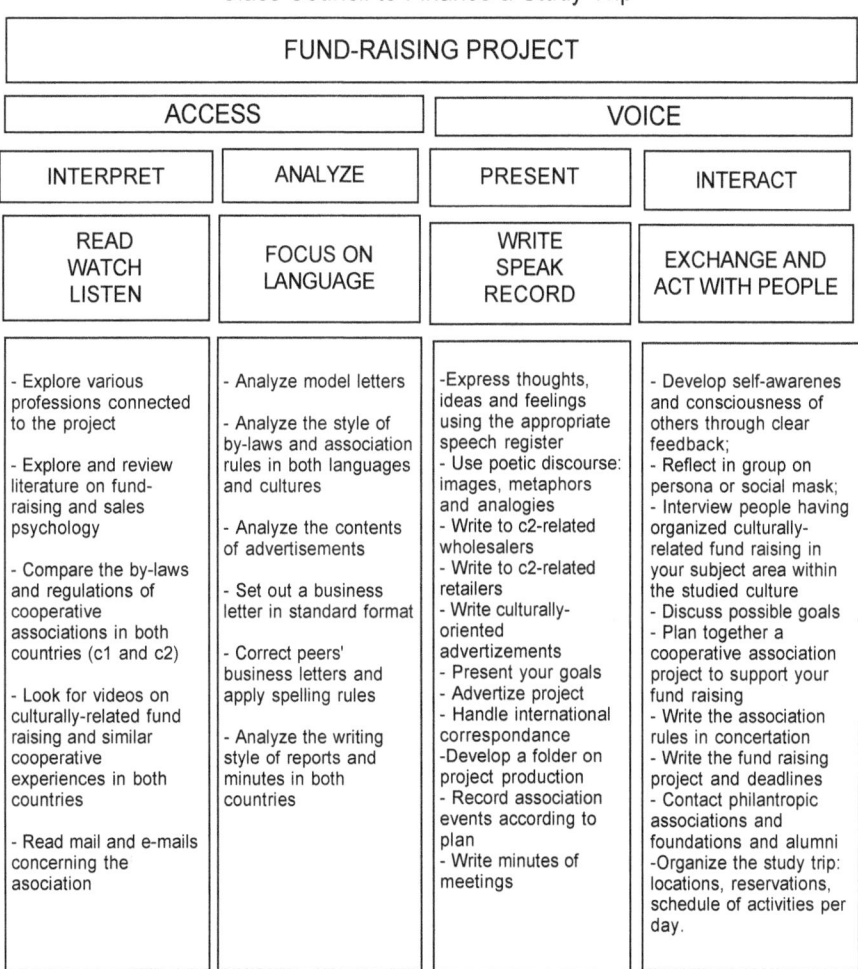

Figure 5.7
Class Council and Study Trip as Experiential Pivots

6. The instructional organizer may change levels at any time to help in developing a new learning unit. These are shifts in pivot. For example, in the case of Figure 5.8, the emphasis shifted from the broader recording project to developing specific dialogic skills. In Figure 5.9, the emphasis was placed, at first, on associative action, then without being perceived, shifted to the thematic organizer, which was about advertising, encouraging the development of other learning units.

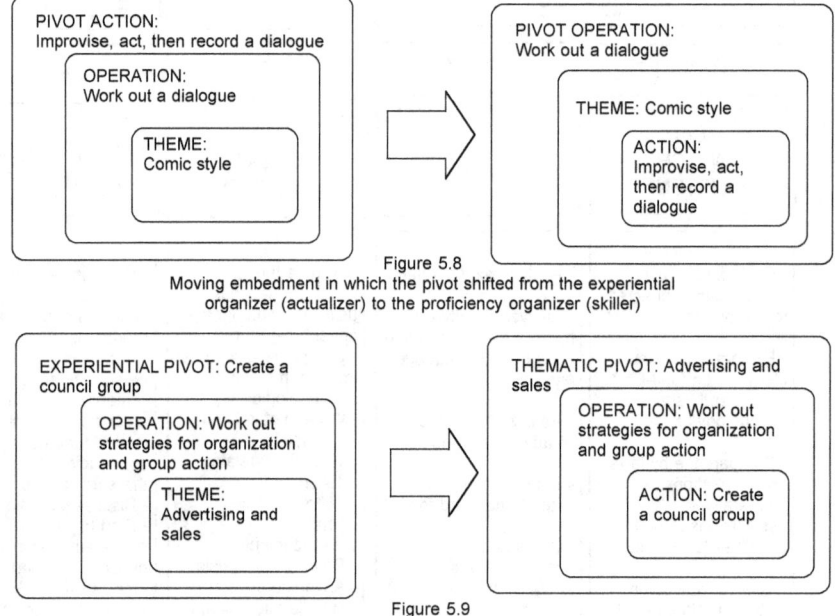

Figure 5.8
Moving embedment in which the pivot shifted from the experiential organizer (actualizer) to the proficiency organizer (skiller)

Figure 5.9
Moving embedment in which the pivot shifted from the experiential organizer (actualizer) to the thematic organizer (narrativor)

An Actual Case: Vegetable Horoscopes

In Table 5.1 illustrates an example of how oral exchange, writing, and reading activities can target the same competence taken from a master program. This illustration depicts an application of the principles that have been underlined. This sketch does not claim to be normative; it represents an actualization, among other possibilities, for application, and does not constitute a model or prototype to be meticulously followed.

Along the lines of this framework, students of French (13-14 years old) were brought to develop the content and strategies contained in the language master plan through a project of their own creation. These contents and strategies were combined into a functional dynamic within a thematic project that they elaborated together.

Table 5.1. Pastiche Planning – Preliminary project for "Mastering the writing techniques of character description".

Tasks in Oral exchange, Reading and Writing	End Task	Competence
-Identifying character descriptions in texts -Applying characterization vocabulary -Using narrative description (form and meaning) -Characterizing persons with names and adjectives -Creating physical and psychological contrasts -Integrating character descriptions into narrative texts -Organizing a character description (sequence, coherence, correspondence, style, etc.) -Associating and contrasting types of characters -Distinguishing between individual specifics and generalities -Synthetically defining interrelationship between characters -Synthesizing physical and psychological types	1. Creating a pastiche with fictional characters 2. Describing characters (physical and psychological portraits) 3. Contrasting characters and specifying their interrelation.	Mastering the writing techniques of the physical and psychological character description

This project brought together two sequences of tasks: (1) characterization and (2) creation of characters. The students chose its title: "Vegetable Horoscopes". Chinese or traditional astrology fascinated a number of students. This theme was therefore used to suggest the creation of a "new" zodiac comprising 12 signs, constituting as many vegetables. The idea of writing a booklet about it strongly motivated the students.

The first phase (Figure 5.10) consisted in learning a number of content elements: vocabulary relevant to characterization, description syntax, antonymy (contrasts), descriptive verbs, etc. Strategies needed to be acquired: transforming characters, detailing out a sketch, enriching a description, applying a discourse typology, comparing psychological characteristics, visualizing a descriptive unit, specifying categories, describing oneself, and so on. These activities are presented as part of a demonstration of a framework that carefully respects a classroom-tested strategy.

INITIATION TO "VEGETABLE HOROSCOPES"

ACCESS

INTERPRET

READ WATCH LISTEN

- Locate character sketches in texts & videos
- Seek out the description of characters portrayed in The Diary of a young girl
- Differentiate between physical and psychological portraits in short texts and determine their impact on the evolution of a short story
- Seek out correspondences between character and nature in excerpts from Romantic literature
- In a state of relaxation, visualize characters on the basis of an oral description
- Relate correspondences between personality and handwriting

ANALYZE

FOCUS ON LANGUAGE

- Replace adjectives with relative clauses
- Formulate antonymic relations
- Correct spelling with the help of a self-evaluative grid (self-correction)
- Review the rules and do the appropriate exercises as needed
- Correct errors of syntax indicated by the teacher
- Check agreement of tenses in descriptions
- Differentiate levels of usage: familiar, neutral, literary

VOICE

PRESENT

WRITE SPEAK RECORD

- Transform the character descriptions in paperback romance novels into a horror sketch and vice versa
- Detail a character sketch in a story
- Enrich a description by means of complex sentences
- Characterize a psychological sketch by assigning names
- Modify a character by means of antonymy
- Keep a record file of the physical and psychological evolution of a character

INTERACT

EXCHANGE AND ACT WITH PEOPLE

- Characterize yourself from a list of personality adjectives
- Characterize a peer (id.)
- Compare various characterizations: contrast your perceptions of others with reality
- Search out contradiction and coherence
- Relate correspondences between appearance and personality
- Characterize fictional characters using imaginary names
- Describe the characteristics of cartoon characters
- Debate the characteristics of characters in a work of short fiction

Figure 5.10
Instructional Framework on Characterization
Time frame: 1-5 weeks, 3 hours per week

In the second phase, these content strategies had to take on dynamic connections by being arranged into units that become interactive on many levels (Figure 5.11).

FIELD APPLICATION OF "VEGETABLE HOROSCOPES" Learning Framework on the Creation of Pastiches			
ACCESS		VOICE	
INTERPRET	ANALYZE	PRESENT	INTERACT
READ WATCH LISTEN	FOCUS ON LANGUAGE	WRITE SPEAK RECORD	EXCHANGE AND ACT WITH PEOPLE
-Read material brought in by the students discussing astrological or graphological profiles that will be imitated -Highlight the vocabulary, expressions; turn of phrase characteristic of this type of text -Research a vegetable: in the library, look for mythological, symbolical, historical, geographical and/or medicinal references -Read classmates' production, evaluate coherence of meaning in these texts	-Respect the syntax of a summary: use 3rd person in the present tense -Recognize the characteristics of a descriptive text -Locate one's own spelling errors with the help of an evaluation grid -Transpose a verb from active to passive form and vice versa -Transpose direct speech to indirect form and vice versa -Proofread classmates' work and locate errors	Each pair of students having chosen a vegetable -Research and write a report on this vegetable's symbolism -Write (in pairs) a short legend explaining the origin of this vegetable -Write the personality profile of the Vegetable-Persons; -Write the personality profile of the Vegetable-Woman -Write the personality profile of the Vegetable-Man; -Join two vegetable-signs as a couple and describe their relationship in a humorous way (e.g., the relationship between "Leek-Woman" and "Tomato-Man", etc.) -Draw up a list of rules for assigning horoscope signs	-Define categories of individuals -Place individuals in predetermined categories (physical or psychological) -Determine correspondence between 12 vegetables and 12 astrological signs and distribute among pairs of students -Each student assumes a Vegetable-Man or Vegetable-Woman role and confronts the other 11 vegetable-signs in order to characterize the resulting relationships (this activity is done in groups of four): both individuals of a sign will meet both individuals of the other sign -Decide on the formula for assigning an astrological sign to a vegetable-sign

Figure 5.11
My Vegetable, my Self.

Time frame: 2-7 weeks, 2 hours per week

The students worked in pairs. Each pair chose a vegetable, as well as a gender for it (example: Mr. Artichoke, Ms. Cucumber). Each pair of students then had to provide an astrological profile for their "Vegetable-Person", and a brief background story for the chosen vegetological sign. The students then proceeded to a description of the Vegetable-Man and Vegetable-Woman for each astrological sign. The students' dynamics integrated self-regulative intentions and social interactive intentions.

Each student responsible for a Vegetable-Woman or Vegetable-Man would be brought to confront all potential "Vegetable-Spouses" for the purpose of writing a synthesis of an eventual match. Obviously, it would be feasible, depending on the students' interest, to organize the horoscope of flowers, cars, musical instruments, furniture, pastry, etc. The possibilities are almost unlimited.

The students elaborated a procedure in which each student would determine their own vegetable sign in order to study one's own vegetological character. This was followed by obtaining knowledge of one's peers and examining potential matches influenced by complementarities between signs. The student-pairs were asked to create at least six vegetable-couples (time restrictions would not allow the creation of the maximum number -144). The students compared physical and psychological sketches, and then humorously described the nature of the relationship produced by pairing off Vegetable-Persons. Table 5.2 presents the overall strategy used in the creation of this pastiche.

Table 5.2. Creating a Pastiche: Actualized Instructional Strategy

1) Verification of students' prerequisites in relation to foreseen plan: a written characterization of a peer.
2) Brief evaluation (unrecorded) of students' knowledge, writing abilities and motivation, based on class discussions. At this point, planning is modified to include a session of characterization vocabulary. Students may contribute personal material.
3) Students bring in books on Chinese astrology and seek out adjectives relating to personality. Following a discussion, propose a thematic project: the creation of an astrological pastiche. Together with the students, name the tasks that must be done in order to achieve the desired result. Specify expectations/directions.
4) Once the general functional dynamics is in place, and the intermediate- and long-term intentions have been determined and modified in relation to the evaluation of prerequisites (Steps 1 and 2), expose possible strategies to the students: the project and its intentions, tasks to be accomplished, means of realizing the intentions (see frameworks shown in Tables 4 and 5).

> 5) Negotiation and implementation of learning strategy (study of adjectives relating to personality, vocabulary relating to physical description, description methodology, the reading of characterizations, descriptive syntax and typology of the descriptive text, pastiche, vegetable symbolism, differentiation and association, improvement of language basics, etc.). This strategy is an "enabling" phase of the thematic project "Vegetable Horoscopes".
> 6) Analysis of each student's production to revise either:
>   - certain intermediate or terminal intentions;
>   - the teaching strategy (if a number of students seem bored with the project, suspend it for 2 weeks, for example);
>   - the content elements (coherence of character sketches or associations, spelling and syntax);
> 7) Remediation of problems identified in Step 6;
> 8) After repeated cycles of a formative evaluation integrated into the instructional strategy (some students may need to revise and improve their work up to five times), final production is undertaken. (Typewritten format is recommended but remains optional. Students may wish to help one another write the final text on a computer).
> 9) Evaluation of students' production and of the thematic project's success.

Within the frame of this thematic project, the students were led to compare the content elements that were being worked in various contexts. They had to transfer knowledge from one domain to another via operations of analysis and synthesis, all while evaluating their own production and that of peers. As transfer is defined by the decontextualization and then recontextualization of knowledge, the student was then brought to recontextualize knowledge in new activities. Functional dynamics implied a higher level of learning by using contents in convergent strategies (see previous chapters). It is possible, in this way, to affirm that project pedagogy can satisfy two types of language requirements: task organization and competence development, as shown in Figure 5.12. The creation of pastiches makes it easy for second language learners to catch a discourse genre and create from there. The focus was on learning about the self, which is so important for adolescents.

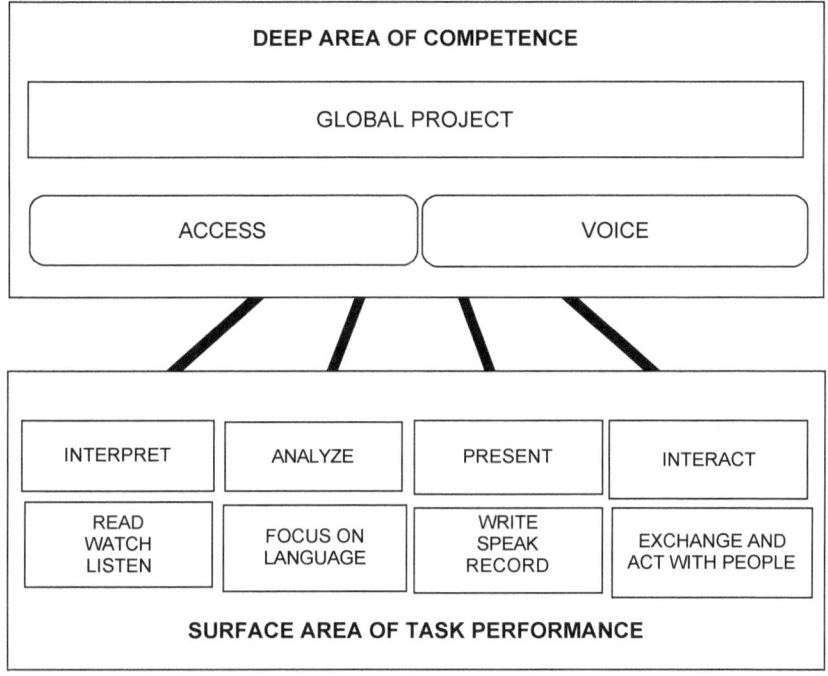

Figure 5.12
When Task Performance Is Not Enough

Discussion

The task performance criterion communicates the intentions and assures, to the degree that it can be assured, an operative planning of learning units. It also facilitates the evaluation of the student's production. The competence criterion implies an extended amount of activity, wide-ranging transfer abilities, and a deep global approach that allows adaptation of learning conditions. Pragmatically, organizing competence is easier than formulating macro-lists of micro-intentions. It energizes teaching by setting into motion a chain-reaction of connected, meaningful learning.

The levels of learning targeted by the school of performance are notably different from the ones targeted by the school of situated competence. The vision proposed here is that both are faces of the same coin. The subordination of the activities' pragmatic organizers to deep dynamics lends a dimension of "contrast" to the traditional instructional sequence. Instrumental rationality then becomes a threshold towards reflective practice and wisdom in action as a project. The sequence's linearity is replaced by a complex, interrelational open universe. This becomes apparent if we reexamine the four dynamic principles of relevance, holism, direction, and connectedness.

1. Rather than starting from a preconceived theory of learning (from simple to complex, arbitrarily), the teacher establishes a principle of instructional relevance, looking to the necessary correspondence of connected units in task domains.

2. The teacher constructs a unifying plan that lends meaning to the content elements to be developed. This way, the student is not assimilating these elements in a void, but rather grasps their usefulness immediately. The plan's totality, as well as the correspondence of instructional domains, leads the student to develop a comprehension of the same phenomenon in different learning situations. Thus, reflection is emphasized in this approach.

3. The path is no longer dictated by the teacher. A production project can be negotiated, taking into account the student's subjective and socio-affective needs, as well as the objective requirements of the curriculum. The production then proceeds from a complex proaction that involves three interlocking levels (content, strategies and experiential dynamics) and four lateral sectors defined as tasks domains (oral exchange, reading, writing, and language basics). The student is thus enabled to assimilate knowledge within a personal creative expression, and is less subject to the teacher's rationale. Students may develop their own way of thinking.

4. The learning, taking place on different levels, is not produced in a linear way, but simultaneously. The interconnection of levels leaves room for the unforeseen, for a functioning disorder--for creativity.

Thus, it has been possible to verify, within the project "Vegetable Horoscopes", what the students had learned simultaneously on many levels. This verification was conducted by a clinical approach. This action-research was to empirically ground the pragmatic validity of an instructional framework and not to experimentally evaluate student productions. It was found that:

- punctuation and spelling had improved because of the need for an impeccable final product (an evaluation guide helped the students find their errors and refer to the appropriate rules);
- vocabulary and syntax were perfected, due to numerous discussions among the students on these very aspects of their spoken language;
- character description was assimilated to such a high degree that, during recesses, the students amused themselves by elaborating morphological and psychological analyses of fellow students, using the choicest and rarest epithets they could glean from a dictionary...
- the pleasure of writing, as well as of speaking and debating, developed;
- the socio-affective relationship between the students matured and the project reinforced group spirit;
- a deepened appreciation of the concepts of the relationships, harmony, personality traits, conflicts, and others resulted from the application of adequate conceptual tools[2];
- the beginnings of an economic and social understanding took root because the students asked questions relating to problems of publication, production, profitability, as well as to those of marriage and divorce, home and work...

---

[2] One student (out of 23) complained that the project "bugged" him. This boy, who was developmentally younger than his physical age, manifested his incomprehension of the concept of "Vegetable-Couples". He was less vegetologically productive than his peers but was nonetheless caught up in their enthusiasm.

- self-evaluation was effected [self-correction with the guidelines (see Chapter 6) and mutual evaluation among peers];
- some degree of self-actualization was noticed, manifested by growth of integrity, autonomy, stability, symbolic representation, and social awareness. This accomplishment was expressed repeatedly, in the course of the year, in personal short stories of excellent quality.

This anecdotal, empirical support indicates that the instructional framework shown targets superior cognitive and affective levels of achievement. These subjective observations arising from the retrospective report of a teacher-researcher are in fact corroborated by a corpus of some hundred typed pages of student work. Such a level of production in a group of students of this age was coupled with a high degree of quality. Further examples of this framework appear in the next chapters.

In such an approach, the learners not only negotiate content, they are curriculum builders. They shape their own projects and find ways to express their subjective needs, along with the paths proposed in the curriculum. Therefore, the teacher is interactively adapting lesson plans to the changing realities of the classroom context. Some groups may work for a longer time on specific projects than others, which is characteristic of personalized, multilevel teaching. Deep teaching functions on the basis of instructional organizers. Organizers focus on input, rather than outcomes. They define processes, rather than products. Nonetheless, they are compatible with clear expectations that can be summarized in a rubric, for example. The rubrics could be adapted to specific projects and form the basics of an agreement. A few instructional organizers are given prime time for a while and become the pivots of learning units. They are the strategic organizers. But this may not last: other important organizers may pop up and take the lead to fulfill the global project. Therefore, embedded maps should be considered as a temporary hierarchy among organizers, which may shift at some point towards other key processes. They constitute a 'heterarchy' (a hierarchy with a moving head) rather than a hierarchy that would be fixed once for all. The rules of coordination, alternation, and subordination help connect tasks within larger projects that respond to this grammar of action. Strategic organizers respond to a principle of convergence of the task domains and a principle of overlapping or embedding of three operational levels: the thematic level of disciplinary content, the instrumental level of interdisciplinary skills, and the strategic, experiential level of general transdisciplinary action. This is what I named the 'unified taxonomy'; the unified taxonomy is the operational principle of the Deep Approach.

To sum up, an instructional model emerged from research on expert language teachers' practices. Seasoned teachers give a lot of freedom to their students. Learners can build up their own educative projects within thematic units. This paradigm shift demonstrates the incompleteness of previous models, yet it eclectically integrates many aspects of previous methods within a broader and deeper approach. It added socioaffective and sociocultural depth to these aspects, as well as a greater freedom to adapt the units to the learners' action.

In Short

Naturalizing as Curriculum Building

Deep teaching is not conceived as a linear path from the simplest to the most complex because what is a simple task for one student may not be for another. The learners themselves select the difficulty level and the resources they prefer. Learning is organized through clear guidelines for a given project that are negotiated in instructional contracts. When implemented, such projects lead the student to build cognitive, socioaffective, and interpersonal enactments of the content, which develop reflection, proficiency and experience in a socializing context. The outcome-directed model manages the curriculum by means of behaviors, at the risk of confusing the standard of competence with its indicator or mistaking performance developed by drills in a controlled setting for actual competence. Deep pedagogy, on the contrary, is aimed at developing proficiency through its expression in an action (the hol-act). Students learn to think in action while handling complex situations that are usual when dealing with native speakers in another speech community.

Instructional organizers are used to designate blurred, subtle, and complex knowledge processes. In naming these subtle processes, they may transform them into things that exist, making tangible the intangible. There is indeed a drawback to any modeling of action. Bourdieu (2004) named this process "naturalizing", which other authors such as Kubota (2004) refer to as "essentializing" or "reifying". It is not uncommon in postmodern literature to deconstruct such designation processes and their contradictions. Postmodern researchers, such as Popkewitz (1998) or Zembylas (2006a) posit that discourse has to be constantly deciphered. Such deconstructing might be the major role of the engaged intellectual: relativizing common sense knowledge when it is used to instigate power games. This issue is political and ontological as well. It relates to how people define what is and is not among competing conceptual interpretations. Whereas many mainstream researchers tend to see their data through the lenses of abstract and universal categories, postmodern researchers see categories and models as discursive constructions that serve social and political goals. They are not abstract, nor are they universal because they are deeply embedded into cultures and communities of practice (McNamara, 2011). The presupposed universalism of concepts such as 'culture' and 'community of practice' require deconstruction as well. Therefore, we are currently witnessing an ontological antagonism between two ways of defining research and action. Considering this opposition, Bourdieu (2000) worked on defining terms and spaces that would be neither subjective nor objective, placing 'field' and 'habitus' theory in an in-between zone of understanding. A similar positioning is being adopted here. Depth is defined in a personal quest for meaning, which is context-sensitive. As a proactive concept, it is neither objective nor subjective. It defines a transdisciplinary, relative and evolving construction of reality. Its transdisciplinary dimension entails that for any R/non-R dualism, there exists another dimension where R is non-R (Lupasco, 1987; Nicolescu, 2002).

Instructional organizers are typical of the curriculum transformation process. They are relative prototypes. Therefore, instructional organizers cannot be criticized for naturalizing concepts: they *are* the naturalizing process, normalizing curricula with the risk that people will take their constructs as *things* that do really exist. They are ways of interpreting curriculum cases and events. They transform the fuzzy, blurred, and complex reality into things that can be taught with levels of intention that can make teaching and learning relevant, meaningful, and successful. The issue with concepts is to keep in mind that they are relative: they represent blurred, complex realities. Part of their process is only discursive. Their power is in sharing understanding. This situates organizers within a very different way of thinking than product-oriented ways of representing curricula, which by the nature of outcomes assessment itself, generalize 'realities' as abstract and universal. These are but tools to reflect on practice.

Adaptive Dynamics for the Language Class

At the beginning of this chapter, the following question was asked: Must a choice be made between performances or competences, or is it possible to use a flexible, practicable framework that combines the organization of performances with holistic dynamics? The educative project, as it is defined here, constitutes a model for short- and medium-term world language planning. It makes it possible to plan definite performances and develop higher-level competences. Projects are not the side-dish of instruction, they are its main meal if proficiency is to be developed (Markham, Larmer & Ravitz, 2003).

Until now, instructional designs rarely allowed teachers to face the variability of learning situations. As presented here, the heterarchical and interconnecting arrangements of the three levels of learning (contents, strategies, and experience dynamics) reduce complexity by way of a convergence principle (Figure 5.12). This proactive sketch may guide the instructional planning forward by linking several levels of intentions with thematic task organizers. The instructional framework proposed in this book is economical in the sense that it combines standards and processes in a coherent wholeness that unifies task domains.

Performances and competences are no longer presumed incompatible. They unite at a higher, pragmatic level. They can be unified by the subordination of content to convergent strategies that drive an engaged experience. They now form complementary planning levels. The organization of performances relates to outer, instructional activity and the global action to actualizing inner competences. Inner activity is then complementary with outer activity. The external activity of performances targets the internal activation of competences. The plan of action inserts contents into a global project by means of convergent strategies.

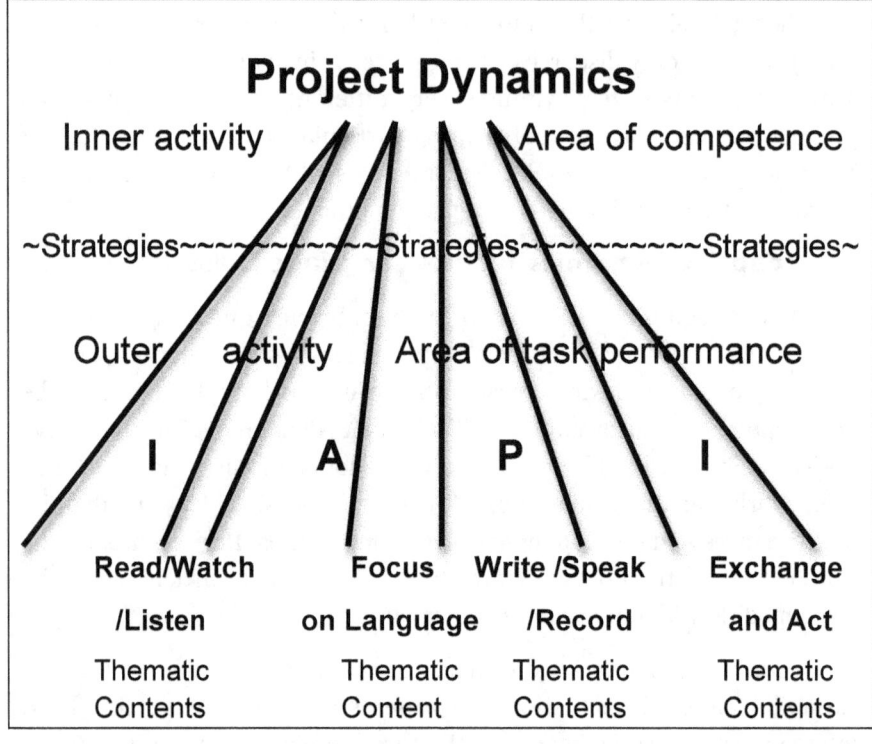

Figure 5.13
Deep Proactive Planning

Last, an apparent paradox needs to be highlighted at this point. It may sound curious to derive a new learning model from research on expert teacher's thinking, which has as a major characteristic giving learners free choice on their projects. The issue most experienced teachers face is to place the responsibility for learning on the learner's shoulders. This helps resolve part of the paradox of educating others to be autonomous. There is tremendous apprenticeship power in self-determination. Tochon (1993) even noted that, besides instructional organizers, expert teachers used "unorganizers" or suspension marks that typically would lead learners to make their own decisions, any guidance being suspended for a while. This comes from the understanding, highlighted by Illich (1969), that humans don't need schools or teachers to learn. Some teachers or forms of teaching even prevent students from really learning.

The Deep Approach is a response to this paradox as students' projects tend to interrupt traditional ways of teaching. This requires sound pedagogy, which is the topic of the next chapter.

Scientific Evidence on the Effectiveness of the Deep Approach to World Languages and Cultures

Tochon's deep, transdisciplinary approach to language and culture was proposed in five Ivy League and Big Ten universities with online instructional materials created for a Deep Approach to Turkish, in comparison to control groups alternating a communicative approach and focus on form activities.

Deep Learning: In the Deep Approach group surface learning decreased while it was stable in the control group. Learning by deep projects made students more reflective and oral proficiency showed a significant increase. Course evaluations were significantly better. The ANCOVAs show a significant difference per factor between the control group and the Deep Approach group, such as a reduction of shallow learning, an increase in strategic learning, and evidence of deeper learning. In addition, the fear of failing was significantly reduced.

Intercultural Learning: The test indicates outstanding results in terms of cross-cultural sensitivity after one semester in the Deep Approach course. The ANCOVAs show significant differences for all factors but one. The following perceived strategies showed significant improvements:

- Strategies used in surroundings that are culturally different;
- Strategies used for dealing with difficult times in another culture;
- Strategies used for making interpretations about another culture;
- Strategies used for communicating with people from another culture;
- Strategies used to deal with different communication styles;
- Strategies used to understand non-verbal communication in another culture.

It is a world first in the fields of Second Language Acquisition and Foreign Language Education. Intercultural learning is a major asset at a time we need an internationalizing of academic programs, countering stereotypes, growth in cross-cultural sensitivity and the development of better strategies to cope with other cultures. The results are being published in: Tochon, F. V., Ökten, C. E., Karaman, A. C., & Druc, I. C. *Teach a Language Deeply. The Deep Approach to Turkish*. Deep University Press.

Chapter 6
Deep Pedagogy:
Organizing Language Hol-Acts

What our world most requires now is the kind of education that fosters love for humankind, that develops character—that provides an intellectual basis for the realization of peace and empowers learners to contribute to and improve society.   Daisaku Ikeda

There is still a current lack of consensus on the best strategies for project-based learning and very few empirical studies in world language education and Second Language Acquisition in particular. The Deep Approach clearly fills a gap in this domain, as it brings a balanced methodology about different ways of organizing educative projects to empower the students and scaffold their new role as curriculum builders. The Deep Approach provides also a sound theoretical framework with the unified taxonomy that can generate multiple educative projects for a broad variety of languages, cultures, and learning situations.

Hol-Acts are holistic actions that frame educative projects. Holistic learning develops proficiency through whole experiences rather than the analysis and dissection of particular items. Project-based methodologies engage students in interrelated activities of an individual or cooperative nature to accomplish concrete projects. A project is a holistic, thematic unit that leads to whole actions. The project can be conceptual (Negueruela & Lantolf 2006). It includes a variety of tasks, which keeps the institutional system open. Such projects facilitate interpersonal exchanges, thereby increasing motivation and creating environments that are rich in meaningful second language use (Netten & Germain, 2002b). Useful knowledge grows empirically. Real-world themes, issues, problems and actions stimulate intrinsic motivation and create reflective situations to solve problems in their context, in a way that respects the autonomy of the student and is conducive to proficiency. Project-based learning compared to other approaches enhances the quality of student learning; it positively affects problem solving and decision making capacities (Thomas, 2000). Projects tend to reduce learners' anxiety and engender positive attitudes toward the discipline (Boaler, 2002).

Many language instructors are accustomed to teaching in a way that involves decontextualized exercises that have been proven ineffective for meaningful Language Acquisition. Empty slot exercises, vocabulary and morphologic manipulation, and an overemphasis on formal aspects of the language are most often developed at the cost of meaning, communication and depth. They force learners to be passive while the teacher makes the curriculum decisions. Therefore, *the first step to truly start with a deeper approach to learning is that teachers must NOT teach, but they must create conditions for the participants to make learning decisions.* Teaching as usual must be interrupted. The role of the teacher will be different. Learners shall be in charge of their own learning; they will be in charge of a large part of the curriculum decisions such as planning educative projects—choosing themes, films, and texts, as well as the grammar complements they need for the projects.

Then what do the teachers do? The language instructors become advisors or counselors and facilitators, and they provide extensive feedback and abundant resources. They propose interactional dynamics where students organize and pursue meaningful tasks clustered within educative projects. In Chapters 2 and 5, we have seen that tasks engage learners in authentic language use, focused on interactional performances, enabling language acquisition and making knowledge operational. In addition, the teacher is available for increased dialogue in the target language (L_2), showing where resources are, and providing feedback on students' writing for their projects. Extensive feedback means much more interaction than usual and longer texts than usual. Thus, what articulates learning is extensive viewing and conversation feedback on extensive reading, intensive expression workshops, as well as individual and group projects.

In project-based learning, the teacher monitors the students' chosen actions, helping the students frame and structure meaningful projects. As a facilitator, the teacher suggests resources appropriate to particular projects, provides extensive feedback, and coaches the development of linguistic knowledge, as well as social and intercultural competences. Within experiential projects, learning is transformed into apprenticeship. Apprenticeship is conducive to acquisition and proficiency. Students learn by and through experience.

Deep Learning Requires Adaptive Teaching

Contemporary reforms toward planned scripted instruction and standards tend to deny the teachers', as well as learners', creativity (Sawyer, 2004, p. 12): "Scripted instruction is opposed to constructivist, inquiry-based, and dialogic teaching methods that emphasize classroom collaboration." As in many types of group management (Farr Darling, Clarke & Erickson, 2007), classroom interactional planning requires adaptation (Baker-Sennett & Matusov, 1997). Experienced teaching is both a complex cognitive skill and an improvisational performance (Borko & Livingstone, 1989). A qualitative study on language teachers' classroom planning and review of their classroom practice illustrated why rigid planning was felt to be inadequate: planning is constantly adapted to students' reactions; it requires instructional flexibility and functional connections; improvisation is a normal feature of the interactive management of content (Tochon, 1993a). Instructional organizers accommodate classroom planning with unorganized events such that students must make decisions in a connected, situated manner with a focus on process, rather than outcomes.

Input-oriented planning requires knowledgeable teachers who are deeply motivated by their subject matter, and by their students and their idiosyncratic learning paths. It requires being able to adapt to the unforeseen—to what students bring to the class, unplanned, but which can still be integrated into classroom projects. It requires substance, invention, creativity, à-propos. Input planning is all about humane content and substance. It involves an in-depth exploration of the field. It responds to another type of logic: heterarchical (conceptual hierarchies have moving heads as things develop), rather than hierarchical, in a spiral, rather than in a sequence, and with rhizomatic–like roots that can reproduce from any part of the tree. We cannot easily design curricula for deep learning within the current normative constraints that prevail in most school and academic contexts. Education administrators must learn certain lessons from homeschooling methods targeting student's autonomy.

A certain number of prior conditions must be met for the Deep Approach to be successful. First, the organizers are to be negotiated and must integrate students' input. The curriculum project specified must align with the project of developing the student's sense of self, which leads to a positive interactional identity. Engagement in such projects implies commitment towards the self. Therefore, a preamble may be necessary for the learner who is initiated to the new approach, such as an agreement with the self to be successful and relinquish anxieties that might prevent the realization of apprenticeship projects (Rogoff, 1990). Second, a level of coherence and harmony among collaborating students must be established to realize optimal learning. Such is the sense of togetherness, or the *agora,* of small groups who communicate harmoniously. Being able to establish a space of harmony is a life skills achievement that will help students live in society, which is mutually beneficial. One rule of the *agora* to reinforce truthtelling that works particularly well is the agreement that any criticisms will be addressed to the person critiqued, and not be told behind his or her back. It can also be agreed not to speak about the group work outside group work. Agreement with the self and *agora* are conditions for the optimal realization of a Deep Approach. In groups of young children, one can witness the *agora* when they harmoniously gather their heads together into a circle to better listen to each other.

The deep teacher ponders a great deal, and suggests plans in response to the impulses coming from students, outlining a framework for general action, leaving the group plenty of latitude for adaptive decisions. The deep teacher changes means or strategy of interaction, while also generously respecting the negotiated curriculum. At the beginning of the course, the students are trained to become curriculum builders. Templates and examples are provided. They examine the resources available and organize themselves in terms of how they want to act or interact with any given material. Extensive knowledge of the instructional materials and deep understanding of subject-matter knowledge lead both teacher and students to scaffold learning projects according to a principle of instructional convergence. This unifies instruction, evaluation, and learning. The plans clarify the possible steps of realization of educative projects. For example, the teacher brainstorms and thinks aloud to show students how they may possibly structure their projects along different avenues in order to encourage expression, interpersonal exchange, individual thought, and personal apprenticeship.

How Projects Are Organized

Educative projects involve abundant input and extensive output on the students' part. Extensive reading, viewing, writing, recording, and reporting involve interconnected interpretive, presentational, and interpersonal tasks, accessing resources and expressing personal voice. As we have seen in Chapter 3, holistic projects effect and affect the junction at which subjective and objective needs of the curriculum intersect. The compatibility of subjective and objective requirements can be achieved by embedding the organization of intentions into a whole project arising from the students' wishes. Holistic actions lie within the gratification of the self-project and of the academic project, in an attempt to reconcile these two plans, one emerging from the subjective aspiration, and the second from the curriculum objects (figure 6.1).

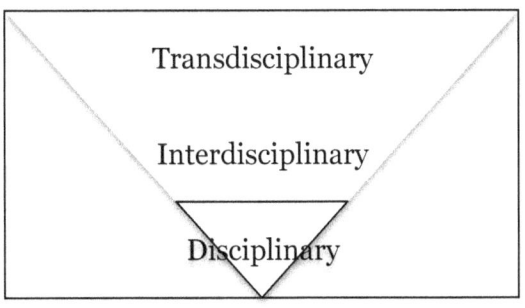

Figure 6.1
Making Education Meaningful
(Complexification of figure 2.1 in chapter 2)

— **Projects' negotiations**. They aim at producing a personal, peer- or group-activity that will satisfy individual aspirations and meet social needs. They integrate learning in a meaningful way, rather than fragmenting it, and link knowledge to a challenge or situation to resolve. The content's practical value is recognized in the context of an action. This goes by transdisciplinary principles (Tochon, 1990) we have seen in Chapter 2:

— **Relevance**: There is no one best way. The path of activity adapts to situations in relation to the students' intentions.

—**Holism**: Reducing complexity may hinder learning as a whole. The dissection of components erases their dynamism. Learning is in dynamic interaction with contexts, situations, and the speech community. Learning by doing is the condition to develop functional proficiency.

— **Direction**: A single gradation can't be a good fit to all students. The student is the one to judge what the best path is.

—**Connectedness**: Planning can't be exhaustive. Too many details favor the addition of elements, rather than a dynamic path of connected units. It is sufficient to specify connected units that are relevant to the project.

Apprenticeship for Deep Learning: When Teachers Stop Working Against the Grain

Pre-action is usually about teacher planning. However in the Deep Approach, teachers change roles. What they prepare in advance are resources for their students to become curriculum planners. Then they are not working against the grain, but getting the flow of energy from the students. That is their approach to learning; an approach that will favor apprenticeship. Teachers don't want to create a situation where students work for extrinsic motives, such as carrying out a task only for a good grade or only to avoid failure (Ellinger, 2004). The focus must be deeper. They work on prerequisites for students to adopt deep learning processes: approaching tasks within a broad transdisciplinary perspective, using interdisciplinary strategies with a passion for the content (Capraro, Capraro & Morgan, 2010). Genuine curiosity and free choice support personal commitment. The learner then relates the material to prior experiences in meaningful contexts.

The preexisting conditions for such an approach to operate include the teacher as well as the students, who all should be released from the usual time pressures, evaluation stresses, and low-level testing that promotes a surface approach (Norton, Tilley, Newstead, & Franklyn-Stokes, 2001). In each department where teachers adopt a Deep Approach, language coordinators should be informed well in advance and, if possible, participate in deep teacher training. They should know that engaged learning activity, peer interaction, project pedagogy, and on-task teacher feedback encourage deep learning and awareness-raising, as students learn how to learn the language (Baillie, Porter, & Corrie, 1996; Clibbens, 2000; Norton & Crowley, 1995). Deep learning involves theorizing about what is being done, using creative, analogical reasoning, and taking exceptions into account. It is not egocentric; it involves free engagement in the task with an interpersonal interest, not merely standardized assessments and requirements. Even a student studying a foreign language for mandatory school/college requirements can be motivated with this way of thinking.

Learners need to feel in charge and competent. They like to relate to others, yet want to keep their autonomy. Their genuine desire for achievement is like an engine that never stops. There is nothing to add to this inexhaustible source of energy. No need to enforce assignments. Anything that goes against intrinsic motivation contradicts its natural drives and fights real progress. Directive teachers contradict the genuine need of the learner for more autonomy and self-regulation in the process of initiating and accomplishing meaningful tasks (Tsai, Kunter, Lüdtke, Trautwein, & Ryan, 2008). Therefore, according to self-determination theory, classroom practices should initiate student relationships that are conducive to the autonomous development of strategic skills and competences in a way that the student controls, not the teacher (Cohen, 2007; Jang, Reeve, Ryan & Kim, 2009).

Project-Based Language Pedagogy

We have seen in another chapter that three motivational theories legitimate project-based approaches: self-efficacy theory, attribution theory, and self-determination theory. They explain why deep projects increase classroom dynamics because the projects benefit from students' intrinsic motivational impulses. A key aspect of intrinsic motivation and engagement is understanding and agreeing with the rationale for the approach (Katz & Chard, 2000). Students like to know that they are in control of the factors of their success. Their source of accomplishment is internal, not external. They develop a sense of ownership over their projects. Self-determination, effort-enhancing attributions, and a sense of self-efficacy form the foundations of the Deep Approach to language learning.

The Deep Approach uses collaborative projects and individual inquiries to bring students to create their own artifacts that serve as evidence of their learning. This differs from the way assessment is organized in many courses. Deep learning engages the students with problems that are relevant to their lives; they feel, therefore, intrinsically motivated, and there is less need for control (Blumenfeld et al., 1991). In the class, students—not the teacher—organize their work and manage their time. Students share experiences, collaborate, and work together to make sense of their discoveries (Kemaloğlu, 2010). Deep learners engage in problem solving from the phases of conception through the phases of design, decision-making, investigation, realization, and reporting. They can choose to work by themselves or in groups; however, there must be a negotiation on the type of process involved, the life situation explored, and the ways it will be explored and accounted for.

One of the major issues that face language instructors who have been accustomed to directive and controlling approaches to language learning is that they need to develop some receptivity to the bottom-up impulses coming from their students. There should be time and space for discussion and a real curriculum negotiation. Teachers should discuss the process and approach with their students, indicating that projects support language socialization and provide environments that are crucial for the development of proficiency. Language instructors are often afraid of not succeeding with such an open approach. They fear that they might not be able to "do" their semester curriculum. The problem emerges from the perception that only directed and controlled environments succeed. This incorrect perception has created a tradition of surface learning in K-

12 and collegiate teaching. Heilman & Stout (2005) indicate possible stages that can help language instructors get a sense of structure and stimulate the creation of educative projects among their students:

A. Generate ideas together and outline projects – what groups will be formed, what will be the role of each one? Teachers should not accept projects' duplication, as each group should do a different theme.

B. Groups need to visualize their anticipated projects and prepare possible scenarios.

C. Internet search and strategic skimming of data; inquiry and summary writing. For interviews: practice with peers the skills needed for contact, warming up, interviewing, and closing before the actual experience.

D. Refining projects for the report phase; preparing and rehearsing presentations.

E. Presenting the individual, peer or group projects; self- and peer-assessment as preps for instructional assessment.

F. Then comes the time for post-active reflection on the work done; students should reflect on what they have learned, the amount of target language use, and the strategies that could have improved their action. This evaluation can be anonymous if the works are numbered or coded.

Project Principles

Here are a few principles for in-depth projects that lead to language apprenticeship. There should be a focus, a pivot organizer, a challenging topic, or a major inquiry question. The end concept should be clarified through negotiation, with a critical discussion on the possibilities and the best strategies for the optimal result. It requires listening skills and communication of perceptions related to the project, its contents, and the way it will be disseminated. The rationale for action should be clear to everyone before starting. Quality is the goal. As we have seen, a key aspect of intrinsic motivation and engagement is understanding and agreeing with the rationale for the approach. Students are proposed to be curriculum-builders: they have choice, decision-making, and voice. They become engaged learners. Projects lead to creation, action, and experience: that is a principle of transdisciplinarity.

Apprenticeship is understood as the creation of entirely new knowledge; knowledge that was not produced by the teacher. Projects are about applying new knowledge, making it useful, functional, and relevant as it is put into action. Critical thinking and collaborative work are crucial in this process; students must develop strategies that will be needed in the workplace and in the world at large. Project-based learning involves in-depth research, ongoing teacher facilitation, adaptation, and long-term achievement. It enacts a variety of task domains connected towards a common purpose. Feedback and revision are the bases for improvements. The products will be submitted to the evaluation of peers and to public critique. Projects involve practices that shape beliefs and develop informed attitudes towards quality work and proficiency in action. They have an impact on personal dispositions, and they contribute to a student's new *habitus* towards self-directed and team-directed work. Bourdieu (1979) defined *habitus* as the set of dispositions to appreciate and do certain things that matter for a person, and have been conditioned by prior experiences. According to this hypothesis, exposing students to new habits of self-directed learning may help them to take charge of their own apprenticeship and proficiency development much better than controlled approaches. Teachers who use this approach quickly feel that they no longer work against the grain, but go with the flow of energy from their students. Similarly, they do not fight against the students' genuine motivation and ambitions they have for their lives.

Tasks in Deep Projects

In many task-based approaches, we find attempts that are somewhat similar to those of Francois Gouin in the late 1800s, which were to help students enact their knowledge in the logical sequence of situated actions that take place in specific contexts. Most languages revolve around the verb, which is the major focus of such series. It is not clear that the situation is the same in less-commonly-taught languages; nonetheless, linking action sequences as steps in the acquisition of discourse in use is a worthwhile idea. Historically, Task-Based Teaching

(TBT) followed the Russian school of pedagogy, which was under the umbrella of activity theory and tasks' organization charts. This approach was later diluted by principles from cognitive psychology and other disciplinary trends in a way that may be confusing to the point where the word "task" may mean anything and can even become synonymous with the word "theme", as I noted in Chapter 2. Some authors, such as Willis and Willis (2007), dissociated TBT from its historical roots and granted superior value to "tasks" over "activities", while in activity theory, "activities" would place the theoretical "tasks" in the situated, practice mode. Handbooks, in which numerous teachers give examples of their TBT practice (such as Leaver & J. Willis, 2004), demonstrate a large variety of uses, giving the feeling that tasks may represent anything, despite the efforts to increase TBT's conceptual coherence. The main flaw of TBT is to focus on mini-tasks and propose an instrumentalist, utilitarian vision. While it is important to know how to act in the target language, cross-cultural pragmatics is in the main absent from the TBT model. Moreover, some of the best reviews of this mainstream trend recognize the lack of a sociocultural dimension in TBT (Lantolf & Thorne, 2006). For example, Ellis (2003, p.333) expresses the need "to go beyond the psycholinguistic rationale for task-based instruction in order to examine the social, cultural, political, and historical factors that contextualize teaching and influence how it takes place. Further, it requires that teachers examine how what they are teaching affects the lives of their students and how they can transform them for the better... discussions of task-based teaching based on psycholinguistic models of language learning do not encompass this wider picture."

Tasks in the Deep Approach take a very different turn. The perspective is broader, its emphasis is sociocultural and ecological, and tasks are embedded into broad educational plans co-created by learners based on a variety of resources they can choose to use or ignore. While we may recognize that project pedagogy has also emerged from experiments in *kolkhozy* (collective farms) and *sovkhozy* (state farms) at the beginning of the 20th century, and therefore, has grown from a similar context as TBT, deep tasks are not minimalist as they convey transdisciplinary aims. There is compatibility between TBT and the Deep Approach, *as long as the tasks are conceived by the students within broader transdisciplinary projects that target identity building and personal actualization through social action for ecological balance, humaneness, and sustainability.*

As we have seen in the previous chapters, converging tasks in different task domains build up projects. Yet the whole picture is more complex and nuanced, as students are the curriculum builders. They need initial training in how to use the IAPI template, as they will choose the nature of the tasks required by their specific project. This planning phase is an important aspect of what stimulates intrinsic motivation and identity investment. The students choose the focus from an open list of possibilities, the teacher shows possible resources adapted to their focus and helps them explore further resources for possible projects; then, the students make their decisions. The requirement is that they start and complete a creative production process that will address their focus, which will contribute to resolve a deep question or complex problem that has implications in real life. Depending on the level, they may need to draft an interview protocol, survey a neighborhood, generate hypotheses and analyze data, and find solutions. Students who love history might dig into the particulars of a specific period to answer one key personal or social question; students who want to specialize in the arts might analyze the target culture from that perspective to create something original and give a lecture, a slide show, or an exhibit; students with an interest in education might look for contacts abroad to do some exchange or have multiple conversations with Skype, Google+, Messenger, Livemocha or WizIQ.

The best projects often require many weeks for their completion. They imply what I described in Chapter 4 as a unified taxonomy of tasks. Disciplinary content is complemented with interdisciplinary strategies to link various disciplines within transdisciplinary experiences. Enjoying the journey is part of the goal. The level of engagement and motivation accelerates Second Language Acquisition (Kroll, 2003). The teacher is a resource person, a facilitator, and a coach charged with giving feedback, NOT with making the decisions for the students. Nonetheless, the teacher can assign roles within the teams, such as in cooperative learning approaches (a secretary, a reporter, a motivator, a prober, etc.). The students can choose their roles. It is not the projects themselves that are motivating; it is the whole environment created to stimulate critical reflection and to realize transpersonal aims. The integration of learning into action implies cultural learning (Yu, 2006; Wu, 2011). The role of the teacher as a resource person needs to be further clarified, which will be done in the next section.

Deep Pedagogy: Teachers as Coaches and Resource Persons with the "Me Project" as an Exemplar

Teachers face a certain number of challenges when they implement projects, namely adapting students' pacing and work to the structure of class periods and managing the administrative pressure to cover the master study plan of their foreign language department (Marx, Blumenfeld, Krajcik & Soloway, 1997). Certainly, research-based projects take time compared to so-called teacher-centered efficiency, but depth is a sounder choice than breadth associated with surface learning (Kristmanson, 2005). Numerous elementary school teachers developed the skill of managing multilayered activities at different levels; this ability to stimulate various groups at the same time in the same class must be developed at other grade levels, including the collegiate level (Turnbull, 1999).

Resources can be online; thus, teachers must update their technological practices (Boss, Krauss & Conery, 2008). Students can build up their projects online in electronic portfolios and linguafolios that have been pre-structured by the teacher (Gulbahar & Tinmaz, 2006). In this way, the teacher plays a crucial role in providing resources and enhancing motivation, and empowering the students to become curriculum builders. Teachers then stimulate, not stifle; they support learners' accomplishments by encouraging their efforts (Blumenfeld et al., 1991). For example, groups may be organized cooperatively within the jigsaw mode.

Imagine the 'Me Project' topic in one intermediate class. The whole group is divided into three smaller groups. Students have viewed an example and acquired basic vocabulary through some readings related with the various tasks as pre-writing organizers. Then, students build a portfolio using PowerPoint slides explaining who they are, what the important events in their life were, what they like, and how they envision their future in relation to the target country, culture and language. They write it in the target language. Each class lasts 50 minutes. The teacher may devote the first 30 minutes to feedback on writing; during this time, students compare their portfolios and explain each slide to each other (for 15 minutes in their group and for another 15 minutes in jigsaw, or recomposed, groups). Thus, the teacher provides writing help and support, possibly with an advanced student volunteering for credit to assist in the projects of intermediate learners. S/he may notice some needs in terms of language techniques, which can be reviewed using grammar videos in small groups, with the grammar book to support their analysis. Students can decide to review these points at home afterwards. Language focus activities are task-related. During the next 20 minutes, half of the class can focus on a film on the topic of their project and discuss it, while the teacher meets the other half of the class for a conversation on the film they viewed during the previous lesson. For that purpose, the students had to scaffold the film conversation with their notes, using the film vocabulary list and its summary in the L_2.

For optimal benefit, conversations with the teacher about the film or the video are generally scaffolded and are usually not unprepared. Thus, much of the emphasis is on pre-oral activities, and the films' pedagogical materials (vocabulary, questions-answers, and summaries) are prepared with this rationale in mind. The film may focus on the biography of a great woman, or it may be paired with a related reading. Culture is present in both the input and the output, as students must connect their interests in their 'Me Project' with the target culture. The other '4Cs' are equally present: students communicate, compare their works and writings, connect disciplines together, relate with biographies from the L_2 community. Assessment can be based on a grid compatible with the European reference framework. Advanced students are proposed as tutors for the intermediate class. They will help with projects, stimulate oral exchange, give some feedback on writing, and help analyze grammar issues.

In the aforementioned example, what is different from earlier conceptions of world language education? What defines depth? First, the approach makes it mandatory for the teacher to change role. The teacher does not teach; rather, she is the world language expert whom students can consult for all kinds of concerns that can be formal, but also cultural, historical, geographical, as well as grammatical. The teacher must have thorough, experiential knowledge of the culture (both c_2 and C_2: popular culture and traditional 'Culture' including the arts, architecture, geography, history, and other social sciences, literature, music, religion, etc.). This allows the teacher to suggest complements to educative projects, guide the students in their explorations and realizations, and provide feedback on what they wrote, or reported. The students are in charge of their own learning. They are not spoon-fed by the teacher. However, the teacher has a tremendous new job, which is to provide feedback on the details of the projects as they are realized.

Through projects, learning develops into a broad apprenticeship, as the students connect the dots across disciplines. The curriculum is built by the students from a huge pool of resources that are visual, cultural, textual, and discursive, as well as humane. Thus, it fills the need for interdisciplinary connections (Capraro, Capraro & Morgan, 2010). Moreover, the humane dimension is always foregrounded. The project must have a transdisciplinary scope: it targets collaboration and shared experience for self-actualization and social action. Then, the teacher helps the students refine their work until it is excellent, no matter which topic they have chosen.

On the next two pages, Table 6.1 (a & b) presents an example of a schedule by projects, using a sequence of two weeks.

Table 6.1.a.
Example of Schedule by Projects

Week 1	Yellow Group	Green Group	Red Group
Mon	Work on ways of proceeding: choose a topic and issue, project guidelines, and come to an agreement; define personalized strategies and roles.	End last weeks' project; apply the self-assessment rubric. Brainstorm for a reinvestment of and write an agreement for the new project.	Decide on one-week individual work within interconnected documentary themes; share guidelines for similar projects, list tasks per domain.
Tues	List tasks per language domain. Specify and enact social roles for project. Engage with contacts abroad: write e-mails using the online dictionary. Print and share L2 e-mails.	Hold a Skype conversation with an exchange team abroad, explain project; one takes notes, one monitors. Prepare the scenario of a video correspondence. Open a YouTube Channel.	Gather individual inquiries on google.docs. Ask friends on livemocha.com for documentation. Take notes in the target languages and type them. Watch L2 YouTube videos on topic.
Wed	Work at home, each one on an aspect of the topic. Give feedback on L2 e-mails.	Meeting with the instructor for feedback on the plans, the rubric, and the scenario.	Focus on language using livemocha.com and peer review. Reach 1000 marks.
Thur	Share internet findings. Summarize documentation. Prepare posters on glogster.com Open a blog on the topic, with each one's contributions.	Compare and improve scenarios. Focus on language. Determine roles for video filming.	Read L2 video editing guide. Download videos through Miro.com, and reedit videos to present the topic in L2.
Fri	Discuss e-mailed information. Meet Green group and watch them prepare their L2 conversation and video with comments.	Rehearse and film a L2 conversation among group participants. Prepare title sequence, credits, and subtitles for the video.	End individualized work, gather results, create a total topical picture on Prezi.com with all the contents that have been gathered on google.docs.

Table 6.1.b
Example of Schedule by Projects

Week 2	Yellow Group	Green Group	Red Group
Mon	Integrate the blog into a mini-website on topic. Request comments and feedback from peers abroad.	Build a video report on the work of red and yellow groups. Discuss titles.	Add cultural pictures to the Prezi slides with L2 comments.
Tues	End project with an exhibit; apply the assessment rubric. Brainstorm for individualized follow-up projects, define tasks per domains.	Edit video; re-film failed shots. Correct language.	Give feedback to the Yellow Group on their exhibit before posting. Gather topic pictures and videos on Animoto.com
Wed	Focus on language, blog sections' peer review.	Work at home: Edit video and L2 off voice comments.	Meet with the instructor for feedback.
Thur	Prepare language night show with the productions of the yellow group	Prepare language night show with the productions of the green group	Prepare language night show with the productions of the red group
Fri	LANGUAGE NIGHT SHOW	LANGUAGE NIGHT SHOW	LANGUAGE NIGHT SHOW

The Deep Approach thus assimilates some principles of inquiry-based teaching. Through their inquiries, students meet a number of task requirements to develop their projects. The projects involve a balance of tasks specific to the various language domains. For example, some instructors report that students are often eager to learn how to develop personal relationships for their next trip. Some students would like the vocabulary and strategies to flirt in the other culture. The teacher may help them extend the scope of their desire to cross-cultural considerations about romantic love, passion, sustainable love, and family life, as points for which cultural choices may differ drastically. Obviously, gender relations are different in each culture and need to be reconsidered from the perspective of inclusivity, engagement and authenticity (Pavlenko, 2004). Pointing to the need for humane, stable relationships that provide peace and stability for society, a deeper level of interpersonal fulfillment is part of the work of a deep teacher. Reconceptualizing flirtation as a threshold towards a deeper level of love through mutual respect may help students in their own lives, whatever their orientation. This will help move society out of the current nonsensical situation in which people are used as objects and money has become the main and leading—if not the only—value.

Thus, deep pedagogy uses the best aspects of previous trends, and it adds one key dimension, which is a transdisciplinary, overarching philosophy. This philosophy must NOT be reduced to any particular, exclusive way of thinking. Additionally, different definitions of depth can be valid as long as the humane dimension is present, and they involve respect for other ways of knowing. The transdisciplinary aim is the icing on the cake of methods; it changes their methods' appearances and meanings and gives a sense of completeness that goes far beyond utilitarianism and social reconstructionism.

Specific functional components of deep pedagogy are reviewed below.

A Conceptual Grammar to Create the 'Deep' Syllabus

Here are broad orientations for the creation of syllabi that match a Deep Approach. Since we want to keep the approach flexible, I don't propose one curriculum or one syllabus, but principles (a grammar) that will allow educators to negotiate curricula with their classes. Models often help visualize what we mean; therefore, I provide examples of modular and flexible syllabi superstructures. Some are on the Deep Approach website (see at the end of the book). They are just food for thought and should not be perceived as formal constraints.

Here are a few principles for decision making in syllabus creation. A syllabus is a picture of what can be done in one period or one semester. It can only focus on part of the instructional materials available. It does not develop the principles on which decisions were based to create the syllabus. Since students must have input in the choice of the modules and themes they will explore, the concept of syllabus changes. Its an open syllabus. This is an important point. The Deep Approach implies that projects are designed for varying degrees of difficulty, which are adapted to the learner's needs. That is the reason why it is so important to let the learners choose their themes and resources. They will spontaneously be directed towards texts and videos adapted to their level. Yet projects require prolonged effort. Students can only be motivated to provide that amount of effort if they feel they are in charge of their work. Therefore, the best structure of a deep syllabus would be like a series of empty slots or units to be invented that can be gathered and articulated with a flexible grammar.

Teachers usually feel pressured to produce a complete syllabus and/or lesson plan of the forthcoming classroom work beforehand, and they are often required by their institution to do so. Here, we propose a superstructure for educative interactions with empty slots for individual projects, peer projects and team projects, each being associated with percentages of alternative assessments. However, the students are the ones to fill the empty thematic slots in the syllabus at the time they gather to create a consensual agreement. They will choose their projects and their optimal duration, and will fill the slots with tasks for each language domain, as shown at the end of this chapter. They can choose their projects from a list that is provided by the instructor, which matches available instructional materials and resources that the teacher specially prepared on certain themes, but the students must be free to choose their own avenues if they wish. The instructional materials proposed can be disciplinary or content-based and interdisciplinary. It is of the utmost importance that all projects target some form of transdisciplinary accomplishment in the realm of personal, social or societal, environmental, spiritual.

In an open syllabus, students can build an instructional contract on their own. Then the instructor plays the role of facilitator, which is usual in project-based learning, providing support to the students in finding relevant texts and videos appropriate to their learning stage. The aim of differentiated projects is to maximize learning, interpersonal and transpersonal growth. Particularly at the low intermediate level after one year of language study, teachers must cope with students of different proficiency levels. A differentiated, open syllabus will help them face this situation. Differentiation personalizes language teaching and learning (Griffiths & Keohane, 2000).

From beginners to intermediate learners, students evolve from open-ended tasks to open-ended projects that match their aspirations and fields of interest. One option is that students can work within homogeneous teams of similar proficiency levels to realize various aspects of projects that require various skills. Another option is that projects can be "tiered" in heterogeneous groups. Tiered projects develop different aspects of a project that involve different levels of complexity, or parallel tasks with varied stages of abstractness and degrees in scaffolding and support. For example, team members can work on different activity levels within the same project. Projects' differentiation requires that the teacher create and maintain a sense of classroom community where learners feel safe and valued. Each participant should get support in maximizing his or her potential. In summary, flexible classroom organization is crucial for deep learning to happen.

A Syllabus with Empty Slots

The level of achievement in a program depends upon the degree of flexibility and autonomy that is provided to the students. Instructional flexibility is the key to program effectiveness.

Thus, teachers must pay attention to this revolutionary change in the conception of what a deep syllabus is. As the syllabus is open, it requires a good grasp of the principles of the Deep Approach. One key to success is a broad variety of resources that will constitute the building blocks of learning projects. For that purpose, the teacher needs an imaginative and stimulating choice of instructional materials in various forms (textual, digital, and audiovisual); including working in rooms with a flexible organization of seats.

Then the teacher can create a syllabus with empty slots where students need to choose their project topics and modules. The slots have characteristics, such as the types of organizers that will lead the way to learning, transforming contents into stories, skills or actions; how activities defined by curriculum concepts (X's) will be connected, will alternate, or will be subordinated to each other. Where instructional modules have been created for a Deep Approach to language teaching and learning, it should be clear that teachers who have their own materials could add these to the proposed lists of topics, instructional materials and modules. Examples with "filled slots" should not be followed *à la lettre*; otherwise, the approach would go back to directed learning. Instructional flexibility is the key to the success of the approach.

Instructional organizers are part of these empty slots that are flexibly adapted to project situations. In Chapter 5, we have seen that seasoned teachers transform the curriculum into thematic stories, operational skills, or actualizing experiences. The curriculum is shaped by key organizers, to which language tasks are subordinated. They were defined in terms of theme, operation, and action. As a reminder, instructional organizers exist for the three levels of the unified taxonomy: disciplinary, thematic narrativors; interdisciplinary, strategic skillers; and transdisciplinary, experiential actualizers. Narrativors transform the language curriculum into stories of experience, skillers transform the curriculum into task operations, actualizers transform the curriculum into interpersonal and transpersonal experiences.

Project participants are provided with multiple options for developing new knowledge, bridging it with past experiences, and making sense of concepts and discourse. Teachers must remain flexible and adjust the curriculum to students' projects, rather than expecting students to conform to an imposed curriculum. Classroom and out-of-class activities are a blend of whole group, team, and individual learning. The premise is that instruction will vary and adapt to individual and diverse learners and proficiency levels. It is a high-quality approach that responds to the diversity of proficiency levels and styles among learners and stimulates deep learning. The embedment of three levels that imbricate disciplinary narrativors, interdisciplinary skillers and transdisciplinary actualizers may be difficult to grasp without an illustration. This action grammar implies multiple embedments, such as in Figure 6.2.

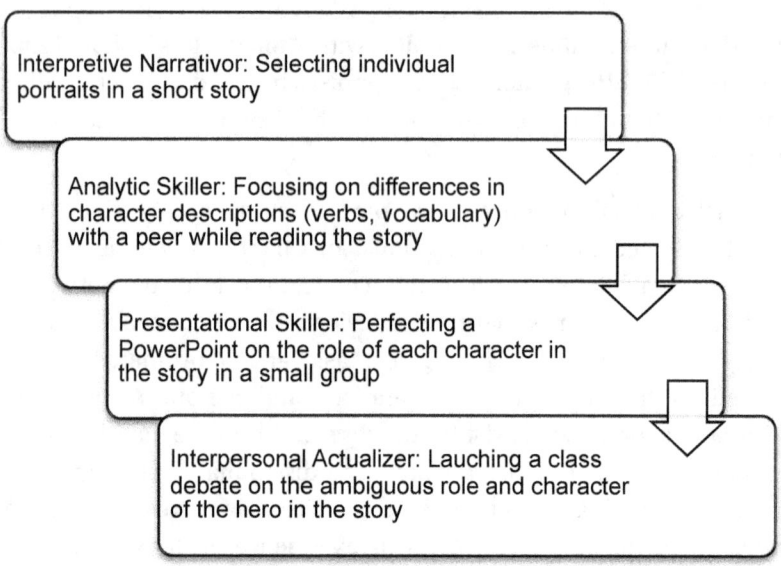

Figure 6.2
Pragmatic Embedment of Narrativors, Skillers and Actualizers in the Realization of a Project

Through embedment, instructional organizers are assembled in a grammar (Tochon, 1991a and 1993b). In Figure 6.3, the organizers are pragmatic modifiers that shape curriculum items for use within certain task domains, which are connected through projects.

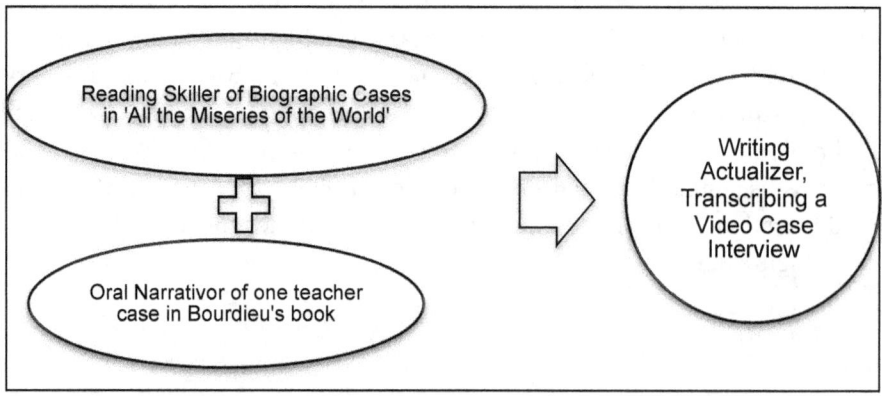

Figure 6.3. Action Grammar Connecting Tasks Domains and Organizers

Table 6.2 gives an idea of the instructional flexibility of project planning in an open slot syllabus. You do not need to learn that algebra! It is just meant to highlight the curriculum organization superstructures.

Table 6.2. The Deep Syllabus - Deep Grammar of Project Planning

PROJECT 1	$\Omega_1 \Delta \sum_1$ @ ACT (audiovisual inquiry) ~ ®$\sum_3$ NAR (geography) / ® $\sum_2$ ACT (exhibit) $\Omega_2 \Delta \sum_2$ NAR (R1 reading) ~ $\Delta \sum_2$ SKI (writing) / $\Delta \sum_1$ ACT (gag performance) Ω_3 © NAR (life events) ~ $\Delta \sum_2$ SKI (writing) / $\Delta \sum_1$ ACT (personal narrative)
PROJECT 2	$\Omega_1 \Delta \sum_1$ NAR (R2 mythology) ~ ® $\sum_1$ NAR (picture analysis) / ©$\sum_1$ ACT (museum visit) Ω_2 ® $\sum_1$ SKI (past tenses) ~ $\Delta \sum_3$ ACT (Journal keeping) / © $\sum_3$ NAR (short story) Ω_3 ® $\sum_1$ SKI (pronunciation) + ® $\sum_1$ (picture comments) / ® $\sum_1$ ACT (slide show)
PROJECT 3	Ω_1 ©$\sum_3$ @ NAR (history) + NAR (dynasty) / ©$\sum_3$ ACT (documentary film) Ω_2 ®$\sum_1$ SKI (indirect speech revision) ~ © $\sum_2$ NAR (comic dialogue) / $\Delta\sum_1$ ACT (TV Show) Ω_3 ®$\sum_2$ SKI (pronunciation) ~ $\sum_1$ ©NAR(R3 Scene Readings) / © $\sum_4$ ACT(R3 theater play)
Etc.	

Slots' Legend

Ω_n Group number
Δ Individual work
® Peer work
© Collaborative group work
@ Internet Contact Abroad
$R_{1...n}$ Resources 1 to n
NAR Narrativor

SKI Skiller
ACT Actualizer
(x) x is a curriculum item
$\sum_n$ Time x n lessons
+ and; coordinated with
~ Alternating with
/ Subordinated

> ### TRANSLATION OF PROJECTS IN TABLE 6.2
>
> **PROJECT 1** (timing is sometimes elided) - Group 1: Alternate a one-hour individual audiovisual inquiry with 3-hour peered geographic storytelling for the purpose of an exhibition with a peer. Group 2: Individual reading of a story available in Resource 1 alternating with writing development, two hours each, to prepare an individual comedy performance. Group 3: Look for stories of life events on the internet as a group in alternation with a 2-hour individual writing session to develop personal narrative that can be presented in a performance during one lesson.
>
> **PROJECT 2** - Group 1: One-hour individual story-telling session on mythology in Resource 2 with one-hour peer work on picture analysis to prepare a one-hour group visit to a museum. Group 2: Peer work on past tenses alternating with individual journal keeping practice to write a short story with group. Group 3: Peer work on pronunciation plus picture commentary to prepare a slide show performance.
>
> **PROJECT 3** - Group 1: For three hours, study history on the internet and follow the stories of a dynasty to prepare a documentary film with the group. Group 2: For one hour, do a peer revision of indirect speech alternating with a group study of comic dialogue to prepare an individual TV show performance. Group 3: Peer work on pronunciation in alternation with group narrative scene readings of Resource 3 to act out a theatrical play with group.

Most curricula rest upon categories and typologies for assessment. No genre typology or discourse typology has been really convincing so far. Nonetheless, typologies can circumscribe aspects of language complexity, such as tenses, hypotheticals, conditionals, and argumentation, which distinguish proficiency levels on scales such as the ACTFL Oral Proficiency Interview criteria or the European Reference Framework. Teachers are encouraged to record stories on language functioning -what I call grammar story telling- with crosscultural pragmatics so students can watch the videos independently when needed. A variety of typologies can be sound for creating a curriculum. With the understanding that the complexity of certain tasks and projects may increase with specific discourse genres, it may be wise to orient students in a way that will lead to the fruitful exploration of the following modalities and discourse genres at each level:

Elementary courses. Tasks gathered in short audio-visual projects; creation of games integrating vocabulary and pictures from the word level to the sentence level and short paragraphs; scaffolded access to texts with visuals; reciprocal teaching; descriptions and conversations; scaffolded interactions; humor, sketched scaffolded improvisation, theater scenes and role play.

Intermediate courses. Narrative storytelling: characters, props and scenarios; observation, detailed description and report; simple persuasion such as advertising; time, goal and comparison subordinates and completives.

Advanced courses. Anticipation, probability and possibility; hypothesizing, debating and arguing for or against; academic and philosophical writing; complex persuasion; subordinates implying concession, condition, cause and consequence.

How Is Evaluation Organized in the Syllabus?

There has been a recent shift in evaluation from a focus on construct reliability to a focus on practicality and social usefulness. Evaluation is to provide constructive feedback and empower participants in their development towards shared, intrinsically motivating projects. Therefore, the interpersonal dimension should be present in the evaluation process. Self-evaluation and peer-evaluation can be integrated in the evaluation model, with the understanding that they are suggestions, and it is the instructor who is in charge of final grading. The Deep Approach is compatible with alternative assessment and self-assessment: can-do-statements, portfolios, linguafolios, participant's diary, and journal-keeping practice. These aspects of what I call a deep evaluation will be developed further in Chapter 8. Expectations should be proactive and positive, rather than normative. The Deep Approach requires various alternative forms of evaluation adapted to the levels of realization of projects, in order to address a broad range of needs in terms of growing strengths.

Deep evaluation is growth referenced and constitutes a progress map to facilitate learners' improvement over time. Its goal is NOT to compare students or performances. Criteria are negotiated and set for each individual or group project. Ongoing, flexible, formative focus is preferable to rigid summative deadlines. Open challenges require neat project organizing and accountability. On the basis of instructional agreements in the form of adaptive mini-contracts that can evolve along with their accomplishments, the teacher must make sure that project participants engage in purposeful and intellectually challenging study. The principle of "evaluation for learning" may sound idealistic, but the readers should note that the most advanced and successful flagship programs for intensive language learning are NOT associated with any other type of assessment. Indeed, the enforcement of formal assessment may generate anxiety, which prevents the growth of genuine proficiency.

Here is a first example of possible evaluation categories for the syllabus, to match the ACTFL reference framework that most teachers use in the U.S.:

- COMMUNICATION: Used a variety of means of communication in projects that have been successfully achieved – 20%
- COMPARISONS: Used the multimedia annotations regularly, focused on language; integrated grammar points and compared language uses and practices systematically while working on projects-20%
- CONNECTIONS: Made exemplary use of interdisciplinary knowledge in other disciplines to accomplish L2 projects – 20%
- COMMUNITY: Contacted L2 community members to realize projects – 20%
- CULTURES: Developed in-depth cross-cultural understanding as illustrated and evidenced in projects – 20%

These categories are very general to meet the 'empty slot' principle. Slots will be filled in the conception and contracting of each project, in the form of a team rubric or tally sheet, for example. Here is a second example of a possible evaluation grid for the syllabus:

- INTERPRET: Film viewing, readings and discussion, answering questions – 20%
- ANALYZE: Integrating grammar in texts and discourse, language awareness activities in the accomplishment of projects, homework, – 20%
- PRESENT: Report on authentic, continuing project tasks (blog, e-mail, iPod, portfolio, PowerPoint, Skype...) 20%
- INTERACT: Quality participation in small group projects; regularity, motivation and empathy – 20%
- IDENTITY-BUILDING: Individual project – 20%

In summary, there are various solutions to organize assessment in a syllabus. Students can create their own evaluation grid for the course at the time of project planning, with specific percentages for certain tasks. They can also propose an assessment grid that matches the IAPI model or the 5Cs, and then negotiate it with the teacher for approval. Or students can go by the assessments proposed in modules they develop, which then are considered part of the course syllabus. Chapter 7 gathers suggestions of work using the IAPI template. Issues related to self-assessment will be examined in Chapter 8. Let's now examine the role of each tasks' domains.

In Guise of Conclusion

In summary, promoting self-determination, effort-enhancing attributions, and a positive sense of self-efficacy are crucial aspects of a Deep Approach to teaching and learning and form the necessary ground for successful project-based learning.

This chapter started by indicating that deep learning requires flexible, adaptive teaching. The Deep Approach is not a given: a certain number of conditions must be met. Students should be placed in a position of curriculum planners. For that purpose, the fundamentals of the approach must be explained to them; they won't be spoon-fed, they will need to design their own coursework and projects. Explaining the rationale for such an approach is crucial. It targets proficiency, not controlled learning in controlled setting, which would make students unable to respond to impromptu requests, tasks, and dialogues on the topics that are dear to their hearts. The approach will go where THEY want to go. They will have to become a bit creative, but it will be rewarding. They will, in large part, design their own assessment as well. This aspect is explored in more details in Chapters 7 and 8. They will work on what is relevant for them, and things will be balanced in terms of the language components involved. Projects will work if students are engaged; they will be engaged if they were the ones making the crucial choices. The teacher won't teach against the grain, but will bring the necessary resources for them to realize their aspirations.

The chapter went on to explain the principles for creating open syllabi and included charts that illustrate the whole flexible planning process. The deep teacher provides assistance to self-directed learning. This aspect must be discussed with the language coordinator or the department head: people should understand that the Deep Approach integrates an alternative accountability structure, yet it can fit within the academic periods and semester. In the deep classroom, participants are generally engaged in challenging projects and have a sense of responsibility for their achievements. If not, then the group should be placed in problem solving mode and examine what the reasons are for the possible lack of interest or motivation of some participants, which may lead to restructuring groups, ways of functioning, or topics. The organizing principles allowing teachers to have various students and groups doing different things in their course match those of differentiated teaching and learning: rich knowledge-base for projects, flexible grouping, ongoing formative evaluations, established work methods that have been negotiated with the learners, and respectful participation.

Chapter 7
The IAPI Model
Access and Voice
for Identity Building

Traditional epistemologies ... systematically exclude the possibility that women could be the "knowers" or agents of knowledge; they claim that the voice of science is a masculine one; that the history is written from only the point of view of men of the dominant class and race... Harding (1987, p. 3)

Identity-Building depends upon Access to knowledge through deep interpretation and critical analysis, and Voice which allows persons of all genders, races, classes, social conditions and statutes to present their thoughts and who they are, and have free interpersonal relations that lead to social action and accomplishments.

This chapter offers a panorama of the means available to Access and Voice in the different task domains, which are:

- INTERPRET: Film viewing, readings and discussion, answering questions

- ANALYZE: Integrating grammar in texts and discourse, language awareness activities in the accomplishment of projects, homework

- PRESENT: Report on authentic, continuing project tasks (blog, e-mail, iPod, portfolio, PowerPoint, Skype...)

- INTERACT: Quality participation in small group projects; regularity, motivation and empathy

The IAPI model serves as a template for planning hol-acts (Fig. 7.1).

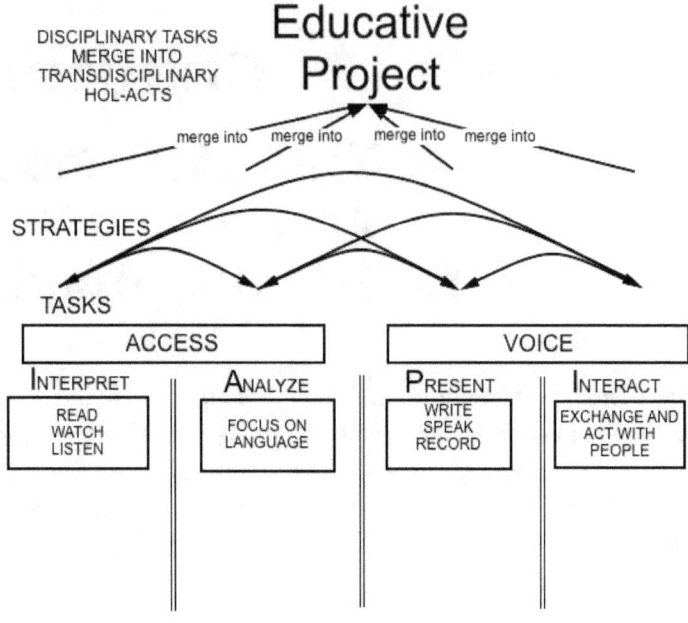

Figure 7.1
The IAPI Model Serves as Planning Template

The major components of this model are ACCESS and VOICE. Both are needed to develop proficiency. ACCESS includes tasks related to *Interpretation* and *Analysis*. VOICE includes *Presentation* and *Interaction* tasks. ACCESS and VOICE tasks unite into identity-building projects. These categories are reviewed below.

Interpret

The interpretation task domain implies tasks that encourage students to read, watch and listen.

THE ROLE OF EXTENSIVE READING – Deep reading is *extensive*. Krashen (2004) used a close concept when he described "free voluntary reading". He qualified it as "the missing ingredient" in foreign language instruction (p.1). The adjective 'intensive', on the contrary, has long been restricted to instructor-selected short readings, to which a series of controlled exercises are associated for appropriate-level readers. Such a traditional approach does not characterize deep, independent learning. Traditional intensive reading can help at the beginner level due to careful scaffolding and ease of reading. However, as soon as possible, the learners should be provided the freedom of confronting real-life readings of their own choosing. This extensive, Deep Approach of reading deserves some explanation. Indeed, it seems to contradict principles around which there was a fair amount of agreement in the SLA community, which come from the initial texts of Stephen Krashen and of the pedagogical interpretation that has been done of Vygotskyan research.

As we have seen in Chapter 2, it was inferred from the 'natural order' of acquisition and the notion of comprehensible input that implies 'i+1' progress, and from Vygotsky's work, that instructors must select readings that are situated within the Zone of Proximal Development (ZPD) of their students. However this comfort zone can be extended with extensive practice, as.our experiences within a Deep Approach indicate: extensive and complex reading can unlock higher levels of understanding and lead to progress of up to one or two OPI thresholds in two semesters depending on the students (Tochon, Ökten, Karaman & Druc, 2012). Instructional designers have inferred from the ZPD principle that *instructors* must choose for their students the appropriate reading level. However each student has his or her own level and vocabulary, different backgrounds with a heterogeneous range of prior experiences, which make it almost impossible, as I shall show in Chapter 8, to really specify the ZPD of each of them.

Students who have the freedom to choose their own readings learn *more* from them and develop new strategies with increased motivation. Allow them the freedom of their choices. Controlled readings may satisfy administrative needs for accountability; however, if the language instructor targets proficiency, this is not the way to go, at least at the intermediate and advanced levels. Here is how the deep, extensive approach to reading can be characterized:

A. The learner chooses readings that correspond to personal or team educative projects at the level of complexity that the learner feels is appropriate. This freedom to read at will what they want is a primer in deep, extensive reading (Rankin, 2005).
B. The choice of the text is open in terms of theme, topic of interest, focus, length, and vocabulary complexity (Day & Bamford, 1998).

Some students may like to challenge themselves more than others, so the choice of the complexity level (from news stories to more abstract texts) is left to the learner, who evaluates his or her Zone of Proximal Development. There is a caveat: texts must be within the range of what is legitimate and appropriate according to context and culture. The educative projects from which they take their legitimacy correspond to transdisciplinary goals for social, societal or personal improvement.

C. Deep learners read extensively to instruct their own project; they choose their pacing—usually quite fast—however, specific time frames are guaranteed within instructional agreements, at home, or in class to make sure such extensive reading can take place.

D. Strategic reading is encouraged, as students should not be restricted to detailed linguistic understanding. Extensive reading will help them develop their own strategies, as they will tend to reduce the use of dictionaries to those elements that are crucial for understanding. They can scan, skim, select, and read thoroughly the elements that are necessary for their project inquiry, as they would do in their mother language.

E. Extensive reading should be intrinsically rewarding. Students tend to enjoy it very much (Tanaka & Stapleton, 2007; Arnold, 2009). It is eye-opening when pleasure and information are meshed in intrinsic motivation. Reading is a mean to an end with the project in process. The motivational impact of extensive readings helps transfer across task domains: there is less anxiety, so students write better and more extensively (Lee, 2005), improve word recognition (Sun, 2003), vocabulary acquisition (Horst, 2005; Mu & Carrington, 2007), mastery over structures (Rodrigo, Krashen & Gribbons, 2004), and seem to improve their abilities to listen, speak, and converse with others (Cho & Krashen, 1994).

F. The teacher, as a resource and facilitator, can help students discover their own strategies, linking their reading to their project, and providing support for the contents of readings in project presentations or in the linguafolio at the time of reporting.

Deep reading is a personal and usually a silent activity, yet some students like non-disruptive music. Reciprocal reading can follow individual reading if it corresponds to the goals of the projects. This scaffolding discussion technique is well suited when there is attunement within a team in verifying their comprehension of the texts they have chosen or encountered online. The reciprocal reading strategy (Palincsar & Brown, 1984) can be augmented with multiliteracy strategies for multimedia reading (Oczkus, 2010) and then integrating:

(1) Project planning, predicting future content, activating prior knowledge, pre-viewing and setting a purpose for the reading activity.
(2) Analyzing the issues and questions that emerge from readings: self-questioning and sharing questions, generating project-focused questions that will guide the next readings.
(3) Monitoring the directions of the reading work, asking whether the text makes sense vis-à-vis the goal of the project, and clarifying the reading process by adapting the strategies.
(4) Specifying and summarizing what has been read. How could it be represented within the frame of the project? Visualizing its contents and creating mind maps and mental pictures, concept maps that synthesize its key ideas. Deciding on the visual or spatial representations of these contents within the project.
(5) Clarifying possible misunderstandings; discussing the difficulties of understanding among peers, examining the most complex sections of the text. Understanding words through strategic vocabulary development, using graphic, phonic, syntactic and semantic cues.
(6) Making conceptual, historical, political, visual and musical connections relating the readings to self, discourse and the world. Valuing and evaluating the contributions of specific texts to the project, making value judgments.

Free resources for reciprocal teaching including flashcards are available here:

http://www.windsorct.org/sagelmc/TEACHERS/ReciprocalTeaching/ReciprocalTeaching.htm

Extensive reading of literary works, as well as authentic texts, such as daily news in the target language, is a way to access the culture and develop a deep understanding of the language in context. In 2007, the Ad Hoc Committee on Foreign Languages of the Modern Language Association (MLA) published a report titled *"Foreign Languages and Higher Education: New Structures for a Changed World"* to address the nation's "language deficit". As mentioned in Chapter 3, the emphasis of the report was about the urgent need to reform academic programs away from narrow models, which separate language courses from literature courses. The lack of integration of the two-track model is at the expense of proficiency growth. The Deep Approach to language teaching and learning helps to bridge this gap between language and literature and resolve this schizoid status. It goes along with the most recent reflections in the fields of MLA, SLA and WLE. In 2009, the MLA proposed a number of ways to relate linguistic disciplinary goals with those of a liberal education for a better integration of language courses and literature:

"Without language, there is no communication, speculative thought, or community; without literature, there is no in-depth understanding of narratives that lead to the discovery of other cultures in their specificities and diversity and to the understanding of other human beings in their similarities and differences." (p. 1).

The committee in charge of this analysis emphasized that

"the arts of language and the tools of literacy are key qualifications for full participation in the social, political, economic, literary, and cultural life of the twenty-first century. It affirmed the centrality of literature and reading to undergraduate education. Interpretation, translation, and cross-cultural communication are essential in today's world." (Executive summary)

The artificial division maintained in language curricula that devalues early language learning while monopolizing upper language courses in the service of literary studies is detrimental to language learning itself, which is highly supported by extensive reading (Tochon, Ökten, Karaman & Druc, 2013). Reading fluency is a most important sign of proficiency (Sayenko, 2011) and there is a positive relationship between reading speed and comprehension (Jodai & Tahriri, 2011). Project environments stimulate speed reading in the inquiry process, and comprehension is further enhanced by the collaboration within learning teams. Cooperative learning that target positive interdependence, individual accountability, equal participation and simultaneous interaction improves significantly reading comprehension and vocabulary learning, particularly for elementary EFL learners (Zarei & Keshavarz, 2011). It can be combined with thinking aloud to produce metadiscourse on reading comprehension, which has been recognized as a pivotal aspect of communication (Hyland, 2005): enhancing awareness of discourse markers in cooperative projects is a way to improve reading comprehension (Hashemi, Khodabakhshzadeh & Shirvan, 2011).

Spontaneously, cooperative learners provide each other as L2 learners with two types of input-providing feedback: recasts (implicit feedback), and explicit corrections. Corrective feedback is rather rare in the learner–learner context (McDonough, 2004). While explicit correction should not be encouraged because it may have negative effects (Adam, Nuevo & Egi, 2011), implicit recasting occurs naturally and can enhance language learning further. A focus on texts may help, in this respect. Literary texts can be the foundation for integrating language and content, which is doable "through the implementation of tasks that reflect the principles of interactive text processing" which is text and reader driven. "Process-oriented instruction includes pre-reading tasks that activate learners' schemata (background and personal information), while-reading tasks that guide comprehension and interpretation (global to detailed), and post-reading tasks that require learners to reconstruct meaning and go beyond plot summary (synthesis and expansion)" (Barrette, Paesani & Vinall, 2010, p.218). Note that the Deep Approach adds one aspect to this edifice: the texts are chosen by the students or through a negotiation with the students after an open series of resources have been proposed. Of particular importance for the acquisition of well formed sentences and paragraph level discourse can be the application of readers theater to world language reading in which learners purposefully interact in class, work with each others, read and write for an audience and enjoy their apprenticeship (Tsou, 2011). Role playing and reader theater and follow up writing are ways to ease curriculum integration.

Extensive reading is a resource-loaded approach used in world language education, in which learners read large amounts of texts for enjoyment, with the intent to improve their vocabulary and fluency. Narrow Reading is a variation of this approach in which the texts are threaded by a common element - such as theme or author - to expose learners to textual redundancy. Both extensive and narrow reading can be valuable to world language students and are part of a deeper approach to language learning. Libraries should consider working in co-operation with teachers to supply Extensive Reading or Narrow Reading projects to areas where there is a known need for material in a given language (Bryan, 2011).

Depth in language acquisition relates to elements that must not be ignored in language courses: the understanding and development of abstract and complex ideas and sensitivity to the aesthetics of language, for which literature remains the major source. Extensive reading is a crucial part of a Deep Approach to languages: it helps address issues at the porous border of first and second language learning and teaching (Silva & Matsuda, 2001). Nowadays, many teachers, with little training or in-service support, may be confronted with issues of linguistic diversity. The border between first and second language varies, and it may differ in the same setting across students and teachers, and differ significantly across regional and state settings. The number of heritage speakers is growing in both L1 and L2 classes, and for now, teachers rarely have solutions. The Deep Approach – because it is project-based and can be tailored to individual and group needs – is a solution because using trandisciplinary principles with this reading emphasis, these linguistic diversity issues can be addressed in a meaningful way.

THE ROLE OF READING ALOUD – Reading aloud is systematically encouraged in the Deep Approach. The way to do it with the limited time in class is to request students or groups to present their texts or readings on audio files, for example a minimum of 30 minutes of week. It will develop the muscles of the mouth and the ear in a way that supports fluency. The instructor can verify briefly if the reading is weak, satisfactory, good, advanced, or superior. Students who reach a superior level for their reading aloud because their phonetics is excellent can be exempted from further reading-aloud. Weak reading-aloud may require a double dose of reading-aloud until a satisfactory level has been reached. Frequent reading aloud may increase comprehension and retention of sentence structure, vocabulary, and cases. Note that the targeted pronunciation is characteristic of a projected lingua franca rather than the mother tongue speakers' norm. World language education has so far been subservient to the myth that native-like proficiency is the goal of language programs, in whatever country. However some aspects of the phonetic matrix of the other language are not accessible unless the person was exposed to this matrix at the time she was developing her first language matrix, before the age of 5. Therefore it seems wiser to teach an adapted pronunciation. For example, in Asian countries, replacing stress by vowel elongation is deemed acceptable (Kirkpatrick, 2010).

THE ROLE OF VOCABULARY – Extensive, integrated vocabulary knowledge sharpens the expression of abstract thought and increases aptness of expression. Students who like to use flashcards can make good use of applications such as Flashcards+, available on mobiles. It is advised to use full sentences and paragraphs as soon as possible, as they provide the necessary interpretive context. Students or instructors can download free computer applications, such as StudyCard Studio Lite and create their own flashcards and quizzes. This can be the focus of projects, with the conditions that (1) full sentences are used, not only isolated words (words can be followed with an example in a sentence); (2) the vocabulary is corpus-related, either linked to a movie being studied, to a newspaper article, or to a literary work or excerpt. This will make sure vocabulary is not used as a goal in itself, but is soon integrated into paragraph and discourse learning. The task should be connected to a broader, transdisciplinary project with interdisciplinary connections.

THE ROLE OF FILMS AND VISUALS – Personal learning environments, video- and multimedia-assisted eLearning provide outstanding ways of organizing language projects. Listening comprehension became a top priority in the language learning agenda in the 1990s with the reform movement based on research advances in child language acquisition and Krashen's hypotheses regarding the role of oral comprehensible input. Yet currently, the high number of studies focusing on the outcomes and products of listening comprehension "is starkly at odds with the current advances in language teaching which advocate a more process-based view towards mastering language skills. Favoring outcome at the cost of the underlying processes will bring about test likeness for the task and anxiety for the learners" (Maftoon, Lavasani & Shahini, 2011, p.110). Broadly, students should benefit from the current online video environments that allow detailed processual descriptions and thematic uses, much more effectively than pictures (Mesri, 2011). A deeper approach based on exploring one's identity on video with prior writing of the script is promising. Video self-modeling improves reading fluency for English language learners and can be a useful tool in world language education. Research with culturally and linguistically diverse students implies that the intervention can be equally effective with these populations. Further research is needed but the existing evidence base demonstrates the potential success of the intervention (Ortiz, Burlingame, Onuegbulem, Yoshikawa & Rojas, 2012).

In our Turkish program, a number of films (around 24 per level) proposed are linked to summaries, questions (and responses) on PDF files and Power Points. The Power Points can be used individually, in group, or by the instructor for the whole class, when needed; for example, to scaffold the choice of modules for the various groups. Some films are presented with L_1 subtitles, and some others, such as interviews, have brief summaries, either orally by the interviewee, or in writing by an assistant. Films have a variety of purposes. First they aim at providing authentic encounters with L_2 people in a variety of professions and situations, many being typical of c_2 and C_2 cultural life. They can introduce students to practices specific to the target culture. Second, they also give access to a large variety of speech used in different regions, not just the capital city or the linguistic pole only. Third, movies, multimedia and video correspondence develop listening comprehension and a greater sensitivity in the interpretive mode. They develop in the listener the ability to discern vocabulary, language structures and cultural aspects, as films can be reviewed as many times as needed.

The films and videoconferences can be used in and outside the classroom. In the classroom, they can be used to prepare and develop projects. Since many films have accompanying materials, such vocabulary lists, subtitles or transcriptions, or summaries and questions in either L_1 or L_2, it is good to prepare the viewing activity with the scaffolding materials. To increase comprehension, students should to watch the films twice, either both times in the classroom (before and after comments or discussion) or once in the class together and the second time at home as homework, associated with questions that they can develop. It is very important to change the process often to avoid tiredness and boredom. Students are the ones to decide what suits best their apprenticeship. This is the reason why I do not advise being systematic in proposing instructional complements to the filmic materials: some questions may have answers or not; some L_1 summaries are proposed by the interviewees, etc.

Nonetheless, it may be useful to present guidelines, summaries and questions in L_1 at the intermediate level, and in L_2 at the advanced level. The variety of the materials is an asset, to make sure that instructors don't start with a routine that will give the impression that the program has been sedimented into a fossil stratum (Goldberg, 2005). This variety can, in turn, help students choose materials in affordance with their level of study. Films and videos are part of the ACCESS component. As such, they can be used both to interpret and analyze the language.

Analyze

The analysis task domain implies tasks that encourage students to focus on language in an autonomous way, using all the resources of language techniques available in the program and on the internet. Such tasks need to be integrated within other task domains, and it needs to be self-directed to become operational. This was presented in the action grammar: tasks are related with connectors such as coordinators, alternators or subordinators (see table 6.2 and its legend). For example, scaffolds that help to understand a video's content at the time of watching can both integrate grammar and make it useful for self-directed learning. Such scaffolded, authentic materials support the motivation to understand and become proficient.

THE ROLE OF GRAMMAR – Grammar has become a controversial issue in Second Language Acquisition, and often teachers report that they teach grammar with guilt. Many teachers indeed continue to apply a deductive PPP approach (Presentation, Practice, Production), which paradigm Lewis had characterized as 'nonsense' in 1994 (p.9). Decisions on how and why to teach grammar are linked to theories of whether its instruction should be implicit and explicit. Krashen & Terrell (1983) argued in favor of implicit acquisition through exposure to comprehensible input and rejected the need to teach grammar formally. In contrast and among others, Swain (1998) and VanPatten (1996) have emphasized how crucial it is to help learners notice language variation, and the role of output for students to process grammatical structures that they have not acquired; getting feedback on their emerging hypotheses is key to formal progress.

A conceptualization of grammar proposed by Larsen-Freeman (2002) views grammar as a higher-order concept having three interrelated dimensions: form, meaning and use (or function). Meaning and use could be integrated in language instruction, in a way that matches Halliday's (1985) model of systemic-functional grammar. What is open to debate is whether rules should be taught explicitly before practice (deductively) or whether contextualized practice should precede a focus on the language organization (inductively). The response by practitioners is most often in favor of a deductive approach to form over inductive meaning and function. Yet the National Standards give precedence to function and meaning over form. Thus in contrast with the 5C Standards, grammar taught in schools and colleges nowadays continues largely to focus on form, with little attention to its functions and meaning, even in recent textbooks. Grammar topics are presented in a guided context with questions for students to notice the structure. The focus is to deductively explain rules before production rather than discovering inductively underlying pragmatic principles. Long (1998, p.136) had condemned such deductive instruction as 'Neanderthal teaching practices'. While deductive PPP is incompatible with current research results in SLA, it is being perpetuated because it is easier to teach and helps managing large classes. Resistance to change and a lack of awareness of possible alternatives also justify the status quo (Evans, 1999).

While the deductive approach to grammar seems rather straightforward once a specific grammar has been chosen (explain the rule and practice its structure), there is no consensus on inductive approaches: learners may discover rules by themselves (i.e. focus on language after extensive reading or personal production), or may focus on specific structures through reflective post hoc session. The 4-stage PACE Model (presentation – attention – co-construction – extension) is an example of hybrid model (Adair-Hauck, Donato & Cumo-Johanssen, 2005) which may be interpreted as an inductive variation of Knopp's (1989) OPDC Model (overview – prime – drill – check), in which drill practice is replace by co-construction. It utilizes an integrated story to highlight a grammar structure. After the input presentation, the instructor focuses learners' attention on a language pattern during a practice session including examples. Then students are asked guiding questions for collaborative understanding of the structure. The instruction is finally extended to give students the opportunity to practice the structure. In this way, "grammar constitutes a 'content' that can be transmitted to students via explicit descriptions and a skill that is developed through controlled practice" (Ellis, 2002, p.161). There is empirical evidence that a guided inductive teaching approach has significant impact on short-term learning of grammatical structures (Vogel, Herron, Cole & York, 2011). However grammar instruction should be determined by the needs of the students on the basis of comprehensibility and acceptability (Swan, 2002). While in the Deep Approach students are free to choose otherwise, there is an emphasis on *post hoc* inductive focus on language rather than focus on form, and guided reflective practice on output. The rationale for this orientation is that deductive grammar exercises practiced mechanically may not be real "skillers".

I propose to extend Mojica-Díaz & Sánchez-López (2010) constructivist approach in a way compatible with self-determined, project-based learning with an inductive focus on language. This approach harmonizes grammar study with the standards, places the instructor as facilitator of learning and stimulates the discovery process by the active participation and decision-making of the students in the analysis, interpretation, and understanding of the discursive structures. Feedback is used to reflect on the dynamic nature of grammar by emphasizing its functions within the larger context of authentic films and texts. To integrate this process learners should:

➢ Use original data, primary sources, and hands-on interactive

materials;
- Structure learning around themes, ideas and concepts that induce logical connections.
- Guide the instructional units in the reciprocal teaching mode, and choose content, plan activities and challenge viewpoints.
- Describe the tasks in each task domain with verbs of action, and specify which focus on language will be useful to their work in the Analysis column of their templates.
- Find contrasted explanations and experiences that contradict their original assumptions and stimulate the debate in their group.
- Mutually feed their curiosity, looking for opportunities to interact and generate questions.

In the Deep Approach, a re-balancing of the role of grammar is proposed: the formal and technical aspects of the language constitute one task domain among others, such as Reading, Writing, and Oral exchange (in the European framework). The focus is on language rather than on form, an activity chosen by the students who are the curriculum builders. Language analysis plays its role to support Interpretive, Presentational and Interactional tasks within educative projects. Indeed, the standards of world language learning with their focus on communication across cultures and communities require far more than grammar knowledge. Learners need to develop sociolinguistic and pragmatic sensitivity and interactive competences to communicate with communities beyond the classroom.

Given the Deep Approach principles, in the main grammar could just be embedded or complementary or just supplementary: let students figure it out themselves when they need it for the tasks, embed it in projects, using reference books, etc. Nonetheless there is something more to the new meaning we propose to give to the term grammar: it reveals the spirit of the language. In the Deep Approach, grammar is concept based (Lantolf, 2006); indeed, grammar forms are best explained by mother tongue speakers when they tell stories that contextualize the meanings being expressed in context by certain expressions and constructions implying wording, sequencing, forming, and sentencing. Researchers who posit that concepts are based on cognitive, i.e. semantic justifications are probably correct for forms that have been sedimented by common use; however, this author posits that concepts are pragmatic features, which are constantly reconstructed in the discourse.

Language apprentices need grammar for a variety of reasons. Grammar provides a metalanguage (a language on language) to express complex understandings about language functioning. It allows for comparisons. Grammar demonstrations allow readers and listeners to analyze language phenomena and present their ideas with precision (Williams, 2011). Thus, grammar serves as a reference for good understanding and correct expression. Moreover, grammar is part of the target culture. There are at least two dimensions that make grammar culturally important in language learning: first, it is a codified translation of cultural rules; second, it is the expression of a specific ontology. The first dimension suggests that it is important to view the language through the traditional grammar used in the target culture, as it provides a cultural introduction to how people see their own language; the second dimension also indicates that accessing grammar the way it is conceived in the other linguistic region may reveal ontological aspects, which should give access to the inner dimension of this cultural beingness: how reality is described from another perspective, within the spirit or *mana* of the other culture. For example, Azocar (2011) proposed a postmodern perspective to touch upon the spirituality of Latin-American peoples and cultures. Grammar in this perspective is the way a world vision is enminded in linguistic frames. The understanding of grammar becomes a way of understanding how agency and meanings are framed in the *mana* or spirit of the other culture. In this language enminding process, a task is an action leading to contact the spirit of another culture through its concepts.

A task-focused concept-based grammar can integrate the focus on language with form improvement, and initiate response-feedback-exchange triads (Hill, 2007). Projects cluster a broad series of tasks. The initial focus, when projects are discussed, is on meaning. Then project planning requires an autonomous attention to language. Later, when the time comes to report experiences, the focus is on clarity and precision. Language access and voice require autonomous periods focusing on language (Willis, 2007). The autonomous analysis of language helps learners become creative, finding opportunities to explore new ways of speaking and writing, and supporting genuine apprenticeship. Over time, autonomous apprenticeship can develop meaningful fluency, as well as formal accuracy.

Reference tools should be provided in the Deep Approach programs. Grammar textbooks are suggested, and grammar topics are proposed for each study course. The grammar topics proposed are those that seem the most appropriate for the proficiency level, and are a good fit with the themes and types of projects developed. The grammar points can be summarized in short video files for students and groups to review or perfect understanding of the grammar topic on their own. Practice is proposed in reading, writing, and recording.

However, the Deep Approach programs may not propose the usual types of exercises you see in textbooks (such as empty slots in sentences to be filled), which have not proven to be proficiency skillers. They can be found anywhere in various textbooks and websites if students want such support. Notwithstanding, the emphasis here is on deep understanding and extensive practice in reading, viewing, writing, recording and interpersonal exchange, which not only replace exercises but should be a better investment for long-term acquisition of grammar in action that is, the spirit of the language.

Present

The presentation task domain implies tasks that encourage students to write, speak, audio and video record and report, and create their own PowerPoints, films, personal learning environments or multimedia.

THE ROLE OF WRITING – As we have seen in Chapter 3, one revolutionary aspect that characterizes the Deep Approach is to reverse one delusory trend that has prevailed for more than two decades. It counters Ferdinand de Saussure's (1916/1977) exclusion of writing and matches Jacques Derrida's (1974) proposition: the text and the writing production process in particular must be the primary focus of language learning and teaching in par with extensive reading. Oral exchange in L2 is most often the by-product of writing and reading. Writing workshops can be defined in proactive terms with instructional organizers that help create an environment conducive to this type of activity. Writing is also the way to crystallize the understanding of rules acquired through reading, viewing, and reflection, while focusing on language. Writing is part of culture, and culture most often constructs its genres. Learning writing through its genres will help learners build thematic projects and get a concept-based grasp of grammar. The deep writing workshop is language-focused on genres and raises awareness to sociocultural cross-pragmatics, but it is not primarily form-focused (Ferreira & Lantolf, 2013). Nonetheless, feedback on writing is an important component and must not be neglected. Audio-recorded feedback is proposed, rather than written feedback. This way, instructors can explain their corrections and the underlying grammar principles with some detail, rather than wasting excessive time on written corrections.

While there are excellent rationales for simplifying grammar in the early stages of study, soon enough, some understanding of the complexity underlying language choices should be beneficial to the whole endeavor of accessing the target culture. In this manner, it could be said that the Deep Approach involves culture-translation. In practice, the characteristics of intermediate and advanced courses should be the same as the characteristics of extensive writing courses.

THE ROLE OF ORAL EXPRESSION – A limitative view of achievement has developed in the world language profession that oral proficiency should be the sole measure of effectiveness. However teacher qualifications go far beyond the ability for their students to reach fluency, and it is not really clear that the way language curricula and textbooks are organized really can lead to such fluency, which certainly is beyond the realm of the teacher's action in the classroom. Kramsch (2010) emitted some doubts that foreign languages as taught in school might target proficiency; rather, with some exceptions, they may well be simply oriented toward a form of sensitivity to other cultures. Whatever the situation, student teachers are advised by ACTFL to reach the Advanced Low proficiency threshold before beginning teaching, a threshold which is now required in 26 states other ones keeping the Intermediate High threshold with a few exceptions (Chambless, 2012). The selection of a threshold raises heated debates. The choice of the Advanced Low level is based upon theories that emphasize the role of input in language acquisition: classroom students should be able to make sense of comprehensible input provided by the student teacher they hear interacting with them. Teachers must be able to rely on their language skills to provide rich and varied input and guide learners to interact, interpret, and negotiate meaning: "teachers who are not at least Advanced Low level speakers [may] have difficulty serving effectively as a facilitator in helping students to negotiate meaning with one another and to function spontaneously in the target language" (ACTFL, 2002). We all hear stories of students comparing their teachers in the school corridors on their ability or inability to use and master the target language.

ACTFL has teamed with the National Council for Accreditation of Teacher Education (NCATE) to impose its threshold. Strategic courses to expedite an increase in oral proficiency are being conceived, and focusing students' attention on the tasks of the next proficiency level (i.e. teaching to the OPI test) results in an increase in proficiency of at least one sublevel in 71% of the cases (Weyers, 2010). I have personally witnessed failing French and Spanish students with an Intermediate Mid official OPI being taught to test by a trained teacher at some costs, and transgressing the Advanced Low threshold in one month for the time of a phone call, which is normally impossible. The business culture of assessment leads us very far from what deep learning might mean. These types of concerns displace the debate over aspects of the profession that are of a rudimentary nature. Teachers lack the necessary availability in time and the funds to travel and increase their language and culture skills (Byrd et al., 2011). First teachers should be provided financial incentives to increase their proficiency and intercultural understanding through regular study abroad and should have the intrinsic motivation to do so. Second, it is possible to teach another language with the resources of today and sound pedagogical knowledge without having reached advanced proficiency yet. Thus, as Chambless (2012) notes, the debate should be over the quality of continuing education and its incentives, and more research is needed in this area.

One way of increasing oral proficiency is through the use of role play and storytelling. "One of the compelling interests of storytelling resides in the power that narrative generates to bring to life for readers classrooms and schools in all their complexity" (Fairbanks, 1996, p.339). Oral narratives help structure reflection upon language learning and what is being lived in the classroom setting, and develop insight into personal, institutional, and social issues that impact education systems: " Learning a language never happens in isolation; it is a work in progress that engages an entire community or peer group" (Polansky et al., 2010, p.308). Audiovisual creation is another way to improve oral expression.

THE ROLE OF AUDIOVISUAL CREATION – Audiovisual creation is part of this apprenticeship. Blogs, glogs, videos, Animoto, or Prezi presentations allow an understanding of cultural subsystems in practice, such as:

- The news and mass media; imaginaries of business, sports, and leisure
- Literature and artwork and their social and historical narratives to inquire into cultural self-understanding, local and national politics, law, economy, education, and welfare
- Local understanding of scientific formation and scholarly work
- Cultural analogies and their relation to national imaginaries
- Stereotypes of self and others negotiated through discourse, videos, and media
- Competing traditions viewing the nation as secularist or religious; testimonies and historiography
- National memory and symbols, including architecture and monuments, historical heroes and popular figures, evolution of currency, gross domestic product and income inequality, cultural products, canons, fashions, and meals.

There is agreement that the two-tiered configuration that artificially separates language learning from literature faculty in language departments is inefficient and antiquated (MLA, 2007, p.2). This "false dichotomy"—because learners need proficiency to engage with literary discourse—is resolved by deeper integrative approaches such as using poetry for a better understanding of culture and creative writing (Melin, 2010). Such integration legitimates as well an approach in which filmic and literary resources can be thresholds for deeper language learning.

Resources for the Deep Approach must be authentic and varied, selected by the students, and should include advanced organizers and scaffolds, which is what we did in the materials created for the Deep Approach to Turkish. For example, reciprocal reading of a narrative video script in small groups may help watch and understand a video of a higher level of complexity than usual. In such context, reading the script aloud and taking a test compared to control groups that did not have the advanced organizer indicates that the prior scaffold increased video comprehension. The learners benefit to similar degrees from access to advanced organizers as their proficiency increases (Ambard & Ambard, 2012).

Authentic video are available on internet at no cost for L2 teaching, and can support oral comprehension, create incentives for oral and written production, model language varieties and regional cultures (Sherman, 2003). They fit into content-based instruction and task-based language teaching and can be threshold toward a Deep Approach. Charlebois (2008) used films to scaffold the development of critical consciousness among learners. Teachers can use films in the L2 classroom as stimuli for information-gathering, problem-solving and peer evaluation, integrating culture and film-related authentic texts (Sturm, 2012).

Interact and Build your Identity

Stimulating identity-building processes is the overarching goal and justification of the whole IAPI model presented at the end of Chapter 2. It implies interaction across cultures. The interaction task domain integrates tasks that encourage students to exchange and interact among themselves and with other people in the target language.

THE ROLE OF EDUCATIONAL TECHNOLOGIES
FROM iPBL TO IDeep.

During their language and culture projects, students invest highly in new technologies, interacting while creating their wikis, web pages, blogs, podcasts, glogs and videos, Second Life encounters, blackboard or Moodle components (Bloch, 2008; Garrett, 2009; Mills, 2009). In 2006, ITJAB proposed the concept of iPBL to designate the use of technologies that support interactional projects. The integration of new technologies into personal and team projects leads to new levels of interactive achievement and communication. PjBL is more than web inquiry. Deep learning projects integrate electronic supports in meaningful ways. Simple eProjects can move to a new dimension I call iDeeP. For example, students can use personal or team learning environments in creative ways to collaborate, research, analyze, synthesize, and report and present their learning (Boss & Krauss, 2007). Personal Learning Environments (PLE) are systems to help learners take control of and manage their own apprenticeship (Attwell, 2007). They are compatible with a Deep Approach to language learning, which provides support for learners to set their own learning goals and manage their learning, both in terms of content and process, and communicate with others in the process, thereby achieving projects that unite multiple sets of tasks in various task domains.

The evaluation of students' and teachers' reactions to TBTL in online courses used from the beginner level suggest that quite a few challenges must be addressed: a) designing an online TBTL syllabus and implementing the task cycle; b) carrying out collaborative tasks; c) the Internet time lag; and d) the exclusive use of the target language (Lai, Zhao & Wang, 2011). However most of the program designers are not specialists of SLA and have a simplistic view of language learning. The classroom arrangement that results from the use of computers is often inflexible, which makes it very difficult to promote real and constructive group dynamics. The spatial arrangement and the relative positioning between the students and vis-à-vis the instructor affect the power structure and is critical. The use of Tablet PCs rather than laptops may resolve part of the dilemma but may perpetuate and amplify risks related to the WIFI environment, to which some students seem to be allergic as it creates nausea, headaches and various forms of sickness (Heroux, 2010), an impact that has been verified by a few biological studies (Adang, 2008). Whatever the situation, the Deep Approach can be used with various types of instructional materials and authentic resources, which doesn't excludes a priori online materials, as exemplified in the case of Turkish, for which a large online material has been provided.

iDeeP is a nice fit with trends, such as life-long learning or using the power of education for emancipation; informal learning throughout personal lives in a variety of settings and contexts (Cross, 2006), with the idea that people use different ways of knowing, learning styles, and intelligences in different contexts and subject-matters, depending upon content knowledge, which involves alternative approaches to assessment. From this perspective, iDeeP might represent the future of learning: it aims at real-life action and communication assisted by various technologies, allowing life apprentices to achieve projects that support their personal and professional identity growth and help enhance society. iDeeP and inquiry learning encourage learners to become independent and creative social actors, life-long learners, and critical thinkers. iDeep could lead to revolutionizing the way we understand schooling. Deep schools are holistic and constitute resources for independent and team projects.

THE ROLE OF INTERCULTURAL AND TRANSPERSONAL EXCHANGE – As we have seen, images can be used springboards to teach culture (Barnes-Karol & Broner, 2010). Or authentic documents can be proposed through digital medias that students use for their projects. Indeed students' perceptions of the other culture becomes more sophisticated when they are exposed to authentic film materials and need to reflect in writing about the plot and its cultural manifestations, note Hammer & Swaffar (2012), who propose a strategy for assessing strategic competences in negotiating cultural difference. An acculturation process that requires a negotiation of cultural meanings may follow an initial culture shock. Acculturation results from "the social and psychological integration of the learner with the target language group" (Schumann, 1986, p.379). Along this line of reflection, organizing reflective peer circles in a foreign community can play a significant role in allowing students to access different worldviews, criticizing local practices, and contrasting everyday living: students immersed in the other culture gather to discuss the experiences with members of their host families, who may be part of the discussion (Karaman, & Tochon, 2010). Supportive host environments are crucial in study abroad and thus such debates over immersive experiences are essential due to the acculturation process that might otherwise negatively impact language learning (Spenader, 2011).

Learning a new language involves interpersonal situations, complex and dynamic contexts, and (dealing with) social differences produced by race, ethnicity, gender, sexual orientation, ability, linguistic status, money, power, and class (Skutnabb-Kangas, 2000; Bhatt, 2005; Motha, in press). For the teacher who facilitates this negotiation process, it is worth having multifold knowledge, multiple ways of knowing and interpreting situations, and the capacity of adapting action within flexible methodologies. Systematic scripted conversations, with scaffolds that are developed through the prior work on themes, films, readings, and peer-sharing, can be thresholds toward interpersonal apprenticeship. Interpersonal exchange is present in group work, as well as through internet connections on sites such as livemocha.org, e-mail conversations, Google hangout, Skype or Messenger, and video correspondence.

Patterns of interaction between people take their meanings from ways of behaving specific to their cultures. These patterned cultural behaviors are dependent upon implicit social rules and agreements about what is common practice. Such rules and behavioral patterns define cultural semiotics or sign meaning-making processes in a particular culture. The patterns and their connections, their rules, and their 'sentencing' may vary across cultures. Breaking behavioral rules that express hidden assumptions about societal roles may explain certain human and social dynamics, such as expressions of cross-cultural uneasiness, social conflicts, interpersonal reactions, discrimination, anger, exclusion, and violence. Social agreements are linked to emotions (Aubé, 1998). Eliciting the cultural grammar and its rules is, therefore, the key to cross-cultural communication, understanding, and instruction (Palou de Carranza, 2004). In turn, cultural grammar can serve as an analyzer of interactions. The procedure for constructing a model of cross-cultural interactions is based upon cross-cultural pragmatics (Wierzbicka, 1999).

Learning a new language is often related to professional goals. Increasing commitment to bridging language programs with the communities around them generates a growing number of partnerships between language departments and local institutions. Service-learning is more and more integrated as a useful aspect of this community connection and figures prominently in these collaborations (Polansky et al., 2010). It is an approach in which thoughtful service freely chosen by the student is conducted to meet the needs of a community in close coordination with the language program. It helps foster transdisciplinary goals such as civic responsibility and enhances the curriculum through structured time for learners to reflect on their crosscultural and crosslinguistic service experience. Frequently students have aspirations such as helping in a foreign language neighborhood in their city or abroad, or doing something with their new language that be helpful to the world. "Most college students believe that a foreign language (L2) will bring value to their training, personal enrichment, and future. However, the use of the L2 is often confined to the classroom" (Grim, 2010, p.605). Thus there is a contrast between the traditional classroom situation and these aspirations due the lack of engagement in teacher-directed classroom learning. In regard, the Deep Approach model allows such learners to be fully engaged in action right for the start of their language study. It obeys one the basic principles of service learning, which is to have youth involved in the planning of active contributions to the community (Bloom, 2008). In the context of World Language Education, community outreach that implies volunteerism, fieldwork, clinical placements or internships must emphasize a balance between learning and service goals. Service learning combines community service with instruction and implies a critical reflection on civic responsibility. Because of their transdisciplinary nature, projects in a Deep Approach can create natural bridges towards service learning and experiences abroad such as those provided by the Peace Corps. Engaged language learning brings new tools and new values for social action (Horst & Pearce, 2010).

Culture is related to knowledge, life choices, and identity. Transcultural understanding relates to the ability to interpret and analyze cultural narratives embedded in advertising, drama, essays, fiction, improvisational performance, legal texts, multimedia, news, poetry, political discourse, popular songs and traditional music. Lack of knowledge and interest in the other culture is a major reason for attrition in language learning. Learning another culture, with its intrinsic variety and complexity, takes much time. It involves prolonged, personal efforts to step outside one's own shoes and adopt new perspectives. Therefore, language learning can't be separated from cultural learning, which is an endeavor that may take many years. It is not a matter that can be addressed in shorthand. This implies that culture and civilization courses, readings, and films that provide contextual clues on how the world is viewed, represented, and interpreted in the other culture and its subcultures can have a major impact on Second Language Acquisition. The Deep Approach is in opposition to approaches that propose an instrumentalist and technical view of languages. Depth requires reflective practice, philosophy, and wisdom.

In Guise of Conclusion

The chapter proposed an overview of the task domains pertaining to the IAPI model. The model serves as a template to plan educative projects. The chapter was a source of inspiration for what could be done in each domain. Nonetheless the IAPI task domains are not meant to be treated separately: they used to be linked by theme, operations and holacts, as we had seen in Chapters 5 and 6. Among the suggestions that were provided, here is a brief summary.

INTERPRET: Organize extensive reading, such as a reading club and systematic reciprocal reading; jigsaw strategies may be useful to organize deep learning. Reading aloud and associative extensions of vocabulary through lexical and semantic networks can be favored as a group endeavor gathering resources to support other activities. Film and visuals are also a great source of linguaculture, as well as videoconferences.

ANALYZE: Video presentations of grammar with examples, grammar storytelling, and text comment are sources of understanding for language in action. Focus on language is connected to a "need to know" principle: topics are explored insofar as they support specific forms of action, for example writing in a specific genre or production of a type of text or discourse. In the Deep Approach methodology, grammar and basics such as verbs and vocab activities are not ostracized as it was in the Communicative Approach. They play their role and are acknowledged as one distinct task domain. However language analysis needs to be connected to and integrated with action in other task domains, which makes such study and analysis meaningful and worthwhile.

PRESENT: In continuation with what was presented in Chapter 3 on the writing workshop, the presentational section of this chapter reemphasized the role of text as primary for a Deep Approach to linguaculture. Writing is also a great way to scaffold and improve oral expression. Deep proficiency goes far beyond casual conversations, it implies passion for knowledge as well as a sense of care and respect for the target linguaculture. Audiovisual creation is another avenue in the development of deep presentational skills, which also support identity investment and growth.

INTERACT: Technologies should not be neglected. Studies on the Deep Approach indicate a positive role of blended learning (Tochon, 2014), on proficiency growth as well as course evaluations (Tochon, 2013). It creates the conditions for deep intercultural learning and deep learning at large (Tochon, in press).

Now that deep pedagogy has been explored as well as the IAPI domains, as thresholds for language access, voice and identity building, Chapter 8 will examine the challenge of organizing pathways to learning autonomy.

Chapter 8
The Democratic Planner and Deep, Reflective Evaluation

Children will never naturally acquiesce to sitting in a class and submitting to knowledge. They must be compelled by a stronger, wiser will. Against which they must always strive to revolt. So the first great effort of every teacher in a... class must be to bring the will of the children into accordance with his own will. And this he can do only by an abnegation of his personal self, and an application of a system of laws, for the purpose of achieving a certain calculable result, the imparting of certain knowledge. Whereas Ursula thought she was going to become the first wise teacher by making the whole business personal, and using no compulsion. She believed entirely in her own personality.
D.H. Lawrence - The Rainbow (1915)

Motivation research demonstrates the crucial importance of autonomy and self-regulation for learning. What are the consequences for assessment? This chapter offers a vision of what deep evaluation could and should be. It examines whether vastly diverse theories of evaluation can be reconciled within a broader, less dogmatic model.

At the time alternative approaches to Second Language Acquisition are emphasized (Atkinson, 2011), what about assessment? An alternative model of evaluation would espouse a high degree of relativism. The polarization of theories is often a question of wording. Yinger (1987) affirmed that the terminology may differ, but the language of practice is a constant, regardless of wording. We may posit, following the transdisciplinary manifesto (Nicolescu, 2002) that for any A and non-A there probably exists an included middle, ie another dimension in which A equals non-A.

This chapter focuses on the advantages and disadvantages of the relativism associated with self-regulated approaches. Then, the functions of evaluation are analyzed in the light of developments in educational research. Differentiated approaches focusing on the needs of the learner have gained widespread acceptance. Allowing learners to plan part of their own learning has been highly commended as well. This could take the form of educative contracts, which incidentally, date from the end of the 19th century. Educative contracts or instructional agreements can define learning intentions and be active within specific units or for course accreditation. They are adaptable to any grade level. Contracts are often associated with formative evaluation in hopes that the learner will progressively achieve fluency.

The practical problems endemic to mastery models are rarely addressed. Supporters bolster their acclamation with astonishing research data. For example, Bloom's followers demonstrated that in a one-teacher-per-student situation, a weak student performed as well as the strongest student in a regular heterogeneous class (Rosenshine, 1986). Logically, it then follows that a proficiency-oriented model, in which clear intentions sustain a formative evaluation, should enable the average student to attain results equivalent to those of the strongest student in a regular classroom. Yet comparative studies have not confirmed these compelling results (Slavin, 1992). In an effort to improve the results of learning, such models have been refined, for example adding new technologies to the panoply of strategies.

This condition favors the emergence of simplistic stands and of new models, which once again will overlook crucial aspects of classroom practice. The bastion of formative evaluation is itself criticized, leading perhaps to the initiation of a serious debate on its merits. Reflecting upon the relationships of learning and evaluation may be a productive exercise at this point. It would be foolish to dismiss thirty years of work in order to develop a new model destined, as have so many others, to perish. This deliberation does not bear polemic intentions; the point lies rather in seeking ways in which models can complement one another, thus retaining the progress that has been made. We are currently posited at an extreme of the pendulum swing, in which teachers must teach to test, not to "leave children behind".

A certain degree of reductionism is almost unavoidable where planning is concerned. New instructional models are often designed to compensate for the deficiencies of older models, but by their very structure, these new models give rise to new deficiencies. These dilemmas fuel more research, and the cycle is perpetuated. It would surely be preferable for all theories to be coherent and complete in themselves, but evidence shows that any theory is only partially useful, and that in the classroom, the teacher must often supplement one theory with elements from a contradictory theory. This criticism does not apply to theories only, knowledge is also filtered to make sure students will conform to a certain model of society. Schools, media, and other social institutions tend in some respects to perpetuate ignorance. For example, literacy reproduces dominant cultural patterns that undermine independent thought and go against the best interests of students (Macedo, 2006). This chapter intends to examine whether vastly diverse theories can be reconciled within a broader, less dogmatic model, open to new knowledge and 'thinking outside the box'. This model would espouse a high degree of relativism, given that one planning option imposes the complementarity of opposing options.

One teacher argued that the constant exposure to opposing models aids professional development better than any other means since no aspect of teaching remains untouched. The analysis of teachers' practice reveals that those who employ the terminology of performance add a cognitive and a social and adaptive dimension to the model to make it functional. They may do this without even being aware of it. Teachers who, on the other hand, advocate discovery or inquiry methods are often compelled to provide guidelines to some students in order to shorten the learning timeframe. The eclectic relativism that exists in practice indicates the need to temper attitudes, avoid extremes, and examine situations as they arise. Theories are analytical tools that shed a particular light on some aspects of the practice of teaching.

Self-Monitoring: A Difficult Project

The opening up of instructional models and the subsequent risk of deviation are often the focus of the debate surrounding these models. Yet without some freedom within the educative system, classroom management becomes tedious, and the learners become bored and/or disruptive. An open plan that fosters thinking skills includes creativity, critical thinking, and unavoidably, a measure of unpredictability. The best teaching plans are, in all likelihood, those that empower the learners by granting them responsibility for part of the planning and are flexible enough to accommodate the unforeseen. For this reason, the deep planning model arranges, within flexible modules, pragmatic organizers that enable the learner to make decisions concerning the activity as it unfolds. Interactive planning is the pivotal element of a learner's freedom within an action.

Simply stated, the educative action is an interactive and dynamic project that targets a concrete production; its planning modalities and classroom management can neither be left unplanned, nor can they be entirely controlled by the students. They need feedback and action develops organically. From the standpoint of learner empowerment, the educative production is a self-determined task that is developed and realized with the teacher's help and support. This interaction involves the active participation of everyone since it springs from personal interests and wishes. The action leads to results that are concrete, material, and communicable (Le Grain, 1985); they have a value or a use relative to the outside world. This definition hides the difficulties of negotiation or contracts based on self-monitoring, on an individual or group basis. In addition, it may be difficult to meet all the required conditions to let the participants decide their learning flow within many schools and colleges (Cziksenmihylahi, 1988).

It has previously been shown that educative projects integrate many knowledge levels and promote the development of competences and knowhow by engaging them in a pragmatic direction within a global action. This hol-act becomes operative due to the subordination of acquisition and transfer organizers to an experiential organizer. Examples of this integration were given in the previous chapters; the pragmatic organizers at all three levels of the deep taxonomy are encompassed within the global conceptualization of an educative process. When condensed into a model, this planning analysis omits a number of important factors, some of which will be examined here.

Hol-acts rest on a consensus regarding the work in the form of agreements, instructional contracts, specification tables, rubrics, or guidelines. Guidelines elaborate templates or models of action on the basis of thematic organizers. All participants in the educative process can continuously refer to these instruments to monitor their progress. If needed, they can be re-negotiated.

One factor that is often overlooked is the difficulty of keeping track of the learner's reactions and level of awareness. It seems easier to teach within a closed system than to leave open the possibility of going off on a tangent or of straying from the foreseen plan. The most competent teachers seem to know how to adapt themselves and motivate their students without losing sight of their basic intentions. They can negotiate pragmatic organizers in such a way as to fulfill the learners' subjective needs as well as the curriculum's objective needs. This is a delicate issue inasmuch as it does not belong to the field of instruction as much as to the psychology of learning. If the planning is based on a principle of non-adaptiveness and closed aims, it will prove inadequate. Planning must consider learning realities that may differ from one group of students to the next. Teaching must include a required degree of foresight in the organization of knowledge that is likely to be activated in the next interactions. This duality is unavoidable because teaching is a social activity oriented toward contents and experiential sharing, as well as toward self-knowledge. Action planning occurs at various levels: cognitive, metacognitive, affective, social and interactional, and it is heavily influenced by the situations and the environment resources that offer affordances for spontaneous learning tasks. Planning, learning, and the ecology of situations are constantly in a dynamic of dialogue.

Teaching and learning cannot be considered separately in practice. This practical inseparability should bring together various strands of research. More bridges are needed to link planning and learning; instruction models will increasingly take the form of syntheses combining discoveries relative to learners' and teachers' cognition. The progress achieved in research and a better understanding of the realities of teaching will hopefully eradicate the dishonest stance that assures teachers that everything is simple and easy if they follow the prescribed steps. The age of methods has almost passed. However, the oversimplified arguments sometimes used to promote integrated language and whole projects have probably worked, in part, against these teaching approaches. A lack of information concerning the practical implication of these models may cause teachers to become discouraged and eventually abandon innovative explorations. This loss is often the technicist model's gain. Experienced teachers tell stories of having often tried, but rarely succeeded, in bringing a global action to a successful close. Nor was the action's negotiation ever without a breakdown at some point or other. The didactivist or pragmatist deviations have been part of many personal experiences. The factors that block the fulfillment of these holistic actions should be carefully studied in order to give the model the fine-tuning it needs. This cannot be done without the help of teachers who are willing to share their success stories, and perhaps more importantly, their failures.

It is only possible to survey the tip of the iceberg and to pinpoint some problems. One highly problematic issue arises when the education action is "initialized" (initialization corresponds to the preparatory phase that ensures the activation of a functional system) since even in this early phase, the student must have some input into the plan of action. When students plan their projects, the teacher must be able to listen without passing judgment. This counseling function is extremely delicate where group activities are concerned. It is vulnerable to the risk of upsetting the precarious balance between subjective needs, objective needs, and the educative project. No model can convey every aspect of the teacher's role or responsibility in a complex, open and dynamic instructional system (Tochon, 1989a; Larsen-Freeman, 2012). Even within those educative projects of smaller scope where success depends upon fewer conditions, there are pitfalls that can jeopardize success.

Students' Input into Course Plans

The action's initialization hinges upon the teacher's creative ability to help students build analogies -to relate the students' expressed wishes to curricular goals. In this way, a metaphor is constructed, establishing a congruity between the two poles—objective and subjective needs. The metaphor becomes active and concrete only in an educative process whose phases are planned by students themselves, with or without the teacher's help. The teacher cannot impose her metaphor upon the students. The most difficult aspect of this task lies in developing guidelines that are acceptable to the students and faithful to the instructional organizers. The following example illustrates this principle of analogy within the development of a project. It becomes immediately apparent that negotiation is a challenge because it must be accomplished in the context of a power struggle. Negotiation is difficult to manage because the arguments are often emotional and contradictory. In this case, the initial student input was minimal.

After a period of investigation, I discovered that my fourth year students had no desire to do anything. That is, anything that is normally done in a World Language class. I undertook to inquire about their personal interests in order to come up with an educative project that would please them and fulfill curricular requirements. A number of students suggested that they were interested in themselves -in their own person. I grabbed the ball and ran. Why not profile your "self"? I was thinking about experience I had had with the personal journals other students had kept in a German class. I was convinced that by getting the students to write about themselves, I would encourage the development of their perception of themselves and of their relationship to the environment. We discussed a theme, a simple one: "Me, Myself and I". Some were reluctant to talk about themselves, so I suggested that they write more chapters about their environment. That way, they would not have to write only about themselves. I wasn't really listening to them, to their reservations. At this point, the only thing that mattered to me was getting this activity off the ground.

I suggested to my students that they describe themselves in various ways: genetically, geographically, culturally, psychologically, symbolically, and so on. It seemed to me that such "Me-Projects" should work. Reactions were favorable, albeit somewhat wishy-washy. Only two students voiced their wish for an individual choice of topic. But at the preceding 6-week period, I had let them choose what they would write about. My concern was to guide the students toward a narrative type of text that could later be used to study the interior monologue and the Diary of a Jung Girl.

The discussion was cut short by the bell.

During the weekend, I prepared the draft guidelines for the writing in order to give them some ideas. I found that some chapters were redundant. I planned that they could spend a total of two hours a week on this writing activity. According to my experience with these students, I figured I could expect 350 lines from every student. I came to class on Monday with this plan (table 8.1), but as I passed by the staffroom, I noticed a memo from the administration concerning an urgent matter to be discussed with the students immediately. That took thirty minutes. I had fifteen minutes in which to hand out photocopies of the writing workshop guidelines. At the time, they didn't react... well, not much. Some protested that 350 lines in five weeks was crazy and that they would never make it. But the topic itself seemed well received. I suggested that they look over the guidelines at home and that we would discuss this again next period. I offered to spend five hours of World Language time the following week to get this workshop started off with a bang.

Table 8.1 Guidelines for self-exploration

Creating a Profile: "Who Am I?"

Requirement: 350 lines

1. Introduction (to be done last since it presents the whole work and the table of contents).
2. Genetic description: my parents, grandparents, family (aunts and uncles), where I might find traces of my physical and personal characteristics.
3. Cultural and geographical description: my culture and my relationship to it, the places that have had an influence on me, such as my country, my city, my neighborhood, my house, my apartment, my room.
4. Historical description: the story of my life, year by year.
5. Environmental description: my friends, my brothers and sisters, my cousins, my class, my school...
6. Pragmatic description: my past and present activities, my hobbies, interests, and extra-curricular activities.
7. Psychological description: my likes and dislikes; my strengths and weaknesses; my values; my habits, good or bad; my personality; what I wish to become like.
8. Sensory description: what I like to eat, touch, see, smell, listen to.
9. Symbolic description: if I were a flower, I would be a... because...

Same thing for a city, a country, a tree, a river, a wind, a color, an animal, an item of furniture, a fabric, an item of clothing, a car, a musical instrument, a tool, a video game...
10. Visual description: of myself and of the things I like: snapshots, drawings, pictures, sketches.
11. Objective description: how ten people in my environment describe me (either write down their opinion or interview them, then transcribe the interviews).
12. Evolutive description: how I am changing, what I am becoming, where I am going.
13. Ideal description: what I would like to become, and why. My personal hero or heroine, my role model.
14. Future description: (a) realistic: what I shall be at 18, 25, 40 years of age if I remain as I am; (b) desirable: what I shall be at 18, 25, 40 years of age if I can change the way I would like to.
15. Conclusion: An account of the positive and negative aspects of this profile, an evaluation of its value for me. What I would like to change within myself, how to go about it, and some concrete resolutions I could make right now.
16. Appendix (optional): adjectives that describe my personality.

By Wednesday, the class was on the warpath. One of my students handed me a petition. Every student had signed it and added a comment. They rejected this activity and claimed to prefer a more traditional approach. Their private life was none of my business. I immediately changed my tactics. I had some texts and exercises on reserve and I improvised a lesson on the integration of completive phrases. I put a lot of emphasis on difficult examples, hoping to wear them down. In two hours, they didn't have a minute to breathe. As they were working, I found out some of the reasons for their revolt. Some parents had no desire of informing me of their personal situation. The chapter entitled "Genetic Profile" was potentially problematic, as certain indiscretions might be leaked.

Five minutes before the bell rang, I rose and announced the date of a test that would cover what had been done that day. I told my students that this way of teaching suited me just fine because it did not require much preparation and corrections were easy. So everybody's happy, right? They didn't look too thrilled. One of the class leaders got up and asked if we could go back to the writing activity, but with fewer chapters, fewer lines and more time. He stated that the whole class had liked the idea of the profile. I asked the class if they agreed, and they all gave it the nod. I had read their comments and had thought of a solution. I would accept fiction; the "self" being described could be an imaginary one, as well as the family and the events. I would accept 275 lines and I would push back the due dates by one week. However, I would not be able to spend more than one hour a week on this activity, aside from the initial week of introduction. I suggested dropping any four chapters they wished. We voted, and all were in agreement to pursue with the workshop. This effort was, from my standpoint as well as from theirs, exceptionally worthwhile. All the work was handed in on time and in the final week of the activity, some extraordinary sharing topped off this educative production.

Negotiation Without Noodles

Without passing judgment on the experience that has just been described, or on the brief consultation period, consider the importance of the true negotiation of contents and of a plan. Negotiation is not a sign of weakness; it requires the skilled and steady instincts that are acquired over years of experience. Negotiating skills stem from knowing how far to go and when to stop. Letting students plan is a matter of knowing with whom, how, and when to do it. Few teachers let their students truly plan because of the great effort required.

In the "Me, Myself and I" workshop, the teacher suggested a metaphor for what he wished to achieve: a deeper self-knowledge for his students. In the "Dungeons and Spelling Dragons" experiment, the analogy channeled the students' needs into an educative process that would meet their needs. The metaphor of "Vegetable Horoscopes" united subjective interests and curricular goals. In every case, negotiation was never a waste of time: it is the act itself of teaching; by and large, the effort yields high dividends. A group reflection on the guidelines helps students understand their implications. This forms the basis of a coherent plan, the interiorization of guidelines, and consequently, a successful educative action. A class discussion on meaning that gives rise to the development of a plan is fundamental to learning. This is a crucial point because some teachers feel guilty if they negotiate with their students, as though they would be shirking their duty, which is pushing the content.

There is a time for both basic content and their reflective assimilation within an expressive context. One does not preclude the other. Even at the university level, content should be complemented by the negotiation of the meaning given to this content. A step in this direction has been taken when, in the syllabus, course intentions and evaluation methods are negotiated with the students. When goals are discussed, when instructional organizers or plans are debated, concepts are being assimilated in terms of values relevant to their choices. This helps counteract a situation in which, most often than not, language evaluation is organized in a way that is undemocratic, and even unethical vis-à-vis certain populations (Shohamy, 2004). The explication and negotiation of guidelines act as advanced organizers in the learning process. The synthesis that precedes the educative action builds the initial metaphor.

Concepts are very often understood and assimilated by the metaphoric route. A new concept is initially perceived as a metaphor, i.e., its first representation within the learner's mind is an approximation based on prior knowledge. By going through various approximations, or compare/contrast loops, the learner concretizes her or his knowledge. The teacher's role is to guide the learner through this process, without forcing it. A teacher will spontaneously relate a new concept to the learner's life experience to help her/him grasp its meaning. In an educative production, the students themselves execute this strategy, starting from a reflection on the guidelines. They assimilate the organizers of meaning within an action. The cognitive links they build help them attain increasingly abstract metaphoric levels to the point where they understand the action and its meaning, and the meaning they wish to create using their own potential (an example is provided later in this chapter). Thus, the learners progress to the awareness of their own style and way of understanding. A personal evaluation of their educative action and of their involvement within the action should lead to the discovery of their own life-action and ways to actualize it. When students plan, they may be weighing their own potential and channeling it into concrete acts.

Reflective Taxonomies Linked to Talk in Interaction

Let us now focus on the knowledge, comprehension, application, analysis, synthesis, and evaluation of the guidelines and results of an educative action. These operations stem from the steps of a gradual evolution toward self-evaluation. To follow up, we will examine the development of the learner's metacognitive evaluation. The difficulty related to the development of authentic learning is brought to light, as well as how the teacher in an institutional situation is compelled to combine incompatible functions, as, for example, in the act of evaluating.

Researchers analyzing "talk-in-interaction" have inquired into how learners' relationships with their peers in classroom contexts (Hellermann, 2008). Others have examined how learners socialize into particular language practices and are socialized by the teacher's discursive patterns (Hall, 2010). This type of study is to establish what connections exist between classroom talk and world language learning, often expressed in the form of guidance. In sociocultural theory, guidance in realizing tasks and solving problems is designated as mediation. It regulation can be provided by others or by the self in the form of private speech (Lantolf & Thorne, 2006; Poehner, 2008). Mediation is stimulated through non linguistic signs such as symbols, visual signs and gesture as well as linguistic signs, and it is then designated as semiotic mediation. The semiotic environment (or *Umwelt*) influences all communication processes including language learning itself. Therefore researchers who want to analyze classroom talk must take into account the sociocultural perceptions of the participants about their respective roles and situate their analysis of interactions into the larger semiotic and cultural frames of institutional beliefs shared by the group participants (Thoms, 2012).

The educative project allows the construction of meaning on the basis of a collective choice. It enriches the learning experience by multiplying the interrelations; it favors authentic learning in action over the straightforward transmission of contents and necessitates an ongoing evaluation. The example "Dungeons and Spelling Dragons" in Chapter 3 (Figures 3.6 to 3.9) is a case in point; students had to continually weigh the impact of their writing on a potential reader/protagonist. This educative project can be categorized among those that regard evaluation as a dimension that is inherent in their realization and where the intentions and processes of evaluation are multiple and varied. Self- and peer evaluations then form the very basis of the project development.

The issues discussed here are related to the functional validity of a complex planning model. The "Dungeons and Spelling Dragons" production has enabled the students to develop the self-evaluation competence demanded by the enterprise itself. This competence worked at many levels, since "Dungeons and Spelling Dragons" encompassed, in the order of simple to complex, the following aspects of self-evaluation:

-a technical process: self-monitoring the spelling and syntax in written communication with the help of the teacher, of peers, reference manuals, and on-line resources. To facilitate this task, an evaluation rubric that included the most common difficulties was available to the students for revising their own texts and those of their peers;

-a descriptive process: self-regulating the coherence within characters and settings; the students wrote character sketches and settings which they later integrated into the sequences of the story;

-a narrative process: self-regulating the coherence, the adopted scenario, and the narrative structure; the class had previously done some work on the analysis and construction of simple story schemas and story grammars; at this level of the production, notions previously learned were being applied;

-a communicative process: judging the usefulness of one's work for others, regulating the motivation of peers in novelling their own adventure, stating clear and comprehensible instructions on how to get from one point to another;

-a teaching process: applying rules to the construction of exercises and constructing evaluative and corrective sequences. The students had to communicate their intentions clearly and they were guided in this by the basic planning guidelines (Figures 2.6 to 2.8 in Chapter 2); the construction of exercises required the assimilation of rules and making planning decisions (A paradox was created since the students were asked to adopt a "structural" learning strategy that targeted problem areas while they were involved in an expressive project based on the development of situated competences).

-a global process: regulating the smooth integration of inner levels of the story and the coherence of one sequence (1/3 of the hero's day) with what precedes it and what follows it in touch with the peer-authors. This level of self-evaluation corresponds to the organizational level of the Hol-Act.

A more detailed description would surely add more items to this list. An analysis is inevitably colored by its modelization; this can hide or create paradoxes whose dynamic synergy is revealed in the field. Such is the case for the formative and summative functions of evaluation; they are opposites in theory, but may often be fused in practice. Summative evaluation generally takes the form of a report made at the end of a unit, followed by the introduction of a new theme. It is graded and has accreditation purposes, usually based on a normative referent; thus, it is selective since it generally draws comparisons between the students (although the summative norms of a passing grade may be sometimes criterion-referenced). Formative evaluation is, in principal, intermediate. It proposes a non-graded but often highly annotated learning process; it is characteristically criterion-referenced and includes one or more remedial phases. Limits of these models of evaluation will be emphasized hereafter. Particularly, it is not sure that summative evaluations in themselves support this higher level of learning: autonomous reflexive evaluation. Reflexive evaluation does not break with the existing models of evaluation, but is rather their logical extension.

This approach to a highly motivating evaluation has received strong support from empirical studies (Reeve, Deci & Ryan, 2004). It is the foundation for major aspects of the Deep Approach. Let us see now how it applies to evaluation. The next two sections examine how teachers can resolve the pitfalls of projects' evaluations in an era of standardized performance assessment.

Evaluating Students' Deep Learning

Alternative procedures have made inroads into world language evaluation. Ross (2005) studied differential language learning growth related to formative assessment, compared with conventional summative assessment. The eight-year longitudinal study (N=2215) growth curves, ratios, and covariate-adjusted gains indicate that alternative formative assessments « yield substantive skill-specific effects on language proficiency growth compared to traditional approaches to assessment. » (p.317) Saito & Fujita (2009) examined (a) the similarities and differences between instructor and peer assessments of L2 group presentations; (b) the utility of peer assessment for discriminating each person's contribution to shared presentations; and they investigated (c) the relationship between the quality of a group product and group cooperation, as measured by peer assessments. The results indicate an overall similarity between peer and instructor assessments. Most group members succeeded in differentiating the degree of each member's contribution to the group project. While caution is advised, these results were encouraging for using peer assessment in group presentations.

Tests often tend to reinforce a surface approach to learning (Newstead & Findlay, 1997). While many teaching methods encourage higher-level thinking, testing often reinforces memorizing rather than critical reflection, the way project-based essays would do (Connor-Greene, 2000). Despite psychological expertise in assessing students' performance, the length of a large number of multiple-choice items cues students to the correct response. Evaluation techniques rarely meet the most basic principles of assessment: they lack standardization, reliability, predictive validity, freedom from bias or manipulation, and fairness; moreover, assessment often has a negative effect on learners (Newstead, 2002; MacSwan & Mahoney, 2008). Since testing does not support conceptual understanding and most often prevents deep learning, language teachers should learn how to support the autonomy of their students, increasing their level of achievement through self-determination (Reeve, 2002). To support student autonomy, teachers should provide resources for a variety of choices and a meaningful rationale for each, as well as acknowledging students' desires (Zinkiewicz, Hammond & Trapp, 2003). Projects are forms of alternative assessments; therefore, the principles of empowerment evaluation apply here (Fetterman, Kaftarian & Wandersman, 1996). Deep evaluation is empowering the apprentice.

The evaluation logic currently used in the educational system is based upon formal criteria that need to be identical for all students. Criterion reference requires an effort to formalize the expectations in terms that can be compared. The 'learning products' need to reach a quality threshold that can be measured by behavioral observations. Such standardization provides a normative perspective because its purpose is to make sure that all students have reached the basics.

In this regard, the deep process perspective allows for a criterion-referenced evaluation if needed; however, it provides a very different view of learning. It has to match a socio-affective taxonomy unifying heart, mind, and emotions in action. The evaluation is on quality processes, and the criteria are adapted to each project. Teachers provide abundant input and resources, and learners develop their own creative projects, so that no real comparisons are possible, except possibly on a scale of engagement. The large variety of possible outputs from a curriculum input is such that assessment changes its role: it focuses on meaningful relevance, rather than formalism. If criterion-referenced rubrics are used to rate accomplishments, it is through a flexible appreciation, including self-appreciation and peer-appreciation of how students or groups of students realize their own projects. It cannot be a surface assessment based on the observation of performances. It focuses on relevance with high-stakes creative action. It parallels flow learning (Csíkszentmihályi, 1998), and empowerment evaluation (Fetterman & Wandersman, 2004).

Optimally, assessments should be integrated within complex tasks that are freely chosen by students. For example, evaluation can be integrated in educative projects that provide choices around many possible finished products and the form they will take (Williams, Saizow, & Ryan, 1999). This form of integrated assessment would go by the principles of attribution theory, self-efficacy theory and identity investment for autonomous and motivating learning. These theories, confirmed by numerous studies, indicate that students are highly motivated when they understand and are responsible for what they are doing. Therefore, their level of production and its quality will increase.

An in-depth review of the literature on language learner attitudes, perceptions and beliefs has been proposed by Wesely (2012). Such research often attempts at correlating attitudes with certain features such as anxiety, self-efficacy and motivation, or certain outcomes such as enjoyment, achievement and proficiency. Other studies have focused on teaching practices, as they reflect or not on learner attitudes, perceptions, and beliefs in the language program. When language teachers share their beliefs with the learners about their approach, the students' beliefs tend to mirror those of their teacher after the class is over. Intercultural inquiry (Altstaedter & Jones, 2009), project-based learning (Mills, 2009) and tutoring feedback focusing on deeper understanding of language (Matthews, 2010) enhance learner attitudes and self-efficacy. The language programs based on these premises produce positive results. Thus, project-based learning takes its energy from learners' intrinsic motivation and self-determination (Liu, Wang, Tan, Ee & Koh, 2009). Students can choose their forms of assessment. It will meet students' needs for relationships, autonomy, competence and identity building (Deci et al. 1991).

The Reflexive Function of Level Evaluation

In the education system, evaluation rubrics focus on disciplinary contents, rarely on the interdisciplinary transfer of knowledge, and almost never on transdisciplinary experience. Evaluation has inherited a normative mandate, made evident by an implicit control revealed through content: socially acceptable knowledge and values; competences and aptitudes that are sanctioned; desired behaviors and attitudes. Traditional evaluation favors measurable goals. Aims that remain unmeasured remain, de facto, undervalued. For example, it is difficult to subject autonomy to an evaluative instrumentation because it cannot be "guided" by the criteria of a grid (even a self-evaluative one). Does it mean that autonomy is not a worthwhile goal? It is not valued in the present state of public and private Education. Goals pertaining to the transdisciplinary level are controlled through disciplinary intentions that transmit implicit transdisciplinary values. Given that evaluation models have a prescriptive function, it is important to question the values that could possibly be linked to transdisciplinary expression. Critical competences are engaged in evaluation and to ignore these might incur the neglect of their development in students. The repercussions of this paradox are sufficiently important to merit closer attention.

The transdisciplinary level of education reaches beyond schooling and influences control and knowledge of self and of the conditions that underlie the enactment of knowledge. The conditions for this emergence can be organized, but this emergence cannot truly be targeted as such. It relates to another kind of evaluation and validation that cannot be predetermined. In the transdisciplinary domain, the establishment of criteria may be contraindicated since it could lead to indoctrination. In last analysis, evaluation could not be transdisciplinary; providing evaluation criteria for transdisciplinary development would be tantamount to contradicting the very nature of autonomy.

This paradox relates to the complications described by Ronald Laing (1967), and to Paul Watzlawick's (1978) "double binds". A more detailed analysis of transdiscipline will shed some light on this contradiction, which is hardly different from what incited Elliot Eisner (1998) to affirm that goals of expression are not evaluable.

Transdiscipline is a curriculum category. Its teaching definition, given in Chapter 4, corresponds to the attempt to activate spontaneous, socially situated experiential awareness and self-knowledge in students. In cognitive psychology, contextual knowledge (the "when" and "why" of learning) pertains to the triggering conditions and context of the procedures acting on specific declarative knowledge. The knowledge of contexts suited to certain types of decisions is a reflective activity that involves self-knowledge and self-mastery, as well as the knowledge and control of strategies. In other words, students achieve transdisciplinary functioning when they reject automatism and think independently. They are creating, rather than repeating, what they already know. Innovation does not easily conform to preset criteria without compromising itself. For this reason, evaluation at the transdisciplinary level is reflective and personal. It belongs to the student. It extends beyond the curriculum framework, and at the same time, represents its realization.

Limits of Instructional Design and Education Policy

The paradox just described is one of the many paradoxes in the education system that teachers must face every day. The public school system would seem to have been built upon anti-institutional ideals (like self-realization) that predate formal instruction (Gusdorf, 1963). The relative stability of the system rests upon the balance between independence and conformity. One logical conclusion to this analysis is that educational institutions resist truly educative, potentially high-risk forces by means of an evaluation that promotes conformity (because it functions on the basis of comparability or on the preselection of criteria). Hence, for example, the articulation of standards. To create a transdisciplinary evaluation would impose conformity on autonomy; this is a self-contradicting equation.

It would be wiser to instead consider a flexible model that targets, at key moments, a student's emancipation by the construction of knowledge within an autonomous action. This stimulates the emergence of reflective evaluation within each student. A student's level of awareness increases. In the aftermath of two decades' worth of idealization, everyone would recognize the foolishness of formalizing transdisciplinarity into a universal model. However, organizing the favorable conditions for this type of development is valid, even knowing that this occurrence is rare, restricted, and difficult to recapture.

To suggest transdisciplinary organizers is to test the limits of didactical logic and even negate it when meaning becomes interiorized and personal. It appears that the evaluation relevant to the development of transdisciplinary goals is individual reflection, i.e. the individual's control over her or his own learning processes, of her or his "becoming". To support this, the body of evaluative research showing the frequent failure of attempts to teach strategies could be cited (cf. Weinstein, Goetz & Alexander, 1988): individual tend to use only those strategies developed by themselves.

When I was researching how language teachers were handling task domains and their grammar of action at the time they were offering much autonomy to the learners, I noticed suspension points in their design: at some point their instructional design would stop and remain open-ended, to leave the decision of the next instructional step to the learner. I named these suspension points "unorganizers" (Tochon, 1991a, 1993b). It was not a matter of creating chaos through which a new, learner-directed order might emerge: it was more like deliberate empty slots, "unplanning" in the instructional matrix creating the necessary flexibility that would allow learners to take initiatives. As we have seen in Chapter 6 when discussing motivation and identity research, students' personal development seems directly related to the measure of decision-making they are given. At every stage of an educative project, the guidelines correspond to decisional operations. In an open system, decisional operations receive input, or information—in this case, guidelines and production output or decisions that operate at the core of the holistic action. The decision-making processes are guided by the nature of the project.

The idea of the hol-act and its pragmatic organizers fits within a paradigmatic change that affects evaluation as well. Some examples that illustrate this difference are: the passage toward a more situated, qualitative focus; the consideration of the complex and fluctuating realities of interactions; the obsolescence of rigid structures, closed systems, prescriptive theories.... A redefinition of evaluation is called for, one that takes into account the coexistence of school systems with open, personal systems. Institutional necessity imposes criteriation and normalization. Criteriation consists of establishing criteria for purposes of evaluation. Normalization is defined here as the act of leading an individual to conform to a group by means of successive comparisons (in evaluation, it corresponds to the notion of a normative reference).

The idea that the institutional forms of assessment, such as prognostic, formative or summative evaluations might trigger reflections on declarative, procedural or contextual aspects of knowing is generalized as a principle, while such process is always tentative (see figure 8.1). The rigid model of assessment has side-effects and creates a conforming mold, but its socializing mode meets major goals of schooling. Even knowing that summative and formative evaluations partly miss the point, it would be impossible to eradicate them without causing serious difficulties in the education system.

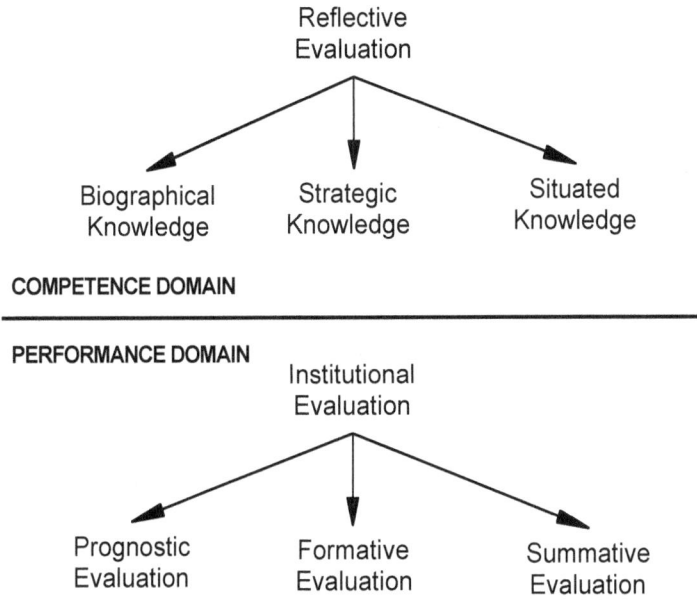

Figure 8.1 A Question of Values
The imperfect match between school evaluation and life-anchored knowledge (Tochon, 2013).

Nevertheless, a place must be made for what some have called the highest achievement of education, the possibility of "something else" outside the system, denoting the flashes of autonomy and of the true creation of meaningfulness. In a sense, what is proposed here is to integrate some of the best aspects of homeschooling as regards learning autonomy within an institutional framework. Generalizing this otherness may not be fully doable; it is feasible, however, to refrain from blocking its possible emergence. Evaluation is an abstraction, regardless of the prevailing paradigm; that even in a numerical form, it is a rationalist idealization, resulting from the projection of structured values onto an evaluated object. Consequently, teachers are wise to be aware of their own prejudices and of the values that may be disseminated by instrumentation, and to choose a functional, empiric, and heuristic system of evaluation. They should feel free to adapt the analytical tools proposed for instruction.

A more integrative and situated model of evaluation that matches experiential learning is presented in figure 8.2. It indicates that both declarative and procedural knowledge are highly context-dependent and influenced by biographic (diachronic) knowledge as well as contextual knowledge present within the interactional situation. Biographic and situated knowledge together constitute the experiential knowledge proper to language apprenticeship.

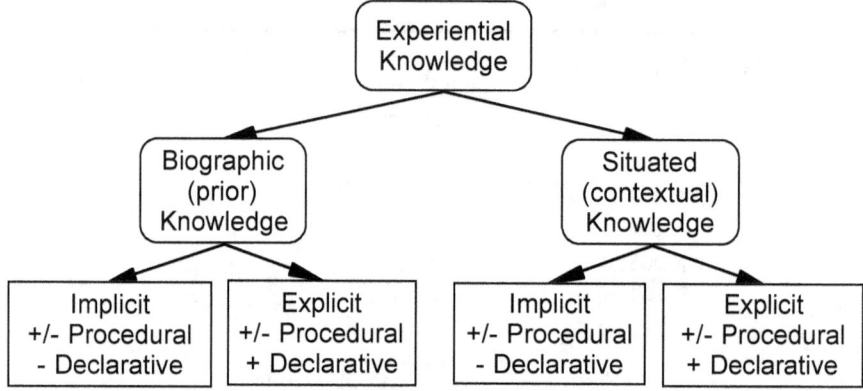

Figure 8.2
Experiential Model Integrating Evaluation and Apprenticeship
(Tochon, 2003)

In an educative project, the management of guidelines involves an evaluation of the activities as they unfold. This type of evaluation works at all levels of the project. In the main, it focuses on the interaction between levels of knowledge. Each task level is an interactive context for another level. Undoubtedly, the self-evaluative management of guidelines in the course of the educative production fills a function that is transdisciplinary (personal and social) and neither prognostic, formative, or summative. This deep function is reflective; it deals with the knowledge and control of oneself and of the learning process. It does not contradict the school functions of evaluation—it simply pertains to another kind of reality. Comparatively speaking, the school functions of evaluation define the sphere of performance, whereas its reflective function pertains to the area of competence. These two orders of reality can be complementary; however, performance assessment should not be organized in a way that doesn't enhance reflection.

We have seen in this section that evaluation must fill a new role; otherwise, it will maintain the conditions of shallow learning. Self-assessment then becomes important, in addition to introspective agreements with the self.

Apprenticeship and Instructional Agreements

The learner is given the floor and the initiative of curriculum decisions; this is of the utmost importance in the Deep Approach. If this condition is not met, learning may rely upon the usual shallow approaches. This principle (placing the learner as curriculum-builder) distinguishes the Deep Approach from most of the current literature on project-based learning (PjBL—Beckett, 2006); often, teachers impose their project on students—this is NOT an approach conducive to deep learning! Initiative can be prepared and scaffolded; prior agreements can be negotiated between the teacher and the apprentice. However, the major agreement is to take place within the learner and his or her own self. The agreement to go consistently deeper in the approach of the target language and culture, investing time and effort from an intrinsic, deliberate and independent impulse, is more important than the rubric's criteria, which is formally written for the sake of classroom management. The agreement with the Self will make the approach deep. It will place the learner as apprentice with an understanding that learning will be self-directed (Knowles, 1975).

Daudelin (1996, p. 70), a specialist of instructional contracts, emphasizes that in any type of agreement, the importance is "the process of stepping back from an experience to ponder, carefully and persistently, its meaning to the self through the development of inferences". Daudelin's review of more than a hundred studies on instructional contracts for self-directed learning and their goals indicates that authors of instructional contracts often use such points as:

- I am/We are going to learn about X and my/our goal is Y.
- I/We will learn it through the following resources using the following strategies:

- I/We will be in charge of the following tasks:
- My/Our project will bring evidence or my/our learning in the following way:
- My/Our learning can be verified with the following criteria for each task:
- I/We intend to complete the work by Z:

"In essence, self-directed learning is seen as any study form in which individuals have primary responsibility for planning, implementing, and even evaluating the effort" (Šliogerienė, 2006, p. 110).

When the rationale for the Deep Approach has been thoroughly explained to the students, they usually agree that their preference is to be able to choose their type of work, their themes, their way of approaching language techniques, and that they wish to remain as close as possible to their central life interests. They most generally love the idea of being the ones responsible for their learning; however, they often want to make sure resources, scaffolding, and flexible instructional organization are ready-made for them to choose from and build upon. In addition, self-directed learning within projects makes it possible for instructors to accommodate different styles of students, from those who have traditional requirements within a major language focus to those more open to creativity and intercultural exchanges. They first need to choose their orientation, build their learning project, and the teacher brings the necessary resources and support.

Alternative forms of assessments are more powerful than traditional forms of norm-referenced evaluation. Criterion reference can handle complexity and thoroughness, treat open and creative questions, and address proficiency. The evaluation criteria can be explored, discussed, negotiated, reworked cooperatively, serving as guides in the accomplishment of projects, and establishing the scale of achievement. The negotiated criteria can form the basis for instructional agreements. Such contracts, even informal, help plan, structure, and personalize the learning process (Šliogerienė, 2006). These agreements can be oral, audio recorded, e-mailed or handwritten, internet-based, pre-formatted, or assembled in the form of tables and criterial rubrics.

Writing a prior agreement creates a favorable condition for real apprenticeship. It promotes a deep, reflexive attitude towards learning. Developing a genuine and personal understanding of the subject matter is central for deep learning. Keeping a log of activities or writing a diary can help link prior knowledge to the current apprenticeship (Liuoliene & Metiuniene, 2009). Writing forces learners to clarify their thinking and is a way to re-enforce an understanding of one's intentions and actions, providing powerful feedback; the writing process becomes quickly self-sustainable and self-motivational, as it clarifies the direction of initial intentions (Doly, 2004). Learning agreements help develop reflective strategies through self-assessment and self-management, a metacognitive training that is conducive to a better level of listening, including listening to the self (Goh, 2008). Quality self-reflection requires training and coached reflection on experience; that is, reflection with feedback (Anseel, Lievens & Schollaert, 2009; Gühn, 2010). Additionally, peer assisted learning is crucial to develop good metacognitive assessments, even when students have individual projects (Shamir, Mevarech & Shamir, 2009).

The advantages of clarifying learning agreements are as follow: (a) proposing a needs-based diagnostic, clarifying the focus; (b) encouraging independent apprenticeship; (c) helping students to structure information and monitor their progress, reflect on their goals, and work at their own pace; (d) teaching how to be synthetic and use metacognitive skills. In summary, projects integrate some features that capture learners' interest and increase motivation: They offer authentic, collaborative challenges over which learners have control; they are realistic and can be accomplished within the limits of the academic schedule; their realization creates real-world accomplishments that can give rise to performance, and can involve social, literary, cultural, aesthetic, or political action. Their results are visible, which sustains motivation, and are compatible with various forms of alternative assessments, such as performance-based assessment. The learners see the link between what they did for their project and the grades they earned.

To sum up, deep projects are framed by a unified taxonomy. Students reflect critically on the coherence between their actions, the tasks that their project involves, and their sense of self. Their increased knowledge of who they are is a powerful stimulus in the accomplishment of projects. Indeed, projects lead students to question why they are doing certain things, and what is good, sound, and fascinating for them. Projects imply a search for the social self, and in this respect, contribute to identity building. They will be even more effective if students can attribute success to their own efforts, anchor their confidence in their abilities to do what they need to do, and perceive that they have the necessary skills to progress in this direction.

Avoid Dogmatisms

It would be possible to argue that the reflective function of evaluation is inseparable from its formative function. Formative evaluation, in effect, integrates several aspects of open system principles: retroaction, regulation by error, consideration of interaction, orientation toward a goal, and relevance. However, formative evaluation has been accused of being reductive, instrumentalist, and linear (Daniel Bain, a specialist of formative assessment expressed: "I denounce the instrumental delusion of which formative evaluation boasts in current practice. I am calling for its complete integration into a psychopedagogical perspective, within a theoretical model of the functioning of the student who is in interaction with an object (subject, concept) to be taught; and I am calling for its complete insertion into a teaching strategy"). Reductionisms arise from the education system's principles governing measurable performances. Even though formative evaluation is more likely to stimulate metacognitive learning than summative evaluation, it belongs to another order—that of the school system.

In a junior high or a high school setting, there are few hours available for the teaching of individual subjects; due to the necessity of grading students within a relatively brief time, the school functions of evaluation tend to merge. Teachers' graded summative evaluations are often used for purposes of diagnosis and remedial intervention. Formative evaluations are based on criteria derived from an initial comparison of students' results. These practices, heretical in theory, seem functional nonetheless. Practice often contradicts theory or calls for its revision. Take, for example, the case of a teacher who revises, after the fact, her/his evaluation criteria according to normative referents to counteract a high rate of failure. Institutional evaluations mess up teachers' flexible and adaptive approaches of assessments.

The analysis of the difficulties endemic to the application of evaluation models could be pushed further yet, if only to ease the mind of worried teachers. Normally, a distinction is made between criterion and normative referents, making these categories of reference illogical. In practical terms, the teacher may develop a scale of evaluation before assessing the students based on predetermined criteria, or after, by comparing students' results. A criterion referent creates a regular scale defined by preestablished criteria. A thorough analysis of concrete examples of application reveals that a teacher who uses criteria ultimately applies a normalizing curve at the heart of those criteria. In other words, the designation of minimum levels of acquisition is useless to the teacher if it does not provide clear information on the seriation of subjects; then the evaluative placement of students, as well as their distribution on the criterial scale, retains its relevance. For example, a high-school teacher who notices that all her students have achieved the level of knowledge mastery would then tend to recalibrate the scale to obtain criteria that are more selective. The teacher who establishes criteria by which to evaluate an upcoming test will refer to her existing scales for the purpose comparing the students among themselves. This is because a fair set of criteria in a selective system must be based on adequate seriation. This proves that the criterial ideal tends to model itself on institutional functioning inasmuch as student populations remain constant (no great differences form one year to the next). In conclusion, criteria are always set on the basis of a sample population, this being the definition itself of a normative frame of reference.

This does not mean that the establishment of criteria and rubrics must be avoided, nor that reflecting on criteria is a wasted effort. Being conscious of the impossibility of obtaining "pure" categories can conquer the lure of proselytizing dogmatics. All theories are limited. Theoretical cogitation is a tool, an imperfect one to the minds of practitioners, but a valuable tool nonetheless. For decades, theories in teaching have come to the fore at the expense of existing ones, although there is no proof that those earlier ones were any less perfect than their successors. This book is an attempt to show that a better understanding of the possibilities produced by the actualization of theories will lead teachers to regard theories as working tools that are complementary rather than irreconcilable. Theory in practice would be the teacher's inductive mental model.

Experienced practitioners indicate that, in evaluation, the prognostic, summative, and formative functions are far from independent and exclusive in the reality of the classroom. These categories are useful in an analysis of who is doing what, why, and how in matters of evaluation. Here however, as in all categorization, care must be taken to avoid a rigid fixation. For example, a meticulous teacher who is preparing a formative evaluation grid would work hard at choosing the goals and standards to be evaluated. Yet this laboriously constructed instrument may be swept away within a few minutes of interaction and prove inadequate if the experience of the class has evolved since the instrument of evaluation was designed. In practice, a teacher quickly learns to rapidly construct instruments that are short-lived; it is still recommended that these instruments be constructed to correspond to the targeted goals.

The discourse on the teaching efficiency that underlies evaluation may hide a movement to water down the selective system. One may find this discourse reassuring until one attempts to apply it. In fact, it imposes a regulative predictive frame that is difficult to manage according to what happens in the classroom. It can be helpful in some circumstances, but this regulative frame could hinder the teacher if the instrumentation is too cumbersome. Teaching has never been a simple matter. The timeliness of instrumentation is generally recognized and few people would dare to contest the good sense of the continued regulation of learning. Institutional evaluations imposed by the states such as 'No Child Left Behind' have a distinct function. Name it a political function. They do not seem to have any usefulness to anyone but in destroying the humane dimension of the public education system, which can benefit private capital.

To be sure, exaggerations should be withheld. For example, the generalization of evaluation grids and rubrics is potentially dangerous. It runs the risk of turning the idea of differentiated and autonomous learning into a socialization process controlled by tiring, repetitive means. It reifies learning. Another risk associated to this type of generalization involves the teacher becoming enslaved to evaluation specialists. Being denied their right to think and to act, teachers would be reduced to handmaidens. The same would apply to students; if they were compelled to check off every autonomous act, mindless activity would be reinforced. Predicting the expected answers might strip students of their right to think. A mechanized approach is geared for intermediate and final tests, whose exaggerated use has been periodically denounced. A student may successfully complete a test on the use of infinitives, but later forgets the same concepts in a written story. This proves the necessity of targeting reflection that stimulates knowledge integration where the school functions of evaluation are concerned. This aim, guardian of the human dimension, hinges on the responsible autonomy of the teacher, her/his professionalism, and intuition.

Autonomy: A Reflective and Complex Phenomenon

There has been a recent recrudescence of interest in complexity and open-systems theory in the field of Applied Linguistics, such that it might be interpreted as the next wave, or next main stream conceptual framework, succeeding to but compatible with neoconstructivism and sociocultural theory. For example, Diane Larsen-Freeman (2012) indicates the advantages to adopt thematic views that transcend the disciplinary borders. She emphasizes the current need for change away from sequential and linear conceptions of instruction, and the necessary opening to multiple paths that adapt to interactions within a dynamic view of language development: "complexity is creative" she mentions (p.207), taking a stand against preformativism ("there is not pre-set patterns", ibid). Larsen-Freeman quotes Whitehead's (1978, p. 339) Process and reality: "Order is not sufficient." As has been demonstrated from the beginning of this book, complex systems dynamics is the integrative factor that explains why rhizomatic thematic connections across task domains stimulate deep language learning. The next pages analyze the role of evaluation from this perspective.

Deep, reflective evaluation is an ongoing activity; it can emerge from prognostic, formative, or summative processes. The evaluation of learning through learning includes not only retroaction cycles, but the principle of autonomy as well. "AUTO" (reference) belongs to the rank of turbulent retroactive cycles" (Morin, 1980, p. 259). It is based in a complex set of causes that cannot be reduced to the straightforward plan of one formative evaluation (see Figure 8.3). This evaluation is holistic, not being limited only to keeping track of errors; it manages "noise" in a productive and multidimensional way, since any growth in complexity is the driving force behind knowledge expansion.

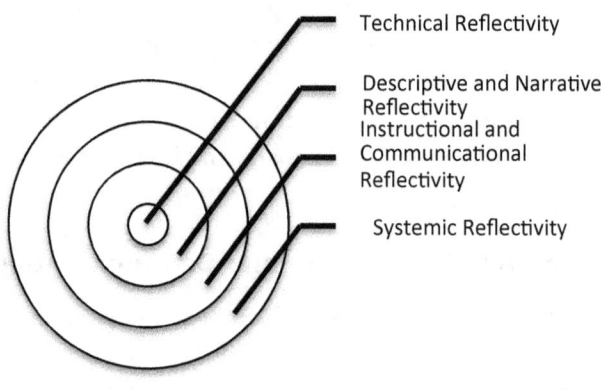

Figure 8.3
Reflective Regulation Levels

Aside from globalism, the autonomy principle and its complex causality, this reflective evaluation permits the management of production via stratified aggregates. For example, in thermodynamic systems, action plans are neguentropic emergences regulating entropy (or disorder) in a constant dynamic of flux. Phase I manifests entropy, which is disorganized energy. Without an action plan, human groups demonstrate such disorganized fluctuations. In Figure 8.4, the little waves represent fluctuations that are first dissipative and entropic, and get organized through direction. In Phase II, system fluctuations are modulated, and a structuring flow suggests plans of action that smooth the dissipative fluctuations. Phase III sees the opening of the system. Concordances or agreements across fluctuations stimulate an evolution within the system. Its complexity breaks prior boundaries. Phase IV results from the system opening. The system dissipates its inner entropy through production processes that exteriorize entropy. This organized flow of energy, named neguentropy, is a balancing factor. It creates a situation which becomes self-regulatory in Phase V. Channeled energy is reaching its environment, which stimulates self-organization and a reorganization. Phase VI (back to square I), in the emptiness of post-production, marks a new phase of entropy within the systemic flow. Indeed, without an action plan, the system comes back to entropy.

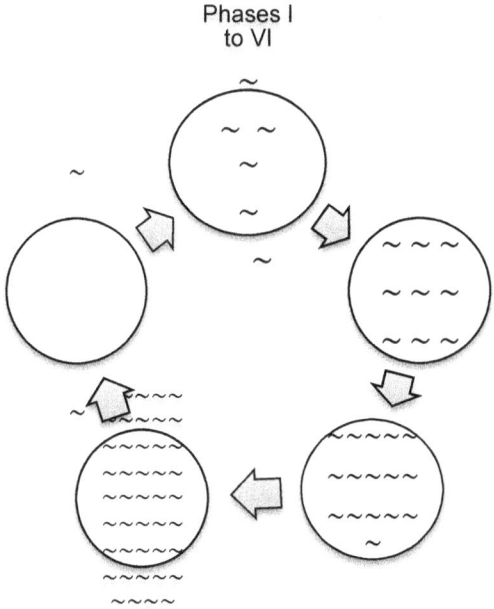

Figure 8.4
The Action Plan: A Metaphor of the Physical World

The principle of entropy, or disorder within a system, is contravened by the informational nature of intrinsically valued and freely chosen rules and guidelines. This reflective evaluation is directional and forward-looking; it operates simultaneously on many different levels (see figure 8.5).

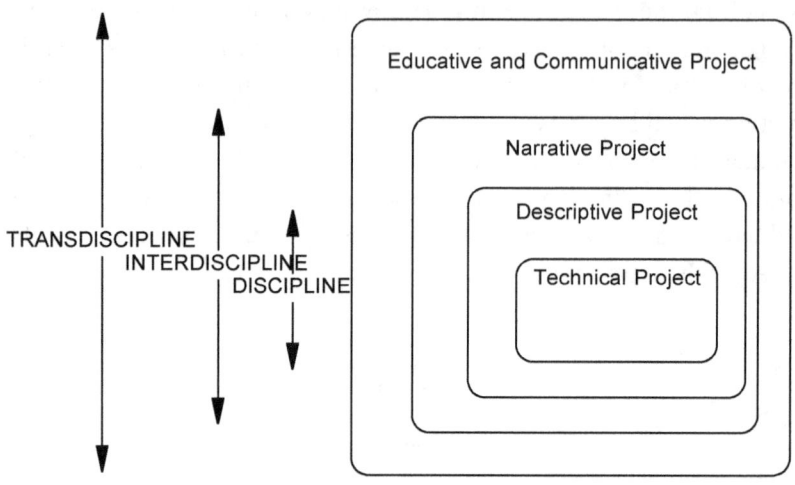

Figure 8.5
The Many Faces of the Hero

The complex end product can never be predicted nor summatively foreseen by anything other than a holistic, approach that motivates its realization. Reflective evaluation is a function of learning. In the presence of heightened awareness, it may be an outgrowth of school evaluation.

To sum up, reflective evaluation is a vital organizing function in an educative process; it regulates activity. Viewed in this way, evaluation is involved at many levels in a reflective model. The feedback dovetails on many planes as shown in Figure 8.5.

The Student Plans for the Protagonist

The linear representation shown above does not adequately depict the complexity of heart and mind involved in concrete action in a classroom setting. The success of the educative production depended upon every student's participation at each of the task levels in an interactive and reflective mode. Every student was compelled to

-engage into active inquiry and search for knowledge (data, methods, meanings);

-link knowledge to life and comprehend (transpose, interpret, make inductions and deductions);
-apply, adapt and integrate;
-frame categories of understanding and analyze (factors, relations, implications, principles of organization);
-conceptualize and synthetize (plan, produce, deduce);
-evaluate (documentation, information, the nature of communication, interactions and action, critical examination both internal and external).

When "Dungeons and Spelling Dragons" was being written by the students, these six operations had to be considered from the protagonist's point of view (see Figure 8.6); knowledge, comprehension, application, analysis, synthesis, and evaluation were mobilized in a practice that led the reader-protagonist to know, comprehend, apply, analyze, synthesize, and evaluate.

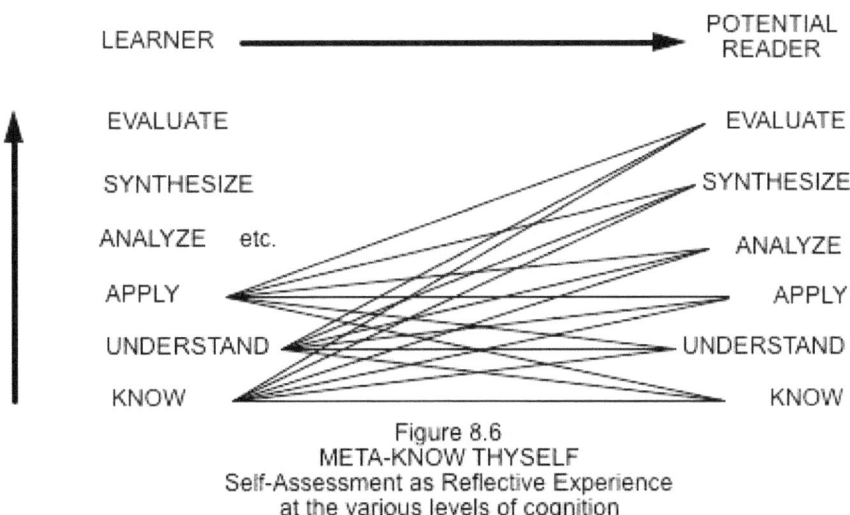

Figure 8.6
META-KNOW THYSELF
Self-Assessment as Reflective Experience
at the various levels of cognition

The students had to know, understand, apply, etc. the knowledge they were teaching. However, they also had to know, comprehend, and anticipate the readers' comprehension, their potential applications, the required analyses and syntheses and, ultimately, the final evaluation. They were therefore called to relate every level of their own skills, abilities, and competences to those of the reader/protagonist. Thus, this educative action is an example of self-evaluation training.

The very definition of an educative project implies a dynamic interrelation that promotes the development of all the reflective levels. This orientation is fulfilling identity growth processes, yet it is not utilitarianist. Indeed Aristotle expressed that the highest values lead to happiness and are disinterested. Their correspondence to the socio-affective levels would then need to be studied, as heart and mind cannot be artificially separated. Does an autonomization project within a group situation promote personal involvement within a positive value system? In the transition from thought to action, there lies the abyss of contingencies, the anarchy of options. In concrete terms, the capacity of evaluation is proportional to the comprehension and shared understanding of the instructional agreement underlying the guidelines' criteria. The action's progression shows that this comprehension is variable and that it develops according to a self-monitoring process, by a progressive enhancement of competence (Figure 8.7).

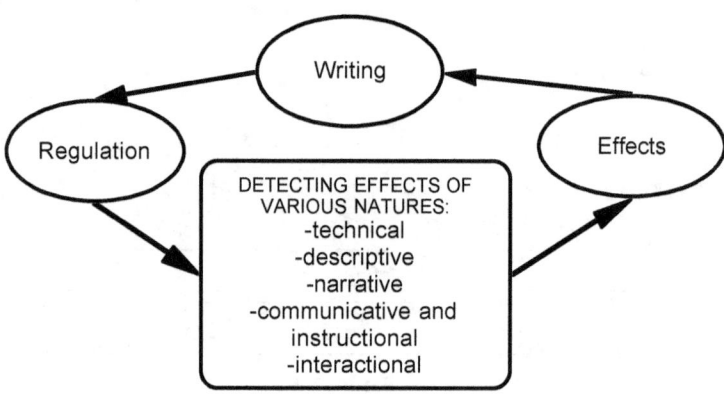

Figure 8.7
Writer's Cramp: Writing Self-Regulatory System

Students create together criteria for their action, which are at the basis of their instructional agreement and map their project as they draft possible guidelines. Then they familiarize themselves with the guidelines, sketch, write, type, or record. They refer again to the guidelines of their instructional agreement. They notice some discrepancies at the technical, descriptive, narrative, communicative, planning, and/or interaction levels. They locate the discrepancies and correct them. That makes their work converge with guidelines again. They are now in a position to go further. The guidelines are reread, reexamined discussed between the students and better understood (transposed and interpreted within their context). The students implement them. Their new writing, typing, or recording creates new discrepancies that are corrected by referring to the guidelines that must be known, understood, and applied in every detail; their factors, association, and organizational principles must be analyzed. Finally, they are synthesized and planned. Everything is then evaluated before proceeding further. In this process, action expands to higher levels of knowledge. Students tend to master guidelines in successive steps of increased comprehension (see Figure 8.8).

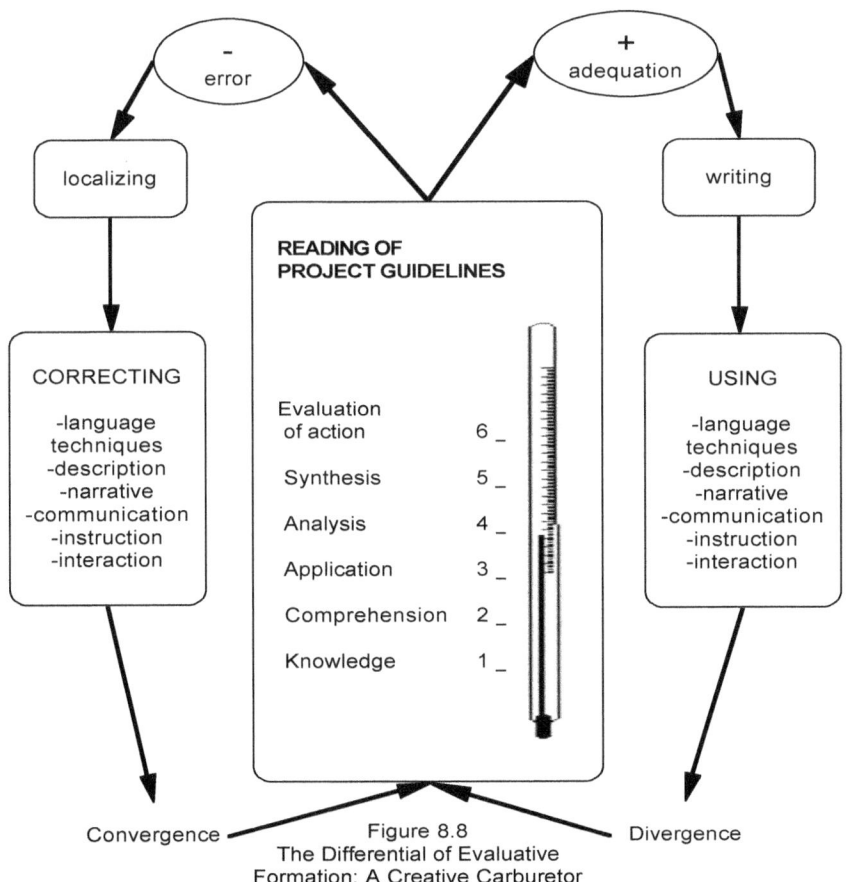

Figure 8.8
The Differential of Evaluative Formation: A Creative Carburetor

Some curriculum specialists propose to organize a diagnostic phase before any project. Students would have to test the guidelines in advance, having a pilot experiment of their instructional agreement. However, it seems difficult to imagine that students could assimilate criteria in a diagnostic phase without having plunged into it first in a real action. In a complex project, the learner cannot realistically organize the necessary competences prior to the actual learning itself. This organization can only be accomplished through extensive practice wrought in the learning process. It is the progressive *differential* development referred to earlier; it appears simultaneously and interactively on many levels of a complex task. The educative project thus conceived and contextualized becomes a differential of formative evaluation. Differential models mark the passage from the learner's knowledge, treatment, and representation to "expert models". The remedial cycle is part of many interactive levels; students learn to improve their self-evaluative competences through numerous, successive readings. The thorough integration of guidelines occurs only after many successive "cycles" of regulation that enable students to deepen their understanding of the chosen action.

No Pain, No Gain
Many Difficulties to Overcome

The level of the work can be reduced to automatism, due to a large measure of practice and taxonomic sliding. However, for an educative project as complex as the one presented here, it could take much longer. The difficulties encountered by the students were spread out in a hierarchy; they pertained to evaluation and mastery at:

- the disciplinary level of contents, pertaining to their focus on language (syntax and spelling),

- the interdisciplinary level of transfer, pertaining to guidelines (ex. converting the "he" guidelines associated to the reader/protagonist to the "you" of the story) and to the descriptive and narrative strategies;

- the transdisciplinary level, pertaining to the relation with peer/reader (intratextual communication) and with peer/author (classmates ensuring the production of the preceding or following text; intertextual and extratextual communication).

The analysis of the class' finished product led to the following conclusions:

1) The instructional organizers relating to disciplinary mastery were generally realized after numerous phases of corrective efforts (interactive and retroactive formative evaluation), even though many students of that age group (13-14 years) have enormous difficulty in avoiding errors, even in copying.

2) The organizers relating to interdisciplinary transfer were achieved more or less satisfactorily. The most arduous phase for the students was in grasping the meaning of the guidelines in all their detail. Many were quick to say that they "got everything" and that they could skip the details of the schema shown in Figures 3.6 to 3.9 of Chapter 3. This incurred some misinterpretations that subsequently had to be revised. Some students made up guidelines or "accidentally" constructed their own schema; which was considered all right, as long they understood the initial project, and their project fit the class' one.

3) The organizers relating to transdisciplinary expression were the most difficult to realize. They pertained to the relation itself; in other words, the relation within an environment, relative to a declared goal, with an active project that is stable yet evolving. The ability to evaluate one's own productions in light of their relation with those of the group was often insufficient. Students who focused on form forgot about function, resulting in a linear series of texts that rarely interacted.

Concluding a partial success should be an incentive to persevere. School should develop high-level processes (analysis, synthesis, and internal and external evaluation). Habitually, many students do not seem to be functioning with their whole potential and motivation. Educating them to analyze and comprehend the meaning of their acts contributes to building a coherent and harmonious collective entity within class projects. Classroom teaching often limits itself to contents and strategies and barely touches upon complex activities and values. This merely fuels the denunciation of the abuse of Cartesian education where causes are emphasized at the expense of function, means and ends are separated for the sake of the "one best way", and the analysis of elements is favored to the detriment of a global outlook. The practice of self-evaluation and reflection must target complex activity, or it will slide into automatism.

In Short

By proposing students various adaptive paths of action through self-determined instructional agreements that they can regulate on their own with the assistance of the teacher who plays an advisory role, educative action projects allow the 5Cs processes to unfold on three levels of self-evaluation:

- self-regulation of disciplinary contents for real communication competences;
- self-regulation of interdisciplinary transfer through comprehension, application, and analysis, thus developing connections and comparative competences;
- self-regulation of transdisciplinary action through synthesis, conceptualizing and cultural re-framing and integration into the larger community, hence developing a reflective competence.

•

Reflection in an open learning project is the basis of evaluative competences—the goal of an education in critical thinking. A differential, evaluative development can take the form of the following model:

A. The integration, within an educative action, of several levels of action and evaluation.

B. The subordination of content to actively engaged strategies.

C. The mapping of the educative action by the creation of regulatory guidelines and an engaged curriculum.

There is usually a tension between instructional flexibility and evaluation aspects of teaching. However, in an educative project, evaluation has to become an integrated part of teaching; its integration is a requisite of a smooth and regulated activity. Shared reflective evaluation that operates on all the taxonomic levels is a fundamental competence to learn, within the project. The creation of criteria for action and reading of guidelines (their knowledge, comprehension, application, analysis, synthesis, and integrative evaluation) will develop within the students work strategies by the organization of contents and competences in engaging situations. Thus, the educative project contributes to the growth of reflection in a way that becomes instrumental in connecting the discipline to life by the integration of increasingly higher levels of tasks into a culture of engagement.

At some point, most learners, as well as teachers, would like to have a reference grid to which they can compare progress, a register of achievements that can be presented to legitimate their learning and teaching. Be it in K-12 schools or at the collegiate level, the academic system requires some form of accountability. We shouldn't try to be too revolutionary on that point because it may still take several decades before humans come to the understanding that we have innate autonomy over our lives and life choices, and we should not need to give an account to anyone but ourselves, as long as our life is compatible with society, and doesn't infringe on the rights of others.

While the Deep Approach would be a delight in the context of the *'free children of Summerhill'*, the proposals in this book are written in a way that makes them compatible with the existing academic systems with their homogenizing pressure, the enforcement of external rules of conduct, and an economically-oriented agenda. The proposals go as far as they can in the direction of freeing young humans from mental slavery, while respecting the functional constraints that keep the system operating within its accountability measures and institutional certifications. Changing this may demand too deep of a change for current society to modify at this stage, while it is true that the institutionalization of values is the seat of oppression, and the certification of competences is the root cause of poverty, as it creates social classes (Illich, 1969).

Within the limited framework that market society imposes, we try to bring some consciousness-raising liberty of action for the learner and the teacher, through the exploration of crucial issues for learning; consequently, we must provide some response to the people concerned by control.

Chapter 9
The Deep Turn Toward Wisdom and Autonomy

We probably have simplified matters too much. We tend to talk about systems thinking and practice as if we knew what they are. The fashionable call for "holistic" or "systems" thinking in ecological issues provides a major example. This much is certain: the quest for comprehensiveness, although it represents an epistemologically necessary idea, is not realizable. If we assume that it is realizable, the critical idea underlying the quest will be perverted into its opposite, i.e., into a false pretension to superior knowledge and understanding. Werner Ulrich (1993, p. 583)

Here is a crucial excerpt from my online article on *Deep Education* (Tochon, 2010b), which had more than 32,000 reads:

Humans are confronted with a choice that Korten (2006) described as, on one hand, the Unraveling with a collapsing environment, violent competition for limited resources, a dieback of the population with a takeover of those who remain by local warlords or, on the other hand, the Turning from imperialism to Earth community, a possibility if we move to a 'politics of consciousness' (*ibid*, p. 43). It consists in moving up from the magical consciousness of people living in dream-like state directed by emotional impulse. Moving out of self-referential and narcissist imperial consciousness, with its primitive sense of justice based on enforcement and retaliation, conforming to the will of authority figures.

Socializing consciousness to share ethical rules of conduct in society, we can internalize cultural norms as well as a sense of community. A sense is developed that security depends upon mutual loyalty. Caring individuals realize what the group interests are and collaborate in this direction. Cultural consciousness then emerges, when the rationales of others can be appreciated in their difference, with the understanding that cultures are social constructs and represents different 'truths'. It constitutes the moral ground for cultural change. The highest expression of this quest for humanity would define spiritual consciousness, which "manifests the awakening to Creation as a complex, multidimensional, interconnected, continuously unfolding whole" (*ibid*, p.47). The transition from cultural consciousness to spirituality would come from the search for deeper, original meanings related to profound encounters with others, each meeting with otherness representing a thorough lesson that gradually increases the awareness that we are connected. Cultural consciousness as well as spiritual consciousness act in favor of a society that is more just, peaceful and mature.

There are some risks at using such heavily connoted wording as 'spiritual consciousness raising' in the context of education (Crossman, 2003). One risk is a return to dualistic stands proper to Platonism; another risk is the resurrection of such elevated educational ideals within obedience networks, which would be just at the opposite of the goal of the present demonstration. Speaking of mindfulness and depth—and meaning it—sound appropriate wording. The word 'depth' should be understood as a continuum rather than an opposition to what 'light' or 'surface' curricula may have been. The directions taken by many disciplines so far have been led by a superficial view of their responsibility towards the world at large and the planet, the humans and the various species who live on it. The deep approach implies a change in scientific ontology. Its integrative ontology does not split the subject from its objects. It takes into account the impacts of the development of objective results on the human subjects, as both subjects and objects are one with their ecosystem. Second, it implies that science and education must shift from a view that is in the main quantitative to creating a world in which quality prevails as evaluated on the scale of deep human values such as social justice, ecological respect, fair information and communication, truthfulness, care for others, intrinsically motivated effort towards improvement, non-interference unless requested.

The Deep Turn for Cross-cultural Understanding

The American Council on the Teaching of Foreign Language's Standards for Foreign Language Learning in the 21st Century describe what "language students should know and be able to do" (2006, p.13). The eleven content standards are divided in five goal domains called the 5C's: Communication, Cultures, Connections, Comparisons, and Communities which represent "facets of language use" with the Culture C being the overarching standard (Byrnes, 2008, p. 106). The 2007 report "Foreign Languages and Higher Education: New Structures for a Changed World" from the Modern Language Association (MLA) calls for the adoption of curricula that increase the translingual and transcultural competence of a broad interdisciplinary range of students. Ideal curricula "situate language study in cultural, historical, geographic, and cross-cultural frames" which is the type of work done in holistic projects or hol-acts; they "systematically incorporate transcultural content and translingual reflection at every level" (MLA Ad Hoc Committee on Foreign Languages, 2007, p. 5) Both the Standards and the 2007 MLA Report recommend that language and culture be taught in an interconnected way. Yet the way to do it is often considered fuzzy and elusive, while clearly intercultural sensitivity is the *raison d'être* of foreign language learning.

While the Communication standard has taken the fore due to the implementation and piloting of the Integrated Performance Assessment (IPA, Glisan, Adair-Hauck, Koda, Sandrock & Swender, 2003) that measures students' interpretive, interpersonal and presentational modes of communication, Schulz (2007) has developed an evaluation framework based on Byram's model of intercultural competence. It is not certain how IPA can be extended to the assessment of Culture in K-16 programs, though (Troyan, 2012). The rebalancing of proficiency and cultural knowledge requires new ways of teaching culture. The National Standards Impact Study (Abbott & Phillips, 2011) reports that most teachers surveyed teach culture in English. Reshaping culture learning into inquiry projects in the hands of the learners might be appealing to the ACTFL designers, if they come to the understanding that increasing evaluation control on complex matters may be at the cost of learning depth. This aspect is equally valid for a deep acquisition of culture (Shaules, 2007).

One goal of the Deep Approach is the internationalization of the mind for better understanding and peace building across cultures. Language is the conduit for connectedness of humanity across continents, nations, cultures and subcultures, allowing speakers to connect the dots and gather the pieces of the puzzle of life that were dispersed due to cultural, epistemological and political fragmentation. I found a reflection of this understanding in the work of the Japanese peace builder Daisaku Ikeda (2010).

Value Creation as one Aspect of the Deep Approach

Ikeda has been a proponent of world language education within the ideal of a human revolution through value creation (or *Soka*). He helped develop a network of *Soka Schools,* which is growing in Asia and in the West, in which language education, guided by Buddhist philosophy, promotes world peace and a form a neohumanism. In the same way Paolo Freire's ideas have applications outside Christian liberation theology, Daisaku Ikeda's proposals have value outside Buddhism. I am interested here in the value of this model for a Deep Approach of languages and cultures. For Ikeda, learning languages allows people to engage in cultural encounters and exchanges:

> "I strongly encourage all of the new students to unremittingly challenge language learning as a steady spiritual struggle toward emitting the light of peace. Learning languages allows you to understand people's hearts, diverse values, and the cultures and histories of countries; it is a direct connection to the path of peace." (Ikeda, 2003, vol 13, p. 27 in Goulah's translation, 2012, p. 6)

Critical Inquiry in Language Studies dedicated a double special issue (vol. 9, 1-2) to Ikeda's theory and work, arguing that his model, akin to Byram's (2003) intercultural acting, transcends simple intercultural being (Goulah, 2012). Ikeda's model appears very compatible with and complementary to deep language learning. It seems that the Deep Approach is the missing element in Ikeda's methodology, as the links he established between foundations, policy, curriculum and learning action is not articulated in depth. On the other hand, Ikeda's concept of value creation offers outstanding arguments in favor of the addition of a transdisciplinary dimension in curricula, which is one taxonomical principle of Deep Education (Tochon, 2010b). I develop these elements below.

First, language learning should not be constructed for the simple purpose of proficiency: it can be organized in a way that fosters the wisdom, courage and compassion of cosmopolitanism for peace, supporting "the intense effort at intercultural dialogue with the other" (Ikeda, 2010a). This circumscribes the role of values to the worldly integration of principles that allow people to share their experience with wisdom, compassion, and courage, making the value model inherent. It targets interculture in action. This bold move characterizes what the Deep Approach curriculum defines as the transdisciplinary level: language studies should educate through and beyond the language.

As in Plato's *Phaedo*, the rejection of languages leads to the rejection of humanity. Yes, language is always incomplete, as linguistic meanings never fully capture experience and tend to reify it. Therefore, language learning and the market logic must be tempered by the logic of humanity, and deeper goals must be targeted (Ikeda, 2010b). Within this deeper perspective, as we have seen in the previous chapters, the logic of testing falls short. Another aspect that contributes to a Deep Approach of languages is extensive reading. Ikeda advises students to move beyond classroom contents, and to have the courage and persistence to access more complex literary works. Students must read extensively in the other language, even large and complex works. They may skip over the most tedious sections and take naps when tired, but persevere in developing their own style of reading (Gebert, 2012) to expand the realm of self and experience. All cultures and subcultures have their own ways of interpreting human experience. Reading and language learning can be enmeshed into a new type of endeavor characterized by the conquest of the soul and the realization of what is at the root of humanity in terms of commonalities, allowing shared and peaceful understanding. Reading becomes a method of transpersonal development through dialogue with the Other as being epistemologically different. Cultures are dynamic and adaptive, which situates learning not as the acquisition of a fixed embodiment of knowledge with its traditions, but as the entry into an intercultural dialogue that stimulates the transformation of cultures towards a deeper cosmopolitan understanding. Because culture is often simplified and reduced, expressed as homogeneous and sanitized, a new standard should be added to language study in reference to the ACTFL model: the Cosmopolitan C supporting social justice and human rights, and responsibility for the world (Starkey, 2007).

The "cosmopolitan turn" (I speak of a *Deep Turn*) in language education goes with the move toward 6Cs standards with the overarching C of Cosmopolitanism as the key to value creation. For Ikeda, the cosmopolitan project is of moral nature and is grounded in virtues "as ways of empowering individual and communities" (Obelleiro, 2012, p. 33). "The essence of education is this process whereby one person's character inspires another" (Ikeda, 2010a, p. 151). Self-transformation and human revolution lead to social reforms on the basis of a global ethic. The language curriculum finds its best expression in a cosmopolitan curriculum promoting global social justice and a "new humanism" (Ikeda, 1996). This "rooted cosmopolitanism" in the terms of Appiah (2005, 2006) implies a continuity of ethical responsibility between the personal, the local, the national and the international. This proposal matches Makiguchi's (1988) idea of creating a world summit of educators to enact changes that support the principle that we must switch from a world in which education is a service to market and society to a world in which society is at the service of education. This matches my understanding that this century must become the Century of Education, or we might be doomed as a species. Social mindfulness leads to a form of engagement that encourages "with maternal care the ultimate potential for good within all people" Ikeda, 2010a, p. 114).

This resembles the Club of Budapest and the Transdisciplinary Manifesto. We need more initiatives in this direction, enmeshing language and culture learning to understanding for the deeper goals of reducing the xenophobia and racism (Schleicher, 2011). Any reflection on cosmopolitanism should not go along without a questioning of its definition: what cosmopolitanism do we want? A cosmopolitan market place? Westernization? Maintaining a balanced world means reaching equilibrium between various life options. In a model that transcends binaries, the concept could be redefined in the inclusive, negotiated way of what a civil planetary society could be.

Ikeda adopts Toda's (1965) criticism that modernity confused knowledge and wisdom: the spiritual illness of modern civilization created a "pathology of divisiveness that blinds humans to their commonalities" (Ikeda, 2010, p. 115). Global citizenship requires the development of virtues of imagination, empathy, and compassion within the acquisition of the other languages and cultures to create an antidote to collective egoism, ethnocentrism, and the pathology of divisiveness. "The question is not whether citizens of the world should learn and experience languages and cultures but rather why and how" (Obelleiro, 2012, p. 52).

A Deep Approach to Linguistic Human Rights

Colonial representations of superior Self and inferior Other involving race, gender, ethnicity, class, and language, are constantly re/constructed in curricula, policies and practices related to foreign languages (Kubota & Lin, 2009). Let us briefly examine the role of the Deep Approach to world languages and cultures in contexts in which systemic linguicism defined by Skutnabb-Kangas (2000), has created a situation of linguistic genocide:

> *Linguicism* refers to the ideologies, structures, and practices that are used to legitimate, create, regulate, and reproduce an unequal division of power and resources (both material and non-material) between groups that are defined on the basis of language (Skutnabb-Kangas & Phillipson, 1989, p.455).

> *Linguistic genocide* refers to a systemic or political situation that created and creates mental and physical harm to a minority population in transferring its children to the majority, "prohibiting the use of the language of the group in daily intercourse or in schools, or the printing and circulation of publications in the language of the group". This definition comes from the original Article III(1) of the final draft of the Convention on the Prevention and Punishment of the Crime of Genocide (E 794, 1948) of the United Nations (Skutnabb-Kangas, 2005).

The Deep Approach to languages and cultures may play the role of empowering micro-policy, forming an interface between government policies and classroom practices. It can help heritage learners broaden the scope of their native proficiency, preserving languages for which there are few sources and instructing learners about language ideologies and attitudes. Indeed minority languages are often underdeveloped in school contexts because of the lack of instructional materials (Heugh, 2009; Hornberger, 2011). When instruction is based on educative projects as shown in chapters 5, 6 and 7, the learning teams can be in charge of gathering the materials needed for their projects, thus providing an effective solution in such contexts. In this fashion, integrating this approach may help counteract attitudes influencing children and parents into believing that their language was worth less than the dominant language, which had a negative influence on the use of minority languages. Thus in the lack of instructional materials to maintain indigenous languages, the Deep Approach can be a response to linguistic genocide (Skutnabb-Kangas, 2005). It can prove that the revitalization of minority languages is not incompatible with proficiency in the dominant language (McCarty, 2009).

The Deep Approach also addresses attitudinal problems that heritage learners may encounter. These students are raised in a home where a non-dominant language is spoken. They speak or merely understand the language inherited from their parents, are somehow bilingual, and they are often deeply affected by dominant language ideologies (Valdés, González, López, García & Márquez, 2008). For example there is a large heritage language community of Turkish speakers in Berlin, Germany, and because of its size and religious difference there was for a long time a form of prejudice against their language and culture. Now after three generations they have their own political representatives (Tochon, 2011).

Most heritage students value language learning highly as it helps them connect to their families and provides strong support to their identity, which is the reason why they apply for optional language courses (Bearse & de Jong, 2008). It is most often difficult in schools and colleges to organize a special track for heritage learners, which actually would be best (Beaudrie & Ducar, 2005). Nonetheless with a project-based approach and critical deepening of knowledge with extensive reading and intensive writing and feedback there is room for having in the same classroom two types of students: L2 learners and heritage learners doing distinct types of projects and having different foci (Lynch, 2008). These students often feel that their first language is an obstacle to their social integration (Beaudrie, 2009). Because of their background and language characteristics which create a vulnerable situation, these students can regain self-esteem through social action projects that reinforce their sense of identity and bring a critical perspective on the language ideologies that are at the root of their discomfort (Correa, 2011).

Discussing Language Status in Teacher Education

Language ideology and language status should be discussed in the context of teacher education, as well as the role that English plays worldwide (Lippi-Green, 2011; Phillipson, 2006; Spolsky, 2004). Student teachers should be trained to recognize linguicism and their own unconscious discrimination of certain people because of their accent and language. Indeed linguicism occurs in the classroom as well. Translanguaging should be more and more accepted in the classroom (Canagarajah, 2011): code switching is the way to create neurological connections between the parts of the brain in charge of the first and second language (Tochon, 2009). Such training will help put the diktat of the dominant language into perspective, and similar guidance is needed on how to deal with diversity at large (Grant, 2003).

Our work as teacher educators underscores the value of student teaching abroad for a better understanding of linguistic human rights, and a deeper approach to issues of cultural difference in education (Karaman & Tochon, 2007, 2010). Our practice has led to the belief that, if student teachers experience otherness—for example through cultural immersion abroad as part of teacher certification—and become receptive to the key issues of multiculturalism, then they will attempt to pursue social justice for underserved students (Nieto, 2005). Yet this does not work without thorough conceptual training and awareness raising (Ladson-Billings, 2001). Rather than detailing empirical findings on these issues, following Gorski's (2006) stand, we propose to "turn the spotlight on ourselves" in challenging the paradoxes inherent with the concept of multilingual and multicultural education itself. Indeed change for social justice implies an underlying definition of morality, a code of conduct that plays a crucial although unacknowledged role in intercultural ethics (Tochon & Karaman, 2010). It requires settings free from the pressure of assessment, such that student teachers feel they can be themselves and express their true feelings, without fear that this information be used against them. Research with non-recorded interviews about graded reflective courses indicated that most student teachers were lying about their true feelings and experiences (Tochon, 2011c): many stories of 'classroom events' were fabricated for the purpose of getting a good grade.

Areas such as world languages have taken up the idea of creating a democratic, culturally responsive curriculum (Ladson-Billings, 2006) and the promotion of respect, tolerance, and recognition of other cultures and languages. Culturally responsive classroom management requires profound training, but first teachers "must recognize we are all cultural beings, with our own beliefs, biases, and assumptions about human behavior" (Weinstein, Curran & Tomlinson, 2003, p.269). Commitment to social justice has also been incorporated into the guiding principles of several other disciplines (North, 2006). Critical forms of intercultural education challenge hegemonic practices within education and society (Hermans, 2002). "The intercultural approach goes beyond equal opportunities and respect for existing cultural differences to the pluralist transformation of public space, institutions and civic culture. It does not recognize cultural boundaries as fixed but in a state of flux and remaking. An intercultural approach aims to facilitate dialogue, exchange and reciprocal understanding between people of different backgrounds" (Wood, Landry & Bloomfield, 2005, p.9). These are aspects contributing to a Deep Approach.

The necessary linking of the Culture standards to the Community standard— which is often neglected in the K-12 classroom for lack of connection with L1 speakers—is rarely alluded to in the research literature. A sociocultural analysis of how language develops in communities of practice may not only suggest that the hierarchy among standards is arbitrary (hence the need for an integrated model), but the Communities standard would need precedence over other areas due to the understanding of where linguistic and cultural interactions take place (Magnan 2008). Furthermore, students understand the crucial nature of communities for language learning and may not understand why this community dimension is often neglected in the curricula while it is clearly of primary importance (Magnan, Murphy, Sahakyan & Kim, 2012). Communication and Cultures are most frequently discussed in schools and districts and are emphasized in the ACTFL Decades of Standards report (ACTFL, 2011). Nonetheless community connection and gathering should be a top priority. Actually it is foundational in the Deep Approach to world languages and cultures because of its transdisciplinary, project-based nature, along with interdisciplinary connections and the integration of the cultural perspective, which are prioritized. Attuned to this understanding from the most recent research literature, the Deep Approach articulates where the next wave of progress will lead us in World Language Education.

Criticality in Content & Language Integrated Learning

Situations in which subject-matters are learned through a target language with the intent to teach the content as well as the language is designated in the U.S. by the terms *Content-Based Instruction* (CBI) and in Europe by the terms *Content and Language Integrated Learning* (CLIL). This approach often implies careful attention to the other culture, thorough readings, intensive writings and projects, thusly entering into a field of compatibility with what I define in this book as a Deep Approach to world languages and cultures. Learning subject-matters such as social studies through an additional language can indeed enhance language proficiency in the target language, a nuanced and pragmatic perception of the other culture, and may develop a positive attitude toward language learning (Coyle, Hood & Marsh, 2010; Madrid & Stephen, 2011). Furthermore it can help develop other aspects such as criticality, international sensitivity and peace, as demonstrated by Byram (2014). Michael Byram discusses exchanges between students from Great Britain and Argentina on the topic of the Malvinas/Falkland war: students interviewed veterans by Skype and exchanged data across groups creating critical, reflective teams. The students were young undergraduate, therefore the 1982 war was history for them. They created blogs and Facebook pages, produced leaflets on Glogster. They took their research outside of the walls of the classroom to outside community by distributing leaflets on the street and in La Plata in Buenos Aires. Later, they taught EFL courses about the topic in secondary schools, posted excerpts on YouTube, and taught a class with a non-governmental organization in a poor neighborhood. This is an example where intercultural world language education integrated competences beyond disciplinary knowledge, with interdisciplinary connections and transdisciplinary action. What Byram (2008) explored in terms of criticality corresponds to transdisciplinary action in the deep model. Transformatory critic leads to actual engagement with higher motivation to act and learn from action.

Critical multiculturalism, aesthetic, political, and cosmopolitan philosophies can also inform the intercultural dimension of the Deep Approach. While anti-racist education has been criticized for its limitations and somewhat negative conceptualizations (Walcott, 1994), its opposition to discrimination on the basis of ethnicity with an open, dialogical approach to education, to avoid 'proselytisation or indoctrination' can significantly contribute to interculturalism (Tormey, 2002, p.18).

Issues in interculturalism have deep connections with moral education. Confucius folded 'fellow-feeling' in moral understanding: shame and resentment yielded the sense of justice. In Aristotle's moral education, happiness defined the highest good that derived from the resolution of injustice. Is it possible to introduce in schools and in the academia a ferment that is partly foreign to their scope? Are there ways of handling intercultural problem solving in education? Helping solve these issues collaboratively with educators may be a path towards building a society in which social inequalities have been reduced, linguistic human rights are respected and governing bodies and international corporations are held accountable for their actions.

The Deep Approach and Transformational Pedagogy

Transformational pedagogy inspired by Paolo Freire and deep pedagogy are related. The major errors of the current social and education system can be described in terms of systemic flow. Since the time Freire wrote *Pedagogy of the Oppressed*, the situation in the world has radicalized, particularly in the United States where the middle class has almost disappeared. The people who were previously in the middle of the spectrum on the salary scale are now representing the bottom 20%; 1% earn 358 times the mean salaries of the 99% (Norton & Ariely, 2011). 147 financial companies direct 40% of the world's finances and have shares in roughly 1,500 partner companies that give them the decision making power for 80% of the global financial resources (Vitali, Glattfelder & Battiston, 2011). Thus the situation now is that at least 85% of the world population are among the oppressed. Most of us are work slaves struggling for our survival in a system of constraints that make our lives more and more unbearable.

The financial system is organized in a way that is detrimental to humanity at large and now only serves a superclass of criminal parasites (de Rivero, 2003; Latouche, 2004; Rothkopf, 2008). We witnessed a situation in which the flow of resources was diverted to go up on the pyramid of power rather than creating balanced exchanges. Money was decoupled from real value in a manner that a few printed paper money out of thin air and sold it with interests to the masses. Then because of the created imbalance, between 2007 and 2014 the wealthy bailed themselves out to an amount close to 25 trillion dollars. The debt was attributed to the population at large, which may create generations of slave workers for the coming century, whose taxes will serve to pay the debt of the rich.

Thus today the contradiction that described Freire is at its maximum, to the point of disequilibrium. Such extraordinary imbalance in which the system is owned by a few who direct the worlds' transactions and decide austerity measures imposed on the whole population characterizes a situation of enslavement of humanity. Surveillance is constant to prevent the inevitable forthcoming revolution. System scientists know the law of systemic homeostasis: complex systems always try to re-equilibrate themselves and they succeed in doing it. When a system reaches a tipping point of imbalance, it suddenly reorganizes itself in a myriad of rebalancing moves from within, which is about to happen.

This situation legitimates pedagogy of social awakening, more than ever. As Freire feared, Education has become an instrument of oppression rather than liberation. The education systems are now top-down hierarchies, dialogue and democratic representation are less and less possible. In particular, the banking concept of education has reached its peak, as global standards are being imposed that target the development of the same outcomes for all rather than personalized inter-subjective and creative growth. Freire's generative themes are great transdisciplinary incentives for open project pedagogy, in which the students freely investigate what matters most in their lives.

Both oppressed and oppressors are part of the same complex living system. It may not be the best idea for the financially dominant to destroy the planet on which they live. Understanding the polarities and binaries through which we grasp the world's situation should help creating spaces for reconstructive dialogue, looking for compatibilities. Oppositions of social class, race and gender may become incentives to transcend the contradictions and start creating a new system. Resistance seems futile because it reinforces opposition. The solution is to create the new system beside rather than within the obsolete imbalanced system. It is what we witness worldwide with the creation of a new international finance system. Both may coexist for a while and then the old corrupted system will mutate. The hope with the Deep Approach is that this rebalancing will be smooth rather than drastic and violent. The same should be done in education.

Deep pedagogy proposes creation as a solution to conflicts. The reader might wonder how this all connects to language education. Again, language is more than language. It establishes contact, dialogue, and cultural action. As Freire (1970) as well as Habermas (1985) demonstrated, dialogical action leads to cooperation, better forms of organization, cultural exchange and greater unity. This relocates the target of world language education in the best interest of all: a world that communicates can be socially uplifting, more balanced, and maintain endangered languages.

While there are clearly similarities, there is a major difference between Freire's pedagogy and deep pedagogy, to the point that the Deep

Approach could be considered neo-Freirean. Indeed in Freire's concept—which appears particularly in his letters to his niece Cristina when he reflected upon his life and work (see *Letter Twelve*, Araujo Freire & Macedo, 2000)—the relation of the student with the teacher was still hierarchical, as the teacher was fully in charge of the learner's awakening. The cultural circles were more than facilitated: they were initiated, guided and monitored. A deeper approach would be for study groups to become autonomous and advisors may become external, playing the role of consultants, like peers in charge of feedback. In reducing the sense of hierarchy, the Deep Approach achieves the goals of pedagogy of the oppressed.

As long as school districts do not have the liberty to free the teachers from the bureaucratic duty of obedience to governmentally imposed forms of knowledge and our governments are the puppets of lobbies, education will be an instrument of oppression rather than liberation. It will be creating servile and dependent customers rather than creative citizens. This applies to so many countries. Zongjie Wu (2014) compared Chinese schooling before 1912 to what is currently being lived: in the 19th Century and earlier, there had been centuries of local schooling, which was the pride of every tiny community. The purpose of pre-modern Chinese Education was to acquire a language that would allow for a deeper understanding and actualizing what ancient wisdom had been proposing. Curricula were open and teachers were considered experts and wise enough to adapt master plans, contents and pacing to the needs of their students. Scholars were highly considered. Nowadays governments are deciding what education policies must be implemented and the way to implement them. The goal of wisdom has been lost, Education focuses on the acquisition of objects. Teachers have a technical role in implementing the decision of others.

Freedom to learn is possible in situations under local, equalitarian control. However governments dictate subject-matters, pacing and disciplinary programming, the forms of delivery and examinations targeting observable performance, this high level top-down control implies a society of un-equals. This is the situation of schooling around the planet.

The time is ripe for a Deep Turn. As system science demonstrates, the terrible imbalance of the current social and educational systems will inevitably create a backlash of high amplitude in the pendulum swing. Depth in education is the forthcoming trend. Deeply knowledgeable free thinkers are required for a society that can address the problems of today, at so many levels. The proposal in this book is to opt for non-violent revolution and awakening: a shared, creative rebalancing of our world.

Starting such a peaceful revolution with world languages education makes sense: languages allow for better communication and cross-cultural understanding. Such accomplishment may only be local, as Freire discussed with Macedo regarding his role in five African countries liberated from Portuguese colonialism (Araújo Freire & Macedo, 2000). In this sense, deep pedagogy is a pedagogy of the heart, and a pedagogy of hope, that accompanies a campaign for deeper literacies.

Avant-garde Methodologies for Social Change

Methodologies proposed for "avant-garde" educational change, second language acquisition and foreign language education often clash because of the lack of an encompassing framework that would make the methodologies compatible. On the contrary, the transdisciplinary framework allows the Deep Approach to language and cultures to flow into Deep Education at large, which actualizes the unified taxonomy and gives it its thorough meaning. We come at a time when we need an approach that gathers the best practices that have been developed so far. In this respect, the Deep Approach represents the next mainstream. The evolution of schooling within the coming decade will inevitably see the development of such a revolutionary approach. Here are the criteria that legitimate the change:

- Deep teaching aims to depth in understanding and reflective, self-sufficient practices. The need to address problematic international rankings will lead more and more educational administrations to adopt models in which teachers and districts adapt existing structures to create conditions for deep learning.

- The world is in shambles and part of the reason is a lack of transdisciplinary focus in education. The Deep Approach responds to a need for social action and action for the planet. "Equity for all" on the basis of everyone doing the same things with standard outcomes has shown that the formula does not work. New schooling will reverse the equation. All children should be permitted to be different and be able to follow their own path. The Deep Approach acknowledges that every person is unique and deserves the right to be recognized in his or her unique characteristics, skills, aspirations, and realizations.

- The need to create cooperation in society will push Japanese, Chinese, and Scandinavian models of collaboration to the fore. Classroom tasks will be focusing on educative projects that can be negotiated and organized individually, among peers, in small cooperative or collaborative groups. The development of social skills will be integrated.

- In the language arena, the struggle between communicative advocates and focus on forms advocates needs to reach its synergic transcendence within an integrative model. The Deep Approach maintains what was acquired in the communicative era with some more flexibility regarding code-switching, and it affirms the primacy of text for deep learning: verbal recordings, literary texts and storied content-based grammar rise as crucial tools for proficiency. There is an emphasis here on "signature" and agency for language learning: connecting situations to authored writing communication and recording.

- With the increasing interest of students in web-based activities, computer-assisted self-directed learning will become a major part of the language programs. Blended learning to work on project will become the rule rather than the exception. This will raise new types of problems that we can't explore here: technologies will need to change to shield humans from their magnetic fields, or to use electromagnetics more wisely and less intrusively (Tochon, 2011a and 2012; Tochon, Karaman & Ökten, 2014).

Educating the Democratic Planner

Communicative Language Teaching (CLT) proposed sound principles for language teaching of a comprehensive nature, with some flexibility and a hands-on way of reaching learners. "However, a tendency among the language-teaching fraternity is to dismiss all previous methods when a new method dominates. What we would like to see is a less triumphalism and superiority claims – which many language teachers seem to have with regard to CLT. We believe basically all 'methods' have merit and that the key is motivation and diligence" (Kirkpatrick & Ghaemi, 2011, p.148). Clearly all methods can be helpful in the eclectic panoply of the language teacher, until s/he feels enough expertise to *be* the method and adapt to the particular way life is being socialized in the class. Yet, research reviewed in chapters 6 and 7 indeed suggests that the socioaffective factors impacting student motivation and leading students to spend enough time learning the language are even more important than teaching methods.

There are clear arguments for going beyond the communicative approach and creating a holistic framework that places intrinsic motivation to the fore. One aspect that supports this move is the re-framing of linguistic concerns within semiotics as an overarching meaning making theory. Language is more than language. Even from a teaching methods perspective, the use of images and films as springboards to teach culture, for example, indicates that understanding lies within broader interpretive frames than the purely linguistic ones and requires that teachers move away from language and culture products and examine cultural perspectives (Barnes-Karol & Broner, 2010; Sturm, 2012). This is precisely the attempt in this book: creating an integrative framework that supports critical reflection in the language teachers' community.

In teacher training workshops, instructors often ask about the difference between project-based learning (PjBL) and the Deep Approach. As we have seen in previous chapters, PjBL is framed in a very particular way in the Deep Approach. Not all project-based activities can lead to deep learning. Certain conditions must be met. First, the project should have input from the student; otherwise, the project will not emerge from and trigger intrinsic motivation. Students must be given choices in terms of topics, ways of processing them, deadlines, pairing, teaming or ways of grouping, roles and the like. If it seems too fuzzy to teachers used to controlled learning, then the terms of the work can be planned in a 'specification table' or a written instructional agreement. The Deep Approach makes projects both more open to many choices made by the students—not the instructor—and at the same time, it requires that projects be better specified in terms of what is being done in each task domains and taxonomic levels. The task domains defined in the IAPI model are different from yet compatible with the framework proposed by the American Council for the Teaching of Foreign Languages (ACTFL). The initial template (oral exchange- reading – writing – language techniques) was compatible with the European framework for languages. As seen in chapter 5, the taxonomic levels are specified in an embedment map describing the narrative organizers, the skillers, and the experiential organizers. Using the unified taxonomy will integrate the transdisciplinary dimension, which is not always present in PjBL as implemented in world languages education.

Already there, you see a world of difference between common uses of PjBL and what the transdisciplinary, Deep Approach adds to it. Thus, when a language instructor tells her students that "your projects are due in two weeks", without scaffolding criteria nor negotiating possible task descriptions balancing all four language modalities within student-chosen holistic actions, her proposal does not fit the Deep Approach and rarely would lead to in-depth learning. More often than not, adapted resources are lacking as well.

The Deep Approach uses projects in a very special way, which leads to broad and thorough, self-directed action, yet quite detailed regarding tasks domains to allow process evaluation to occur. This is where World Language Education and Deep Education merge.

Depth Is Not Stultifying

Another dimension of depth is that the traditional positioning of what Rancière (2004) named the "stultifying pedagogue" is not acceptable in the Deep Approach. The *Ignorant Schoolmaster* was a meditation on the work of Joseph Jacotot, a French professor of the early

19th century, who became famous in demonstrating with his students that he could teach them another language at a high level of proficiency without a method other than their self-directed ways of approaching texts for which they had translations. At the end of the year at the written exam, Jacotot's Dutch students' French was brilliant, which he proved to the academic world by having a panel of experts compare their results and read their dissertations. Jacotot had broader claims such as the equality of intelligences, which is denied by the process of teaching itself, in which the master positions some knowledge and his own status as superior. Doing so, the teacher deprives the students from ownership of their own learning. It was a call for intellectual emancipation, against the 'stultification' of the institutionalized system (Rancière, 1999).

Not to be a stultifying teacher requires flexibility, openmindedness, efforts, understanding, a vast resource of knowledge, and self-training, but not the type of training that makes one dependent upon the guidance of someone else (Vieira & Alfredo Moreira, 2008). This is one paradox of the Deep Approach, no different from the apparent contradiction of teaching students towards autonomy. It is true that some wording and direction are provided and some conceptual framing is broadly and flexibly proposed, yet the key decisions regarding instructional content should not be made by the instructor. Thus, the contradiction is only partial.

Over the past decade, there has been a marked shift in the focus of world language education. Students are now being encouraged to learn how to learn and use the foreign language. Effective learning and use strategies enhance students' efforts to reach increased proficiency. "Strategies-based instruction provides the most efficient way for learner awareness to be heightened" expresses Cohen (2011, p.265). There are various arguments in favor of making language learners more autonomous, as I mentioned in Chapter 8: being reflectively engaged in their learning strategies renders these strategies more personal and focused, and therefore more effective, as they serve the learners' own agendas; the higher level of commitment resolves motivation issues, as learners have a positive attitude toward the orientation proposed; and it puts communication and discursive strategies into use in a context of social autonomy, which is what real-life immersion normally provides (Cummins, 2009).

Self-Regulated Learning Strategies and Autonomy

This section briefly reviews some results of research on language learning strategies, their relation to autonomy and the role of the teacher in this context, as well as the strategy-related factors that influence proficiency. It indicates that it is important to discuss students' existing beliefs on how they learn best, challenge them and legitimize new ways of approaching learning that support the growth of language awareness in creative and open sociocultural contexts.

There is no consensus in research on the types of strategies needed by world language students, while there is some evidence that students who use strategies are deeper learners and develop proficiency faster (Fazeli, 2011). The crucial debate is whether strategies can be taught. Macaro (2006) mentions a whole series of problems faced by research on language learning strategies, when researchers try to decontextualize the concept of learning strategy to analyze its types and occurrences, and teach strategies out of context. Their definition is fuzzy. There is no real consensus on what strategies are: "Do they consist of knowledge, intention, action, or all three?" (p.325). We do not know whether strategies survive across learning situations, tasks, and contexts, and it is not clear if they are integral to language processing or might depend upon social support. Strategy teacher trainers are reifying abstract concepts that may well not correspond to the genuine effective strategies of their students. Strategies might be very personal and situational. They might evolve over time. Their relation to skills and processes is hypothetical for lack of definition of these terms. How strategies lead to language learning and skill development over the long term is unknown.

Thus there is increasing suspicion that the best strategies might be idiosyncratic and personalized to the point that students forget them at higher levels of proficiency (Rivera-Mills & Plonsky, 2007). Learning styles and strategies seem interdependent (Cohen, 1998). This means that teaching strategies that are foreign to the students may contrary their belief system, their vision of what works for them, their motivation and ultimately their growth towards proficiency (Garrett & Shortall,

2002; Morris & Tarrone, 2003). Moreover strategies are not only inside the mind, they are also negotiated with the outer world and partly social and cultural. Hence the need for the teacher to discuss the students' belief systems, socioaffective perceptions and attitudes (Kern, 1995). Socioaffective strategies indeed play a neglected and important role in language learning, as well as social strategies (Oxford, 1990). Student beliefs, their philosophy of learning and language learning behaviors are interconnected (Wenden, 1998). These beliefs need to be discussed; otherwise, for example if the student feels that only vocabulary repetition and translation exercises may help, deeper strategies won't be able to develop (Horwitz, 1988; Truscott, 1999).

Instrumentalized Autonomy

In a sense, research on learning strategies has instrumentalized autonomy: autonomy has been understood as the expression of a set of self-directed and motivation-oriented strategies aiming at increasing the potential of success in the person's endeavors (Macaro, 2006). Awareness plays a crucial role in this instrumental process, not only at a cognitive level, most often very active in beginner learners, but also at a metacognitive and reflexive level, which indicates an enhanced and more mature level of language learning (Sheorey & Mokhtari, 2001). But even autonomy, once understood as an internal factor, is socially situated and negotiated (Bown, 2009). Self-regulatory practices that apprentices undertake in their growth towards proficiency need in large part to be legitimized in a context (Oxford, 2003), which explains why the Deep Approach may help, after an initial phase of dialogue and legitimization, develop a new set of attitudes that can be highly motivating, as supports to personal and linguistic growth.

To sum up, in a domain in which researchers argue for rigor and precision, strategic research has revealed to be particularly inconsistent, ill-defined, contradictory and elusive. My stand is that strategies can rarely be taught fruitfully because these would be the strategies of someone else; nonetheless students can be placed in complex production situations that require the development and use of their own, personal or team strategies to succeed. The position adopted in this book is that thinking strategy out of context when most motivational aspects are socially built may only keep us backward in our understanding of the ways of stimulating proficiency growth. However reflecting on the role of identity, agency, cooperation and shared autonomy in language learning through critical discussions with the students appears to be a key point that teachers should never neglect.

Pedagogy for Autonomy and Value Creation

We have seen that self-regulation is necessary to language learning (Noels, 2001). Autonomy, which implies self-regulation, is tied to motivation (Dörnyei, 2003). Asking students how they prefer to learn is a first step in a Deep Approach, as it supports the identity-building process and value creation.

A brief survey at the beginning of the academic year may help teachers understand the styles and strategic approaches of their students (Rivera-Mills & Plonsky, 2007). This implies that the teacher must also be aware of her personal style and strategies. Becoming a diagnostician and learner trainer rather than 'instructor' will also help re-shape the role of the teacher as one resourceful participant in a process initiated by the students (Weaver & Cohen, 1998). Deep learning may have different characteristics for different students in the various situations and projects they face. The active participation of the student in the learning process is crucial (van Lier, 2007).

Pedagogy for autonomy and value creation is not a simple task for the teacher, however. It requires a change of mindset in both teacher and students (Jiménez Raya & Lamb, 2008). The current shift from a communicative approach to a larger, holistic action-based orientation, such as the one described in this book, represents a leap from previous practices that were clear cut, functional with the classroom controlled setting, and professionally satisfying because both teacher and students had the feeling things were uniform, and they 'had done something', even if it did not lead to proficiency. In the provisional definition of Little (1991, p.4), the capacity to be an autonomous learner implies "detachment, critical reflection, decision-making and independent action". Thorough language learning presupposes that "the curriculum now comes from within the learner, as a product of his (or her) past experience and present and future needs" (p.7). "Despite the ever-expanding literature, learner autonomy remains a minority pursuit, perhaps because all forms of 'autonomisation' threaten the power structures of educational culture" notes Little (2002a), even though the *European Language Portfolio* was conceived as a support for this orientation (2002b) and a comparison of European reforms indicates they often use that vocabulary without providing the necessary resources to make it happen, "as the relationship between policy and practice is problematic" (Lamb, 2008, p.36).

Teachers who start with the new orientation toward deep language learning may have at first the perception that they are entering situations that they don't fully control, with messy classes and expectations from students they did not anticipate about matters they may not always know. "The development of learner autonomy in the language classroom is a long and difficult process—especially for the teacher. Letting go and trusting in the learners' ability to take hold... seems to be the biggest problem" (Dam, 1995, p.78). Thus, the transition may be slightly uncomfortable, depending the individual and the group of students. The Deep Approach requires thorough training, expertise, relevance and aptness, delicacy and tact, and a new rapport with the students' lives, who must be considered as adult learners, grown-up with the potential of leading their projects, even in the K-12 grades. Teachers may start with the Deep Approach for an hour a week or so until they feel comfortable with it and their students understood why it is crucial to language proficiency.

Marsh, Richards and Smith (2001, p. 389) remark that students "simply do not know what they do not know and how to come to know it". The hypothesis underlying previous teaching methods was that teachers and teacher educators know better. Actually, teaching lies upon assumptions that come from their own 'studenting', experience and training, and the reality of each student might differ. Hence, there is a need for negotiating the path toward progress. By negotiating, I mean that there are at least two decision makers involved—one teacher and one student—each with various epistemic interests and foci, who need to tune their instruments to orchestrate harmonious projects. There might be jarring notes at the beginning.

For Little (2002b), the problematic concept of autonomy has often been confused with self-instruction and it is very difficult to define it in terms of strategy. Obviously, such skills require a focus on methodological aptitudes, so students can cope with a situation in which they are no longer spoon-fed, which can be partial at first, and may decrease over time; or there can be moments of spoon-feeding during the week, on an individual or group basis, with time devoted to independent projects at other times. This implies much negotiation, and the teacher must develop a comfort zone, vis-à-vis the unexpected. Carson (2010) analyzes the learner's necessary scaffolding of autonomy in her article *Language learner autonomy: Myth, magic or miracle?* She notes that many language learners do not come in class with the prior ability of setting their goals, reflecting on their progress and helping each other, being in charge of their learning. Sociocultural understanding of how 'real' learning takes place leads to a holistic approach of the ways to scaffold autonomy in language learners. It suggests that "designing a syllabus of learning activities without taking into account learners' prior knowledge is unlikely to enhance linguistic proficiency" (Carson, ibid, p.84).

Various attempts have followed such orientation. Thomsen (2000) used logbooks for the learners to draft their work agenda as a dialogical communication process tool for each instructional unit. Language modules have been created by the Trinity College of Dublin with thematic resources to scaffold autonomous, individual, or small group learning. Their task-based curriculum is precast, but students can choose their projects with some flexibility. Students develop up to four projects over two semesters and take full responsibility for their learning activities for half of the weekly lessons. They use this approach even at the lowest proficiency levels, with much physical gesture and acting, and specific times devoted the grammar and vocabulary points related to what emerges from projects: designing a travel brochure, organizing a topical seminar; debating a theme; creating a thematic website; preparing a newsletter; performing a short piece of drama, improvising comic scenes; or re-writing a story together. Thus, authentic documents and communication are based on students' desires, needs and interests, and lead to tangible products in real life.

Deep Creative Pedagogy Does Not Focus on Control and Order

When order is emphasized in classroom interaction, conformity models are produced that do not support much creativity: only legitimate moves are part of the intelligibility system, in which legitimacy is defined from the point of view of the authority. In classroom discourse where the perspective of the teacher is privileged, "whatever students do other than what the teacher specifies is invisible or anomalous" (Pratt, 1991, p.38). However humorous talk is not always a disruptive, off-task behavior: jocular talk allows learners to construct new classroom identities and it occasions complex and creative speech acts. While humor may express resistance to monotonous and face-threatening classroom practices, it can also create a pedagogical safe space.

It is important, then, to "consider how learners negotiate competing subject positions in conflicting discourse communities" and to understand "how these struggles shape their practices of language learning" (Canagarajah, 2004, p. 117). Students' conflicting reactions might be better understood in the light of what Janks (2004) named the "access paradox". While teachers base their position on their mastery of the language being taught, which may tends to reinforce a dominant participation style, access to participation in classroom activities should not depend upon forms of interaction that delegitimize minority languages or marginalize users (Miller & Zuengler, 2011).

In this respect, we need to reimagine different ways of organizing practices, and the Deep Approach is such a proposal. For example, teachers need to be open to humor in the development of projects as it contributes to a healthy classroom climate and create a pedagogically safe house in the foreign language classroom (Pomerantz & Bell, 2012).

The experience of teachers can vary tremendously from group to group depending the schedule, the environment, the participants' history and the special composition of the class including the characters assembled as a group with its own dynamic (Dörney & Murphy, 2003). Understanding why some classes "feel good" and others don not is the focus of some psychosocial research, as the group dynamic is emotionally laden and, as it develops, it creates interpersonal connections that have tremendous impact on individual learning (Schmuck & Schmuck, 2001). In the world language arena in particular, the interaction between students is "the pivot on which language learning turns" (Burton & Clennell, 2003, p. 1). It is precisely in this area that a Deep Approach to language learning can be beneficial as classroom climate impacts learning positively (Gascoigne, 2012).

Deep teacher education is homologous to the self-directedness of the Deep Approach: self-chosen training matches personal and prolonged efforts along a professional development plan, grown from within, to find a personal definition of depth and the practices that correspond to it (Karaman, Ökten & Tochon, 2012). It requires the firm willingness to do better in a less than ideal world, and continue on this impulse to free others from the bondage of formal schooling by becoming a resource rather than the enforcing agent of institutionalized stultification. These are the terms used by Jacotot, in the 19th century, when demonstrating the virtues of autonomous learning over controlled teaching. The Deep Approach goes as far as is institutionally doable against indoctrination within the schooling and academic systems.

The Theory/Practice Dilemma

At this point, let us further examine crucial aspects mentioned in earlier chapters. Curriculum planning lacks a unified theory, and the concept itself implodes when the learner is introduced as curriculum builder and decision maker. Previously, clear conceptions of what should be done were given to teachers as prescriptions for the classroom. SLA, as a field, has somehow perpetuated the myth of the unification of paradigms, as if SLA were a meta-paradigm. The inadequateness of SLA theory has been substantiated (Firth & Wagner, 1997). However, without theory, how may an idea of autonomy, growth and interiorization of knowledge be shaped? Where this question is concerned, some think it is better to have a bad theory than none at all and be at the mercy of the implicit. Another dilemma: theories are based on concepts, yet every day practice escapes description. As explained in Chapter 1, description is always an "afterword". Hence, the emphasis in the "rabbit story" of the introductory chapter was on the inexpressibility of the Deep Approach and the role of non-cultivation in the construction of autonomy.

Some postmodern researchers have ironized that John Dewey's educational ideals were fantasies ignoring the complexities of social life. Deweyan reconstructionism may be a dream, and future-oriented imaginaries may well have a quasi mythic socio-affective charge, yet a positive use of symbolic language is certainly to be preferred to its political misuse for the sake of a self-serving class. The use of symbolics is almost inevitable in any form of "educational speak"; it is up to us to judge if it is used to delude others or to stimulate their self-determination (Tochon, 2013). Here, the intention behind the use of symbols and concepts is to motivate teachers in the move towards freeing their students from numerous institutional encumbrances. The Deep Approach project is to ensure the transcendance of both construction (A) and deconstruction (-A) in a third space where both are dialectically engaged in a new dynamic. The transdisciplinary principle of the included middle (Nicolescu, 2002) is applied here in Figure 9.1.

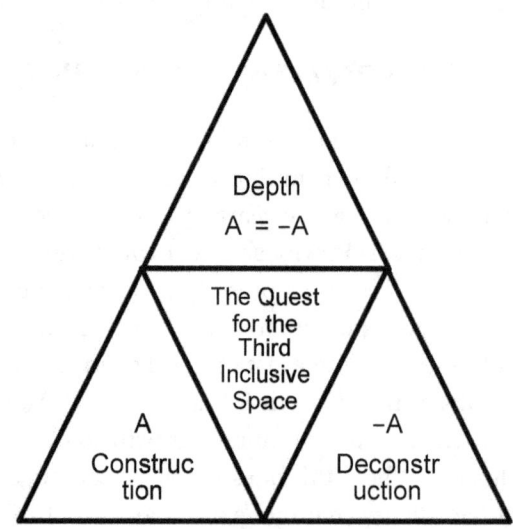

Figure 9.1
Searching for the Included Middle or Third Space

The modern lesson is that progress is possible and humans can direct it with good will. Its flaw is the belief in objectivity, as if objects existed independently from the mind (Deely, 2009). The postmodern lesson is that good will and good words have been twisted and used abusively to enslave humanity for the benefit of a small minority. The mind must take precedence over forms. I propose an orientation that defines a third space along the lines of Henri Lefebvre's (1991) work, in which Depth is relative, not an absolute. Each layer of dialogue between construction and deconstruction opens a new breach into a new depth. The dialectic, dialogical learning process becomes more important than the outcomes. Some plans might temporarily lead to wrong ways, but feedback loops will embed opportunities for increased awareness and regulation into the projected path. Yes, planning should be well organized but subordinated to an autonomous educative production. The paradox of impracticable pragmatic theories mirrors that of predictive planning for use in an unpredictable field. Throughout this, the teacher helps organize possible pathways for deep apprenticeship.

Analyses reveal the difficulties linked to the elaboration of an instructional plan. The teacher is torn between theory and practice, organization and creativity, rigidity and flexibility, scoring and sharing, the intellectual and the affective, the technical factor and the human factor. As a general note, planning by standard outcomes has clearly been met with mixed reactions. Teachers speak of it in terms of impersonality and restriction, of recipes and compartmentalization, as opposed to "other alternatives where solutions don't come "off-the-rack". Teachers cannot always explain their actions in rational terms; they may juxtapose contradictory theories or force them to correspond to some situations and not others. Most researchers who were in search of a coherent model have since come to see that a mechanical model, conceived out of context and omitting the relational factor, does not respond to learners' needs and expectations. Teachers work with conflicting theories not out of apathy, but because most of the problems they face are unsolvable dilemmas.

In foreign language education in particular, teachers have been over-trained to operant conditioning, in which they switch activities every 3-4 minute to keep students alert. Such conditioning does not respect the students' choices and motivation. It surfaces the identity issue: learning a new language and culture is a matter of deep identity change. The capacity to use stylistic and social variation in a meaningful way relates to the ability by the learners' to negotiate their identities in relation to the second language in their past, present, and future lives, more than anything else such as formal learning (van Compernolle & Williams, 2012). The learners' agency then entails considering the language learners as sensible people, "whose history, dispositions toward learning, access to sociocultural worlds, participation, and imaginations together shape the quality of their achievement" (Kinginger, 2004, p.241). The Deep Approach creates a frame in which learning is changing of mental space. Learning occurs creatively when one adapts to the new, vibrant intellectual environment.

Growth and Interiorization

As an example, a stance supporting identity-building and the pedagogy of growth has been taken in this book. Without reaching for a unified theory, many concepts were evoked in a parallel fashion, be they individuation, actualization, or the process of shared personalization. In every case, these concepts were mentioned to draw the reader's attention to the fact that the path from a concept to its transmission, inasmuch as a socio-affective goal is concerned, incurs unsolvable problems. A language planning design that includes complex, high-level goals touches on creativity and its growth on the development of the learner's autonomy. Therefore, what needed to be brought to light was the paradox of the formulated transposition of the concept of independence, without adhering to one psychological theory or another.

Another issue is that there is a subtle shift, from one interiorization theory to another. Any effort of synthesis retains only the common denominators, the recurring elements from the concepts cited, while trying to avoid simplification or metaphoric interpretation. The interiorization theory that served as the underpinnings of the works of David Krathwohl and his collaborators (1964) is complex, not to mention hybrid, because it assembles many antecedent concepts, as shown in chapters 3 and 4. How did they reconcile this conception with the interiorization-influenced behavioral theses and with the constructivist theses of that time? How do we reconcile today this conception with deeper, socio-cultural understandings of the sedimented layers of *habitus*—these agglomerates of social experience (Bourdieu, 2002)? Vygotskyan interiorization (1930) is but a socially-mediated mentalization of action (Lantolf & Thorne, 2006; Pavlenko, 2005) and does not articulate the possibility of autonomous depth, autopoietic attunement with a content field, and connectivity and resonance across individuals (Tochon, 2007).

It is not possible here to avoid the discussion of foundations. "Personable" views of psychological development have been rejected by sociocultural theorists, most of whom have forgotten that Vygotsky was describing aspects of the socialization of thought and did not develop the extent to which heredity makes each of us unique, despite our shared, socialized vocabulary of this uniqueness through local cultures. Sharing a culture and identity in a society in which practice is clothed within similar choices that, in turn, influence the way each of us expresses his or her identity, does not imply that we are only social constructions. Any parent with two or more children raised in the same social milieu could share their experience and testify that whatever they did, siblings would drastically differ in numerous ways, which would not entirely be accounted for by sociocultural theory.

If once again we applied the inclusive principle in search of a third conceptual space, we might articulate a semiotic niche in which the developmental psychology of the human would be compatible with its sociocultural integration and sharing. We are biological *and* historical beings. The common denominator is life—life as bio-organically and biographically lived, life as a search for deep meaning within the limitations of our organisms, societies, and cultures. The Deep Approach embraces Deep Ecology (Naess, 1973) in the search for a life paradigm. Life is biological, personal, social, and cultural. Yet life differs deeply, and the difference applies as well in the way each of us perceives concepts and their connection to life situations. Therefore, depth is plural, multivalent, and relative to the variety of microworlds that constitute our visions of reality as a space filled by the mind.

Language is not *one*. It is necessary to go beyond the various hypotheses, demonstrating their convergence to ensure a coherent basis for a planning strategy. Is planning not the pragmatic process of generalizing learning situations, allowing the representation of processes within their functional use, without subscribing to an entire system of psychological explanation, which, in any case, is constantly changing?

This is what many curriculum designers have done: opt for a functional approach whose justification would come *a posteriori* in its activation. This strategy's persistence, relative to more sophisticated theories that are complex but less pragmatic (those of J.P. Guilford or Robert Marzano, for example), grants it exemplary status, despite all the arguments that could be advanced regarding its use. At a time when teachers are reclaiming their autonomy and action research or exploratory practice (Allwright, 2003) tends to assign them an intermediary role between the education sciences and the practical classroom setting, the question of the legitimacy of theories of reference is slowly being addressed.

It took curriculum theorists more than fifty years to realize the obsolescence of their outcome-based strategy. One cannot organize schooling on a bad economic model that focuses on basic performance yet keep up with high-level goals. They were finally measuring the pulse of the field when a backlash occurred to a hardline definition of science, separating it from wisdom in practice. There is more than one teaching model, just as there is more than one psychological model. We dare to say that teachers are at liberty to adopt whichever model best serves a given group of students in a given situation. The same cannot be said for psychological models. Presently, no one theory can circumscribe practice - unless that model adapts, self-regulates, emerges from "life-action", and merges with learning in action. To this end, an effort has been made, in this book, to sort out the heterogeneity of theories and show the complementarity that exists among some of them. Far from being reductive, this effort recognizes the complexities of practice that cannot be addressed by a univocal theory. Linear reasoning cannot circumscribe the intertwined realities of practice. The coexistence of seemingly opposed, yet essentially complementary, trends is a fact of life. Therefore, a science dealing with everyday life and its synchrony is compelled to take this into account. The synthesis of opposites that enters into a dialogue with life's contradictions could very well become the method (in reference to Edgar Morin's complex systems' method) or one of the methods in an emerging educative pragmatism. Practitioners' knowledge would constitute a pragmatic, "life-action" science.

Like their students, teachers are creators who continuously develop, complicate and test their personal theories of the world around them. This approach requires adaptive models; research on teachers' thinking has indicated the importance of flexible, non-linear methodologies that span the disciplines (Tochon, 2000). The link between the prescriptive research into curriculum and the descriptive research into teachers' thinking is destined to profoundly affect school programs, teachers' training and continuing education, and any innovation related to teaching itself. This book's argument for a deeper, pragmatic paradigm hopes to advance this movement.

In Conclusion

This chapter briefly reviewed problems related to language ideology, discrimination and linguistic human rights that legitimate the Deep Turn. It proposed teachers and educators to build deeper understanding of the implications of multilingualism and multiculturalism.

As Osborn (2006) expressed, we now need to teach world languages for social justice. The Deep Turn to other languages and cultures may play the role of empowering micro-policy, forming an interface between government policies and classroom practices. It can become the 21st Century success story, starting new forms of dialogue, and also help heritage learners broaden the scope of their native proficiency, preserving languages for which there are few sources and instructing learners about language ideologies and attitudes.

Current changes in pedagogic practices motivate numerous comparisons between methodological worldviews of the past and of the present. What is unthinkable nowadays is that for centuries Chinese teachers never taught the language, but taught philosophy through the language. The learner's language had to reach perfection through learning philosophy. The absence of language pedagogy was deliberate, as this absence itself could bring the essence of educational intelligibility and depth (Wu, 2012). This book was an attempt at reconciling Deweyan project-based learning with deep philosophy, wisdom and the quest for mindful autonomy.

Shallow teaching places the learner in front of pre-formatted curricula and textbooks with extrinsic demands for a specific series of minimal achievements. Fear of failing stimulates extrinsic motivation to get good marks. In contrast, deep learning requires contextualized, holistic experiences in which the identity narrative can expand with new life meanings. The Deep Approach has, for its purpose, to stimulate deep learning. Among the many conceptions of learning, deep learning does emphasizes quality, relevance, and purposefulness rather than rote learning.

Learning a new language is understood as a process of cultural accommodation and abstraction, which is tied to a variety of subtle meanings and situational elements that need to be related to perceive the whole. Such meaningful, intrinsically motivated and active learning supports deep re-interpretations of reality as being partly shaped by the complexities of cross-cultural pragmatics (Goddard, 2011).

Partnering in peace building between the West and the East is crucial at this stage to stop warmongering elites from destroying humans and our environment. This eventually is the invaluable deep focus of learning other languages and cultures, as much as the emancipation from obsolete models of schooling enslaving humans through normative and normalized perpetuation of status quo. Language policies should be at the service of moral, transdisciplinary values rather than focusing on critical targets. This can also be interpreted as a call for changing the role of the military towards real peace maintenance and work for a sustainable world.

Conclusion

> *Recent calls for an early start for foreign language education by President Barack Obama, former Secretary of State Condoleezza Rice, and Utah Governor Gary Herbert, among others, have emphasized the need for linguistically competent, globally competitive students in the 21st century, and language educators are poised to respond by offering well-designed, well-articulated, proficiency- and standards-based curricula and instruction.* Nancy C. Rhodes (2014, p. 116)

U.S. Senator Akaka stated in 2005 that "Americans need to be open to the world; we need to be able to see the world through the eyes of others if we are going to understand how to resolve the complex problems we face" (MLA, 2007, p.235).

For numerous years, policy makers, educators, parents, leaders and research associations called for a better preparation of students to become competent world citizens communicating with some fluency in various languages (Jackson & Malone, 2009). However recent budget cuts with unintended adverse impacts of No Child Left Behind legislation have negatively affected elementary and secondary world language programs (Center on Education Policy, 2009).

World languages are in free fall in the U.S., as a number of politicians have the illusory perception that the whole world now speaks English. Tochon's (2009) review—awarded as the best Review of Education Research of the year by the American Educational Research Association—indicated on the contrary that the number of English speakers worldwide has been in slight decrease in relative percents during the last few years and the trend continues.

A national survey of a representative sample of more than 5,000 U.S. public and private elementary and secondary schools has identified the current patterns and shifts over time in key areas of K–12 world language education (Pufahl & Rhodes, 2011). The results show that "despite some positive developments, overall foreign language instruction has decreased over the past decade and the achievement gap has widened" (p.258). Language programs should start early and be more intensive. K-12 schools need to offer a large number of major languages at multiple, well coordinated levels. An approach to teaching organized on the basis of small group thematic learning projects would help enhancing such coordination. The lack of a specific certification for Elementary language teachers as well as the shortage of teachers must be addressed.

Research and school programs are under funded in world language education. The message is that world languages are less important than Sciences, Technologies, Engineering and Mathematic (STEM), which are supposed to lead the economy. But currently the economy and high finance are growing outside the U.S. This stand favoring STEM also neglects the strong evidence that learning languages improves STEM achievement and is crucial to build the new economy: not an economy of outsourcing but an economy of collaborative, international partners. Specific funding should be made available for world language education at both state and federal levels. This is the condition for the U.S. to be more welcomed in the community of nations. We need to transform the imperial image with its delusive ambition into the image of what the large majority of its population is really: a deeply peaceful and democratic people, willing to live in harmony with our neighbors, curious of new venues and open to so many worthwhile and fascinating other cultures.

Learning How to Deal with Complexity

Outcome-directed theory, born of a rationalist context, is shedding its old skin. It is now on steroids with the standards movement. Stripped of superfluous doctrine, what will it slough off to reinvent itself? It will likely preserve its teleological axis, i.e. the educative project. Operational criteria for evaluation have a limited usefulness, in rubrics that can be renegotiated during projects, and in highly structured subject areas, but they might become an obstacle to active learning. These are best left to psychometricians because of their utility in test management (in the strictest sense). The specification of observable performance can be a useful tool, but there is a tendency to confuse the task with its indicator. The fact remains that very few action verbs are truly unequivocal. There is no longer any question of "previsional exhaustivity": it is impossible to specify all the tasks of a project in advance. Besides, the learner needs a margin of freedom, adaptability and flexibility in the face of the unpredictable that is offered by differentiated approaches. The spontaneity factor can be framed, but within terminal tasks proper to each task domain that stipulate the expected global performances, rather than their supposedly operational dissection. Seasoned teachers recognize that a too-detailed rubric becomes an embarrassment. Pragmatic organizers whose results are not dictated *a priori* by evaluation can accommodate projects in a more creative way.

The organization of instructional units has always been problematic and it is probably here that the research of the deep paradigm will bring solutions. It is natural for people to go forward rather than backward. How can a teacher decide what is simple or complex without input from students? In Deep Approach classes, students learn how to deal with complexity from the start. The definition of tasks maintains some coherence between the conceptual approach and the procedures of evaluation. The search for a pragmatic coherence between strategy and evaluation has been an on-going concern. If models based on performance are expanded to include communicational and intercultural competence, the adoption of flexible organizers seems easier than that of "well-defined" tasks and outcomes. At some point, they may even be complementary, the former sustaining reflexive evaluation, the latter constituting institutional evaluation.

From Sequenciation to Complex Dynamics

When closely examined, it becomes apparent that the sequencing of tasks has always been left up to empiricism. Certain principles, such as that of immediate feedback (operant reinforcement), suggest that teachers should sequence instruction for themselves and proceed linearly from simple to complex. Thinking about prerequisites amounts to relying upon intuition, not to mention the lack of planning designs specific to certain subject areas like less-commonly taught languages. This serious flaw should be redressed by exploratory practice and action-research adjunctive to descriptive, ethnomethodological research.

Other than for the purposes of preparing standardized tests, stipulating criteria and conditions of evaluation for every action seems a wasted effort. Instructional operationalization leads to the fragmentation of learning and favors lower level tasks. The type of sequencing suggested by SLA theory masks the need for the teacher's empiricism under an ostensibly rigorous linearity. Teachers themselves remain the best judges of which resources are best suited for their areas of instruction, their groups of students, and the intricate web of circumstances and projects in which they labor. The linearity of a closed system is at the expense of an indispensable adaptation to the learners and, in World Language Arts, goals of expression. Finally, the omission of the socio-affective aspect in the specification of outcomes confers a degree of sterility to the approach (except perhaps in some advanced and flexible conceptions compatible with learners' self-determination), because motivation follows interest and interest necessitates freedom of choice.

Some teachers describe the Deep Approach as a "non language specific approach". Here is a good place to address this remark. The need for language specific methods emerged from the view that the teacher must be in control as the sole expert (yet informed by applied linguists). This view is only partly true. It is true that teachers need to develop language specific expertise. The feedback and resources they will provide will be more accurate and precise. Nonetheless, if they come to understand the necessity to having the learners in control of their learning, then specific forms of sequencing and their generalization for the whole class no longer make sense. It entails a new and complex dynamic. Therefore, since in the Deep Approach the learners develop a sense of their own zone of proximal development when choosing resources, this selection will always be language specific. The zone of proximal *identity development* becomes even more important, which is identity-specific (Tochon & Lee, 2011).

Conceptualizing Social Action as Deeply Educative

An educative approach based on projects does not attempt to develop content linearly, in a simple-to-complex fashion, disassociated from their application in a socio-affective and cultural context. On the contrary, the educative process operates on many levels simultaneously intradisciplinary, interdisciplinary, transdisciplinary. It operates by regulating the flow of knowledge in a complex interaction. The theory and practice of this educative process are appealing inasmuch as they appear to encompass the more desirable aspects of task-based analysis, while preserving aims of personal expression. But they carry a permanent risk of favoring action at the expense of content, and the project of self at the expense of the educative project or vice versa. It would be necessary to assimilate one to the other, which again is not without some problems related to the negotiation of appropriate choices. This compatibility paradoxically requires rigor in planning (to clarify processes and to map expectations), as well as openness.

It may be feared that a lack of systematic organization may culminate in the demise of the education action project. This danger is real, as demonstrated by the history of this type of learning as well as the evolution of so-called liberation workshops. Thus, in an effort to manage error productively and keep track of learning, this author suggests the association of a unified taxonomy for action with the specification of three levels of instructional organizers. This would allow at least the operative regulation, if not the measure, of the social action project within each task domain, making a global, expressive activity compatible with the thematic structuring of contents. In this model, the educative action project may be defined as an event occurring simultaneously at three levels in a unified taxonomy, which is integrated by a pragmatic direction. The relation between performances in different task domains allows room for the development of global competences through experiential modules supporting value creation.

Content-rich Experiential Learning

The proposals set forth in this book aim for an awareness of learners' deeper needs and of teachers' rationale in planning models. In order to de-emphasize cognitive planning tactics or a compartmentalized approach, it has been suggested herein that the concept of outcomes be refined by a flexible, better-contextualized articulation of instructional organizers that are arranged in thematic modules. Thematic organizers are pragmatic and allow simultaneous action on many levels and the elaboration of sequences that are guided by a well-planned improvisation. In fact, the thematic organizers are not used in the sense of a fragmentation of knowledge in a linear curriculum whose every step would be geared to evaluation. Pragmatic organizers, on the contrary, represent modules of expression and strategies that activate contents within a hol-act. In this way, contents acquire purpose, or significance. The creation of meaning and value is not accomplished in steps but in simultaneous, multiple interactions driven by the educative process itself. It is not a question of confining the student (or the teacher) to a closed learning system, dictating *a priori* the modalities of progression. It is a case of expanding the possibilities for individual expression related to the development of an action involving multi-level learning.

Potential benefits arise from an interrelation between language modalities and task domains. Some attempts have been made, notably in the management of creative expression workshops. However, the lack of organization in these "autonomy workshops" has engendered reaction from teachers whose experience revealed that liberation without a complementary dialectical structuring is not possible. Table 10.1 aims at defining some characteristics of the third educative space.

Table 10.1.
Dialectical Processes Inherent with Educative Projects

1. Planning	2. Teaching	3. Educating
Diachrony	Synchrony	Synergy
Structuring	Free expression	Creation
Organizing	Acting	Managing
Reflecting	Contextualizing	Living

From Routine to Experience via Operative Images

Lee Shulman (1986) has postulated that a teacher's knowledge crystallizes into situational agglomerates in the form of case images, lived experiences and positive examples. In this question, he pursued the work of Donald Schön (1983) whose analysis revealed that professional thinking and planning springs from a bank of practical knowledge that generates examples (cases, anecdotes) or metaphoric images allowing the grasp of new events.

Modular planning that progresses from the integration of interactions between language modalities leaves room for the teacher's routines, or operative images mentioned in the introduction, the metaphors arranging the teacher's language of practice into inspirational mental models. Planning is a means to simplify procedures in order to increase efficiency within a given time. Routine procedures ensure the coordination of action models. Even if project planning should be incapable of always predicting the learning relation, the context, the results of an educative action, and activities of free expression, it can provide the foundations for ensuring the forthcoming interactions through the adoption of an open system of organizers that activate knowledge within a concrete experience. Modular planning that progresses from the integration of interactions between the language modalities leaves room for metaphors and symbolic appeal, arranging the language of practice into inductive models.

The more competent a teacher is, the more liberty she takes. This liberty taken amidst the strong constraints imposed by the system can be explained by the ongoing need for adaptation in the field and to the interaction with the learner. Routine procedures are established to ensure the coordination of behavior. These routines figure so prominently that planning can be defined as a choice made regarding the selection, the organization and the arrangement of routines (Yin, 2003).

This suggests that teachers need time to adapt to a new model of behavior. They might need to start using it for a few weekly hours at first until they feel comfortable with it and become confident that they can handle deep learning situations.

Modeling Experiential Innovation

The IAPI modeling of educative projects introduces new routines with improvisational potential. Its template helps students integrate new tasks within a methodological structure they grow accustomed to. It helps them focus on the crucial aspects of their projects and get on task.

The methodical process of organizing knowledge tends to become automatic in the learner, who comes to grips with new resources through an action-based modeling format. The learner interiorizes a structure of accommodation, i.e. a group of procedures that allows the automatic transposition of knowledge into mind maps, rubrics and models formatting action. This interiorized organizational frame is soon deeply entrenched in learners' minds, which provides a path to deep learning. Teachers report that this format helped students create their own modules. Thus, the process of developing plans occurs in the moment, when content is being assimilated, as well as during the mental or written preparation of projects. Planning includes two phases: the first phase, accommodating and ascending, targets the construction of flexible mental models, and alternates with a second, descending phase corresponding to the use of these models in the project planning process.

Routinization cannot be discounted in any innovation that fosters links between old and new strategies. Besides, innovation can only be conceived in terms of ongoing reflection, giving time to interiorize new modules. These modules crystallize into routines that free learners from preoccupations over content, allowing them to be attentive to the social and affective aspects of their projects. They can progress from planning to learning in the sense of a conceptual awareness of their actions. Thanks to well-formed routines based on the IAPI model, learners can excel in the area of content to be acquired—which they manipulate at will when they have been interiorized—as well as in the adaptive area of their relation to their projects. To these ends, project participants are not in need of a linear prescriptive model as much as a flexible framework that embraces their deep aspirations.

Crucial Changes Are Needed in the Teacher's Role

The role of the world language teacher is changing from instruction to pedagogical scaffolder, cross-cultural resources librarian and methodological counselor. In addition, many beginning and early intermediate learners prefer having a non-native teacher (Karaman, Serpil & Black, 2008). There are a variety of reasons for that: the non-native teacher is better able to create the necessary cognitive links between L2 and L1, the pedagogy is adapted to the first culture, and bridges towards the target culture can be set to attenuate culture shock. Moreover, feedback is usually lighter and more lenient than if it came from a native speaker, who may not always be aware of all the difficulties language learners may meet. The downside of it is that the other culture tends to be prototyped, if not stereotyped, and modeled according to the assumptions of the first culture (Azocar, 2011).

From a certain threshold up, probably somewhere at the end of the intermediate proficiency spectrum, conversing and getting feedback from native speakers, as well as having a teacher who is a native speaker, often helps in evolving toward advanced and superior levels of proficiency. This is a loaded statement, which deserves further comment. The current and shared understanding of languages as *linguae francae* implies that non-native learners may not easily operate within the phonetic matrix and morphosyntax of the native speakers. There is no one and unique correct language variety, as the unity of a language is, in large part, a construction of grammarians (Reagan, 2012). Nevertheless, well-trained and pedagogically wise mother tongue speakers, whatever their social class and regional variation, are useful helpers in uncovering a wide variety of local and cultural resources, have historical knowledge that non-native speakers might not have, and may help in contextualizing information. This means, that generally—and there are many exceptions of highly proficient non-native teachers having spent many years in the other country and culture—there are legitimate reasons to recommend that advanced level language and culture teachers preferably be mother tongue speakers. Further refining of this recommendation is that they should be well trained and well rounded for a Deep Approach of their language and culture. Indeed, native speakers may tend to be more directive and less inclined to be patient with the initial chaotic phase of project-based learning. Thorough feedback on intensive writing is also highly demanding.

A correlate of this change in the role of the teacher is that—if the resources for a Deep Approach are available—beginning and early intermediate teachers could scaffold learning of a family of languages, not simply one language. This may be a very shocking statement at a time when universities try to cut down on 101 – 102 – 203 - 204 language courses, which appears counterproductive if only for economic reasons:

these language levels are in high demand and institutionally profitable; moreover, they are important to support graduate students in providing positions for teaching assistants. We can reflect on the changes the new format could bring in K-12 school districts. *IF* the resources were created with modules and applications, allowing students to creatively format elementary and intermediate projects in blended and scaffolded e-learning environments, such as the one we developed for Turkish. Spanish or French teachers could scaffold language apprenticeship for learners of Italian or Portuguese as well, for instance.

Transcribed videos with captions, recorded conversation associated with role-playing would go a long way if associated with interactive websites providing video chats and peer tandems with native speakers of their age. Grammar use could be recorded in the storytelling mode to complement film excerpts and modules. This would fit an emerging need in many school districts for language programs in less-commonly-taught languages due to the growing numbers of heritage speakers. It matches the principles of multilingualism (Troncy, 2014). Besides providing autonomous learning to non-native speakers, the Deep Approach is a particularly good fit for heritage speakers (Tochon, 2011a).

As Henry Jacotot demonstrated in his own experience, teachers can teach languages when they are familiar with the structure and culture, even if they do not speak them, until a native language teacher is available. Yet the view of what a native language speaker is should not be framed into this stereotypical image of someone having lived most of his or her life in the capital of the major country associated with that language, since a variety of native languages are welcome and the definition of language is becoming more fluid. This conclusion—another shocking hypothesis in the search for a deeper approach to language learning—has far reaching implications and should be a focus for future research. If the trend were adopted that language teachers be placed in a position to scaffold deep learning for a family of languages, teacher education should be adapted as well to give them a more methodological sense of their role, and to equip them with some comparative understanding in the chosen family of languages.

New Avenues for Deep Research

The fact that the Deep Approach template emerged from field research explains how and why its flexible guidelines work in the field. They match the natural practice of seasoned practitioners. The model came from the stories that highly experienced language teachers reported about their genuine ways of organizing learning interactions into projects.

This book has described the basis for the deep model and its templates. They emerged from research on expert language teacher thinking, through protocols comparing the preactive, interactive and post-active phases of teaching. This was mainly done in K-12 schools. It was considered the Phase I of research on the Deep Approach, which was ethnocognitive in methodology. Seasoned teachers would explain their plans, then their classes would be observed, and that was followed with a post-active interview on what happened and what the rationale was for the organization of these events. This highlighted instructional flexibility and variability, and the task domains used by these teachers in their actual practice, as well as the focus of these teachers on process organizing rather than outcome-based planning. Since this research was held in several countries, two models were derived, one with task domains that match the European framework, and one with task domains that match activities framed for the American classroom.

Then a Phase II of this research started with the creation of instructional material for a specific language and program assessment with a forum to support primarily college-level teaching, while I was also contacted by secondary teachers, teachers from private schools, as well as self-taught learners using this online material. I chose a less-commonly taught language for this demonstration: indeed, there was a lack of instructional materials in this area and the Deep Approach could bring fresh air into a dynamic language association. Deep Approach materials were created online for the Turkish language, thanks to a Title VI grant awarded by the U.S. Department of Education. This led to the creation of templates that can serve as guides for other languages. Program evaluations were conducted in Big Ten and Ivy League universities, and other universities are joining the program. The instructional materials are copyrighted, but are freely available on the internet. The results, published in Tochon (2013), Tochon, Karaman and Ökten (2014), and Tochon, Ökten, Karaman and Druc (2014), indicate higher proficiency compared to control groups, reduced fear of tests, deeper learning and significant improvements on most factors of cross-cultural learning. The aforementioned report details the instructional material that was created for the Deep Approach, and how to use it.

One concern rises from offering such instructional material online: some instructors start using these instructional modules with no understanding of the importance of self-determination and self-directedness in deep, project-based apprenticeship. The good side of this is that it indicates the quality and compatibility of the materials with other approaches, yet these instructors lose the depth that could be achieved with better training. Thus, research on deep teacher education is needed (Karaman, Ökten & Tochon, 2012). It could be done through video study groups: see Tochon (1999) for a how-to guide designed for self-sufficient teachers who would like to organize their own professional development.

This book has touched on many topics regarding deep language teaching and learning. In order to better define the nature of depth in learning and teaching and the relationship between depth, the factors that affect a Deep Approach, and its possible benefits for language and culture learning as well as for broader transdisciplinary goals, new research is needed. Although deep learning has been shown to benefit learners, research must investigate whether self-regulated projects and self-directed thematic preference is indicative of inherent characteristics that learners bring with them to the classroom. Perhaps more importantly, we need studies of the extent to which student beliefs about their ability or inability to work autonomously towards language learning can be altered. The Deep Approach to learner apprenticeship is strategic and has enormous potential. Instead of training students with strategies that have been generalized from existing studies, we need to guide students to discover their own strategies, which should be more effective and long-lasting. This new perspective to learning strategies training could change the beliefs that students have about learning a language, and stimulate students' motivation for successful and autonomous language learning.

Research on the Deep Approach focuses on questions to students, to teachers, and to policymakers, such as: what do you consider deep in your activity, and what is shallow? What are the criteria associated with depth and surface action? What would legitimate going deeper? Why are surface approaches potentially detrimental to sound, shared development in your work? In your field? Can you give example in your daily life? What is your own sense of depth? What would change in your activity if you targeted depth? How could you organize globally to reach such a deep purpose? What are the aids and the obstacles? What are the constraints in your environment that prevent the change from taking place? With whom should you negotiate the changes? How can you share your definition of what is deep, and why it should be reached? Is there a connection between depth and a better life?

Final Warnings

The rationale for these warnings is that the Deep Approach is not a dogmatic doctrine: it is inquiry-based.

The first warning is that this book brings crucial ideas and principles for education that cannot really be fixed to an institutional system of schooling; not that it is impossible to introduce it in schools. On the contrary, the ideas and principles emerge from the careful study of seasoned teachers' practices when they were allowed by a particularly flexible principal or superintendent to go by their genuine impulses and knowledge to teach 'a third way'.

The book requires the teacher to think in terms of finding the time to become a knowledgeable resource person, to deeply understand cultural differences, otherness, language discrimination and linguistic human rights, to create the space to introduce more freedom in the learning system, to take the student's self-determination into account, and to change mass instruction into a deep personalized apprenticeship adapted to the interests and motives and values brought by the learners.

The solutions proposed in this book can be integrated in the life of some language programs to variable degrees, depending on the flexibility that school stakeholders are ready to provide for individual teams of teachers to change trends and revolutionize their conception of learning, as well as the type of subordination that is being created by the process of teaching and schooling itself. The propositions in this book are serious, in the sense that these solutions work, they have been tested by experience, and teachers may and can adapt them as they see fit. The key aspect is 'as they see fit', which makes the whole endeavor touchy. Like any professional endeavor, change from old to new practices may require perseverance, strength, courage, and depth.

I have given workshops on the Deep Approach to Language and Cultures to many K-12 teachers and teaching assistants since 2008. As a teacher educator, I already see that the force of this book, from those who could read some chapters before their publication and experimented with the new approach, will rapidly make it a trend. The Deep Approach is already becoming a buzzword. Herein lies the second danger: because of the buzz, some people might adopt the word without even exploring the deep conceptualization behind it or knowing what it represents to re-center on Deep Education (Tochon, 2010b). They may ignore the effort needed for understanding one's own discipline another way, and what commitment is needed to make schooling a whole different adventure because of the perseverance, prolonged effort, unique knowledge, and the willingness to learn by oneself. Those who make the effort will convey to their students, like Socrates: the only thing I know is that I know nothing; the understanding is yours! Such a humble statement of the unfathomable depth of otherness will be the basis for taming Rancière's (1991) concept of ignorant master, becoming able to un-teach, un-helping others to be themselves and choose and build their path on their own. Better your own path than the path of another, even wiser, advised Bhagavat Gita, in an Indian story about life as a game of power, of which the rabbit story at the beginning of the first chapter was just an echo.

The second warning is thus: that if this book brings a model of teacher expertise, it also indicates that expertise is something personal that takes time to develop. It is after much conceptual work and original reflection that one can realize what meaning, as an educator, one wants to give to the word depth, and how it can be enacted within one's environment and society, with one's character, qualities, and limitations. At that moment, the model will probably become diaphanous, transparent, and it will be referred to as a possible discourse only, as what will take priority will be action and value creation to match the level of transdisciplinary depth that has been reached by personal reflection and professional practice. This book is on a particular grammar of action, the grammar of world languages' apprenticeship. It is the story of these teachers who have reached expertise such that they now intend to free their students of their omnipresence, to meet their students' needs—leaving them free to choose what they want to learn, their pacing, and how they want to learn it—; giving benchmarks that require negotiation and re-negotiation as understanding and projects grow.

To Sum Up

Why Do We Need a New Approach to Foreign/Second Language Teaching?

Here are a few issues with the current language methods that sum up the propositions made in this book:

- Controlled teaching for controlled learning rarely leads to proficiency. With outcome-based learning, students are limited in their development by the pre-specified goals that are assigned to them.

- Reductionist approaches tend to reify the concepts taught within a monolithic view of the language. Educational outcomes reify competences as if one could 'learn' proficiency. When outcomes are solidified into sub-standards, the bureaucratic view of education tends to reduce the scope of what is being taught and learned. The tendency is increasingly to teach to test, and teach only the core knowledge.

- Language courses are limited by the reference to applied linguistics. However, language is more than language. We need to frame the approach within the broader framework of applied semiotics, which integrates cross-cultural pragmatics, language policies, the issues related to language status and linguicism, and action in a complex and subtle environment which requires a better understanding of linguistic human rights. Socio-cultural features are an inherent part of the approach. Such a deep semiotic approach bridges language, aesthetics, and meaningful action in context.

- In settings of controlled learning, students often note a lack of opportunities for self-directed learning, as most current approaches do not take into account the results of motivation research. Teaching is then based on extrinsic motivation, and there is not much room for student's self-determination. The new approach matches the results of motivation research and identity research.

- At a time when the takeover of education tends to enslave students in the market ideology and its forms of social oppression, we need to reclaim the right to be different and individualized rather than standardized, as all of us have a right to be unique. While it is true that knowledge is socially constructed, knowledge relates to personal experience; our experiential perceptions may differ greatly from each other. Genetics, heredity, and the unique components of stratified *habitus* and identity make us entirely unique as human beings. We need an approach that returns the humane to the fore, in the sense of a deeper account of humanity and humaneness in the education system, and language classes in particular.

- A lack of critical depth and deep content is often noted in language instruction. A number of researchers and practitioners have alluded to the importance of reaching instructional depth. Taking depth into account will help re-conceptualize the field in a way that will support a paradigmatic shift. Deep learning requires deep understanding and implies ethnorelativism and critical thinking.

- In most current language methods, the teacher or the applied linguist is the curriculum builder. In contrast, self-directed learning requires that the student become the curriculum builder on the basis of broad resources provided by the instructor, who takes a role of facilitator and gives regular and thorough feedback on writing practices and extensive reading, film watching, reflective analysis of the language and open discussion toward social and environmental action.

- Current language methods often lack higher dimensions and life values beyond the disciplinary content being taught; in contrast, the new approach is transdisciplinary, targeting higher level, Earth-based values that imply humaneness, a unity of knowledge, social action, and intellectual and spiritual emancipation.

- In the current communication era, the primacy given to oral expression prevents a deeper account of the language complexity and culture. The primacy should be given back to the text as an inscription of knowledge, without neglecting oral, interpersonal exchange.

- Content is rarely fully integrated into the language methods while the coherence between methodology and epistemology requires such integration; the new approach is content-based, immersive and interdisciplinary. It uses instructional materials from a variety of disciplines to develop language proficiency.

- Current educative approaches are normative; the Deep Approach is process-focused; deep instructional modules and master plans refer to task organizers rather than outcomes. Input and output are balanced, and open. Projects require input from the learner as to the topics being developed, the strategies and types of projects, and the formation of pairs or teams.

- Most other language learning methods are sequential. Then students are at loss when immersed abroad. A non-sequential approach to the language in context, with many opportunities for the learners to untangle the parts they work on, will prepare them better for future immersion.

- Presently, the use of new technologies is still relatively scarce; there is a lack of linguistic immersion and contact with native speakers that new technologies could provide, if they were integrated as an integral part of the curriculum. Blended learning with social networking, video and multimedia may create thresholds to deeper language learning.

In summary, the Deep Approach requires new ways of understanding language learning as a life project. The roles of the learner and the teacher are different. One way to stimulate deep learning is to free students from surface, linear curricula and to allow them to organize their own projects with an abundance of resources. With the Deep Approach, the fields of World Language Education, Second Language as well as Third Language Acquisition have found their higher goal.

Decolonizing Foreign Language Education
An Afterword

by
Donaldo Macedo
University of Massachusetts Boston

François Tochon's new book, *Help Them Learn a Language Deeply!*, is at once brilliant and humble. Its brilliance lies in Tochon's ability to courageously join a select group of scholars such as Tim Reagan, Claire Kramsch, and Terry Osborn, among others, all of whom have studiously and rigorously challenged "the marginalization of foreign language education." Their challenges rupture the yoke of colonialism that informs and shapes the relationship between foreign language education and literary studies—a relationship unavoidably tainted by colonization since, by and large, most foreign language programs are housed in foreign literature departments that, by and large, reproduce values of the dominant ideology.

Tochon's humility enables him to transcend the arrogance that has traditionally permeated foreign language literature studies and relegated foreign language teaching to a sub-disciplinary status in the academy. Unfortunately, literature professors who make decisions about the curriculum know little about the very complex nature of the foreign language they have learned to read and write primarily to gain access to that language's literary texts. These foreign literature professors know even less about the multifaceted processes of second language acquisition and how universal principles of grammar determine and predict certain linguistic realizations. I am reminded of a seminar organized many years ago by a former professor of foreign languages at Harvard—a seminar that focused on the principles of textbook sequencing. After listening to her prescriptive rationale as to why grammatical concepts needed to follow specific sequencing (i.e., the present tense is followed the perfect tense which, in turn, is followed by the imperfect tense, the future tense, etc.), I felt unconvinced and politely asked her to reconcile her conclusions with the current emerging research on second-language acquisition spearheaded by Michael Long, Lidia White, Suzanne Flynn, Derek Bikerton, Stephen Krashen, Roger Anderson, and John Schuman, among others—studies that suggest convincingly that the stages of second-language acquisition, like first-language acquisition, are determined by universal principles that must meet at least one fundamental condition: maximal learnability.

It was not my intent to engage my colleague from Harvard in a debate regarding the theoretical status of learnability as some have suggested. I simply felt it would be rewarding to engage her and the audience in a discussion that considered the role of universal grammar (UG) in determining accessibility to structures. She abruptly interrupted me, suggesting that the second-language acquisition literature was tentative and inconclusive. Given my youth at the time and my enthusiasm for the important insights that the second-language acquisition studies were reporting, I pushed the issue further by insisting that stages of second language acquisition were governed by principles of universal grammar (UG), thus predictable. I more aggressively suggested she would have to consider the role of the theory of markedness in her determination of tense sequencing. That is, the more marked the structure, the later the acquisition, and that the least marked structures are more accessible and thus more easily learnable. My foray into debating a senior professor from Harvard who commanded undivided and uncritical attention from an audience made up largely of literature professors with little to no understanding of linguistic and language acquisition theories, was quickly cut short as she interrupted me for the second time: "Young man, you are out of order. We are not going to wait for second-language research findings to write foreign language textbooks." Clueless about academic protocols at the time, I ventured to have the last word by saying, "Thank goodness the medical field does not prescribe cancer treatments in the same manner, without scientific evidence to support their medical interventions." Needless to say, I was never invited back.

I learned a painful lesson about academic hierarchy from this incident. It also taught me how pernicious the arrogance of ignorance derived from institutional authority can be and how it can often lead to the fragmentation of bodies of knowledge, giving rise to a misguided elitism that, in turn, creates tensions and contradictions between theory and practice. Often theorists devalue practice while practitioners dismiss theory as unnecessary and cumbersome while not realizing that there is always a theory that explains practice, acknowledged or not. On learning stages, Tochon takes two strong theoretical stands that are directly informed by practice. First the way of organizing learning sequences backward from the targeted goal is restrictive and may limit learners to shallow learning predetermined by specific outcomes. We should leap way from this restrictive way of building sequences and adopt a creative, generative sequence that allows a variety of outcomes. Second, he emphasizes that teachers or textbook designers are not the best people to select the ideal learning sequence. Only the learner can sense and choose his or her zone of proximal development. This leads to greater autonomy in curriculum design, which in large part should be assumed by the learner. Yes, says Tochon, stages of progression are predictable, yet the best persons to evaluate maximum learnability are the learners themselves, if they are placed in an environment of rich and culturally authentic resources. Otherwise "spoon feeding" may deprive them for their power on their own learning process.

I am reminded of former classmates of mine while doing research as a visiting scholar in MIT's Linguistics and Philosophy Department. They considered themselves "pure" linguists and had little appreciation or tolerance for issues of language instruction and the role of language in society, particularly along the lines of gender, class, culture, and ethnicity, including the linguistic hybridity that results from languages in contact. This misguided elitism also seeps through the field of applied linguistics and gives rise to a hierarchy demarcated by sub-specializations such as foreign language education, heritage language studies, English as a foreign language (EFL), ESL education, bilingualism studies, and bilingual education, the latter having the least prestige.

In the United States, for example, ESL education is often linked with images of lower-class immigrant students that populate urban schools in major cities. Thus, it enjoys less prestige within the academy even though the field of applied linguistics is characterized by "those areas of language description and analysis that locate themselves within the social world, and which understand language use as a form of social practice."[1]

Tochon's humility allows him to transcend the arrogance of disciplinary rigidity and status hierarchies while unabashedly embracing an interdisciplinary approach to language analysis and teaching that factor in cross-cultural variables. He convincingly argues for "methodologies associated with language arts and first language literacy [that] must now be integrated into the second/foreign language classroom for a deeper, integrated apprenticeship of languages and cultures. What makes *Help Them Learn a Language Deeply!* unique is the author's profound understanding of culture that goes beyond the elitist and often reductionist view of culture that, with rare exception, continues to dominate literary studies and to reproduce dominant values throughout the field of foreign language education. It is these values that perpetuate myths of supremacy that provide individuals, according to Vaclav Havel, with "the repository of something 'supra-personal,' an objective [that] enables people to deceive their own conscience and conceal their true position and their inglorious modus vivendi, both from the world and from themselves."[2] The elitist conception of culture (high culture) that permeates literary studies reproduces a philosophy that functions in the interest of the dominant ruling elites rather than in the interest of the subordinate groups that are the object of policies of cultural reproduction. In other words, if one critically analyzes the integration of culture in even some progressive approaches to foreign language teaching, it soon becomes apparent that many foreign language textbooks and methods of teaching are nothing more or less than a sophisticated tourist guide selectively shepharding students through the great deeds of "civilized" cultures and archeological sites associated with the language being taught. They celebrate and focus primarily on the "great" cultural deeds of mostly former colonial powers and literacy. The foreign language curriculum is constructed as a set of practices that function to disempower those who, through an accident of birth, are not part of a class structure where literacy serves as fundamental cultural capital.

Foreign language educators seldom make explicit that they are teaching a dominant discourse in the target language, denying learners who are not middle and upper class nuances that are imperative in the foreign language acquisition process. What foreign language textbooks and methodologies often hide is the underbelly, the true cultural reality, of the countries whose languages we are teaching. For instance, the integration of French culture into the French language lessons teachers are charged to teach would certainly give students a comprehensive tour of France through the prism of great museums and historical sites. If the teacher considers himself/herself a liberal, the integration may even include café life and casual encounters with ordinary French speakers, but what will never be allowed is the role of French culture in the dehumanization of other cultural beings so painfully captured by Franz Fanon in his book *Wretched of the Earth*. What will not be allowed is a cultural tour of the quasi-apartheid life in Paris where North Africans and Muslims are reduced to subhumanity. What will certainly not be encouraged is the analysis of the relationship between, for example, the colonization of Algeria and the Algerian immigrant life in the ghettoes of Paris—an analysis where students could even read the great French philosopher Jean-Paul Sartre when he protested that the "conquest [of Algeria] occurred through violence and over-exploitation, and oppression necessitates continued violence, so the army is present. There would be no contradiction in that, if terror reigned everywhere in the world, but the colonizer enjoys, in the mother country, democratic rights that the colonialist system refuses to the colonized."3

In this more progressive scenario in the French classroom, students learning French would be encouraged to develop critical tools that would enable them to link France's colonial past with its present neocolonial system that regulates the immigrant life in Paris. They would be able to clearly hear and understand the painful cries of a Roma woman in French, "Why did God even create us, if we are to live like this?", as bulldozers moved in to tear down the camp in Gennevilliers on the outskirts of Paris,3 leaving elderly Roma men, women, and children homeless and hungry. Foreign language textbooks and methodologies are not designed to expose the barbarism and primitivism that characterize the colonial legacy that informs present immigrant life in major colonial metropolises. These texts and methodologies are also not designed to expose policies that threaten to eradicate the cultural expressions of the members of those groups who, by virtue of their race, ethnicity, language, or culture are not treated with the dignity and respect warranted in a true democracy. The colonial model of cultural literacy, implicit in most foreign language education today, is designed to mostly reproduce dominant values through programs that are, in general, discriminatory, mediocre, and based on verbalism."[4] The integration of culture in foreign language education is hugely class based and generally ignores the rich and complex fabric of diverse cultures subsumed under the dominant class's culture. Consequently, the expected role of integration of culture in foreign language textbooks and methodologies muffles cultural diversity through a process that "attempt[s] to view culture as a soothing balm—the aftermath of historical disagreement—some mythical present where irrationalities of historical conflict have been smoothed out."[5]

It is against this backdrop of a "disingenuous view of culture [which is also] profoundly dishonest"[6] that *Help Them Learn a Language Deeply!* stands out as a remarkable book. It is characterized by its emphasis on the development of critical skills in language teaching and learning by "integrating structure and agency to meet deeper, humane aims"—critical tools that would reject the teaching of selective cultural knowledge, which produces a disarticulation of this same knowledge by dislodging it from a critical and coherent comprehension of the world that informs and sustains it. This disarticulation of knowledge anesthetizes consciousness, without which one can never have clarity of reality. It is for this reason that conservative and even some liberal language teachers would more readily embrace mechanistic methodologies based on language instrumentality and would avoid Tochon's call to "deepen language curriculum and instruction in ways that are respectful to language and culture differences." To "deepen language curriculum" would necessarily call for a different approach to language teacher education, one that takes cross-cultural education seriously and incorporates "broader projects that meet higher values and aims such as deep ecology, deep culture, deep politics and deep humane economics."

Tochon's proposal to teach language deeply is in direct opposition to traditional foreign language education that sustains a notion of ideology that systematically negates rather than makes meaningful the cultural experiences of members of subordinated linguistic groups who are, by and large, the objects of its policies. Traditional foreign language education was designed to produce cultural homogeneity rather than authentic cultural democracy. Although there has been great progress in diversifying foreign language education, it remains largely class based, as attested to by the success of dual language immersion programs populated mostly by middle-class white students and the endemic failure of bilingual education populated generally by lower-class immigrant and linguistic minority students.

Dual language immersion programs include mostly a middle-class socialization and provide greater space for cultural production where the curriculum is viewed as an integral part of the ways students produce, transform, and reproduce meaning and develop their capacity for critical and independent thinking. On the other hand, transitional bilingual education, with its focus on English language acquisition, is based on cultural reproduction where the cultural experiences of lower-class and linguistic minority students, including their native languages, are devalued if not eradicated. The sad irony is that, after losing their native languages and distancing themselves substantially from their cultural experiences, these lower-status students, in the future, will probably encourage their grandchildren to enroll in heritage language education that the dominant society now celebrates. What remains veiled is that in order for the society to have heritage language programs, these languages had to have been eradicated in some point in time in the first place. This blatant contradiction is seldom unpacked given the insidiousness of the ideology that views the education of immigrant students in transitional bilingual programs as a matter of simply learning standard English language and manifests its logic with renewed emphasis on memorization or technical reading and writing skills.

The inability to make linkages between the promotion of heritage language programs and the concurrent eradication of transitional bilingual programs in states such as Alabama, Arizona, California, and Massachusetts, among others, is predicated on the dominant ideology that falsely denies that language education is an eminently political phenomenon. But it should always be analyzed within the context of a theory of power relations and an understanding of social and cultural reproduction and production. How else can one explain the contradiction inherent in the Massachusetts language policy that forbids, for instance, instruction of content subject matter in the students' native Spanish language while, at the same time, Spanish is taught down the hall as a foreign language to mostly mainstream white native English-speaking students who are generally middle-class and are enrolled in college-bound tracks. The contradiction is more glaring when the same school system requires these same students—denied literacy in their native language through the imposition of English as the only language of instruction—to later relearn their forgotten mother tongue as a foreign language if they are to be college bound. This complicity prevents an infusion of criticity the language curriculum that would otherwise create pedagogical spaces for the following questions to be asked: "What culture, against what, for whom and against whom?" Language educators would have to consider the cleansed "civilizing" role of the dominant culture in the exclusion of other cultural beings who are often relegated to the status of half citizenry. It is this need for self-examination and change among language educators that creates opposition to even a mild request to study language deeply and critically.

Tochon's proposal for deep language education, through which students could develop critical skills that enable them to easily see the contradictions inherent in the dominant language policies that regulate their (mis)education, is very attractive to educators who have democratic convictions and are committed to a humane pedagogy that requires critical reflection and action. It is simultaneously threatening to both conservative and vacillating liberal educators who pay lip service to the integration of culture in foreign language teaching but remain complicit with the dismantling of bilingual and bicultural programs for mostly lower-class immigrant and linguistic minority students.

I am reminded of a discussion that took place in our Applied Linguistics Department concerning the profile of our next faculty hire. Because our department is Freirean inspired and several faculty members consider themselves to be language critical educators, one colleague cautioned us that "we should not hire any more critical pedagogues," but rather, a "pure applied linguist." Notwithstanding that the construction "pure applied linguist" is an oxymoron, this colleague revealed her deep ignorance of critical theory and critical pedagogy. Along the lines of Paulo Freire's thinking, I have always rejected reductionist proposals that reduce critical pedagogy to a method. Critical pedagogy is not a method. It is a way of being in the world and with the world. Hence, one does not teach critical pedagogy in abstraction disarticulated from the subject matter one is charged to teach. What Freire emphasizes in his writings is that teachers teach all subject matters critically, including language.

While Tochon does not explicitly claim to have been directly influenced by Freire, his deep approach to language teaching and his passionate insistence that "value-loaded projects [should be] chosen in order to revolutionize the current state of affairs, in increasing our sense of responsibility for our actions as humans vis-à-vis our fellow humans and our home planet," renders his humanely written book deeply Freirean. It is Freirean to the degree that it calls for revolutionary actions in language teaching, not only in the teaching/learning process, but also through a deep communion with the "wretched of the earth" whose native languages have been asphyxiated by the colonial languages we teach. *Help Them Learn a Language Deeply!* is Freirean because it requires a deep communion with the very people about whom we make our careers, denouncing their human sufferings and oppressive conditions. It is also Freirean in that it condemns those who prey on human suffering and oppressive conditions to establish a platform for career building while avoiding linguistic and cultural conviviality with the oppressed—a conviviality that can serve as "theoretical context in which [the people we write about and us] together [analyze] the concrete events they [are] living through and planned the strategy of their action."[7]

Tochon's book is more than a treatise on language pedagogy. It "presents a grammar and [plans] the strategy of [their] action "for deep instructional planning, a grammar for action [which implies understanding] of adaptive and complex cross-cultural situations [that should] be the prime focus of such a hermeneutic inquiry." Consequently, we should increase our sense of responsibility to understand deeply that writing about education, particularly the education of the culturally "other," when our only contact with those individuals is when they come to our university classrooms or when we visit their classrooms and their communities to collect research data, constitutes inauthentic communion that benefits mostly those who already hold privileged positions.

Finally, *Help Them Learn a Language Deeply!* is revolutionary in its recognition that "only praxis in the context of communion makes conscientization a viable project." Concientization [which can only be achieved via a deep mastery of language] is a joint project in that it takes place in ...[people] ... among other [people] united by their action and by their reflection upon that action and the world."[8] Foreign language education, if carried out critically along the lines suggested by Tochon, is, par excellence, an important and perhaps essential venue for action in the world for the transformation of dehumanizing conditions—a transformation that indignantly denounces any and all forms of injustices and human misery while yearning for an ever-increasing expansion of our humanity.

REFERENCES OF THE AFTERWORD

1. Cited in Bessie Mitsikopoulou, *Rethinking Online Education: Media, Pedagogies, and Identities* (Boulder, CO: Paradigm Publishers, forthcoming).
2. Vaclav Havel, *Living in Truth* (London: Faber and Faber, 1989), 41.
3. Jean-Paul Sartre, "Introduction," in Albert Memmi, *The Colonizer and the Colonized* (Boston: Beacon Press, 1991), xxiv.
4. Paulo Freire and Donaldo Macedo, *Literacy: Reading the Word and the World* (South Hadley, MA: Bergin & Garvey, 1987), 143.
5. Peter McClaren, "Collision with Otherness," *American Journal of Semiotics* 9, nos. 2-3 (1993): 52-64.
6. Ibid.
7. Paulo Freire, *The Politics of Education: Culture, Power and Liberation* (South Hadley, MA: Bergin & Garvey, 1985), 84.
8. Ibid., 85.

Glossary

Academia: Cultural community of practice engaged in education and research to collaborate in the fixation of beliefs in every branch of learning. The akademeia outside Athens was Plato's famous learning center, or gymnasium.

Accuracy: Normed language production.

Achievement test: A test supposed to measure what students have learned from a program of study; evaluative part of most language programs, which attempts at matching the goals of the language course. Expression of a reductionist trend hypothesizing that achievement can be defined and measured is ways that can be generalized for all students in the same manner. Very few such tests measure deep learning; on the contrary, these tests often tend to induce shallow learning.

Active learning: process whereby learners are actively engaged in the learning process, rather than "passively" absorbing lectures. Active learning involves reading, writing, discussion, and engagement in solving problems, analysis, synthesis, and evaluation. Active learning often involves cooperative learning.

Activity Theory: A Soviet psychological framework rooted in the socio-cultural approach of Alexei Leontyev and S. L. Rubinshtein. It became one of the major theories for applied psychology, education and work psychology.

Aim and objective: An aim expresses the broad purpose of an educational unit whereas an objective states a specific goal which participants are expected to demonstrate at the completion of an instructional unit.

Alternative education: non-traditional approach to teaching and learning for students of all ages and all levels of education.

a posteriori: in retrospect, after the fact

Apprenticeship: Situated, in practice training of skilled crafts practitioners.

a priori: in principle

Assessment: Is the validation of learning activities with a logic of accountability that may, in many cases, be counterproductive and backlash in reducing the power to learn.

Assignment: Lesson, task, homework, project or other course deliverable that can be assigned to the learners to complete on their own, without instructional assistance.

Audiolingualism: Behavioral language learning stressing listening and speaking before reading and writing; activities such as dialogues and drills, formation of good habits and automatic language use through much repetition; exclusive target language use in the classroom.

Aural: Related to listening.

Authentic text: Natural or real teaching material; often this material is taken from newspapers, magazines, radio, TV or podcasts. Authentic materials are resources that have been developed specifically for native speakers. These include print, audio, and visual materials.

Autodidactism or autodidacticism: Self-education or self-directed learning, one of the conditions for deep learning. An **autodidact** is a mostly self-taught person, who has an enthusiasm for self-education and a high degree of intrinsic motivation.

Autopoietic: system embedded in a dynamic of changes such as sensory-motor coupling; living element showing attributes that include responsiveness, feedback, growth, homeostatic self-regulation, energy transformation, ability to generate new forms and reproduce.

Backward design, also called **backward planning**: teacher-centered plan of a unit or lesson by identifying the intended end task or product, then working in reverse to identify the prerequisite tasks and assessment. Form of mind programming that leads to shallow, identical learning for all.

Belief: A conviction to the truth of a proposition, acquired through perception, contemplation or communication. According to the semiotician Charles Peirce, science is the result of the process of fixation of beliefs.

Bilingual education as various definitions:
- two languages are used for teaching;
- help is provided for children to become bilingual (such as two-way bilingual education);
- regional or native language is first used, followed by mainstreaming in classes in the national of official language;
- regional or native language is used with minimal instruction the other language.

Biliteracy: being literate in two or more languages, and considered stronger than being simply bilingual, as reading and writing are added to proficiency in listening and speaking.

Blended learning: Learning in an alternation of instructional modes, such as face-to-face teaching and online learning.

Brainstorming: Producing ideas individually or sharing ideas in a group by free associations for enhancing creativity in order to generate a large number of ideas leading to an improved concept. As ideas come to the mind, they are written or recorded and stimulate the development of better ideas. Listing all thoughts or ideas on a topic to be narrowed down later.

Brainwashing: Use of covert or overt coercion to change the beliefs or behavior of people for ideological, moral, educational, religious, economic or political purposes.

Classroom climate: Socio-affective environment created in the classroom by factors that can be physical (seats, location, postings) and psychosocial such as the interrelationship between teacher and learners, and among learners.

Classroom management: Process of organizing classroom instruction to run smoothly without disruption from students, within a shallow learning perspective based on extrinsic motivation. Includes classroom procedures, groupings, how instructions for activities are given, and management of student behavior. The most thorny aspect of teacher learning is to develop the ability to move away from classroom management based on extrinsic motivation to forms of self-management in which the learners are in charge and work on the basis of their intrinsic motivation.

Coaching: A coach is a learning facilitator who teaches and trains another person via encouragement, feedback and offer motivational support and advice.

Code-switching: Interlingual switching by bilingual speakers or intralingual switching between discourse types. Switching between subcodes in any sign system.

Cognitive mapping (mental mapping, mind mapping, or mental model): Mental processing and structural transformation of information by which a learner can code, store, recall, and decode information about the relative locations and attributes of phenomena in a metaphorical spatial environment. Mental models can be mapped and sketched into cognitive maps, scripts, schemata, and frames of reference.

Communicative competence: One of the key goals of language learning, achieved through:

- how well a person has learned features and rules of the language (**grammatical competence**), which includes vocabulary, pronunciation, and sentence formation.

- how well a person speaks and is understood in social contexts (**sociolinguistic competence**), which depends on factors such as status, purpose, and expectations.

- how well a person combines grammatical forms and meanings to achieve different genres of speaking or writing (**discourse competence**).

- how well the person uses both verbal forms and non-verbal communication to compensate for lack of other competences (**strategic competence**).

Communicative Language Teaching: an approach to world language learning that emphasizes communicative competence, as a reaction away from grammar-based approaches such as the audio-lingual approach. Communicative teaching focuses on expression and understanding of functions such as requesting, describing likes and dislikes, using language appropriately in various situations, performing tasks, solving puzzles, or using language for social interaction with other people. Not incompatible with a Deep Approach if integrated with extensive reading and watching, such as reading clubs and video clubs, and intensive writing such as writing workshops.

Community of practice: Process of social learning occurring when learners or teachers who have a common interest in some discipline, topic or problem collaborate over an extended period to share plans and projects, look for solutions, and create innovations.

Comprehensible input: Language understandable to learners.

Concept map: Diagram helping visualize the result of cognitive mapping and indicate the relationships between concepts. Concepts are then connected with labeled arrows, either from the center of the map or in a vertically hierarchical structure. One goal of concept mapping is to elicit knowledge and mental models of individuals, teams and organizations. Another is to capture knowledge from written documents and represent its structure. The addition of resources, such as colors, shapes, files or videos, reports or spreadsheets, to the nodes significantly improves meaningful learning.

Constructivism: Constructivism views all of knowledge as constructed, because it does not reflect any external transcendent reality; it is contingent on convention, perception and social experience. An extreme expansion of social determinism, it assumes that representations of physical and biological reality, including gender and race, are socially constructed. Set of assumptions about the nature of human learning guiding active learning theories and teaching methods: constructivism values developmentally appropriate, learner-centered learning that is initiated and directed by the student.

Constructivist epistemology: A development in philosophy which criticizes essentialism, whether it is in the form of realism, rationalism, positivism or empiricism. It originated in sociology under the term social constructionism and has been given the name constructivism when referring to philosophical epistemology. Constructionism and constructivism are often used interchangeably. The common thread between various forms of constructivism is that they do not focus on an ontological reality, but on reality construction.

Controlled practice: Teacher-controlled practice of language forms.

Cooperative learning: Proposed in response to traditional curriculum-driven education. In cooperative learning environments, students interact in purposely structured heterogeneous group to support the learning of one self and others in the same group.

Cooperating teacher: Mentor teacher welcoming a student teacher in his or her class to provide the student teacher with feedback on experimental practice.

Critical pedagogy: A teaching approach which attempts to help students question and challenge domination, and the beliefs and practices that dominate. In other words, it is a theory and practice of helping students achieve critical consciousness. In this tradition the teacher works to lead students to question ideologies and practices considered oppressive (including those at school), and encourage liberatory collective and individual responses to the actual conditions of their own lives.

Critical thinking: Consists of a mental process of analyzing or evaluating information, particularly statements or propositions that people have offered as true. It forms a process of reflecting upon the meaning of statements, examining the offered evidence and reasoning, and forming judgments about the facts. Critical thinkers can gather such information from observation, experience, reasoning, and/or communication. Critical thinking has its basis in intellectual values that go beyond subject-matter divisions and which include: clarity, accuracy, precision, evidence, thoroughness and fairness.

Cultural learning: The way a group of people within a society or culture tend to learn and pass on new information. Learning styles are greatly influenced by how a culture socializes with its children and young people.

Culture: The sum of the beliefs, attitudes, behaviors, habits and customs of a group of people.

Curriculum (plural **curricula**): The set of courses and their contents offered by an institution such as a school or university. In some cases, a curriculum may be partially or entirely determined by an external body. In the United States, the basic curriculum is established by each state with the individual school districts adjusting it to their desires. A designated set of related courses focused on a field of study.

Deductive teaching: Also known as deduction, from the verb "to deduce"; a teaching technique in which the teacher presents language rules and the students then practice those rules in activities. Deductive teaching is usually based on grammar-based methodology and proceeds from generalizations about the language to specifics. (See "Inductive teaching".)

Deep Approach: Deep, reflective language learning stressing reading and writing before listening and speaking; promoting open project-based activities such team and peer work, placing the student as curriculum builders on the basic of intrinsic motivation; code-switching and scaffolding among peers is considered a natural part of deep second and third language development, which results not from automatism but from reflexive output in writing accompanied with extensive reading and listening or watching, and then in speaking.

Deictic: Property of discourse markers specifying identity or spatial or temporal location from the perspective of the participants in an interaction, either in a situation or in surrounding discourse.

Dialogical: in the form of dialogue, or relating to or using dialogue; of, pertaining to, or characterized by dialogue

Diaphaneity, diaphanousness: fineness and translucency

Discourse: system of representation including a repertoire of concepts and codes for creating and maintaining worldviews within an ontological domain or discursive field.

Distance education or **distance learning**) A field of education that focuses on the pedagogy/andragogy, technology, and instructional systems design that is effectively incorporated in delivering education to students who are not physically "on site" to receive their education. Instead, teachers and students may communicate asynchronously (at times of their own choosing) by exchanging printed or electronic media, or through technology that allows them to communicate in real time (synchronously). Distance education courses that require a physical on-site presence for any reason including the taking of examinations is considered to be a hybrid or blended course or program.

Educational evaluation: Characterizing, valuing and appraising some aspect of education. No criteria can be exempt from subjectivity in the assessment process, even automated. Educational evaluation is a matter of choices on what to value and devalue, and therefore is social and political.

Educational organization: Organization for the purpose of education. This does not mean organizing the educational system as a process; it rather deals with how organizational theory applies to educating humans.

Education policy: Collection of explicit and implicit rules that govern the behavior of persons in schools. Education policy analysis is the scholarly study of education policy and common policy practices in a particular education setting.

Education reform: Policy, program, plan or movement attempting to bring about a systemic change in education theory and practice across a school system, school district(s), community, a nation, or society.

Efficacy: Measured on the basis of educational evaluation. Related to a paradigm or conceptual framework that defines what is to be considering important in terms of efficacy. Any evaluation paradigm may shadow possibly crucial aspects of learning and teaching.

Empirical knowledge: Propositional knowledge obtained by experience or sensorial information.

Encoding: Producing text or discourse in actualizing relevant codes, foregrounding some meanings and backgrounding others.

Engagement: The sentiment a student or teacher feels or does not feel towards learning or teaching, or the educational environment.

Epistemology: Branch of philosophy that deals with the nature, form, origin and scope of knowledge. Analysis of the way of knowing, focusing on the nature and type of knowledge and how it relates to verisimilitude, truth, trustworthiness, and belief, with a concern for the justification of knowledge claims.

Experience: Perception or knowledge of, skill in or observation of things or events gained through involvement in or exposure to these things or events. Accumulation of such knowledge and understanding in terms of procedural knowledge, know-how and expertise rather than propositional knowledge.

Experiential education, learning by doing: The process of actively engaging students in an authentic experience that will have benefits and consequences. Students make discoveries and experiment with knowledge themselves instead of hearing or reading about the experiences of others. Students also reflect on their experiences, thus developing new skills, new attitudes, and new theories or ways of thinking. Experiential education is related to the constructivist learning theory.

Facilitator: A concept related to a teacher's approach to interaction with students. Particularly in communicative classrooms, teachers tend to work in partnership with students to develop their language skills. A teacher who is a facilitator tends to be more student-centered and less dominant in the classroom than in other approaches. The facilitator may also take the role of mentor or coach rather than director.

Feedback: Reporting back or giving information back, usually to the teacher; feedback can be verbal, written or nonverbal in the form of facial expressions, gestures, behaviors; teachers can use feedback to discover whether a student understands, is learning, and likes an activity.

Fluency: Natural, normal, native-like speech characterized by appropriate pauses, intonation, stress, register, word choice, interjections and interruptions.

Form-focused instruction: The teaching of specific language content (lexis, structure, phonology). See "language content".

Forward planning: A concept developed by Francois Victor Tochon that implies thematic design, the teacher plans a unit or lesson by first identifying the transdisciplinary theme and project, then identifying the tasks pertaining to each language domain or skill that can bring this experience forward.

Functional syllabus: Syllabus based on communicative acts such as making introductions, making requests, expressing opinions, requesting information, refusing, apologizing, giving advice, persuading; this type of syllabus is often used in communicative language teaching.

Genre: The category a piece of literature belongs to (ex: science fiction, biography).

Grammar translation: A method of language teaching characterized by translation and the study of grammar rules. Involves presentation of grammatical rules, vocabulary lists, and translation. Emphasizes reading rather than communicative competence.

Graphic Organizer: Visual aids which helps organize thoughts and ideas (ex: Venn Diagram, T Charts, KWL).

Guided practice: An midway stage in teaching - between controlled and free practice activities; this stage implies limited guidance from the teacher who works as a facilitator.

Heritage speaker: Student who is exposed to a language other than the official or national language at home. Some students have full oral fluency and literacy in the home language; others may have full oral fluency but their written literacy was not developed because they were schooled in English. Another group of students -- typically third- or fourth-generation -- can speak to a limited degree but cannot express themselves on a wide range of topics. Students from any of these categories may also have gaps in knowledge about their cultural heritage. Teachers who have heritage speakers of the target language in their class should assess which proficiencies need to be maintained and which need to be developed further. See also native speaker.

Heuristic teaching: helping students to learn through discovery and investigation; a method of teaching allowing pupils to learn things for themselves.

Hidden curriculum: Idea that schools do more than simply transmit knowledge written in the curricula: curricula may have invisible agendas, social implications, political underpinnings, and cultural outcomes.

Hol-act: Holistic action within the frame of an educative project.

Holistic: related to holism, non-binary, integrative and responding the transdisciplinary principle of the inclusive third in its relation to the whole rather than the parts of a complex system.

Home education or home schooling: An educational alternative to public or private schools, in which children learn at home and in the community, in contrast to compulsory education organized in dedicated institutions.

Homeostasis: process by which a complex system keeps balance within stable conditions of functioning whatever the conditions in its environment.

Homologous: having a related or similar position, structure

Illocutionary: of or relating to the intention of a statement rather than it's overt meaning

Immersion: In this model, most commonly found in elementary schools, general academic content (the primary educational goal) is taught in the target language, and language proficiency is a parallel outcome. Individual districts design their programs such that English is introduced at a given grade level, with a gradually increasing percentage of time given to English language instruction. Partial immersion programs differ in the amount of time and number of courses taught in English and in the target language.

Individualized instruction: A method of instruction in which content, instructional materials, instructional media, and pace of learning are based upon the abilities and interests of each individual learner.

Inductive teaching: Also known as induction, from the verb "to induce"; a facilitative, student-centered teaching technique where the students discover language rules through extensive use of the language and exposure to many examples. This is the preferred technique in communicative language teaching. (See " Deductive teaching".)

Informal assessment: During an informal assessment, a teacher evaluates students' progress while they are participating in a learning activity, for example, a small-group discussion. Results are typically used to make decisions about what to do next, namely, whether the students are ready to move on or whether they need more practice with the material.

Input hypothesis: Hypothesis that states that learners learn language through exposure to language that is just beyond their level of comprehension.

Interference: A phenomenon in language learning where the first language interferes with learning the target or foreign language.

Interlanguage: The language a learner uses before mastering the foreign language; it may contain features of the first language and the target language as well as non-standard features.

Interlocutor: In a conversation, this refers to the person you are speaking to.

Interpretive community: Group of people sharing the same codes.

Inquiry education: A student-centered method of education focused on asking questions. Students are encouraged to ask questions which are meaningful to them, and which do not necessarily have easy answers; teachers are encouraged to avoid speaking at all when this is possible, and in any case to avoid giving answers in favor of asking more questions.

Instructional design: The analysis of learning needs and systematic development of instruction. Instructional designers often use instructional technology as a method for developing instruction. Instructional design models typically specify a method, that if followed will facilitate the transfer of knowledge, skills and attitude to the recipient or acquirer of the instruction.

Instructional scaffolding: The provision of sufficient supports to promote learning when concepts and skills are being first introduced to students.

Instructional theory: A discipline that focuses on how to structure material for promoting the education of humans, particularly youth. Originating in the United States in the late 1970s, *instructional theory* is typically divided into two categories: the cognitive and behaviorist schools of thought. Instructional theory was spawned off the 1956 work of Benjamin Bloom, a University of Chicago professor, and the results of his Taxonomy of Education Objectives — one of the first modern codifications of the learning process. One of the first instructional theorists was Robert M. Gagne, who in 1965 published Conditions of Learning for the Florida State University's Department of Educational Research. Renowned psychologist B. F. Skinner's theories of behavior were highly influential on instructional theorists because their hypotheses can be tested fairly easily with the scientific process.

Integrative learning: A learning theory describing a movement toward integrated lessons helping students make connections across curricula. This higher education concept is distinct from the elementary and high school "integrated curriculum" movement.

Intrinsic motivation: Evident when people engage in an activity for its own sake, without some obvious external incentive present. A hobby is a typical example.

Knowledge transfer: In the fields of organizational development and organizational learning, is the practical problem of getting a packet of knowledge from one part of the organization to another (or all other) parts of the organization. It is considered to be more than just a communication problem.

Language education: Teaching and learning of languages, usually as foreign or world languages.

Language skills: In language teaching, this refers to the mode or manner in which language is used. Listening, speaking, reading and writing are generally called the four language skills. Speaking and writing are the productive skills, while reading and listening are the receptive skills. Often the skills are divided into sub-skills, such as discriminating sounds in connected speech, or understanding relationships within a sentence.

Learning: The process of acquiring knowledge, skills, attitudes, or values, through study, experience, or teaching, that causes a change of behavior that is persistent, measurable, and specified or allows an individual to formulate a new mental construct or revise a prior mental construct (conceptual knowledge such as attitudes or values). It is a process that depends on experience and leads to long-term changes in behavior potential. **relatively permanent change in an individual's behavior or behavior potential (or capability) as a result of experience or practice**

Learning outcome: The term may refer to course aims (intended learning outcomes) or may be roughly synonymous with educational objectives (observed learning outcomes). Usage varies between organisations.

Learning standard: Standardized Approaches to Content Development, Itemization, Publication, Assessments, Presentation, Feedback, Transmission and Runtime Packaging. There are various related and unrelated Learning Standards. Name any that apply to the specific piece of content.

Lesson plan: A teacher's detailed description of the course of instruction for an individual lesson. While there is no one way to construct a correct lesson plan, most lesson plans contain similar elements. A writing noting the method of delivery, and the specific goals and timelines associated to the delivery of lesson content. An outline or plan that guides teaching of a lesson; includes the following: pre-assessment of class; aims and objectives; warm-up and review; engagement, study, activation of language (controlled, guided and free practice); and assessment of lesson. A good lesson plan describes procedures for student motivation and practice activities, and includes alternative ideas in case the lesson is not long enough or is too difficult. It also notes materials needed.

Lifelong learning: The concept that "It's never too soon or too late for learning", a philosophy that has taken root in a whole host of different organizations. Lifelong learning sees citizens provided with learning opportunities at all ages and in numerous contexts: at work, at home and through leisure activities, not just through formal channels such as school and higher education.

Literacy: The quality of being educated and literate, and the ability to read and write with mastery over specific fields of knowledge. In modern context, the word means reading and writing in a level adequate for written communication and generally a level that enables one to successfully function at certain levels of a society. Literacy is now *deictic*, in other words sensitive to spatiotemporal changes, and is continually changing as technologies and social practices emerge while older practices fade away. Two features of contemporary literacies are: (1) the use of digital technologies for accessing, producing, interacting with and sharing meaningful content; (2) their hybrid and distributed, collaborative and participatory nature.

Mastery learning: An instructional method that presumes all children can learn if they are provided with the appropriate learning conditions. Specifically, mastery learning is a method whereby students are not advanced to a subsequent learning objective until they demonstrate proficiency with the current one.

Meta: In epistemology, which is the study of the ways of knowing, the prefix **meta-** is used to mean *about (its own category)*. For example, metadata is data about data (who has produced it, when, what format the data is in and so on). Similarly, meta-memory in psychology means an individual's intuition about whether or not they would remember something if they concentrated on recalling it. Any subject can be said to have a *meta-theory*, which is the theoretical consideration of its foundations and methods.

Metacognition: Refers to thinking, perceiving, observing, noticing, grasping one's thought process. Metacognition can be explicit, that is conscious and factual, or implicit, unconscious and procedural. The ability to think about thinking is to regulate one's own cognition and maximize one's potential to think, learn and process information.

Metalanguage: Language used to describe, analyze or explain another language. Metalanguage includes, for example, grammatical terms and the rules of syntax. The term is sometimes used to mean the language used in class to give instructions, explain things, etc. – in essence, to refer to all teacher talk that does not specifically include the "target language".

Methodology: Strictly speaking is the study and knowledge of methods; but the term is frequently used pretentiously to indicate a method or a set of methods. In other words, it is the study of techniques for problem-solving and seeking answers, as opposed to the techniques themselves.

Motivation: The driving force behind all actions of human beings and other animals. It is an internal state that activates behavior and gives it direction. Emotion is closely related to motivation, and may be regarded as the subjectively experienced component of motivational states. Paradox: Students' main motivators are factors the teacher has little control over (integrated versus instrumental motivation, which heavily influence time on task), yet motivation is critical to learning.

Native speakers: Those who speak English as their mother tongue. A native speaker considers the target language to be his or her first language. Teachers seek opportunities for students to communicate in person or through technology with native speakers. Students in foreign language classes who are first- or second-generation immigrants and who use the language extensively outside the classroom are also considered native speakers. These students typically maintain the cultural norms of their heritage in certain situations. See also heritage speaker.

Negotiation of meaning: In this process, teachers and students try to convey information to one another and reach mutual comprehension through restating, clarifying, and confirming information. The teacher may help students get started or work through a stumbling block using linguistic and other approaches.

Neguentropy: reverse entropy; negative entropy of a living system that it exports to keep its own entropy low; it lies at the intersection of entropy and life.

Objective: An educational objective is a statement of a goal which successful participants are expected demonstrably to achieve before the course or unit completes. Also called lesson objectives or aims; statements of student learning outcomes based on student needs; objectives state specifically what the students will be able to do in a specified time period; objectives are measurable and therefore involve specific and discrete language skills.

Oral: Related to speaking. Oral exchange implies both speaking and listening.

Ontology: the branch of metaphysics that deals with the nature of being; the set of entities presupposed by a theory.

Paradigmatic shift: The term first used by Thomas Kuhn in his 1962 book The Structure of Scientific Revolutions to describe the process and result of a change in basic assumptions within the ruling theory of science. Don Tapscott was the first to use the term to describe information technology and business in his book of the same title. It has since become widely applied to many other realms of human experience as well.

Pastiche: a work of art that mixes styles, materials; a work of art that imitates the style of another time or artist.

Peace education: The process of acquiring the knowledge and developing the attitudes, skills, and behaviour to live in harmony with oneself and with others. Peace education is based on a philosophy that teaches nonviolence, love, compassion, trust, fairness, cooperation, respect, and a reverence for the human family and all life on our planet. It is a social practice with shared values to which anyone can make a significant contribution.

Pedagogy: The art and science of teaching children, often used, by extension, for adult education. The term comes from the Greek *paidagogos*, the slave who took little boys to and from school. "Paidia" means 'children', which is why pedagogy is normally meant for children and andragogy is meant for adults. The Latin word for pedagogy, education, is more widely used.

Peer correction or review and feedback: in writing, an activity whereby students help each other with the editing of a composition by giving each other feedback, making comments or suggestions; can be done in pairs or small groups.

Personal development (self-development or personal growth): Comprises the development of the self. The term may also refer to: traditional concepts of education or training; counseling and coaching for personal transformation; New Age movement and spiritual beliefs & concepts - including "inner pathways" to solve social and psychological issues; or professional development educators treating the whole person instead of the profession only).

Ponerology: Interdisciplinary study of evil phenomena and traumatic social issues that result in aggressive war, ethnic cleansing, tyranny and genocide, from the perspective of various sciences such as psychology, sociology, philosophy, theology and history. Concept proposed by the psychiatrist Andrzej Lobaczewski. Example: the Shock Doctrine of Naomi Klein.

Praxis: the practice and practical side of a profession or field of study, as opposed to the theory

Prescriptive grammar: Grammar that is described in terms of grammar rules of what is considered the best usage, often by grammarians; prescriptive grammar may not agree with what people actually say or write.

Problem-based learning (PBL): Instructional transfer of active learning in College education, yet being adapted for use in K-12 education. The defining characteristics of PBL are: learning is driven by messy, open-ended problems; students work in small collaborative groups; and "teachers" are not required, the process uses "facilitators" of learning. Accordingly, students are encouraged to take responsibility for their group and organize and direct the learning process with support from a tutor or instructor. Advocates of PBL claim it can be used to enhance content knowledge and foster the development of communication, problem-solving, and self-directed learning skill.

Project: An extensive task purposely and collectively undertaken by group or individuals to apply knowledge and skills toward a targeted goal which will result in a product, within a certain timeframe.

Procedural knowledge or know-how: The knowledge of how to perform some **task**. Know-how is different from other kinds of knowledge such as propositional knowledge in that it can be directly applied to a task. Procedural knowledge about solving problems differs from propositional knowledge about problem solving. For example, in some legal systems, this knowledge or *know-how* has been considered the intellectual property of a company, and can be transferred when that company is purchased.

Proficiency level: Describes how well a student can use the language. Proficiency describes how well a person functions in a language. The American Council on the Teaching of Foreign Languages further defines proficiency with a set of guidelines for assessing communicative abilities. The guidelines cover how an individual performs across three criteria: function, content/context, and accuracy. When combined, these criteria determine the student's communicative ability to be Novice, Intermediate, Advanced, or Superior.

Proficiency tests: General tests that provide overall information on a student's language proficiency level or ability; can be used to determine entry and exit levels of a language program or to adjust the curriculum according to the abilities of the students.

Programmed instruction: A field first studied extensively by the behaviorist B. F. Skinner. It consists of teaching through small lessons, where each lesson must be mastered in order to go on to the next. Students work through the programmed material by themselves at their own speed. After each step, they are presented with a question to test their comprehension, then are immediately shown the correct answer or given additional information.

Propositional or declarative knowledge: Knowledge that some proposition is either true or false. This distinguishes propositional knowledge from know-how or procedural knowledge, which is the knowledge of how to perform some task. This article discusses propositional knowledge from a variety of perspectives, including philosophy, science, and history.

Professionalism: More than simple vocational practice, professionalism characterizes an ethical attitude in professional problem solving, which indicates working with a conscience.

Push-down principle or principle of reduction: according to the law of least effort, cognitive responses tend to "slide" toward the lower end of the taxonomic scale. What was initially a complex problem-solving situation becomes, by force of habit, a simple regurgitation of stocked responses.

Rapport: Relationship, usually a harmonious one, established within a classroom between teacher and students and among students.

Reify: to consider or make (an abstract idea or concept) real or concrete

Rhizomatic: rhizomatous: of or relating to a thick horizontal underground stem (called a rhizome) of plants such as the mint and iris whose buds develop new roots and shoots.

role-playing: Role-playing is an activity in which students dramatize characters or pretend that they are in new locations or situations. This activity challenges students by having them use language in new contexts.

Rote learning: A learning technique which avoids grasping the inner complexities and inferences of the subject that is being learned and instead focuses on memorizing the material so that it can be recalled by the learner exactly the way it was read or heard.

Rubric: Set of criteria and standards linked to learning objectives, used to assess students' performance, such as on a test, project, or essay. A type of assessment in which a score is derived from a list of expectations.

Schooling: Teaching and learning that takes place in formal education environments.

Self-concept or self-identity: The mental and conceptual awareness and persistent regard that sentient beings hold with regard their own being. Components of a being's self-concept include physical, psychological, and social attributes; and can be influenced by its attitudes, habits, beliefs and ideas. These components and attributes can each be condensed to the general concepts of self-image and the self-esteem.

Self-efficacy: The belief that one has the capabilities to execute the courses of actions required to manage prospective situations. Unlike efficacy, which is the power to produce an effect (in essence, competence), self-efficacy is the belief (however accurate) that one has the power to produce that effect. It is important here to understand the distinction between self-esteem and self efficacy.

Self-esteem relates to a person's sense of self-worth, whereas self efficacy relates to a person's perception of their ability to reach a goal. For example, say a person is a terrible rock climber. They would likely have a poor efficacy in regard to rock climbing, but this wouldn't need to affect their self-esteem; most people don't invest much of their self-esteem in this activity.

Self-study: The content is intended to be used as a medium of study that relies on one's own self to follow through on learning tasks related to a course, module, lesson or lab medium which are all also self-contained in a unit of medium or as a file type.

Service learning: A method of teaching, learning and reflecting that combines academic classroom curriculum with meaningful youth service throughout the community. As a teaching methodology, it falls under the category of experiential education. More specifically, it integrates meaningful community service with instruction and reflection to enrich the learning experience, teach civic responsibility, encourage lifelong civic engagement, and strengthen communities.

Situated learning: Education that takes place in a setting functionally identical to that where the learning will be applied.

Skill: An ability, usually learned, to perform actions.

Social constructionism: A sociological theory of knowledge developed by Peter L. Berger and Thomas Luckman with their 1966 book, The Social Construction of Reality. The focus of social constructionism is to uncover the ways in which individuals and groups participate in the creation of their perceived reality. As an approach, it involves looking at the ways social phenomena are created, institutionalized, and made into tradition by humans. Socially constructed reality is seen as an ongoing, dynamic process; reality is re-produced by people acting on their interpretations and their knowledge of it.

Social context: Environment in which meanings are exchanged. It can be analyzed in terms of the field of discourse, tenor of discourse, and mode of discourse. The field of discourse refers to what is being discussed; the tenor of discourse refers to the participants in the exchange of meaning, including who they are and their relationships with each other (for example, teacher and students); the mode of discourse refers to what part the language is playing with what production channel (writing or speaking).

Spiraling: the process of teaching a theme or language rule to different levels of learners by creating multiple tasks that are increasingly complex. For example, a lesson on weather can be spiraled as follows: (1) Novice students can describe the weather in short formulaic sentences; (2) Intermediate students can talk about the weather and its effect on their activities, or gather information from broadcasts or newspapers; and (3) Pre-Advanced students can tell a story about a frightening weather-related event or follow a description of weather in a literary piece.

story grammar or story map: A story map is a graphic organizer that leads students to discover specific elements from a, written or oral text. It is built upon common elements such as characters and characteristics, place, plot, resolution, and moral or lesson, or a "who, what, when, where, how, and why" format.

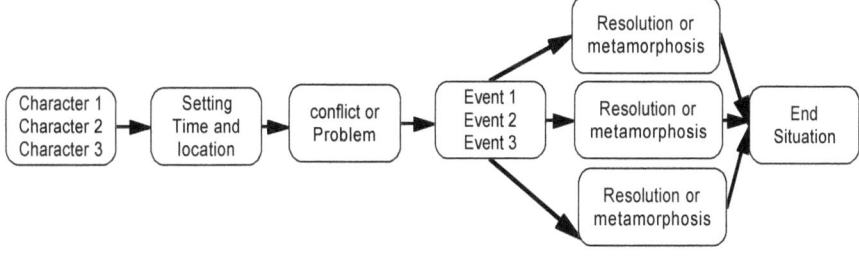

Student activism: A form of youth-led community organizing that is specifically oriented towards engaging students as activists in order to create change in the educational system.

Student-centered learning: An approach to education focusing on the needs of the students, rather than those of others involved in the educational process, such as teachers and administrators. This approach has many implications for the design of curriculum, course content, and interactivity of courses. Also called learner-centered, a way of teaching that centers on the goals, needs, interests and existing knowledge of the students. Students actively participate in such classrooms and may even be involved in setting learning outcomes. Teachers in student-centered classrooms ask students for input on their goals, needs and interests and on what they know before providing them with study topics or answers to questions (for example, grammar rules). They may also ask students to generate (help produce) materials. The teacher is seen more as a facilitator or helper than the dominant figure in the classroom.

Student teacher: Pre-service teacher having initial classroom experiences and practical training under the supervision of a cooperating teacher, or mentor teacher.

Student voice: the distinct perspectives and actions of young people throughout schools focused on education itself.

Stultify: to make useless, futile, or ineffectual, esp. by routine; to cause to appear absurd or inconsistent, to dumb down.

Syllabus: An outline or a summary of the main points of a text, lecture, or course of study.

Syntax: Sometimes called word order; how words combine to form sentences and the rules governing sentence formation.

Synthesis: Integration of two or more pre-existing elements that results in a new creation.

Task-based syllabus: A syllabus organized around a sect of real, purposeful tasks that students are expected to carry out; tasks may include telephone use, making charts or maps, following instructions, and so on; task-based learning is purposeful and a natural way to learn language.

Taxonomic sliding: see *Push-down principle*.

Taxonomy: the science or practice of classification, An educational taxonomy that classifies educational objectives into three domains: cognitive, affective, and psychomotor.

Teachable moments: Times in a language class in which the teacher realizes that a point of information not in the lesson plan will help students understand a language point; teachable moments digress for a brief time from the lesson plan and can be valuable in helping student learning and keeping students engaged.

Teacher: In education, one who teaches students, a course of study that requires planning instructional units, enabling the development of practical skills, including learning and thinking skills. There are numerous ways to teach and help students learn, often referred to as pedagogy. When deciding what teaching method to use, a teacher usually considers the students' prior knowledge, the environment, and school genres, standards and curricula set by their school district. However the teacher rarely considers the ways to free the students from the system of alienation put into place to provide more space for autonomy and deep learning.

Teacher talk: The language teachers use when teaching; involves simplifying speech for students; it may be detrimental to learning if it is childish or not close to the natural production of the target language.

Teaching: the purposeful direction and management of fruitful conditions for deep learning processes to happen.

Thematic Unit: Lessons complimenting and working together under one common topic, often cross curricular. Thematic units are designed using content as the organizing principle. Vocabulary, structures, and cultural information are included as they relate to the themes in each unit.

Whole language: A term used by reading teachers to describe an instructional philosophy which focuses on reading as an activity best taught in a broader context of meaning. Rather than focusing on reading as a mechanical skill, it is taught as an ongoing part of every student's existing language and life experience. Building on language skills each student already possesses, reading and writing are seen as a part of a broader "whole language" spectrum.

Wisdom: Intangible quality gained through experience, ability to make correct judgments and decisions, foreseeing consequences and acting to maximize beneficial results. From a complex system theory perspective, wisdom would be the attainment of homeostatic equilibrium, the balance between opposites. Wisdom is pragmatically determined by common sense, cultural, philosophical and spiritual sources.

Writing: (a) Inscribing characters on a medium, with the intention of forming words or concepts and record information in natural language or in coded form; (b) creation of materials conveyed through written language. Both activities may occur at the same time.

Workshop: Brief intensive hands-on seminar or series of meetings emphasizing interaction and exchange among a small number of participants.

Activism: Engagement in community organizing for social change and meaningful involvement.

Appendix
Proactive Planning Practice

1st Proaction: From Curriculum to Dynamic Activities

Following the framework given in Chapter 2 (Table 2.2 or Figures 2.4 and 2.5), choose a main unifying goal from the course curriculum. In each of the four columns, indicate related activities you will organize for your class to develop this competence in your students:

ORAL EXCHANGE	WRITING	READING	LANGUAGE FOCUS

Project description:

Its main organizers:

Narrativor

Skillers

Actualizer

Processes:

INTERPRET	ANALYZE	PRESENT	INTERACT

2nd Proaction: A Comedy Routine

This time, you are to proceed differently. With the help of the following Tables, sketch a project on paper. The competence you wish to develop is "Writing a Short Comedy Sketch". Within the task domains of your action plan, insert organizers for transposing direct speech to indirect speech and vice-versa. Once you have finished your first draft, recopy your plan and examine it. Is it satisfactory? You may wish to include other activities mentioned in the course curriculum that would tie your plan together better. Table A.1 shows one planning possibility. You may wish to compare it to your own.

PROJECT: Writing a Short Comedy Sketch

INSTRUCTIONAL ORGANIZERS and EMBEDMENT MAP

WRITING A SHORT COMEDY SKETCH			
ACCESS		VOICE	
INTERPRET	ANALYZE	PRESENT	INTERACT
READ/WATCH /LISTEN	FOCUS ON LANGUAGE	WRITE/SPEAK /RECORD	EXCHANGE AND ACT

THEME:

ACTION:

OPERATIONS:

3rd Proaction: Documenting a Profession

Try to imagine a more ambitious project: "Document a Profession" for more advanced students. Jot down a few key words in each domain shown below, just to recall the organizers of this type of activity. Then, on paper, visualize your project. Combine simple and complex issues, linking parts, such as presentation of the completed document to the strategies themselves. Define what you expect from the students and determine the key organizers of their action. Then reread your plan, modifying as needed, in order to ensure that the apparent links between the task domains unify the whole project. Table A.2 is the culmination of much reflection and experience.

PROJECT: Documenting a Profession

INSTRUCTIONAL ORGANIZERS and EMBEDMENT MAP

DOCUMENTING A PROFESSION			
ACCESS		VOICE	
INTERPRET	**ANALYZE**	**PRESENT**	**INTERACT**
READ/WATCH /LISTEN	**FOCUS ON LANGUAGE**	**WRITE/SPEAK /RECORD**	**EXCHANGE AND ACT**

THEME:

ACTION:

OPERATIONS:

4th Proaction: An Informative Challenge

High school language teachers often have a predilection for argumentative discourse. How would you go about developing, in your students, a reflection on the media? Why not propose a challenge to succeed in getting their letter to the editor abroad, online or on paper, written in response to an article, published in the readers' page of a daily newspaper, community journal, or on a blog? Your plan of action will surely include, in each task domain, an introduction to media, an introduction to argumentation and an introduction to correspondence. This may require a month. Which organizers are you using to build a project? Before consulting Table A.3 (a and b) for ideas, let your imagination link your knowledge of your students to your wish to accomplish a fascinating project.

PROJECT: Get a letter of opinion printed in the readers' page of the foreign newspaper

INSTRUCTIONAL ORGANIZERS and EMBEDMENT MAP

GET A LETTER OF OPINION PRINTED IN THE READERS' PAGE OF THE FOREIGN NEWSPAPER			
ACCESS		VOICE	
INTERPRET	ANALYZE	PRESENT	INTERACT
READ/ WATCH/ LISTEN	FOCUS ON LANGUAGE	WRITE/ SPEAK/ RECORD	EXCHANGE AND ACT

THEME:

ACTION:

OPERATIONS:

5th Proaction: On Your Own

Let us now proceed to an original project for your class. Find a group of concepts from the curriculum that could become part of a unifying action. Let the ideas come freely and write them down. Broach the project with your students and find out what their plans and interests are. Eventually, you will find a way to synthesize the disparate concepts you have assembled, taking the students' motivation into account in an original manner. With your students, define directions for a unified plan. Then, open yourself up to dynamic, innovative connections.

Project: Interactive Plans of Action

ORAL EXCHANGE	WRITING	READING	LANGUAGE FOCUS
_____	_____	_____	_____
_____	_____	_____	_____
_____	_____	_____	_____
_____	_____	_____	_____
_____	_____	_____	_____

Processes:

INTERPRET	ANALYZE	PRESENT	INTERACT
_____	_____	_____	_____
_____	_____	_____	_____
_____	_____	_____	_____
_____	_____	_____	_____
_____	_____	_____	_____

Now, reread the directions, verifying their coherence and clarity. Each set of directions could include production criteria. Discuss these in detail with your students to ensure comprehension.

Table A.1. Project: Writing a Short Comedy Sketch

WRITING A SHORT COMEDY SKETCH			
ACCESS		VOICE	
INTERPRET	ANALYZE	PRESENT	INTERACT
READ /WATCH /LISTEN -Read a comic play; -Practice active listening; -Reflect on the effect or purpose of repetition in comedy.	FOCUS ON LANGUAGE -Seek repetitions of spoken lines in the form of indirect speech (often used to create a comic effect); -Respect verb tenses; -Make necessary transformations related to indirect speech: pronouns, tenses, demonstratives, subordinates.	WRITE/SPEAK /RECORD -Write a comic dialogue; -Rewrite this dialogue in indirect form; -Respect rules of punctuation of dialogue; -Vary introductory verbs (He said...) in the transposition to indirect speech; -Transpose a comic story into a dialogue; -Write an original short comedy using three stereotyped characters. For enhanced comedic effect, one character acts as "translator" and repeats, in indirect form, what is said by the other two characters.	EXCHANGE AND ACT -Improvise dialogue corresponding to the following acts of speech: begging, ordering, affirming, denying, questioning, suggesting, etc. -Relate a comic dialogue; -Relate "how" comic dialogue works; -Transpose, as rapidly as possible, a spoken question or affirmative statement into indirect speech; -Transpose, as rapidly as possible, indirect speech into direct speech; -Read orally a comedy written by peers.

Table A.2. Pre-Professional Brainstorming: Profiling a Profession

DOCUMENTING A PROFESSION			
ACCESS		VOICE	
INTERPRET	ANALYZE	PRESENT	INTERACT
READ/ WATCH/ LISTEN	FOCUS ON LANGUAGE	WRITE/SPEAK/ RECORD	EXCHANGE AND ACT
-Respond to a questionnaire on profession-oriented questions; analyze responses; -Practice systematic self-documentation; -Read at least one book related to the chosen profession; -Choose photos, pictures, articles or excerpts from books that complement the interviews; -Find prospectuses or other information to complete the profile; -Organize the research to fit the outline plan; -Read and evaluate the work of peers.	-Punctuate a dialogue; -Transpose spoken form into written form; -Write complete sentences; -Use accurate spelling and proofread for spelling mistakes in others' written work; -Do self-corrected exercises to review rules of grammar and spelling; -Rewrite the text of the profile until it is free of mistakes related to syntax or spelling; -Verify spelling, subject-verb-agreement and syntax before submitting final copy to the teacher.	-Prepare an interview of 15-20 questions to an apprentice or a professional; -Transcribe interviews; -Take notes and summarize material that is read; -Write an introduction and commentary on the documentation; -Write a presentation that synthesizes information obtained on the chosen profession; -Choose a format for the profile that organizes the various parts and submit it for the teacher's approval; -Write the final draft as neatly as possible, including adjunct material (pictures, photos, articles, prospectuses) and other "extras" to add color and interest; -Work on an attractive presentation for the profile (title page, graphics, color, etc.); -Present the profession chosen for profiling.	-Organize professions into categories; -Choose the theme for your profile: the profession you wish to practice; -Brainstorm the aspects and conditions of a profession; -Characterize a profession according to categories selected by the class; -With the class, outline a plan that indicates the direction and limits of the profile; -Prepare a questionnaire; verify the relevance of questions by testing them on a peer; -Eliminate yes/no questions and improve long-answer questions; -Interview three persons on tape, allowing time for reflection and thorough replies; -Evaluate the work of peers.

Table A.3a. Yours Truly
Project: Get an opinion letter published in the readers' page.

GET A LETTER OF OPINION PRINTED IN THE READERS' PAGE OF A FOREIGN NEWSPAPER	
ACCESS	
INTERPRET	ANALYZE
READ/WATCH/LISTEN	FOCUS ON LANGUAGE
-Read newspapers online regularly; -Select articles for use in a newscast; -Using an evaluative grid, analyze the work of peers; -Refine an introduction; -Seek out the neutral passages, notice the absence of argument in an introduction; -Compare various introductions from the perspective of syntax, style, and originality; -Evaluate various introductions, using predetermined criteria; -Id. for the conclusion, seek out the various forms of synthesis; -List the arguments used in the body of an opinion letter; -Discern between stated position, argument and example; -Analyze and critique argumentative paragraphs written by peers; -Analyze and critique newspaper articles on the basis of pre-established criteria (introduction/development, argument/conclusion).	-Compare various argumentative paragraphs; -Use correct spelling and syntax, self-correct texts based on teacher's comments; -Use conjunctions that mark transition or linkage; -Use a standard level of language; -Use appropriate tenses and persons; -Use pronouns correctly; -Use subjunctive and conditional tenses correctly.

Table A.3b. Yours Truly
Project: Get an opinion letter published in the readers' page.

GET A LETTER OF OPINION PRINTED IN THE READERS' PAGE OF A FOREIGN NEWSPAPER	
VOICE	
PRESENT	INTERACT
WRITE/SPEAK/RECORD	EXCHANGE AND ACT
Introduction to written correspondence	ORAL EXCHANGE
-Write a letter of request, demand or proposition;	Introduction to media
-Explain the circumstances justifying the request, demand or proposition;	-Discuss the main themes currently appearing in newspapers and relate the different points of view, as well as treatment of news stories;
-Clearly formulate, order, and justify the points on which the request, demand or proposition rests;	-Express a critical viewpoint on the news, news media;
-Argue for the adopted point of view;	-Listen to a newscast and report on its structure, compare its information with that of print media;
-Adopt standard letter format and arrange the body of the letter in a logical sequence;	-Create a newscast: distribute tasks into groups related to content areas (national, local, sports, etc.), and present a summary of the main highlights of an event;
-Use correct form of address and introduction, salutation and conclusion;	-Create a televised newscast on video, id.
-Correctly address the envelope.	Introduction to argumentation
Introduction to argumentation	After hearing arguments related to a list of polemic themes,
From a list of themes:	-Determine if the arguments are in favor of a stated thesis;
-Write the introduction for an opinion paper;	-Provide a counterargument;
-Write the conclusion, (id.);	-Provide an argument that supports the thesis;
-Write an argumentative paragraph "pro", as follows: a) state position taken, b) argument, c) example: id. "con".	-Differentiate between argument and example;
	-Explain the concept of argument;
	-Respond to a newspaper article in the form of an opinion letter.

6th Proaction: Commedia dell' Hol-Act

A tri-level organization is easier to grasp with a concrete, practical example. Go back to what you finalized in the 2nd application and reorganize it in an interlocking composition with the disciplinary narrativor(s), the interdisciplinary skiller(s), and transdisciplinary actualizer(s) – see Figure A.1. Be sure to distinguish these three levels: the contents to master (independently of the oral exchange/writing/reading/language focus task domains), the operations that are likely to be transferred from one task domain to another, and the expressive, unifying work.

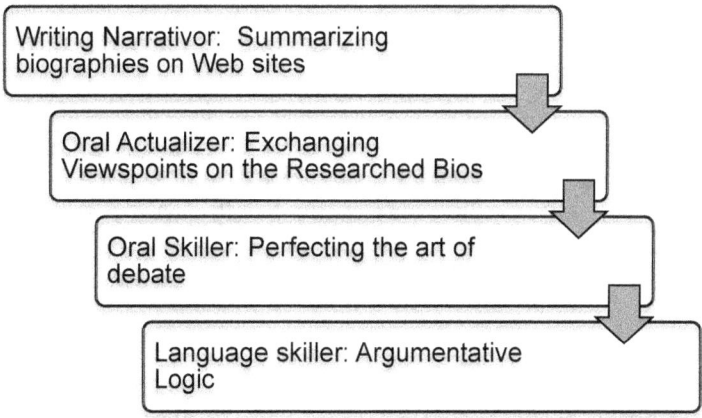

Figure A.1. Choose the Pragmatic Embedment

Through embedment, instructional organizers are assembled like a grammar. In Figure A.2, the organizers are pragmatic modifiers that impact curricular concepts for classroom use within certain domains, connected through projects.

You will see for yourself the utility of these categories. You have discovered a new way to plan a holistic action and to bring out the juice of it. That merits special attention. A well-balanced Hol-Act deals with four domains of tasks and contains specific work guidelines on three strategic levels. Sure, there are challenges in trying to make tasks compatible with holistic projects (Nunn, 2006).

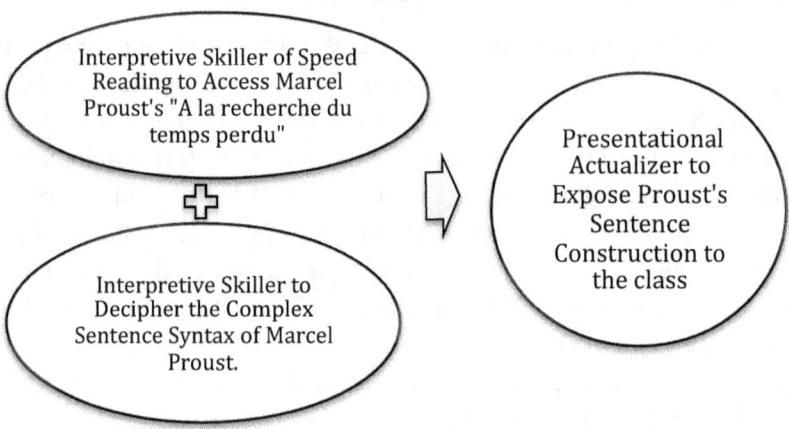

Figure A.2
Organizers and IAPI Task Domains
Help Decipher the Grammar of Projects

The 6th Proactive application was a good way to verify this balance, and thus, served as a specification table. An alternate method of balancing your classroom plan is to construct a matrix on which the three levels of planning are represented by the horizontal coordinates and the four task domains by the vertical coordinates. Then decide where to situate your pragmatic organizers. In any case, the classroom remains the best place to verify your choices and to negotiate them.

References

Abbott, M., & Phillips, J. (2011, November). *A decade of foreign language standards: Influence, impact, and future directions: Survey results* [Electronic report]. Alexandria, VA: American Council on the Teaching of Foreign Languages. Retrieved from http://www.actfl.org/files/public/StandardsImpactSurveyApr2011.pdf

ACT (2013). The Condition of College & Career Readiness 2012. ACT. 2013-08-21. From: http://www.act.org/research-policy/college-career-readiness-report-2012/

ACTFL - American Council on the Teaching of Foreign Language (2002). *ACTFL/NCATE program standards for the preparation of foreign language teachers (Initial level-undergraduate and graduate) (For K–12 and secondary certification)*. Alexandria, VA: American Council on the Teaching of Foreign Languages. Retrieved from http://www.actfl .org/files/public/ACTFLNCATEStandardsRevised713.pdf

ACTFL - American Council on the Teaching of Foreign Languages. (2006). *Standards for foreign language learning in the 21st century*. Lawrence, KS: Allen Press.

ACTFL Task Force on Decade of Standards Project. (2011, October). *A decade of foreign language standards: Influence, impact, and future directions* [Electronic report]. Alexandria, VA: American Council on the Teaching of Foreign Languages. Retrieved from http://actfl .org/fi les/public/national-standards-2011.pdf

Adams, R., Nuevo, A. M., & Egi, T. (2011). *The Modern Language Journal, 95*, Supplemental Issue, 42-63.

Adang, D. (2008). *Impact des ondes GSM sur la mortalité de 124 rats de laboratoire avec groupe contrôle*. Louvain, BE : Université Catholique de Louvain.

Adorno, T. (2008). *Lectures on negative dialectics: fragments of a lecture course 1965/1966* (ed. R. Tiedemann, trans. R. Livingstone). Cambridge: Polity.

Akbar Hessami, M., and Sillitoe, J. (1990). *Deep vs. surface teaching and learning in Engineering and Applied Sciences*. Footscray: Victoria University of Technology.

Alan, B., & Stoller, F. L. (2005). Maximizing the benefits of project work in foreign language classrooms. *English Teaching Forum, 43*(4), 10–21.

Alberty, H. B. (1927). *A study of the project method in Education.* Columbus, OH: Ohio State University Press.

Allen, H. W. (2009). A literacy-based approach to the advanced French writing course. *The French Review, 83*(2), 368-387.

Allmark, P. J. (2008). An Aristotelian account of autonomy. *Journal of Value Inquiry, 42*(1), 41-53.

Allwright, D. (2003). Exploratory practice: rethinking practitioner research in language teaching. *Language Teaching Research, 7*(2), 113–14.

Altstaedter, L. L., & Jones, B. (2009). Motivating students' foreign language and culture acquisition through web-based inquiry. *Foreign Language Annals, 42*, 640–657.

Alvarez, I., Guasch, T., & Espasa, A. (2009). University teacher role and competencies in online learning environments: a theoretical analysis of teaching and learning practices. *European Journal of Teacher Education, 32*(3), 321-336.

Ambard, P.D., & Ambard, L.K. (2010). Effects of narrative script advance organizer strategies used to introduce video in the foreign language classroom. *Foreign Language Annals, 45*(2), 203-228.

American Council on the Teaching of Foreign Languages – See ACTFL.

Anderson, L. W., & Krathwohl, D. R. (2001). *A taxonomy of learning, teaching, and assessing: A revision of Bloom's taxonomy of educational objectives.* New York: Longman.

Anseel, F., Lievens, F., & Schollaert, E. (2009). Reflection as a strategy to enhance task performance after feedback. *Organizational Behavior and Human Decision Processes, 110,* 23–35.

Appiah, K. A. (2005). *The ethics of identity.* Princeton, NJ: Princeton University Press.

Appiah, K. A. (2006). *Cosmopolitanism: Ethics in a world of strangers.* New York, NY: Norton.

Apple, M. W. (1990). *Ideology and curriculum.* New York: Routledge.

Araújo Freire, & Macedo, D. Eds. (2000). *The Paolo Freire Reader.* New York: Continuum.

Aristotle (2004). *The Nicomachean Ethics.* Translated with Introduction and Notes by J. A. K. Thompson; new revised edition with Notes and Appendices by Hugh Tredennick. London: Penguin.

Arnold, N. (2009). Online extensive reading for advanced foreign language learners: an evaluation study. *Foreign Language Annals, 42*(2), 340-366.

Atkinson, D. (2011). *Alternative approaches to Second Language Acquisition*. New York, NY: Routledge.

Attwell, G. (2007). Personal Learning Environments – the future of learning? *eLearning Papers, 2*(1). Retrieved from: http://www.elearningeuropa.info/files/media/media11561.pdf

Ausubel, D.P. (1978). In defense of advanced organizers: a reply to the critics. *Review of Educational Research, 48*(2), 251-57.

Ausubel, D. P., & Robinson, F. G. (1969). *School learning: an introduction to Educational Psychology*. New York: Holt International Edition, 1971 (first published by Holt, Rinehart and Winston).

Azocar, A. (2011). *From researching Others to researching the Self: an autoethnography of early Spanish education using poststructuralist storytelling*. Unpublished dissertation. University of Wisconsin-Madison, School of Education, World Language Education, Department of Curriculum and Instruction.

Baillie, A., Porter, N., & Corrie, S. (1996). Encouraging a deep approach to the undergraduate Psychology curriculum: An example and some lessons from a third-year course. *Psychology Teaching Review, 5*, 14-24.

Baker-Sennett, J., & Matusov, E. (1997). School performance: improvisational processes in development and education. In R. K. Sawyer (Ed.), *Creativity in performance* (pp.197-212). New York: Ablex.

Bandura, A. (1986). *Social foundations of thought and action: a social cognitive theory*. Englewood Cliffs, NJ: Prentice-Hall.

Barab, S. A. & Wolff-Michael Roth (2006). Curriculum-based ecosystems: supporting knowing from an ecological perspective, *Educational Researcher, 35*(5), 3-13.

Barnes-Karol, G., & Broner, M. A. (2010). Using images as springboards to teach cultural perspectives in light of the ideals of the MLA Report. *Foreign Language Annals, 43*(3), 422-445.

Barrette, C. M., Paesani, K., & Vinall, K. (2010). Toward a integrated curriculum: maximizing the use of target language literature. *Foreign Language Annals, 43*(2), 216-230.

Bearse, C., & de Jong, E. J. (2008). Cultural and linguistic investment: Adolescents in a secondary two-way immersion program. *Equity and Excellence in Education, 41*, 325–340.

Beaudrie, S. (2009). Receptive bilinguals' language development in the classroom: The differential effects of heritage versus foreign language curriculum. In M. Lacorte & J. Leeman (Eds.), Español en Estados Unidos y otros contextos de contacto: Sociolingüística, ideología y pedagogía (pp.325–346). Madrid: Iberoamericana/Vervuert.

Beaudrie, S., & Ducar, C. (2005). Beginning level university heritage programs: Creating a space for all heritage language learners. *Heritage Language Journal, 3*, 1–26.

Beckett, G. H. (2006). Project-based second and foreign language education. In G. H. Beckett & P. C. Miller (Eds.), *Project-based second and foreign language education. Past, present, and future* (pp.3-16). Charlotte, NC: Information Age.

Beckett, G. H., & Miller, P. C. (2006). *Project-based second and foreign language education. Past, present, and future*. Charlotte, NC: Information Age.

Bhabha, H. K. (1994/2004). *The location of culture* (2e ed.). New York: Routledge.

Biggs, J. B. (1987). *Student approaches to learning and studying*. Melbourne: Australian Council for Educational Research.

Biggs, J. B. (1989). Approaches to learning in two cultures. In V. Bickley (Ed.), *Teaching and learning styles within and across cultures: implications for language pedagogy* (pp. 421-436). Hong Kong: Institute of Language in Education, Education Department.

Biggs, J. B. (1993). What do inventories of students' learning process really measure? A theoretical review and clarification. *British Journal of Educational Psychology, 83*, 3-19.

Biggs, J. B., & Telfer, R. (1987). *The process of learning* (2nd ed.). Englewood Cliffs, NJ: Prentice Hall.

Bitchener, J., & Knoch, U. (2010). Raising the linguistic accuracy level of advanced L2 writers with written corrective feedback. *Journal of Second Language Writing, 19*(4), 207-217.

Blake, R. (2008). *Brave new digital classroom: Technology and foreign language learning*. Washington, DC: Georgetown University Press.

Bloch, J. (2008). *Technologies in the second language composition classroom*. Ann Arbor: MI: The University of Michigan Press.

Bloom, B. S. (1956). *Taxonomy of educational objectives, handbook I: the cognitive domain* (2nd Ed). New York: Wesley.

Bloom, M. (2008). From the classroom to the community: Building cultural awareness in first semester Spanish. *Language, Culture and Curriculum, 21*, 103–119.

Blumenfeld, P. C. (1992). Classroom learning and motivation: clarifying and expanding goal theory. *Journal of Educational Psychology, 84*(3), 272–281.

Blumenfeld, P. C., Soloway, E., Marx, R. W., Krajcik, J. S., Guzdial, M., & Palincsar, A. (1991). Motivation project-based learning: sustaining the doing, supporting the learning. *Educational Psychologist, 26*, 369–398.

Boaler, J. (2002). Learning from teaching: exploring the relationship between reform curriculum and equity. *Journal for Research in Mathematics Education, 33*(4), 239–258.

Bobbit, F. (1918). *The curriculum*. New York: Houghton.

Borko, H., & Livingstone, C. (1989). Cognition and improvisation: Differences in mathematics instruction by expert and novice teachers. *American Educational Research Journal, 26*(4), 473-498.

Boss, S., & Krauss, J. (2007). *Reinventing project-based learning: your field guide to real-world projects in the digital age*. Eugene, OR: International Society for Technology in Education.

Boss, S., Krauss, J., & Conery, L. (2008). *Reinventing project-based learning: your field guide to real-world projects in the digital age*. Eugene, OR: International Society for Technology in Education.

Bourdieu, P. (1969). Intellectual field and the creative project. *Social Science Information, 8*, 89–119.

Bourdieu, P. (2000). *Pascalian Meditations*. New York: Polity.

Bourdieu, P. (2004). *Esquisse pour une auto-analyse* (Draft for Self-Analysis). Paris: Éditions Raisons d'agir, collection Cours et Travaux.

Bown, J. (2009). Self-regulatory strategies and agency in self-instructed language learning: a situated view. *Modern Language Journal, 93*(4), 570-583.

Bradley, C. (1994). Evidence of sex bias knocked out by blunt instrument? A comment on Hartley (1992). *Psychology Teaching Review, 3*, 19-23.

Brandon, L. & Tochon, F. V. (1996). *COACH – Computer Observation and Analysis of Coaching*. Pascal++ on Macintosh. Application funded by the Social Sciences and Humanities Council of Canada. Sherbrooke: QC: Université de Sherbrooke.

Breault, D., & Breault, R. (2005). *Experiencing Dewey.* Indianapolis: Kappa Delta Pi.

Brophy, J. (1989). *Teaching for meaningful understanding and self-regulated learning.* Greenwich, CT: JAI.

Brown, J. S., Collins, A., & Duguid, P. (1989). Situated cognition and the culture of learning. *Educational Researcher, 18,* 32-42.

Bru, M., & Not, L. (1987). *Où va la pédagogie du projet?* (Where goes project pedagogy?). Toulouse, France: Editions Universitaires du Sud.

Bruner, J. (1986). *Actual minds, possible worlds.* Cambridge, MA: Harvard University Press.

Bruner, J. (1990). *Acts of meaning.* Cambridge, MA: Harvard University Press.

Bryan, S. (2011). Extensive reading and narrow reading: a review of literature. *Australian Library Journal, 60*(2), 113-122.

Buck Institute for Education (2009). PBL Starter Kit: To-the-Point Advice, Tools and Tips for Your First Project. Introduction chapter free to download at: http://www.bie.org/tools/toolkit/starter

Bunch, G. C., Abram, P. L., Lotan, R. A., & Valdes, G. (2001). Beyond sheltered instruction: rethinking conditions for academic language development. *TESOL Journal, 10*(2/3), 28-33.

Bussey, M., Inayatullah, S., & Milojević I. (2008). *Alternative educational futures: pedagogies for emergent worlds.* Rotterdam: Sense Publishers.

Byram, M. (2003). On being bicultural and intercultural. In G. Alread, M. Byram, & M. Fleming (Eds.), *Intercultural experience and education* (pp. 50-66). Clevedon, UK: Multilingual Matters.

Byram, M. (2008). *From foreign language education to education for intercultural citizenship. Essays and reflections.* Clevedon, UK: Multilingual Matters.

Byram, M. (2014, April). Content Based Instruction in Foreign Language Education. Invited lecture sponsored by the Doctoral Program in Second Language Acquisition, with the Department of African Languages and Literature, Department of German, Language Institute, and Department of Slavic Languages and Literature. Madison, WI: The University of Wisconsin-Madison. April 17, 2014.

Byrd, D. R., Cummings Hlas, A., Watzke, J., & Montes Valencia, M. F. (2011). An examination of culture knowledge: a study of L2 teachers' and teacher educators' beliefs and practices. *Foreign Language Annals, 44*(1), 4-39.

Byrnes, H. (2005). *Re-sourcing the content of language teacher's knowledges: a sociocultural literacy approach.* Plenary presentation given at the 2005 Conference on Language Teacher Education. Minneapolis, MN: University of Minneapolis, CARLA.

Byrnes, H. (2008). Articulating a foreign language sequence through content: A look at the culture standards. *Language Teaching, 41,* 103–118.

Byrnes, H., & Sprang, K. A. (2004). Fostering advanced L2 literacy: a genre-based, cognitive approach. In H. Byrnes & H. H. Maxim (Eds.), *Advanced foreign language learning: a challenge to College programs* (pp. 47-85). Boston: Heinle.

Calderhead, J. (1987). *Exploring teachers' thinking.* London: Cassell.

Calderhead, J. (1996). Teachers' beliefs and knowledge. In D. C. Berliner and R. C. Calfee (Ed.). *Handbook of educational psychology* (pp. 709-725). New York: Macmillan.

Cammarata, L., & Tedick, D. J. (2012). Balancing Content and Language in Instruction: The Experience of Immersion Teachers. *The Modern Language Journal, 96*(2), 251-269.

Canagarajah, S. (2011). Codemeshing in Academic Writing: Identifying Teachable Strategies of Translanguaging. *The Modern Language Journal,* 95, 401-417.

Capraro, R.M., Capraro, M.M., & Morgan, J. (2010). *A companion to interdisciplinary STEM project-based learning.* Boston, MA: Sense Publishers.

Cadierno, T. (1995). Formal instruction from a processing perspective: An investigation into the Spanish past tense. *The Modern Language Journal, 79,* 179–193.

Carroll, S. E. (2001). *Input and evidence: The raw material of second language acquisition.* Philadelphia: John Benjamins.

Carson, L. (2010). Language learner autonomy: Myth, magic or miracle? Proceedings of the international conference, 'From teaching to learning: current trends in English Language Teaching' (pp.77-100). South East European University, Macedonia, April 2010.

Castells, M. (2004). *The power of identity.* Malden, MA: Blackwell.

CECRL (2001). *Cadre européen commun de référence pour les langues – apprendre, enseigner, évaluer.* Paris: Didier.

Center on Education Policy. (2009). *Compendium of key studies of the No Child Left Behind Act: Curriculum and instruction.* Retrieved from http://www.cep-dc.org/_data/n_0001/resources/live/Curriculum%20and%20Instruction.pdf

Chambless, K.S. (2012). Teachers' oral proficiency in the target language: research on its role in language teaching and learning. *Foreign Language Annals, 45*(S1), S141-S162.

Champagne, A., Bergin, K., Bybee, R., Duschl, R. & Gallagher J. (2004, November). *NAEP 2009 Science framework development: issues and recommendations.* Washington, DC: National Assessment Governing Board.

Charlebois, J. (2008). Developing critical consciousness through film. *TESL Canada Journal, 25,* 124–132.

Cho, K., & Krashen, S. D. (1994). Acquisition of vocabulary from the Sweet Valley Kids series: adult ESL acquisition. *Journal of Reading, 37,* 662–667.

Choi, B.C.K., Pak, A.W.P. (2006). Multidisciplinarity, interdisciplinarity and transdisciplinarity in health research, services, education and policy: 1. Definitions, objectives, and evidence of effectiveness. *Clinical Investment Medical, 29*(6), 351–364.

Clark, C. M., & Peterson, P. L. (1986). Teachers' thought processes. In M. C. Wittrock (Ed.), *Handbook of research on teaching* – 3rd ed (pp. 255-296). New York: Macmillan.

Clark, C. M., & Yinger, R. J. (1987). Teacher planning. In J. Calderhead (Ed.), *Exploring teachers'* thinking (pp. 84-103). London: Cassell.

Clibbens, J. (2000). Group discussion workshops in advanced undergraduate teaching: an evaluation. *Psychology Teaching Review, 9,* 11-15.

Cohen, A. D. (2007). *Language Learner Strategies: 30 years of Research and Practice.* Oxford, UK: Oxford University Press.

Cohen, A. D. (2011). *Strategies in learning & using a second language* (2e ed.). Englewood Cliffs, NJ: Prentice Hall.

Connor-Greene, P. A. (2000). Assessing and promoting student learning: blurring the line between teaching and testing. *Teaching of Psychology, 27,* 84-88.

Confucius (1979). *The Analects.* New York: Penguin Classics.

Cook-Sather, A., & Shore, E. (2007). Breaking the rule of discipline in interdisciplinarity: Redefining professors, students, and staff as faculty. *Journal of Research Practice, 3*(2), Article M15. Retrieved from http://jrp.icaap.org/index.php/jrp/article/view/101/93

Correa, M. (2011). Advocating for critical pedagogical approaches to teaching Spanish as a heritage language: some considerations. *Foreign Language Annals, 44*(2), 308-320.

Council of Europe (2001). *The Common European Framework of References for Language Learning, Teaching, and Assessment.* Retrieved from: http://www.coe.int/

Coyle, D., Hood, P., & Marsh, D. (2010). *Content and Language Integrated Learning (CLIL).* Cambridge, MA: Cambridge University Press. Retrieved from: http://www.cambridge.org/servlet/file/9780521112987c04_p48-73.pdf?ITEM_ENT_ID=5633692&COLLSPEC_ENT_ID=7

Cross, J. (2006). *The low-hanging fruit is tasty, internet time blog.* Retrieved from http://internettime.com/?p=105

Crossman, J. (2003). Secular Spiritual Development in Education from International and Global Perspectives. *Oxford Review of Education, 29*(4), 503-520

Csíkszentmihályi, M. (1990). *Flow: the Psychology of optimal experience.* New York: Harper and Row.

Csíkszentmihályi, M., & Selega-Csíkszentmihályi, I. (1990). *Optimal experience: psychological studies of flow in consciousness.* New York: Cambridge University Press.

Csíkszentmihályi, M. (1998). *Finding flow: the psychology of engagement with everyday life.* New York: Basic Books.

Cummins, J. (2009). Bilingual and immersion programs. In M. Long and C. J. Doughty (Eds.), *The handbook of second language teaching* (pp. 161-181). Oxford, UK: Blackwell Publishing.

Cummings Hlas, A., & Hlas, C. S. (2012). A Review of High-Leverage Teaching Practices: Making Connections Between Mathematics and Foreign Languages. *Foreign Language Annals, 45*(S1), S76-S97.

Dam, L. (1995). *Learner autonomy: from theory to classroom practice.* Dublin: Authentik.

Damron, J. (2009). An analysis of student evaluations of native and non native Korean foreign language teachers. *Journal of the National Council of Less Commonly Taught Languages, 7,* 81-102.

Daudelin, M. W. (1996). Learning from experience through reflection. *Organizational dynamics, 24*(3), 36–48.

Davidson, D. E. (2010a). Study abroad: when, how long, and with what results? New data from the Russian front. *Foreign Language Annals, 43*(1), 6-26.

Davidson, D. E. (2010b, October). *L2 gain, time-on-task, and language use in Arabic and Russian overseas Flagship programs.* Lecture given at the Language Institute, College of Letters and Science, University of Wisconsin-Madison on October 26, 2010 for the American Councils for International Education.

Day, R. D., & Bamford, J. (1998). *Extensive reading in the second language classroom.* Cambridge, UK: Cambridge University Press.

De Bot, K., Lowie, W., Thorne, S. L., & Verspoor, M. (2013). Dynamic Systems Theory as a comprehensive theory of second language development. In M. del Pilar Garcia Mayo, M. J. Gutierrrez Mangado & M. Martinez Adrian (Eds.), *Contemporary Approaches to Second Language Acquisition* (pp.199-220). Philadelphia: John Benjamins.

Deci, E. L., Vallerand, R., Pelletier, L., & Ryan, R. (1991). Motivation and education: The selfdetermination perspective. *Educational Psychologist, 26,* 325-346.

Dennis, I., & Newstead, S. E. (1994). The strange case of the disappearing sex bias. *Assessment & Evaluation in Higher Education, 19,* 49-56.

Derrida, J. (1974). *Of Grammatology.* Baltimore: John Hopkins University Press.

Descartes, R. (1637/1943). *Discours de la Méthode* (Discourse on Method). Paris: Cluny.

Dewey, J. (1916/2010). *Democracy and Education: an introduction to the philosophy of education.* New York: CreateSpace.

Dewey, J. (1938). *Experience and education.* New York: Collier.

Ding, H. (2008). The use of cognitive and social apprenticeship to teach a disciplinary genre. *Written Communication, 25*(1), 3-52.

Dolence, M. G. (2004). The curriculum-centered strategic planning model. *EDUCAUSE Center for Applied Research, 10.* Boulder, CO: ECAR. Retrieved from: http://net.educause.edu/ir/library/pdf/ERB0410.pdf

Doly, A.-M. (2004). Metacognition to learn how to write texts at school and to develop motivation to do it. *Effective Learning and Teaching of Writing. Studies in Writing, 14*(2), 381-392.

Dörnyei, Z. (2003). Attitudes, orientations,and motivations in language learning: Advances in theory, research, and applications. *Language Learning, 53*, 3-32.

Dörnyei, Z., & Murphy, T. (2003). *Group dynamics in the language classroom.* Cambridge, UK: Cambridge University Press.

Doughty, C., & Long, M. (2003). Optimal psycholinguistic environments for distance foreign language learning. *Language Learning & Technology, 7*(3), 50-80.

Du-Babcock, B. (2003). An analysis of long-distance internet cultural communication: a Hong Kong project. *Intercultural Communication Studies, 12*(1), 1-16.

Edelsky, C. (1990). Whose agenda is this anyway? A response to McKenna, Robinson, and Miller. *Educational Researcher, 19*(8), 7-11.

Ellinger A.D. (2004) The concept of self-directed learning and its implications for human resource development. *Advances in Developing Human Resources 6*, 158–178.

Ellis, N. (1998). Emergentism, connectionism and language learning. *Language Learning, 48*, 631-664.

Ellis, R. (1991). *Second Language Acquisition and language pedagogy.* Clevedon: Multilingual Matters.

Ellis, R. (2002). Methodological options in grammar teaching materials. In E. Hinkel& S. Fotos (Eds.), *New perspectives on grammar teaching in second language classrooms* (pp. 155–179). Mahwah, NJ: Lawrence Erlbaum

Ellis, R. (2003). *Task-based language learning and teaching.* Oxford, UK: Oxford University Press.

Ellis, R. (2007). *Task-based language teaching: sorting out the misunderstandings.* Auckland: University of Auckland, Department of Applied language Studies and Linguistics.

Ellis, E. S., & Friend, P. (1991). Adolescents with learning disabilities. In B. Y. L. Wong (Ed.), *Learning about learning disabilities.* New York, NY: Academic Press.

Entwistle, N. J. (2000, November). *Promoting deep learning through teaching and assessment: conceptual frameworks and educational contexts.* Paper presented at TLRP Conference, Leicester, Great Britain.

Entwistle, N. J., & Ramsden, P. (1983). *Understanding student learning.* London: Croom Helm.

Entwistle, N. J., Tait, H., & McCune, V. (2000). Patterns of response to an approach to studying inventory across contrasting groups and contexts. *European Journal of Psychology of* Education, 15, 33-48.

Evans, D. (1999). *A review of PPP*. Birmingham: University of Birmingham, UK.

Farr Darling, L, Clarke, A., & Erickson, G. (2007). *Collective improvisation: sustaining a cohort in teacher education*. Tilbury, Netherland: Kluwer Academic.

Fazeli, S. H. (2011). The exploring nature of definitions and classifications of language learning strategies in the current studies of second/foreign language learning. *Language in India*. (ERIC ED523602)

Fetzer, A. (2007). *Context and appropriateness: Micro meets macro*. Amsterdam: John Benjamins.

Ferreira, M. & J. Lantolf (2013). A concept-based approach to teaching writing through genre analysis. In J. P. Lantolf & M. E. Poehner (eds.), *Sociocultural Theory and the Pedagogical Imperative in L2 Education: Vygotskian Praxis to Eliminate the Research/ Practice Divide*. New York, NY: Routledge, ESL & Applied Linguistics Professional Series.

Fetterman, D. M., Kaftarian, S. J., & Wandersman, A. (1996). *Empowerment evaluation: knowledge and tools for self-assessment & accountability*. Thousand Oaks, CA: Sage.

Fetterman, D.M. & Wandersman, A. (2004). *Empowerment evaluation principles in practice*. New York: Guilford.

Fortune, T. W., & Tedick, D. J. (2008). One-way, two-way and indigenous immersion: A call for crossfertilization. In T. W. Fortune & D. J. Tedick (Eds.), *Pathways to multilingualism: Evolving perspectives on immersion education* (pp.3–21). Clevedon, England: Multilingual Matters.

Foucault, M. (2011). *Leçons sur la volonté de savoir. Cours au Collège De France, 1970-1971* (Lessons on the willingness to learn, 1970-1971 College of France Course), followed by "Le savoir d'Œdipe" (Oedipe's knowledge, dir. F. Ewald, A. Fontana & D. Defert). Paris: Gallimard/Seuil, "Hautes études".

Frederiksen, C. H., and Breuleux, A. (1989). Monitoring cognitive processing in semantically complex domains. In N. Frederiksen, R. Glaser, A. Lesgold, and M. Shafto (Eds.), *Diagnostic monitoring of skill and knowledge acquisition*. Hillsdale, NJ: Erlbaum.

Freire, P. (1970). *Pedagogy of the oppressed* (transl. M. Bergman Ramos). New York: Continuum.

Freire, P. (1996). *Letters to Cristina. Reflections on my life and work.* New York: Routledge.

Freitas (de), L., Morin, E., & Nicolescu, B. (1994). *Charter of transdisciplinarity.* Adopted at the First World Congress of Trandisciplinarity, Convento da Arrábida, Portugal, Nov. 2-6, 1994.

Fried-Booth, D. L. (2002). *Project work* (2d ed.). Oxford, UK: Oxford University Press.

Friedman, J. (2000). Using online projects to enhance learning. http://www.more.net/~janice/

Fromm, E. (1956). *The Art of Loving.* San Francisco: Vintage Books.

Firth, A., & Wagner, J. (1997). On discourse, communication, and (some) fundamental concepts in SLA research. *Modern Language Journal, 81*(3), 285-300.

Gagne, R. M. (1985). *The conditions of learning* (4th ed.). New York: Holt, Rinehart & Winston.

Gagné, R. M., & Briggs, L. J. (1974). *Principles of instructional design* (2nd ed.). New York: Holt, Rinehart, and Winston.

García, O. (2009). *Bilingual education in the 21st Century. A global perspective.* Malden, MA: Wiley-Blackwell.

Garrett, N. (2009). Technology in the service of language learning: trends and issues. *Modern Language Journal, 93*(S1), 697-718.

Garrett, P, & Shortall, T. (2002). Learners' evaluations of teacher-fronted and student-centered classroom activities. *Language Teaching Research, 6*, 25-57.

Gascoigne, C. (2012). Toward an understanding of the relationship between classroom climate and performance in postsecondary French: an application of the Classroom Climate Inventory. *Foreign Language Annals, 45*(2), 193-202.

Gass, S. (1997). *Input, interaction, and the second language learner.* Mahwah, NJ: Lawrence Erlbaum.

Gebert, A. (2012). Daisaku Ikeda and the culture of translation. *Critical Inquiry in Language Studies, 9*(1-2), 15-32.

Gee, J. (2007). *What video games have to teach us about learning and literacy* (Revised edition). New York: Palgrave Macmillan.

Genosko, G. (2003). "Félix Guattari: towards a transdisciplinary metamethodology". *Angelika, 8*(1), 29.

Germain, C., and J. Netten (2005). Fondements d'une approche transdisciplinaire en FLE/FL2 : le français intensif au Canada. *Cahiers du français contemporain, 10*, 13–33.

Gibbons, A. (1998). *Higher Education relevance in the 21st century.* Paris: UNESCO & World Bank.

Glisan, E. (2010). Envisioning foreign language education through the lens of high-leverage practices. *Foreign Language Annals, 43*, 359–360.

Glisan, E. W., Adair-Hauck, B., Koda, K., Sandrock, S. P., & Swender, E. (2003). *ACTFL integrated performance assessment.* Yonkers, NY: ACTFL.

Goddard, C. (2011). *Semantic analysis: a practical introduction.* Oxford, UK: Oxford University Press.

Goh, C. (2008). Metacognitive instruction for second language listening development: theory, practice and research implications *RELC, A Journal of Language Teaching and Research, 39*, 188-213.

Goldberg, A. (2005). *Constructions at work: the nature of generalization in language.* Oxford, UK: Oxford University Press.

Goldstein, L. M. (2005). *Teacher written commentary in second language writing classrooms.* Ann Arbor, MI: University of Michigan Press.

Gorski, P. (2006). Complicity with conservatism: The de-politicizing of multicultural education. *Intercultural Education, 17,* (2): 163-77.

Goulah, J. (2012). Daisaku Ikeda and language: An introduction. *Critical Inquiry in Language Studies, 9*(1-2), 1-14.

Grant, C. A. (2003). *An education guide to diversity in the classroom.* Boston: Houghton Mifflin.

Griffiths, G., & Keohane K. (2000). *Personalizing language learning.* Cambridge: Cambridge University Press.

Grim, F. (2010). Giving Authentic Opportunities to Second Language Learners: A Look at a French Service-Learning Project. *Foreign Language Annals, 43*(4), 605-623.

Grossman, P., & McDonald, M. (2008). Back to the future: Directions for research in teaching and teacher education. *American Educational Research Journal, 45*, 184–205.

Gühn, B. (2010). Quality self-reflection through reflection training. *ELT Journal, 64*(4), 126-135.

Gulbahar, Y., & Tinmaz, H. (2006). Implementing project-based learning and e-portfolio assessment in an undergraduate course. *Journal of Research on Technology in Education, 38*(3), 309–327.

Guo, Y. (2007). Project-based ESL Education: promoting language and content learning. ATESL Conference, Mont Royal College, Calgary, AL. October 19th, 2007. Retrieved from: http://www.atesl.ca/cmsms/home/newsletters/december-2007/project-based-esl-education/

Habermas, J. (1985). *Theorie des kommunikativen handels (The theory of communicative action).* Frankfurt: Suhrkamp Verlag.

Hall, J. K. (2010). Interaction as method and result of language learning. *Language Teaching, 43,* 202–215.

Hall Haley, M., & Austin, T. Y. (2004). *Content-based second language teaching and learning: an interactive approach.* New York: Allyn & Bacon.

Halliday, M.A.K. (1985). *An introduction to functional grammar.* London: Edward Arnold.

Halverson, E. R. (2010). Film as identity exploration: a multimodal analysis of youth-produced films. *Teachers College Record, 112*(9).

Hammer, J., & Swaffar, J. (2012). Assessing strategic cultural competency: holistic approaches to student learning through media. *The Modern Language Journal, 96*(2), 209-233.

Harris, K. R., Graham, S., & Mason, L. H. (2006). Improving the writing, knowledge, and motivation of struggling young writers: effects of self-regulated strategy development with and without peer support. *American Educational Research Journal, 43*(2), 295-340.

Harrow, A.J. (1972). *A taxonomy of the psychomotor domain.* New York: David McKay Co.

Hashemi, M. R., Khodabakhshzadeh, H. & Shirvan, M. E. (2011). The effect of metadiscourse on EFL learners' reading comprehension. *Modern Journal Language Teaching Methods, 1*(2), 112-125.

Hauenstein, A. Dean (1998). *A conceptual framework for educational objectives: a holistic approach to traditional taxonomies.* Lanham, MD: University Press of America.

Heilman, J., & Stout, M. (2005). Putting projects into practice. In K. Bradford-Watts, C. Ikeguchi, & M. Swanson (Eds.), *JALT 2004 Conference Proceedings* (p. 587-591). Tokyo: JALT. Retrieved from: http://jalt-publications.org/archive/proceedings/2004/E113.pdf

Hellermann, J. (2008). *Social actions for classroom language learning.* Clevedon, UK: Multilingual Matters.

Heroux, P. (2010). *Health effects of Electromagnetic. Biomedical Course Instruction Materials.* Montreal, QC: McGill University. Retrieved from: http://www.invitroplus.mcgill.ca/Ftp/Health%20Effects%20of%20Electromagnetism%20CourseNotes%202010.pdf

Heugh, K. (2009). Literacy and bi/multilingual education in Africa: Recovering collective memory and expertise. In T. Skutnabb-Kangas, R. Phillipson, A. K. Mohanty, & M. Panda (Eds.), Social Justice through Multilingual Education (pp.103-124). Buffalo, NY: Multilingual Matters.

Hill, K. (2007). Concept-based grammar teaching: an academic responds to Azar. *Teaching English as a Second Language, TESL-EJ, 11*(2), 1-10.

Hirvela, A. (2004). *Connecting reading and writing in second language writing instruction.* Ann Arbor, MI: University of Michigan Press.

Holliday, A. (2008). Standards of English and politics of inclusion. *Language Teaching, 41*(1), 119-130.

Hornberger, N. H. (2011). *Can schools save indigenous languages? Policy and practice on four continents.* New York: Palgrave Macmillan.

Horst, M. (2005). Learning L2 vocabulary through extensive reading: A measurement study. *Canadian Modern Language Review, 61*, 355–382.

Horst, E.E., & Pearce, J. M. (2010). Foreign Languages and Sustainability: Addressing the Connections, Communities, and Comparisons Standards in Higher Education. *Foreign Language Annals, 43*(3), 365-383.

Horwitz, E. K. (1988). The beliefs about language learning of beginning university foreign language students. *Modern Language Journal, 72*, 283-294.

Hosie, L. (1999). Project-based learning and language learning strategies in the ESL classroom. A case study in teaching ESL with project based curriculum. Retrieved from: www.edventures.com/corporate/media/pdf/esl_in_payette.pdf

Huberman, M. (1993). *Lives of teachers.* New York: Teachers College Press.

Hudson Kam, C. L., & Newport, E. L. (2009). Getting it right by getting it wrong: when learners change languages. *Cognitive Psychology, 59,* 30-66.

Huhn, C. (2012). In Search of Innovation: Research on Effective Models of Foreign Language Teacher Preparation. *Foreign Language Annals, 45*(S1), S163-S183.

Hyland, K. (2004). *Genre and second language writing.* Ann Arbor, MI: University of Michigan Press.

Hyland, K. (2005). *Exploring interaction in writing.* London: Continuum.

Hyland, K., & Hyland, F. (Eds.) (2006). *Feedback in second language writing: contexts and issues.* New York, NY: Cambridge University Press.

Ikas, K., & Wagner, G. (2008). *Communicating in the third space.* New York: Routledge.

Ikeda, D. (1996). *A new humanism: The university addresses of Daisaku Ikeda.* New York, NY: Weatherhill.

Ikeda, D. (2000). Peace through dialogue: A time to talk, thoughts on a culture of peace (pp. 1-20). Tokyo, Japan: Soka Gakkai.

Ikeda, D. (2003). *Manabe, manabe! Doryoku seyo! Kimi jishin no dodai wo kizuke!* (Learn, learn! Exert effort! Build your foundation!) 1995-2010, vol. 13. Tokyo, Japan: Iwanami Shoten.

Ikeda, D. (2010a). *Soka education: For the happiness of the individual.* Santa Monica, CA: Middleway Press.

Ikeda, D. (2010b). *A new humanism: The university addresses of Daisaku Ikeda* (Rev. ed.). London, UK: I.B. Tauris.

Illich, I. (1970). *Deschooling society.* New York: Marion Boyards.

Jackson, P. W. (1968). *Life in classrooms.* New York: Holt, Rinehart & Winston.

Jackson, F. H., & Malone, M. E. (2009). *Building the foreign language capacity we need: Toward a comprehensive strategy for a national language framework.* Washington, DC: Center for Applied Linguistics. Retrieved from http://www.cal.org/resources/languageframework.pdf

Jang, H., Reeve, J., Ryan, R. M., & Kim, A. (2009). Can self-determination theory explain what underlies the productive, satisfying learning experiences of collectivistically oriented Korean students? *Journal of Educational Psychology, 101,* 644-661.

Janks, H. (2004). The access paradox. *English in Australia, 139,* 33–42.

Jeon-Ellis, G., Debski, R., & Wigglesworth, G. (2005). Oral interaction around computers in the project-oriented CALL classroom. *Language Learning & Technology, 9*(3), 121-145.

Jiménez Raya, M., and Lamb, T. (2008). *Pedagogy for autonomy in language education*. Dublin, Ireland : Authentik.

Jodai, H., & Tahriri, A. (2011). Reading rate and comprehension. Modern Journal of Language Teaching Methods, 1(3), 122-131.

Jung, C. G. (1973). *Synchronicity: an acausal connecting principle*. Princeton, NJ: Princeton/Bollingen.

Karaman, C., Ökten, C., & Tochon, F. V. (2012). Learning the Deep Approach: language teachers' voices. *Porta Linguarum, 18*, 79-95.

Karaman, A. C, & Tochon, F. V. (2007). International student teaching in world language education: Critical criteria for global teacherhood. *Critical Inquiry in Language Studies, 4*(2-3), 237-64.

Karaman, A. C., & Tochon, F. V. (2010). Worldviews, criticisms, and the peer circle: a study of the experiences of a student teachers in an overseas school. *Foreign Language Annals, 43*(4), 583-604.

Karaman, A. C., & Tochon, F. V. (2010). Worldviews, Criticisms, and the Peer Circle: Experiences of a Prospective Teacher Student Teaching Abroad. *Foreign Language Annals, 43*(4), 583-604.

Katz, L. G. & Chard, S.C. (2000). *Engaging children's minds: the project approach*. Stamford, CT: Ablex.

Kemaloğlu, E. (2010). *Project-based foreign language learning: theory and research*. New York: Lambert Academic Publishing.

Kern, R. G. (1995). Students' and teachers' beliefs about language learning. *Foreign Language Annals, 28*, 71-92.

Kern, R. G. (2000). *Literacy and language teaching*. Oxford, UK: Oxford University Press.

Kerne, A. (2005). Doing interface ecology: the practice of metadisciplinary. Proceedings of the ACM SIGGRAPH 05 electronic art and animation catalog. Los Angeles, CA: August 1-4, 2005. Retrieved from: http://portal.acm.org/citation.cfm?id=1086057.1086144

Kilpatrick, W. H. (1918). The project method. *Teacher's College Record, 19*(4), 319-335.

Kinginger, C. (2004). Alice doesn't live here anymore: Foreign language learning and identity. In A. Pavleko & A. Blackledge (Eds.), *Negotiation of identities in multilingual contexts* (pp. 219–242). Clevedon, England: Multilingual Matters.

Kirkpatrick, A. (2007). *World Englishes: Implications for International Communication and English Language Teaching*. Cambridge: Cambridge University Press.

Kirkpatrick, A. (2010). *English as a Lingua Franca in ASEAN: a multilingual model*. Hong Kong: Hong Kong University Press.

Kirkpatrick, R., & Ghaemi, H. (2011). Beyond the communicative approach in language teaching. *Modern Journal of Language Teaching Methods, 1*(3), 143-149.

Klein, J. T. (1996). *Crossing boundaries: knowledge, disciplinarities, and interdisciplinarities*. Charlottesville, VA: University Press of Virginia.

Korten, D., C. (2006). *The great turning. From Empire to Earth community*. San Francisco: Berrett-Koehler, Kumarian.

Knowles, M. (1975). *Self-directed learning: a guide for learners and teachers*. New York: Association Press.

Koike, D. A., & Palmiere, D. T. L. (2011). First and second language pragmatics in third language oral and written modalities. *Foreign Language Annals, 44*(1), 80-104.

Kramsch, C. (2006). From communicative competence to symbolic competence. *Modern Language Journal, 90*, 249–252.

Kramsch, C. (2010). *The multilingual subject*. Oxford, UK: Oxford University Press, Applied Linguistic Series.

Kramsch, C. (2010, March). *Language departments as privileged sites for the study of meaning*. The 12th annual Graduate Student Conference of the German and Dutch Graduate Students Association. Madison, University of Wisconsin-Madison.

Krashen, S. (1985). *The input hypothesis: issues and implications*. New York: Longman.

Krashen, S. D. (2004). *The power of reading: insights from the research*. Portsmouth, NH: Heinemann.

Krashen, S., & Terrell, T.D. (1983). *The Natural Approach*. New York: Pergamon.

Krathwohl, D. R., Bloom, B. S., and Masia, B. B. (1964). *Taxonomy of educational objectives, handbook II: affective domain*. New York: David McKay Co.

Kristmanson, P. (2005). Beyond time on task: strategy use and development in intensive core French. In J. Cohen, K.T. McAlister, K. Rolstad, and J. MacSwan (Eds.), *ISB4: Proceedings of the 4th*

International Symposium on Bilingualism (pp.1235-1251). Somerville, MA: Cascadilla Press.
Kroll, B. (Ed.) (2003). *Exploring the dynamics of second language writing.* Cambridge, UK: Cambridge University Press.
Kronman, A. (2007). *Education's end: why our Colleges and Universities have given up on the meaning of life.* New Haven: Yale University Press.
Kubota, R. (2004). The politics of cultural difference in second language education. *Critical Inquiry in Language Studies, 1*(1), 21-39.
Kubota, R., & Lin, A.M.Y. (2009). *Race, culture, and identities in second language education: exploring critically engaged practice.* New York: Routledge.
Ladson-Billings, G. (2001). *Crossing over to Canaan: The journey of new teachers in diverse classrooms.* San Francisco: Jossey Bass.
Lai, C., Zhao, Y., & Wang, J. (2011). Task-based language teaching in online ab initio foreign language classrooms. *The Modern Language Journal, 95*, Supplementary Issue, 81-108.
Lamb, T. (2008). Learner autonomy in eight European countries: opportunities and tensions in education reform and language teaching policy. In M. Jiménez Raya and T. Lamb (Eds.), *Pedagogy for autonomy in language education* (pp.36-57). Dublin, Ireland: Authentik.
Lampert, M. (2010). Learning teaching in, from, and for practice: What do we mean? *Journal of Teacher Education, 61,* 21–34.
Lantolf, J. P. (2006). Conceptual knowledge and instructed second language learning: a sociocultural perspective. In S. Fotos & H. Nassaji (eds.), *Form focused instruction and teacher education: studies in honour of Rod Ellis* (pp. 35-54). Oxford, UK: Oxford University Press.
Lantolf, J. P. & Thorne, S. F. (2006). *Sociocultural theory and the sociogenesis of second language development.* New York: Oxford University Press.
Larmer, J., Ross, D. & Mergendoller, J.R. (2009). *PBL starter kit.* Novato, CA: Buck Institute for Education.
Larsen-Freeman, D. (2002). The grammar of choice. In E. Hinkel & S. Fotos (Eds.), *New perspectives on grammar teaching in second language classrooms* (pp. 103–118). Mahwah, NJ: Lawrence Erlbaum.

Larsen-Freeman, D. (2012). Complex, dynamic systems: a new transdisciplinary theme for applied linguistics? *Language Teaching, 45*(2), 202-2014.

Latouche, S. (2004). *Survivre au développement* (Survive development) Paris: UNESCO, Mille-et-Une-Nuits.

Lattuca et al. (2006). Does interdisciplinarity promote learning? Theoretical support and researchable questions. *The Review of Higher Education, 28*(1), 23-48. Retrieved from: http://www.teaglefoundation.org/learning/pdf/2006_ssrc_whitepaper.pdf

Lave, J., & Wenger, E. (1990*). Situated learning: legitimate peripheral participation.* Cambridge, UK: Cambridge University Press.

Leaver, B. L., & Willis, J. R. (2004). *Task-based instruction in foreign language education.* Washington, DC: Georgetown University Press.

Lee, I. (2002). Project work made easy in the English classroom. *The Canadian Modern Language Review, 59*(2), 282–290.

Lee, S. (2005). Facilitating and inhibiting factors in English as a foreign language writing performance: A model testing with structural equation modeling. *Language Learning, 55,* 335–374.

Lefebvre, H. (1991). *The production of space* (D. Nicholson-Smith, trans.). Cambridge : Blackwell.

Leinhard, G. (1986, April). *Math lessons: A contrast of novice and expert competence.* Paper presented at the annual meeting of the American Educational Research Association (AERA), San Francisco.

Lenoir, Y. (2006). Practices of disciplinarity and interdisciplinarity in Quebec elementary schools: Results of twenty years of research. *Journal of Social Science Education, 5*(2), 19-36.

Lemke, J. (1994). *The coming paradigm wars in education: Curriculum vs information access.* Computers, Freedom, and Privacy Conference; The John Marshall Law School, Chicago, March 1994.

LeMoigne, J.-L. (1984). *La théorie du système général. Théorie de la modélisation* (General Systems Theory. Modeling Theory). Paris: Presses Universitaires de France.

Levine, G. (2011, February). *Blessings of Babel: principles for code choice in the foreign language classroom.* Presentation made at the Language Institute of the University of Wisconsin-Madison. Madison, WI: February 8, 2011.

Lewis, M. (1994). Implications of a lexical view of language. In D. Willis & J. Willis (Eds.), *Challenge and Change in Language Teaching* (pp.9-16). New York: Macmillan Heinemann.

Lippi-Green, R. (2011). *English with an Accent: Language, Ideology, and Discrimination in the United States* (2d Ed.). New York: Routledge.

Little, D. (1991). *Learner autonomy: definitions, issues, problems.* Dublin: Authentik.

Little, D. (2002a). Learner autonomy and second/foreign language learning. In The guide to good practice for learning and teaching in languages, linguistics and area studies. Retrieved from http://www.llas.ac.uk/resources/gpg/1409

Little, D. (2002b). The European Language Portfolio: structure, origins, implementation and challenges, *Language Teaching, 35*(3), 182-9.

Little, D. (2007). Language Learner Autonomy: some Fundamental Considerations Revisited. *Innovation in Language Learning and Teaching, 1*(1), 14-29.

Liu, W. C., Wang, C. K., Tan, O. S., Ee, J., & Koh, C. (2009). A self-determination approach to understanding students' motivation in project work. *Learning and Individual Differences, 19*, 139-145.

Liuoliene, A., & Metiuniene, R. (2009). Students' Learning through reflective journaling. *Coactivity, 4*, 32-37.

Lobaczewski, A. M. (2007). *Political ponerology. A science on the nature of evil adjusted for political purposes* (2d ed.). Grande Prairie, AB: Red Pill Press.

LOGSE – Ley Orgánica General del Sistema Educativo (1990). In S. Castillo Arredondo (Ed.), *Compromisos de la evaluación educativa* (pp.73-88). Madrid, Spain: Prentice Hall.

Lupasco, P. (1951). *Le principe d'antagonisme et la logique de l'énergie: prolégomènes à une science de la contradiction* (Antagonism principle and the logic of energy: prolegomenon to a science of contradiction). Paris: Hermann.

Lupasco, S. (1987). *Le principe d'antagonisme et la logique de l'énergie* (Antagonism principle and the logic of energy - 2^d ed). Paris: Le Rocher.

Lynch, A. (2008). The linguistic similarities of Spanish heritage and second language learners. *Foreign Language Annals, 41*, 252–281.

Macaro, E. (2006). Strategies for Language Learning and for Language Use: Revising the theoretical framework. *Modern Language*

Journal, 90(3), 320-337.
Macedo, D. (2006). *Literacies of Power: What Americans Are Not Allowed to Know (Expanded Edition)*. Boulder, CO: Westview.
MacSwan, J. & Mahoney, K. (2008). Academic bias in language testing: A construct validity critique of the IPT I Oral Grades K-6 Spanish Second Edition. *Journal of Educational Research and Policy Studies, 8*(2), 85-100.
Madrid, D. (2002). The power of the FL teacher's motivational strategies. CAUCE, *Revista de Filología y su Didáctica, 25*, 369-422.
Madrid, D., & Stephen, H. (2011). *Studies in bilingual education*. New York: Peter Lang.
Maftoon, P., Lavasani, M., & Shahini, A. (2011). Broadening the listening materials in second/foreign language context. *Modern Journal of Language Teaching Methods, 1*(3), 110-121.
Mager, R. (1962/1975). *Preparing instructional objectives* (2nd Ed.). Belmont, CA: Lake.
Magnan, S. S. (2008). Reexamining the priorities of The National Standards for Foreign Language Education. *Language Teaching, 41*, 349–366.
Magnan, S. S. Murphy, D., Sahakyan, N. & Kim, S. (2012). Student goals, expectations, and the standards for foreign language learning. *Foreign Language Annals, 45*(2), 170-192.
Makiguchi (1988). *Makiguchi Tsunesaburo zenshu* (The complete works of Tsunesaburo Makiguchi), 10 vols. Tokyo, Japan: Daisan, Bunmeisha.
Manchón, R. (Ed.) (2009). *Writing in foreign language contexts: learning, teaching, and research*. Clevedon, UK: Multilingual Matters.
Markham, T., Larmer, J., & Ravitz, J. (2003). *Project based learning handbook: a guide to standards-focused project based learning for Middle and High School teachers* (2d Rev Spl ed.). Novato, CA: Buck Institute for Education.
Marsh, C., Richards, K., & Smith, P. (2001). Autonomous learners and the learning society: systematic perspectives on the practice of teaching in Higher Education. *Educational Philosophy and Theory, 33*(3&4), 381-395.
Marton, F., & Säljö, R. (1976). On qualitative differences in learning. I. Outcome and process. *British Journal of Educational Psychology, 46*, 4-11.

Marton, F., Dall'Alba, G., & Beaty, E. (1993). Conceptions of learning. *International Journal of Educational Research, 19*, 277-300.

Marx, R. W., Blumenfeld, P. C., Krajcik, J. S., & Soloway, E. (1997). Enacting project-based science: challenges for practice and policy. *Elementary School Journal, 97*(4) 341–358.

Marzano, R. J. (2001). *Designing a new taxonomy of educational objectives.* Thousand Oaks, CA: Corwin Press.

Maslow, A. (1998). *Toward a Psychology of Being.* New York: Wiley.

Matthews, P. H. (2010). Factors influencing self-effi cacy judgments of university students in foreign language tutoring. *Modern Language Journal, 94*, 618–635.

Mathews-Aydinli, J. (2007). *Problem-based learning and adult English language learners. CAELA Brief, April 2007.* Washington, DC: Center for Adult English Language Acquisition.

Matsuda, P. K., Ortmeier-Hooper, C., & You, X. (Eds.) (2006). *The politics of second language writing: in search of the promised land.* West Lafayette; IN: Parlor Press.

Mayer, R.E. (1979). Can advance organizers influence meaningful learning? *Review of Educational Research, 4*(2), 371-383.

McCarty, T. L. (2009). Empowering Indigenous languages – What can be learned from Native American experiences? In T. Skutnabb-Kangas, R. Phillipson, A. K. Mohanty, & M. Panda (Eds.), *Social Justice through Multilingual Education* (pp.125-139). Buffalo, NY: Multilingual Matters.

McDonough, K. (2004). Learner–learner interaction during pair and small group activities in a Thai EFL context. *System, 32*, 207–224.

McKenna, M. C., Robinson, R. D., & Miller, J. W. (1993). Whole language: a research agenda for the nineties. *Educational Researcher, 19*, 3-6.

McManus, T.F. (2000). Individualizing instruction in a web-based hypermedia learning environment: nonlinearity, advance organizers, and self-regulated learners. *Journal of Interactive Learning Research, 11*(3), 219-251.

McNamara, T. (2011). Multilingualism in Education: A poststructuralist critique. *The Modern Language Journal, 95*, 430-441.

Meijer, P. C., Verloop, N., & Beijaard, D. (1999). Exploring language teachers' practical knowledge about teaching reading comprehension. *Teaching and Teacher Education, 15*(1), 59-84.

Melin, C. (2010). Between the lines: When culture, language, and poetry meet in the classroom. *Language Teaching, 43*, 349–365.

Mesri, F. (2011). Using different presentations of pictures and video clues and Iranian EFL learners' listening comprehension. *Modern Journal of Language Teaching Methods, 1(3)*, 132-142.

Miller, E. R., & Zuengler, J. (2011). Negotiating Access to Learning Through Resistance to Classroom Practice. *The Modern Language Journal, 95*, Supplementary Issue, 130-147.

Mills, N. (2009). A Guide du Routard simulation: increasing self-efficacy in the standards through project-based learning. *Foreign Language Annals, 42(4)*, 607-639.

Mitchell, S., Foulger, T. S., & Wetzel, K., Rathkey, C. (February, 2009). The negotiated project approach: project-based learning without leaving the standards behind. *Early Childhood Education Journal, 36(4)*, 339-346.

MLA – Modern Language Association Ad Hoc Committee on Foreign Languages (2007). *Foreign Languages and Higher Education: new structures for a changed world.* New York: The Modern Language Association of America.
Retrieved from: http://www.mla.org/pdf/forlang news pdf.pdf

MLA (2009). *Report to the Teagle Foundation on the Undergraduate Major in Language and Literature.* New York: The Modern Language Association of America.

Moje, E. B., & Luke, A. (2009) Literacy and identity: examining the metaphors in history and contemporary research. *Reading Research Quarterly*. International Reading Association.

Mojica-Díaz, C. C., Sánchez-López, L. (2010). Constructivist Grammatical Learning: A Proposal for Advanced Grammatical Analysis for College Foreign Language Students. *Foreign Language Annals, 43(3)*, 470-487.

Morgan, A. (1993) *Improving your students' learning.* London and Philadelphia: Kogan Page.

Morin, Edgar (2001). *Seven complex lessons in Education for the future* (Education on the Move). Paris: UNESCO.

Morris, E, & Tarone, E. (2003). Impact of classroom dynamics on the effectiveness of recasts in second language acquisition. *Language Learning, 53*, 325-368.

Moss, D., & Van Duzer, C. (1998). Project-based learning for adult English language learners. Washington, DC: National Center for

ESL Literacy Education. Retrived from www.cal.org/caela/digests/ProjBase.htm

Mu, C., & Carrington, S. (2007). An investigation of three Chinese students' English writing strategies. *TESL-EJ, 11*. [Electronic version]. Retrieved from http:// tesl-ej.org/ej41/a1.pdf

National Standards in Foreign Language Education Project (1999). *Standards for foreign language learning in the 21st century*. Lawrence, KS: Allen Press.

Negueruela, E. & J. P. Lantolf. (2006). A concept-based approach to teaching Spanish grammar. In R. Salaberry & B. Lafford (eds.), Spanish second language acquisition: state of the art, (pp. 79-102). Washington, D.C.: Georgetown University Press.

Netten, J. & Germain, C. (2002a). Transdisciplinary approach and intensity in second language learning/teaching. *Canadian Journal of Applied Linguistics/La Revue canadienne de linguistique appliquée*, 3(1-2), 107-122.

Netten, J. & Germain, C. (2002b). *L'apprentissage intensif du français: Rapport Final (Intensive French Learning: Final Report)*. Ottawa, ON: Department of Canadian Heritage.

Neuman Allen, K., & Friedman, B. D. (2010). Affective learning: a taxonomy for teaching social work values. *Journal of Social Work Values and Ethics, 7*(2), online journal: http://www.socialworker.com/jswve/fall2010/f1oneuman.pdf

Newstead, S. E. (2002). Examining the examiners: why are we so bad at assessing students? *Psychology Learning and Teaching, 2*, 70-75.

Newstead, S. E., & Findlay, K. (1997). Some problems with using examination performance as a measure of teaching ability. *Psychology Teaching Review, 6*, 14-21.

Newstead, S. E., Franklyn-Stokes, B. A., & Armstead, P. (1996). Individual differences in student cheating. *Journal of Educational Psychology, 88*, 229-241.

Nicolescu, B. (2002). *Manifesto of transdisciplinarity*. Cresskill, NJ: Hampton Press.

Nicolescu, B. (2005). *Towards transdisciplinary education and learning*. Paper presented at the Metanexus Institute for the 'Science and Religion: Global Perspectives' Conference. Philadelphia, PA, June 4-8, 2005.

Nieto, S. (2005). *Why we teach*. New York: Teachers College Press.

Noble, T. (2004). Integrating the revised Bloom's taxonomy with multiple intelligences: A planning tool for curriculum differentiation. *Teachers College Record, 106,* 193.

Noels, K. A. (2001). Learning Spanish as a second language: Learners' orientations and perceptions of their teachers' communication style. *Language Learning, 51,* 107-144.

North, C. (2006). More than words? delving into the substantive meaning(s) of "social justice" in education. *Review of Educational Research, 76,*(4), 507-35.

Norton, L. S. (2001a). *Encouraging students to take a deep approach to learning: Tutor pack.* Retrieved from http://ltsnpsy.york.ac.uk/LTSNPsych/Specialist/Norton/Introduction.htm

Norton, L. S., & Crowley, C. M. (1995). Can students be helped to learn how to learn? An evaluation of an approach to learning programme for first year degree students. *Higher Education, 29,* 307-328.

Norton, L. S., Tilley, A. J., Newstead, S. E., & Franklyn-Stokes, A. (2001). The pressures of assessment in undergraduate courses and their effect on student behaviours. *Assessment and Evaluation in Higher Education, 26,* 268-284.

Norton, M. I., & Ariely, D. (2011). Bulding a better America – One Wealth Quintile at a Time. Perspectives on Psychological Science, 6(1), 9-12. Retrieved from: http://www.people.hbs.edu/mnorton/norton%20ariely%20in%20press.pdf

Nowotny, H. (2004). The potential of transdisciplinarity, in *Rethinking interdisciplinarity*, January 2004. Retrieved from: www.interdisciplines.org/interdisciplinarity/papers/5/24

Nowotny, H., Scott, P., Gibbons, M. (2001). *Re-Thinking Science: Knowledge and the Public in an Age of Uncertainty.* Oxford, UK: Polity.

NSFLP - National Standards in Foreign Language Education Project (1999). *Standards for foreign language learning in the 21st century.* Lawrence, KS: Allen Press.

Nunn, R. (2006). Designing holistic units for task-based teaching. *Asian EFL Journal, 8*(3), 69-93.

Obelleiro, G. (2012). A moral cosmopolitan perspective on language education. *Critical Inquiry in Language Studies, 9*(1-2), 33-59.

Oczkus, L. D. (2010). *Reciprocal teaching at work: strategies for improving reading comprehension* (2nd Ed.). New York: International Reading Association.

Ong, J., & Zhang, L. J. (2010). Effects of task complexity on the fluency and lexical complexity in EFL students' argumentative writing. *Journal of Second Language Writing, 19*(4), 218-233.

Ortega-Martín, J.L. (2004). La atención a la diversidad en el aula de idiomas. *Porta Linguarum, 1,* 121-140.

Ortiz, J., Burlingame, C., Onuegbulem, C.,Yoshikawa, K., & Rojas, E. D. (2012). The use of video self-modeling with English language learners: Implications for success. *Psychology in the Schools, 49*(1), 23-29.

Osborn, T. A. (2006). *Teaching world languages for social justice. A sourcebook of principles and practices.* Mahwah, NJ: Lawrence Erlbaum Associates.

Oxford, R. L. (1990). *Language learning strategies: What every teacher should know.* Boston: Heinle & Heinle.

Oxford, R. L. (2003). Relationships between second language learning strategies and proficiency in the context of learner autonomy and self-regulation. *Revista Canaria de Estudios Ingleses* [Canarian Journal of English Studies], 38, 109-126.

Paige, R. M., Cohen, A. D., & Shively, R. L. (2002). Assessing the impact of a strategies-based curriculum on language and culture learning abroad. *Frontiers Journal, 10,* 10-15.

Palincsar, A. S. & Brown, A. (1984). Reciprocal teaching of comprehension-fostering and comprehension monitoring activities. *Cognition and Instruction, 1*(2), 117-175.

Palou de Carranza, E. (2004). Vers une grammaire culturelle et civilisationnelle capable de donner sens à une appropriation intégrée des langues (Towards a cultural and civilization grammar able to give meaning to the integrated acquisition of languages). *Le Français à l'Université, 9*(4), 2.

Paquette, Gilbert (2002). *Modélisation des connaissances et des compétences, pour concevoir et apprendre* (Modeling knowledge and competencies to conceptualize and learn) Sillery, QC: Presses de l'Université du Québec.

Paquette, G., Rosca. I, Mihaila S. and Masmoudi A. (2006). TELOS, a service-oriented framework to support learning and knowledge management. In S. Pierre (Ed), *E-Learning networked environments and architectures: a knowledge processing perspective.* New York: Springer-Verlag. Retrieved on October 6, 2008 from: http://www.igi-pub.com/downloads/excerpts/1599043394ch1.pdf

Park, H-Y. (2008). Linguistic minority children's heritage language learning and identity struggle. Unpublished dissertation. Madison, WI: University of Wisconsin-Madison, School of Education, Department of Curriculum & Instruction, World Language Education.

Pavlenko, A. (2004). Gender and sexuality in foreign and second language education: critical and feminist approaches. In B. Norton & K. Toohey (Eds.), *Critical pedagogies and language learning* (pp.53-71). New York: Cambridge University Press.

Pavlenko, A. (2005) *Emotions and multilingualism.* Cambridge, MA: Cambridge University Press.

Petrina, S. (2007). Communicating and planning for instruction. Idea group. Retrieved from:
http://www.igi-pub.com/downloads/excerpts/1599043394ch1.pdf

Phillipson, R. (2006). English, a cuckoo in the European higher education nest of languages? *European Journal of English Studies, 10*(1), 13-32.

Piaget, J. (1926/1960). *The child conception of the world.* Totowa, NJ: Littlefield, Adams & Co.

Poehner, M. (2008). *Dynamic assessment: a Vygotskian approach to understanding and promoting second language development.* Berlin: Springer.

Polansky, S. G., Andrianoff, T., Bernard, J. B., Flores, A., Gardocki, I. A., Handerhan, R. J., Park, J., & Young, L. (2010). Tales of tutors: the role of narrative in language learning and service-learning. *Foreign Language Annals, 43*(2), 304-323.

Pomerantz, A., & Bell, N. (2012). Humor as safe house in the foreign language classroom. *The Modern Language Journal, 95,* Supplementary issue, 148-161.

Popkewitz, T. (1998). Dewey, Vygotsky, and the social administration of the individual: constructivist pedagogy as systems of ideas in historical spaces. *American Educational Research Journal, 35*(4), 535-70.

Popkewitz, T. (2008). *Cosmopolitanism and the age of school reform: Science, education and making society by making the child*. New York: Routledge.

Popper, K. R. (1962). Philosophy of science: a personal report. In K. R. Popper (Ed.), *Conjectures and refutations: the growth of scientific knowledge* (pp. 33-65). New York: Basic Books.

Prabhu, N. S. (1987). *Second language pedagogy*. Oxford, UK: Oxford University Press.

Pufahl, I., & Rhodes, N. C. (2011). Foreign language instruction in U.S. schools: results of a national survey of elementary and secondary schools. *Foreign Language Annals, 44*(2), 258-288.

Ramsden, P. (1985). Student learning research: retrospect and prospect. *Higher Education Research and Development, 5*, 51-70.

Ramsden, P. (1992). *Learning to teach in higher education*. New York: Routledge.

Rancière, J. (1991). *The ignorant schoolmaster: five lessons in intellectual emancipation*. Stanford, CA: Stanford University Press.

Rancière, J. (2004). *The emancipated spectator*. Keynote lecture given at the Academy of Arts Marten Spangberg. Online text.

Rankin, J. (2005). Easy reader: a case study of embedded extensive reading in intermediate German L2. *Die Unterrichtspraxis/Teaching German, 38*, 125–134.

Ransdell, S., & Barbier, M. (Eds.). (2002). *New directions for research in L2 writing*. Boston: Kluwer Academic.

Reagan, T. G. (2002). Chapter 2. "French isn't a real class": the marginalization of Foreign Language Education. In T. Reagan, *Language, Education, and ideology. Mapping the linguistic landscape of U.S. schools*. Westport, CN: Praeger.

Reagan, T. G. (2012, May). *Toward a critical epistemology of world language teaching and learning*. Paper presented at the Fifth International Conference of English as a Lingua Franca. Istanbul, Turkey. May 24-26, 2012.

Reagan, T. G., & Osborn, T. A. (2002). *The foreign language educator in society. Toward a critical pedagogy*. Mahwah, NJ: Lawrence Erlbaum.

Reeve, J. (2002). Self-determination theory applied to educational settings. In E. L. Deci & R.M. Ryan (Eds.), *Handbook of self-determination research* (pp. 193-203). Rochester, NY: University of Rochester Press.

Reeve, J., Deci, E. L., & Ryan, R. M. (2004). Self-determination theory: a dialectical framework for understanding socio-cultural influences on student motivation. In D. M. McInerney & S. Van Etten (Eds.), *Big theories revisited* (pp. 31-60). Greenwich, CT: Information Age.

Reigeluth, C. (1999). *Instructional-design theories and models: a new paradigm of instructional theory,* Vol. 2 (Instructional design theories & models). New York: Routledge.

Révész, A. (2012). Task Complexity, Focus on L2 Constructions, and Individual Differences: A Classroom-Based Study. *The Modern Language Journal, 95,* Supplementary Issue, 162-181.

Rhodes, N. C. (2014). Elementary school foreign language teaching: Lessons learned over three decades (1980-2010). *Foreign Language Annals, 47*(1), 115-133.

Ribero (de), O. (2003). *The myth of development: the non-viable economies of the 21st century.* New York: Zed Books.

Richards, J. C., & Lockhart, C. (1996). *Reflective teaching in second language* classrooms. Cambridge, MA: Cambridge University Press.

Ringer, F. (1990). The intellectual field, intellectual history, and the sociology of knowledge. *Theory and Society, 19,* 269–294.

Rivera-Mills, S. V., & Plonsky, L. (2007). Empowering Students With Language Learning Strategies: A Critical Review of Current Issues. *Foreign Language Annals, 40*(3), S35-S48.

Rodrigo, V., Krashen, S., & Gribbons, B. (2004). The effectiveness of two comprehensible-input approaches to foreign language instruction at the intermediate level. *System, 32,* 53–60.

Rogers, C. R. (1969). *Freedom to learn.* Columbus, OH: Charles E. Merrill.

Rogers, C. R. (1986). *Freedom to learn: a view of what Education might become* (2d ed.). Columbus, OH: Charles Merrill.

Rogoff, B. (1990). *Apprenticeship in thinking: cognitive development in social context.* New York, NY: Oxford University Press.

Rogoff, B., Baker-Sennett, J., & Matusov, E. (1994). A sociocultural perspective on the concept of planning. In M. Haith, J. Benson, B. Pennington, & R. Roberts (Eds.), *Future-oriented processes* (pp. 353-373). Chicago: University of Chicago Press.

Roekel (van), D. (2008). Standards: a limited tool for Education improvement. *A NEA Policy Brief, PB18.* Washington, DC: National Education Association. Retrieved from:
http://www.nea.org/assets/docs/mf_PB18_Standards.pdf

Romizowski, A. J. (1981). *Designing instructional systems: decision making in course planning and curriculum design*. New York: Kogan Page/Nichols.

Roschelle, J. (1999). Transitioning to professional practice: a Deweyan view of five analyses of problem-based learning. *Discourse Processes: A Multidisicplinary Journal, 27*(2), 231–240.

Ross, S. J. (2005). The Impact of Assessment Method on Foreign Language Proficiency Growth. *Applied Linguistics, 26*(3), 317-342.

Rossiter, N. (2006). Organized networks, transdisciplinarity and new institutional forms. *Intelligent Agent, 6*(2). Retrieved from: http://www.intelligentagent.com/archive/ia6_2_transvergence_rossiter_transdisciplinarity.pdf

Rothkopf, D. (2008). *Superclass: the global power elite and the world they are making*. New York: Farrar, Straus and Giroux.

Sacks, P. (2000). *Standardized minds. The high price of America's testing culture and what we can do to change it*. Cambridge, MA: Perseus Books.

Sarhady, T. (2011). The impact of consciousness-raising on learning grammar: interval between teaching and practice or not? Modern Journal of Language Teaching Methods, 1(3), 24-38.

Saito, H., & Fujita, T. (2009). Peer-assessing Peers' contributions to EFL group presentations. *RELC, A Journal of Language Teaching and Research, 40*(2), 149-171.

Saljo, R. (1979). Learning about learning. *Higher Education, 8*, 443-451.

Sandrock, P. (2002). *Planning curriculum for learning world languages*. Madison, WI: Wisconsin Department of Public Instruction.

Saussure, F. de (1916/1977). *Course in general linguistics* (trans. W. Baskin). Glasgow: Fontana/Collins.

Sawyer, K. (2004). Creative teaching: collaborative discussion as disciplined improvisation. *Educational Researcher, 33*(2), 12–20.

Sayenko, T. (2011). Reading speed in L1 and L2. In A. Stewart (Ed.), JALT 2010 Conference Proceedings. Tokyo: JALT. Retrieved from: http://jalt-publications.org/proceedings/articles/1045-reading-speed-l1-and-l2

Schleicher, A.F. (2011, April). *Teaching culture through language*. Lecture presented at the annual meeting of the African Language Teachers Association, National Council of Less commonly taught languages. Madison, Wisconsin. April 7-11, 2011.

Schmuck, R., & Schmuck, P. (2001). *Group processes in the classroom* (8th ed.). Boston: McGraw-Hill.

Schneuwly, B., & Dolz, J. (1997). Les genres scolaires. Des pratiques langagières aux objets d'enseignement (School genres. From language practices to teaching objects). *Repères, 15*, 27-40.

Schön, D. A. (1987). *Educating The Reflective Practitioner*. San Francisco: Jossey-Bass.

Schulz, R. A. (2007). The challenge of assessing cultural understanding in the context of foreign language instruction. *Foreign Language Annals, 40*, 9–26.

Schumann, J. H. (1986). Research on the acculturation model for second language acquisition. *Journal of Multilingual and Multicultural Development, 7*, 379–392.

Schunk, D. H. (1991). Self-efficacy and academic motivation. *Educational Psychologist, 26*, 207–232.

Scott, V. M., Liskin-Gasparro, J. E., & Lacorte, M. E. (2009). *Double Talk: Deconstructing Monolingualism in Classroom Second Language Learning*. Upper Saddle River, NJ: Prentice Hall.

Shamir, A., Mevarech, Z.R., & Shamir, C.G. (2009). The assessment of meta-cognition in different contexts: individualized vs. peer assisted learning. *Metacognition and Learning, 4*(1), 47-61.

Shaules, J. (2007). *Deep Culture: The Hidden Challenges of Global Living*. Clevedon, UK: Multilingual Matters.

Shavelson, R. J., & Stern, P. (1981). Research on teachers' pedagogical thoughts, judgments, decisions, and behavior. *Review of Educational Research, 51*(4), 455-498.

Sheorey, R., & Mokhtari, K. (2001). Differences in the metacognitive awareness of reading strategies among native and nonnative readers. System, 29, 431-449.

Sherman, J. (2003). *Using authentic video in the language classroom*. Cambridge, UK: Cambridge University Press.

Shohamy, E. (2004). Assessment in multicultural societies: applying democratic principles and practices to language testing. In B. Norton & K. Toohey (Eds.), *Critical pedagogies and language learning* (pp.72-92). New York: Cambridge University Press.

Shrum, J. L., & Glisan, E. W. (2010). *Teacher's handbook: Contextualized language instruction* (4th ed.). Boston: Cengage.

Sieloff-Magnan, S., & Tochon, F. V. (2001). Reconsidering French pedagogy in terms of the crucial role of the teacher and teaching. *French Review, 74*(6), 1092-1112.

Silva, T., & Matsuda, P. K. (Eds.) (2001). *On second language writing.* Mahwah, NJ: Lawrence Erlbaum Associates.

Skehan, P. (1998). *A cognitive approach to language learning.* Oxford: Oxford University Press.

Skutnabb-Kangas, T. (2000). *Linguistic genocide in Education.* Mahwah, NJ: Lawrence Erlbaum.

Skutnabb-Kangas, T. (2005). Linguistic Genocide. In D. Shelton (Ed.), *Encyclopedia of Genocide and Crimes Against Humanity, 3 vols* (pp.653-654). New York: Macmillan Reference.

Skutnabb-Kangas, T., & Phillipson, R., (1989). 'Mother Tongue': The Theoretical and Sociopolitical Construction of a Concept. In U. Ammon (Ed.), *Status and Function of Languages and Language Varieties.* Berlin, New York: Walter de Gruyter.

Šliogerienė, J. (2006). *Learning contracts in Second Language Acquisition.* Santalka. Filologija. Edukologija,14(2), 1822–4318 online: http://www.coactivity.vgtu.lt/upload/filosof_zurn/j_sliogeriene_filologija_nr2.pdf

Soja, E. W. (1996). *Thirdspace. Journeys to Los Angeles and other real-and-imagined places.* Padstow, Cornwall: Blackwell.

Spenader, A. (2011). Language learning and acculturation: lessons from high school and gap-year exchange students. *Foreign Language Annals, 44*(2), 381-398.

Spolsky, B. (2004). Language practices, ideology and beliefs, and management and planning. In B. Spolsky, *Language policy* (pp.1-15).

Starkey, H. (2007). Language education, identities and citizenship: Developing cosmopolitan perspectives. *Language and Intercultural Communication, 7*(1), 56-71.

Stewart, J. A. (2010). Using e-journals to assess students' language awareness and social identity during study abroad. *Foreign Language Annals, 43*(1), 138-159.

Stoller, F. (2002). Project work: a means to promote language and content. In J. C. Richards & W. A. Renandya (Eds.), *Methodology in language teaching: an anthology of current practice* (pp. 107-119). Cambridge, MA: Cambridge University Press.

Sturm, J. L. (2012). Using film in the L2 classroom: a graduate course in film pedagogy. *Foreign Language Annals, 45*(2), 246-259.

Sun, Y. C. (2003). Extensive reading online: an overview and evaluation. *Journal of Computer Assisted Learning, 19*, 438–446.

Swain, M. (1985). Communicative competence: Some roles of comprehensible input and comprehensible output in its development. In S. Gass & C. Madden (Eds.), *Input in second language acquisition*. Cambridge, MA: Newbury House.

Swain, M. (1998). Focus on form through conscious reflection. In C. Doughty & J. Williams (Eds.), *Focus on form in classroom second language acquisition* (pp. 64–82). Cambridge: Cambridge University Press.

Swain, M. (2000). The output hypothesis and beyond: Mediating acquisition through collaborative dialogue. In J. Lantolf (Ed.), *Sociocultural theory and second language learning*. Oxford, UK: Oxford University Press.

Tanaka, H., & Stapleton, P. (2007). Increasing reading input in Japanese high school EFL classrooms: An empirical study exploring the efficacy of extensive reading. *The Reading Matrix, 7*, 115–131.

Thomas, J. W. (2000). *A review of research on project-based learning*. San Rafael, CA: Autodesk Foundation.

Thoms, J. J. (2012). Classroom Discourse in Foreign Language Classrooms: A Review of the Literature. *Foreign Language Annals, 45*(S1), S8-S27.

Thomsen, H. (2000). Learners' favoured activities in the autonomous classroom. In D. Little, L. Dam & J. Timmer (Eds.), *Learning rather than teaching: why and how?* Dublin: Trinity College, Centre for Language and Communication Studies.

Tochon, F. V. (1988). *Didactique du français* (French curriculum & instruction) Geneva, Switzerland: University of Geneva, Cahiers de la Section des Sciences de l'Éducation n° 51.

Tochon, F. V. (1989a). La planification des objectifs, de l'organisation des performances au fonctionnement systémique (Goal-based planning, from performances organizing to open-system functions). *Education et Recherche, 1*, 61-81.

Tochon, F. V. (1989b). L'organisation du temps en didactique du français (Time organizing in French curriculum & instruction). *Revue internationale Les Sciences de l'Education pour l'ère nouvelle, 2*, 31-51.

Tochon, F. V. (1989c). L'atelier d'écriture, du projet aux organisateurs didactiques (Writing workshop, from planning to instructional organizers). *Pratiques, 61*, 91-110.

Tochon, F. V. (1989d). La pensée des enseignants, un paradigme en développement (Teacher thinking, a growing paradigm). *Perspectives documentaires en Sciences de l'Education, 17*, 75-98.

Tochon, F. V. (1989e). Vous avez dit trois niveaux d'objectifs ? (Did you say three levels of objectives?) *Mesure et Evaluation en Education, 11*(4), 27-48.

Tochon, F. V. (1990a). *Well planned improvisation.* Winnipeg, MA: University of Manitoba, CUSB.

Tochon, F. V. (1990b). *Didactique du français: de la planification aux organisateurs cognitifs* (French curriculum & instruction: from teacher planning to cognitive organizers). Paris: Editions Sociales Françaises.

Tochon, F. V. (1991a). *L'enseignement stratégique: transformation de la connaissance dans la pensée des enseignants* (Strategic teaching: knowledge transformation in teacher thinking). Toulouse: Editions Universitaires du Sud (South University Press).

Tochon, F. V. (1991b). Entre didactique et pédagogie: Epistémologie de l'espace/temps stratégique (Between curriculum & instruction and pedagogy: epistemology of the strategic space/time). *Journal of Educational Thought, 25*(2), 120-133.

Tochon, F. V. (1991c). Les critères d'expertise dans la recherche sur les enseignants (Expertise criteria in research on teachers). *Mesure et Evaluation en Education, 14*(2), 57-81.

Tochon, F. V. (1993a). Le fonctionnement improvisationnel de l'enseignant(e) de langue expert(e) (Well-Planned improvisation of language expert teachers). *La Revue des Sciences de l'Education, XIX*, 437-462.

Tochon, F. V. (1993b). From teachers' thinking to macrosemantics: catching instructional organizers and connectors in language teaching. *Journal of Structural Learning and Intelligent Systems, 12*(1), 1-22.

Tochon, F. V. (2000a). Recherche sur la pensée des enseignants: un paradigme à maturité (Research on teacher thinking: a mature paradigm). *Revue française de pédagogie, 133*, 1-23.

Tochon, F. V. (2000b). When authentic experiences are "enminded" into disciplinary genres: crossing biographic and situated knowledge. *Learning and Instruction, 10*, 331-359.

Tochon, F. V. (2002). *Tropics of teaching: productivity, warfare, and priesthood.* Toronto, ON: University of Toronto Press.

Tochon, F. V. (2003a). The Deep Approach: world language teaching for bilingual education. In F. V. Tochon & D. Hanson (Eds.), *The Deep Approach: second languages for community building* (pp. 11-28). Madison, WI: Atwood Publishing.

Tochon, F. V. (2003b). *L'effet de l'enseignant sur l'apprentissage en groupe* (Teacher's impact on group learning). Paris: Presses Universitaires de France (France University Press).

Tochon, F. V. (2009). The Key To Global Understanding: World Languages Education. Why Schools Need to Adapt. *Review of Educational Research. 79*(2), 650-682. 2010 AERA Award of Best Review of Research published in 2009.

Tochon, F. V. (2010a). Portfolio électroniques et socialisation du changement en formation des maîtres. *Formation et pratiques d'enseignement en questions, 11*(1), Juin 2010.

Tochon, F. V. (2010b). Deep Education. *Journal for Educators, Teachers and Trainers (JETT), 1*, 1 - 12. http://www.ugr.es/%7Ejett/articulo.php?id=1

Tochon, F. V. (2010c). A Deep Approach to Language Multimedia and Evaluation: For a more Colorful Future. Invited Keynote Speech. *Proceedings of the Fourteenth international conference of APAMALL* (pp.73-92). Kaohsiung, Taiwan: National Kaohsiung Normal University.

Tochon, F. V. (2011a, September). *The Deep Approach to Turkish language as a response to hybridity in immigrants' Urban Education.* Presentation made at the European Education Research Association (EERA), University of Berlin, Berlin, Germany, September 12-16, 2011.

Tochon, F. V. (2011b). Research on the Possible Implications of Multimedia Language Education with iPad or Tablet PC. Keynote Speech. *Proceedings of the Fifteenth international conference of APAMALL and ROCMELIA* (pp.15-27). Kaohsiung, Taiwan: National Kaohsiung Normal University.

Tochon, F. V. (2011c). Reflecting on the paradoxes of foreign language teacher education: a critical system analysis. *Porta Linguarum, 15*, January, 7-24.

Tochon, F. V. (2011d). Le savoir-évaluer comme politique éducative: Vers une évaluation plus profonde (Evaluative Knowledge as Educational Politics : Towards Deeper Evaluation). *Mesure et Évaluation en Éducation, 34*(3), 133-156.

Tochon, F. V. (2013). Effectiveness of deep, blended language learning as measured by proficiency and course evaluation. *Journal of the National Council of Less Commonly Taught Languages*, 11.

Tochon, F. V. (2013). *Signs and Symbols in Education: Educational Semiotics*. Blue Mounds, Wisconsin: Deep University Press.

Tochon, F. V. (2014). *L'azione dell'insegnante sull'apprendimento in gruppo*. Roma, Italy: Aracne Editrice.

Tochon, F. V., Karaman, A. C., & Ökten, C. E. (2014). Online instructional personal environment for deep language learning. *The International Online Journal of Education and Teaching* (IOJET), 1(2). http://iojet.org/index.php/IOJET/article/view/32

Tochon, F.V., Ökten, C. E., Karaman, A. C., & Druc, I. C. (2014). *Teach a Language Deeply. The Deep Approach to Turkish*. Blue Mounds, WI: Deep University Press.

Tochon, F. V., & Black, N. (2006). Psychosemiotic Analysis of Reflective Conflict and Equilibrium in a Video Study Group. *International Journal of Applied Semiotics, 5*(1-2), 219-233.

Tochon, F. V., & Black, N. J. (2007). Narrative analysis of electronic portfolios: preservice teachers' struggles in researching pedagogically appropriate technology integration. *CALICO Monograph Series "Preparing and developing technology-proficient L2 teachers", 6*, 295-320.

Tochon, F. V., & Dionne, J.-P. (1994). Discourse analysis and instructional flexibility: a pragmatic grammar. *Pragmatics and Language Learning, Monograph Series, 5*, 64-87.

Tochon, F. V. & Hanson, D. (2003). *The Deep Approach: world language teaching for community building*. Madison, WI: Atwood Publishing.

Tochon, F. V., & Karaman, A. C. (2009). Critical reasoning for social justice: Moral encounters with the paradoxes of intercultural education. *Intercultural Education, 20*(2), 135-149.

Tochon, F. V. & Lee, H. J. (2011). *Internet-mediated videoconferencing and the Zone of Proximal Identity Development (ZPID) in second language education*. Working paper. University of Wisconsin-Madison, School of Education.

Tochon, F. V., & Munby, H. (1993). Novice/expert teachers' time epistemology: a wave function from didactics to pedagogy. *Teaching and Teacher Education, 9*(2), 205-218.

Tochon, F. V., & Ökten, C. E. (2010). Curriculum mapping and instructional affordances: sources of transformation for student teachers. *Transnational Curriculum Inquiry, 7*(1). Online: http://ojs.library.ubc.ca/index.php/tci

Tochon, F.V., Ökten, C. E., Karaman, A. C., & Druc, I. C. (2008). *The Deep Approach to Turkish Teaching and Learning*. Title VI grant proposal to the U.S. Department of Education, International Research Studies. Awarded 2009-2012.

Tochon, F.V., Ökten, C. E., Karaman, A. C., & Druc, I. C. (2012). *The Deep Approach to Turkish Teaching and Learning*. Blue Mounds, WI: Deep University Press.

Tochon, F.V., Ökten, C. E., Karaman, A. C., & Druc, I. C. (in press). *Teaching Turkish Deeply. The Deep Approach to Language and Culture*. Blue Mounds, WI: Deep University Press.

Toda, J. (1965). *Toda Josei zenshu* (The complete works of Josei Toda), 5 vols. Tokyo, Japan: Wakosha.

Tormey, R. (2002). Celebrating difference, promoting equality: Intercultural education in the primary school classroom. Limerick, UK: CEDR.

Toth, P. (2006). Processing Instruction and a Role for Output in Second Language Acquisition. *Language Learning, 56*(2), 319-385.

Tristán, Agustín, & Molgado, Deyanira (2006). *Compendio de taxonomías. Clasificaciones para los aprendizajes de los dominios educativos*. San Luis Potosí, México: Instituto de Evaluación e Ingeniería Avanzada.

Troncy, C. (2014). *Didactique du plurilinguisme* (Multilingual Curriculum & Instruction). Rennes, France: Presses Universitaires de Rennes.

Troyan, F. J. (2012). Standards for foreign language learning: defining the constructs and researching learner outcomes. *Foreign Language Annals, 45*(S1), S118-S140.

Trudel, P., Gilbert, W., & Tochon, F.V. (2001). The use of video in the construction of knowledge and meaning in Sport pedagogy. *International Journal of Applied Semiotics, 2*(1-2), 89-112.

Truscott, J. (1999). What's wrong with oral grammar correction. *Canadian Modern Language Review, 55*, 437-456.

Tsai, Y., Kunter, M., Lüdtke, O., Trautwein, U., & Ryan, R. M. (2008). What makes lessons interesting? the role of situational and individual factors in three school subjects. *Journal of Educational Psychology, 100*, 460-472.

Tsou, W. (2011). The application of Readers Theater to FLES (Foreign Language in the Elementary Schools) reading and writing. Foreign Language Annals, 44(4), 727-748.

Tsui, A. B. M. (2003). *Understanding expertise in teaching. Case studies of ESL teachers*. New York: Cambridge University Press.

Turk, M. (2002). Case study: learning in the affective domain with two undergraduate IT subjects. *Group & Organizational Management, 1*(1), 99-116.

Turnbull, M. (1999). Multidimensional project-based teaching in French second language (FSL): a process-product case study. *Modern Language Journal, 83* (4), 548-568.

Ulrich, W. (1993). Some difficulties of ecological thinking, considered from a critical systems perspective: a plea for critical holism. *Systems Practice, 6*(6), 583-611.

Valdés, G., González, S., López García, D., & Márquez, P. (2008). Heritage languages and ideologies of language: Unexamined challenges. In D. Brinton, O. Kagan, & S. Bauckus (Eds.), *Heritage language education: A new field emerging* (pp. 107–130). New York: Routledge.

Van Compernolle, R. A., & Williams, L. (2012). Reconceptualizing Sociolinguistic Competence as Mediated Action: Identity, Meaning-Making, Agency. *The Modern Language Journal, 96*(2), 234-250.

van Lier, L. (2007). Action-based teaching, autonomy, and identity. *Innovation in Language Teaching, 1*, 46–65.

van Lier, L. (2010). Agency, Self and Identity in Language Learning. In B. O'Rourke & L. Carson (Eds.), *Language learner autonomy: Policy, curriculum, classroom* (pp. ix-xviii). Bern: Peter Lang.

VanPatten, B. (2004), Processing instruction: Theory, research, and commentary. Mahwah, NJ: Lawrence Erlbaum.

Varner, P. (2003). Learning from learning journals. *Journal of management education, 27*(1), 52–77.

Vieira, F. and Alfredo Moreira, M. (2008). Reflective teacher education toward learner autonomy: building a culture of possibility. In M. Jiménez Raya and T. Lamb (Eds.), *Pedagogy for autonomy in language education* (pp.266-282). Dublin, Ireland : Authentik.

Vitali, S., Glattfelder, J. B., & Battiston, S. (2011). The network of global corporate control, System Design, 2, 1-36. Retrieved from: http://arxiv.org/PS_cache/arxiv/pdf/1107/1107.5728v2.pdf

Vogel, S., Herron, C., Cole, S. P., & York, H. (2011). Effectiveness of a Guided Inductive Versus a Deductive Approach on the Learning of Grammar in the Intermediate-Level College French Classroom. *Foreign Language Annals, 44*(2), 353-380.

Vygotsky, L. (1934/1986). *Thought and language* (revised edition). Cambridge, MA: Massachusetts Institute of Technology Press.

Walcott, R. (1994). The need for a politics of difference: Challenging monolithic notions. *Orbit, 25*(2), 26-9.

Weaver, S. E, & Cohen, A. D. (1998). Making strategy training a reality in the foreign language curriculum. In A. D. Cohen (Ed.), *Strategies in learning and using a second language* (pp. 66-106). New York Addison Wesley Longman.

Weiner, B. (1986). *An attribution theory of motivation and emotion.* New York, NY: Springer-Verlag.

Weinstein, C., Curran, M., & Tomlinson, S. (2003). Classroom Management in a Diverse Society. *Theory Into Practice, 42*(4), 269-276.

Weissberg, R. (2006). *Connecting speaking and writing in second language writing instruction.* Ann Arbor, MI: University of Michigan Press.

Wenden, A. L. (1998). Metacognitive knowledge and language learning. Applied Linguistics, 19, 515-537.

Wesely, P. M. (2012). Learner attitudes, perceptions, and beliefs in language learning. *Foreign language Annals, 45*(S1), S98-S117.

Weyers, J. R. (2010). Speaking strategies: meeting NCATE oral proficiency standard. *Foreign Language Annals, 43*(3), 384-394.

Wierzbicka, A. (1999). *Emotions across languages and cultures: diversity and universals.* Cambridge, UK: Cambridge University Press.

Williams, G. C., Saizow, R. B., & Ryan, R. M. (1999). The importance of self-determination theory for medical education. *Academic Medicine, 74*, 992-995.

Williams, L. (2011, February). *Concept-based grammar of French*. Paper presented at the University of Wisconsin-Madison, Department of French & Italian. February 21, 2011.

Willis, D. (1996). Accuracy, fluency and conformity. In J. Willis and D. Willis (Eds.), *Challenge and change in language teaching* (pp. 17-30). New York: Heinemann Macmillan.

Willis, J. (1996). *A framework for task-based learning*. Harlow, UK: Longman.

Willis, J. (2004). Perspectives on task-based instruction: understanding our practices, acknowledging different practitioners. In B. L. Leaver & J. R. Willis (Eds.), *Task-based instruction in foreign languages education* (pp.3-45). Washington: Georgetown University Press.

Willis, D.S, & Willis, J. (2007). *Doing task-based teaching*. New York: Oxford University Press.

Wood, P., Landry, C., & Bloomfield, J. (2005). *Cultural diversity in britain. A toolkit for cross-cultural co-operation*. York, UK: Joseph Rowntree Foundation.

Woolgar, S. (2002). *Virtual society? Technology, cyberbole, reality*. Oxford, UK: Oxford University Press.

Wortham, S. (2006). *Learning identity. The Joint Emergence of Social Identification and Academic Learning*. New York: Cambridge University Press.

Wu, Z. (2011). Interpretation, autonomy, and transformation: Chinese pedagogic discourse in a cross-cultural perspective. Journal of Curriculum Studies, 43(5), 569-590.

Wu, Z. (2014, April). Speak in the place of sages: rethinking modes of pedagogic signification. Invited lecture given at the University of Wisconsin-Madison, Department of Curriculum & Instruction, Monday April 14, 2014.

Yinger, R. .J. (1987, April). *By the seat of your pants: an inquiry into improvisation and teaching*. Paper presented at the meeting of the American Educational Research Association, Washington, DC.

Young, R. F. (2001, February). *The entextualization of talk*. Paper presented at a joint symposium on "Defining and Assessing Speaking Ability" held at the annual meeting of the American

Association for Applied Linguistics and the Language Testing Research Colloquium. February 24, 2001, St Louis, Missouri, USA.

Young, R. F. (2009). *Discursive practice in language learning and teaching*. Malden, MA and Oxford: Wiley-Blackwell.

Young, R. F. (2010). The practice of multimedia in English learning and teaching. *Proceedings of the Fourteenth international conference of APAMALL and ROCMELIA* (pp.93-118). Kaohsiung, Taiwan: National Kaohsiung Normal University, Republic of China Multimedia English Learning Instruction Association.

Young, R. F. (2011). Interactional competence in language learning, teaching, and testing. In E. Hinkel (Ed.), *Handbook of research in second language teaching and learning* (Vol. 2, pp. 426-443). London & New York: Routledge.

Yu, L. (2006). *Cultural variance of reflection in action learning*. Geneva, Switzerland: University of Geneva, Centre for Socio-Economic Development.

Zarei, A., & Keshavarz, J. (2011). Effects of two models of cooperative learning on EFL reading comprehension and vocabulary learning. *Modern Journal of Language Teaching Methods, 1*(2), 39-54.

Zembylas, M. (2005). *Teaching with emotion: A postmodern enactment*. Greenwich, CT: Information Age Publishing.

Zembylas, M. (2006a). Work-based learning methodologies, politics and power: developing a Foucauldian research ethic. *Journal of Education and Work, 19*, 291-303.

Zembylas, M. (2006b). Witnessing in the classroom: the ethics and politics of affect. *Educational Theory, 56*, 305-324.

Zhao, W. (2009, August). *Weaving Western mind into Chinese Xin/heart-mind-body systems of reason*. Madison, WI: UW-Madison, School of Education, Dept of Curriculum & Instruction.

Zheng, D., Young, M., Wagner, M., & Brewer, R. (2009). Negotiation for action: English language learning in game-based virtual worlds. *Modern Language Journal, 93*, 489–511.

Zinkiewicz, L., Hammond, N., & Trapp, A. (2003). Applying Psychology disciplinary knowledge to Psychology teaching and learning. A review of selected psychological research and theory with implications for teaching practice. *LTSN Psychology, Report and Evaluation Series*, 2, March. Retrieved from: http://www.psychology.heacademy.ac.uk/docs/pdf/p20030321_r2p.pdf

Index

5Cs, 37, 65, 86, 293
21st Century, 315

A

ACTFL, 65, 85, 241-242, 293, 301, 309
actional, 37
actualizer, 168-170, 174, 216-217
adaptive classroom dynamics, 71-73, 190-192
administrative straightjacket, 54
agency, 85, 153, 238, 308, 319
agora, 200
alternative assessment, 274
anticipatory mental models, 63
advanced organizers, 160
analyze, 234-239
anti-racist education, 301
apprenticeship, 129, 159, 202-203, 273-276
assessment, 61, 264-267, 274
authentic learning, 164
autonomy, 279, 311-316

B

backward design/planning, 45, 93
bilingual, 22, 165
buzzword, 324

C

Cartesian principles, 71-73, 202
CBI/CLIL, 301-302
Chinese philosophy, 35, 324

CEFR - Common European Framework of Reference for Languages, 37, 74, 76, 85
communication, 293, 301
communicative language teaching, 307
competence/performance, 185, 192-193
complexity, 67-68, 70, 94, 123, 266, 279, 317, 322, 324, 327
computer-mediated communication, 103
conceptual grammar, 214, 218-220
conflicting needs, 62
connectedness, 72
content, 91
control, 89, 92, 315-316, 329
cosmopolitanism, 155, 296-297, 301
creativity, 105, 197, 315-316
criterion-referenced evaluation, 266
cross-cultural pragmatics, 324
cultural consciousness, 292
cultural grammar, 246
cultural spaces, 161
cultural turn, 84, 295-297
culture, 211, 293-297, 300, 320
curriculum design, 89
curriculum transformation, 170

culturally relevant pedagogy, 300

D
decontextualized teaching, 43
Deep Approach principles, 83-84, 110, 122-123, 166, 170-172, 196-198, 203-204, 211, 219-220, 237, 242, 293
Deep Education, 60, 291-294, 301-307, 328
deep culture, 83, 294
deep ecology, 321
deep learning, 59, 197-198, 201
deep pedagogy, 62, 190, 197-198, 209, 214, 261, 311-312
deep taxonomy, 130-132, 138-153, 158, 170, 329
deep teaching, 34, 190, 302
deep turn, 293-297, 306-309, 321, 323, 328
depth and transdisciplinarity, 153
depth as a continuum, 292
diachrony, 87, 162-163
diagnostic tests, 51
difference between project-based learning and Deep Approach, 308
direction, 72
disciplinary field, 128, 130, 162
discipline: 130,150
discrimination, 298-305, 327
Dynamic Systems Theory, 80-82, 302-306, 322

E
Earth-based values, 331
Earth community, 291

educative contract, 252-254, 274-276
engaged intellectual, 190
engagement, 190, 289
English/EFL/ESL, 22, 165
enminding, 238
entropy, 281
evaluation, 61, 264-267, 274
examples of schedule by projects, 212-213, 257-260
experienced teachers, 73, 325, 328
experiential learning: 329-332
expert teacher, 166-167, 208, 325, 328
exploratory practice, 40, 59, 311, 313, 317
extensive reading, 83, 225-230

F
facilitator, 196-197
films & visuals, 232, 324
finding one's own path, 30-32, 35
first language in the language classroom, 84
flexible planning, 34
focus on language, 58, 86
forward planning, 159, 174-185
fragmentation of subject-matter, 67, 88, 95, 133, 320
freedom of choice, 47

G
grammar, 86, 234
growth, 319-321

H
habitus, 320, 330
heritage learners, 109, 298-299,

324
holism, 72, 196
holistic action / hol-act, 89, 96, 108, 111-120, 174-178, 196, 200, 254-256, 308
humor, 219, 315-316

I

IAPI Model, 77, 185, 193, 208, 223-225, 248-249, 308, 322
identity-building, 91, 198, 208, 223-224, 243, 319
idiosyncratic strategies, 311-312
immersion programs, 76
imperial consciousness, 291
included middle, 24, 318, 321
indicators of performance, 62
indoctrination, 317
input, 32-33
inexpressibility, 35, 317
instructional agreement, 109, 273-276
instructional design, 54-55, 64, 69, 172-173, 268-270
instructional flexibility, 77, 217-220, 289
instructional objectives, 29
instructional organizer, 25, 78, 160-165
instructional planning, 38, 54-55, 82, 172-173, 217
instructional sequence, 47, 66, 93
instructional unorganizers, 194
integrative ontology, 292
intensive writing, 83
intention, 48-49, 92
interact, 243-247

intercultural, 197, 245, 293, 300-301
intellectual fields, 128
interdisciplinarity, 154
interdiscipline, 130-131, 150
internationalization, 42, 293-301
interpersonal, 221, 244-248
interpret, 226-235

K

Knowledge society, 55
Knowledge types, 101, 272

L

language deficit: 230
language ideology, 299
language of practice, 34, 61
language education policy, 268, 293, 298, 315-316, 324
language status, 299-301
learning strategies, 306-307
life paradigm, 317
limitations of outcome-based models, 45-48
lingua franca, 22, 323
linguicism, 297-299
linguistic genocide, 297-299
linguistic human rights, 297-299
literacy, 85 – see MLA Report

M

mana, 238
mental models, 161
mental slavery, 289
methods, 108, 306-307, 326
MLA task force report, 23, 230, 242, 293
moral education, 301

motivation, 40, 196, 203-206, 209, 224, 228-229, 234, 241, 263-275
multicultural, 299-300
multidisciplinarity, 131
multilingual, 106-107, 300
myths about language learning, 36

N
narrativor, 168, 218
national master plan, 57
naturalizing, 190
next mainstream, 19, 302
No Child Left Behind (NCLB), 291, 311
non-cultivation, 35, 317
non-interference, 292
non-language-specific approach, 314
non-linear, 63, 109
Normative curricula, 56
novice teacher, 39, 65

O
objectification, 164
open syllabus, 214-218
open system dynamics, 71-79, 80-82, 93, 202, 279-288
operant conditioning, 319
OPI – oral proficiency interview, 74, 240-241
Oral expression, 241-242
Outcast in the system, 56
outcomes, 33, 45, 49-55
outcome-based models, 49-55, 67, 93-98
output, 32, 85
overloaded curricula, 57

P
peace building, 45, 211, 291-297, 324
pedagogically safe space, 315-316
pedagogy for autonomy, 312-315
pivot, 172, 180
planning, 38, 54-55, 82, 172-173, 217, 321-322
ponerology, 158
portfolio, 54, 103, 155, 313
post-methodology, 98
power point thinking, 84
prescriptive models, 64
present, 239-243
primacy of text, 83
prior experiences, 63
process, 63, 79-81, 161-162, 331
process philosophy, 63, 123
process-oriented curricula, 61, 161-162
product-oriented curricula, 55-58
proficiency growth, 86, 326
project-based learning, 87-92, 172-173, 203-206, 244-247, 308
project pedagogy, 173-174, 203-206, 244, 308
push-down principle, 94, 286

R
rabbit story, 30-32
reading: 226-233
reading aloud, 231
reductionism, 98, 253, 329
reflexive evaluation, 267-271, 276

reification, 53
relevance, 71
repetitive obedience, 61
research, 325-328, 335-337
rhizomatic approach, 53, 197, 279
role of reflection, 33-34, 199, 203
root cause of poverty, 289
rubric: 327

S

scaffolding deep learning for a family of languages, 324
school genre, 128
scripted instruction, 198
seasoned teacher, see experienced/expert teacher
self-determination, 90, 168, 310-316
semantic organizers, 160-161
semiotics, 23, 321, 329
service learning, 247
skills, 4 skills, 74-75, 85
skiller, 169, 216
SLA, 40, 61, 88, 161, 227, 251, 318, 332
social change, 302-307
social justice, 323
socioaffective taxonomy, 135-137
sociocultural, 36, 48, 85-86, 189, 205, 319
spirit, 238
spiritual dimension, 156, 239, 291-292
standards, 37, 65, 210, 293, 300, see 5Cs

standard-based planning model, 50, 57-58, 85
STEM, 316
strategies, 310-311
structuralist reductionism, 98, 252-253
student as curriculum builder, 167, 170, 202-203, 209, 211, 330
student teacher, 154-155, 167
study abroad, 86
stultification, 309-310
syllabus, 39, 214-217, 225-227
synchrony, 87, 162-163
synthesis of opposites, 317-318, 322
systemic, 71-73, 79-81, 202, 279-288, 322

T

task-based planning, 58-60, 66-68, 206-208, 244
task domains, 73-79
TBTL - task-based teaching and learning, 58-60, 66-68, 206-208, 244
task performance, 49, 58-59, 218
taxonomic sliding, 94, 286
taxonomy, 127-128, 132, 134
teacher education, 299, 314, 316, 332-334
teacher planning, 65, 172-173, 197, 319
teacher research, 321
teaching to test, 252, 265
TESOL, 22
textbook, 29, 69, 329

thematic project (example), 179-189
thingification, 39
third space, 24, 153-154, 318, 321
trans-action, 22
transdiscipline, 131, 151-156, 317-318
transdisciplinarity, 153-156, 317-318
transformational pedagogy, 302-305
transpersonal exchange, 245-246

U
unified taxonomy, 130-132, 138-153, 158
unorganizers, 193
Unraveling, 291

Z
ZPD -Zone of proximal development, 68-70, 227-228, 328
ZPID - Zone of proximal identity development, 328

un-teach, 328

V
value creation, 294-297

W
warnings, 327-328
what makes the Deep Approach distinct, 17, 25-27, 83-84, 110, 196-198, 204, 223-224, 298, 303-307, 313-315
what the Deep Approach is NOT, 36, 220, 247
why do we need a Deep Approach, 329-332
wisdom of practice, 40
world language education, 22, 40, 74, 88, 195, 210, 247, 294, 310, 319, 325-326
Writing, 239
writing workshop, 99, 103-120

DEEP UNIVERSITY PRESS
SCIENTIFIC BOARD MEMBERS

Dr. Gilles Baillat, Rector, ex-Director of the Conference of Directors of French Teacher Education University Institutes (CDIUFM), University of Reims, France

Dr. Niels Brouwer, Graduate School of Education, Radboud Universiteit Nijmegen, The Netherlands

Dr. Yuangshan Chuang, President of Asia Pacific Association of Multimedia Assisted Language Learning, NETPAW Director, Department of English, Kun Shan University, Taiwan, ROC

Dr. José Correia, Dean, Faculty of Education, University of Porto, Portugal

Dr. Muhammet Demirbilek, Assistant Professor and Head, Educational Science Department, Suleyman Demirel University, Isparta, Turkey

Bertha Du-Babcock, Professor, Department of English for Business, City University of Hong Kong, Hong Kong, China

Marc Durand, Professor, Faculty of Psychology and Education, University of Geneva, Switzerland

Dr. Paul Durning, Emeritus Professor, ex-Head of the Doctoral School, first Director of the French National Observatory (ONED), First vice president of EUSARF. University of Paris X Nanterre, Paris, France

Dr. Stephanie Fonvielle, Associate Professor, Teacher Education University Institute, University of Aix-Marseille, France

Dr. Mingle Gao, Dean, College of Education, Beijing Language and Culture University (BLCU), Beijing, China

Dr. Liliana Morandi, Associate Professor, National University of Rio Cuarto, Cordoba, Argentina

Dr. Joëlle Morrissette, Professor, Department of Educational Psychology, Université of Montreal, Quebec, Canada

Dr. Thi Cuc Phuong Nguyen, Vice Rector, University of Hanoi, Hanoi, Vietnam

Dr. Shirley O'Neill, Associate Professor, President of the International Society for leadership in Pedagogies and Learning, University of Southern Queensland, Queensland Australia

Dr. José-Luis Ortega, Professor, Foreign Language Education, Faculty of Education, University of Granada, Spain

Dr. Surendra Pathak, Head and Professor, Department of Value Education, IASE University of Gandhi Viday Mandir, India

Dr. Shen Qi, Associate Professor, Shanghai Foreign Studies University (SHISU), Shanghai, China

Dr. Timothy Reagan, Professor and Dean of the Graduate School of Education, Nazarbayev University, Kazaksthan

Dr. Antonia Schleicher, Professor, NARLC Director and NCTOLCTL Executive Director, ACTFL Board member, Indiana University-Bloomington, USA

Dr. Kemal Silay, Professor and Director of the Flagship Program, Department of Central Eurasia, Indiana University-Bloomington, USA

Dr. Ronghui Zhao, Director, Institute of Linguistic Studies, Shanghai Foreign Studies University, Shanghai, China

Other referees may be contacted depending the Book Series or the nature and topic of the manuscript proposed.

Contact: publisher@deepuniversity.net

Author's Biosketch

Dr. Francois Victor Tochon is a Professor in the Departments of Curriculum & Instruction and French & Italian at the University of Wisconsin-Madison where he headed World Language Education for 6 years. He was born in Geneva, Switzerland. He has a Ph.D. in Applied Linguistics (Université Laval) and a Ph.D. in Educational Psychology (Ottawa University), and received the equivalent of Honorary Doctorates from two universities in Argentina and Peru. Prof. Tochon was the co-editor and Chief editor of the International Journal of Applied Semiotics. Briefly on the Board of the Semiotic Society of America, he worked on intercultural semiotics and was the president of the special interest group of Semiotics in Education of the American Educational Research University, looking for deeper ways of organizing teaching and learning. In 2009-2011, Prof. Tochon received an award from the U.S. Department of Education to create, research and evaluate personal learning environments for a "deep approach" to languages and cultures, with a focus on Turkish. It allowed his research team to format an innovative interface between language policies and classroom curricula and practices. In 2007-2008, he was awarded grants from Spencer and Tubitak—National Science and Technology Foundation of Turkey—to study ways to internationalize Education through e-portfolios, world languages and intercultural semiotics. With twenty-five books and more than hundred fifty articles and book chapters to his credit, Prof. Tochon has also been Visiting Professor in several universities including Akershus (Norway), Arizona, Brussels (Belgium), Freiburg (Switzerland), Granada (Spain), Lyon, Paris V Sorbonne, Nanterre, Reims, Rennes, West Indies (France), Arizona and Princeton (USA), Rio Cuarto (Argentina), Yildiz (Turkey), etc. He is currently published in 11 languages among which English, French, Italian, Portuguese, Spanish, Turkish, and Vietnamese, and forthcoming translations are planned for Chinese. Among his books are: "The Foreign Self: Truth Telling as Educational Inquiry" (Atwood); Tropics of Teaching: Productivity, Warfare, and Priesthood" at University of Toronto Press. His article "The Key To Global Understanding: World Languages Education. Why Schools Need to Adapt" published in the Review of Educational Research (79/2) received the 2010 Award of Best Review of Research from the American Educational Research Association (AERA). He received the 2012 Award of International Excellence from the University of Granada, Spain. Professor Tochon is President of the International Network for Language Education Policy Studies (INLEPS):

http://www.languageeducationpolicy.org

YOU MIGHT WANT TO READ :

SIGNS AND SYMBOLS IN EDUCATION
EDUCATIONAL SEMIOTICS

François Victor Tochon, Ph.D.
University of Wisconsin-Madison, USA

In this monograph on Educational Semiotics, Francois Tochon (along with a number of research colleagues) has produced a work that is truly groundbreaking on a number of fronts. First of all, in his concise but brilliant introductory comments, Tochon clearly debunks the potential notion that semiotics might provide yet another methodological tool in the toolkit of educational researchers. Drawing skillfully on the work of Peirce, Deely, Sebeok, Merrell, and others, Tochon shows us just how fundamentally different semiotic research can be when compared to the modes and techniques that have dominated educational research for many decades. That is, he points out how semiotic methods can provide the capability for both students and researchers to look at this basic and fundamental human process in inescapably transformational ways, by acknowledging and accepting that the path to knowledge is, in his words "through the fixation of belief."

But he does not stop there – instead, in four brilliantly conceived studies, he shows us how semiotic concepts in general, and semiotic mapping in particular, can allow both student teachers and researchers alike insights in these students' development of insights and concepts into the very heart of the teaching and learning process. By tackling both theoretical and practical research considerations, Tochon has provided the rest of us the beginnings of a blueprint that, if adopted, can push educational research out of (in the words of Deely) its entrenchment in the Age of Ideas into the new and exciting frontiers of the Age of Signs.

Gary Shank
Duquesne University

SEE REVIEWS HERE: http://www.deepuniversity.com/book1.html

Deep Language Learning Book Series

Language learning needs to be reconceptualized in two ways: first, as an expression of dynamic planning prototypes that can be activated through self-directed projects. Second, integrating structure and agency to meet deeper, humane aims. The dynamism of human exchange is meaning- producing through multiple connected intentions among language task domains.

Language-learning tasks have a cross-cultural purpose which then become meaningful within broader projects that meet higher values and aims such as deep ecology, deep culture, deep politics and deep humane economics. Applied semiotics will be a tool beyond the linguistic in favor of value-loaded projects that are chosen in order to revolutionize the current state of affairs, in increasing our sense of responsibility for our actions as humans vis-à-vis our fellow humans and our home planet. In this respect, deep instructional planning offers a grammar for action. Understanding adaptive and complex cross-cultural situations is the prime focus of such a hermeneutic inquiry.

For more, see here:

http://deepuniversity.com/deeplanguage.html

Guide to Authors

What our Publishing Team can offer:

- An international editorial team, in more than 20 universities around the world.

- Dedicated and experienced topic editors who will review and provide feedback on your initial proposal.

- A specific format that will speed up the production of your book and its publication.

- Higher royalties than most publishers and a discount on batch orders of 25+ copies.

- Global distribution and marketing through Amazon in the U.S., UK, Australia, and other countries.

- Fast recognition of your work in your area of specialization.

- Quality design and affordable sales pricing. Using the latest technology, our books are produced efficiently, quickly and attractively.

- A global marketing plan, including electronic and web marketing and review mailing.

- Book Series: Deep Education; Deep Language Learning; Signs & Symbols in Education; Language Education Policy; Deep Professional Development; Deep Activism.

    http://www.deepuniversitypress.com/universitypress.html

    - **Contact : publisher@deepuniversity.net**

Deep University Online !

For updates and more resources
Visit the Deep University Website:

www.deepuniversity.com
www.deepapproach.com

For the Turkish language:
www.deepapproach.wceruw.org

Contact : **publisher@deepuniversity.net**

❖ Online Certificate and Courses on Deep Education:
http://www.deepuniversity.com/graduatecourses.html

❖ Facebook group on Deep Language Learning :
https://www.facebook.com/groups/deep.approach/

❖ Forum: http://deepapproach.wceruw.org/forum.html

❖ Twitter: http://twitter.com/Deep_Approach

Correspondence

Francois Victor Tochon, Department of Curriculum & Instruction, Teacher Education Building, UW-Madison, 225 North Mills street, Madison, Wisconsin 53706 USA.

Fax: (608) 263-9992. E-mail: ftochon@education.wisc.edu

www.ingramcontent.com/pod-product-compliance
Lightning Source LLC
Chambersburg PA
CBHW071234300426
44116CB00008B/1037